Sickness and Healing

A Case Study on the Dialectic
of Culture and Personality

edition afem
mission academics 11

Robert Badenberg

This book ist part of the series edition afem – mission academics,
ed. by Klaus W. Müller, Bernd Brandl,
Thomas Schirrmacher and Thomas Mayer.
http://www.missiologie.org

Bibliographic information published by Die Deutsche Bibliothek
Die Deutsche Bibliothek lists this publication in the Deutsche National bibliografie; detailed bibliographic data are available in the Internet at http://dnb.ddb.de.

ISBN 978-3-937965-96-3
(VTR Publications) http://www.vtr-online.de

ISBN 978-3-938116-53-1
(VKW Culture and Science Publ.) http://www.vkwonline.de

ISSN 0944-1077 (edition afem – mission academics)

© 2008 by Robert Badenberg
2nd revised edition

All rights reserved.
No part of this book may be reproduced in any form or by any means without permission in writing from the publisher,
VTR Publications, Gogolstr. 33, 90475 Nürnberg, Germany,
vtr@compuserve.com, http://www.vtr-online.de.

Cover Illustration: VTR

Printed in the UK by Lightning Source

My parents
My parents-in-law
&
Old friends of childhood days

ET IN MEMORIAM
Chewe

CONTENTS

FOREWORD 11
ACKNOWLEDGMENTS 13

CHAPTER 1 INTRODUCTION 15
   1. REASON FOR THE STUDY 15
      1.1 General Injunctions 15
      1.2 Scope of Problem 16
   2. SIGNIFICANCE OF THE STUDY 17
      2.1 Sickness and Healing: Context Variables 17
      2.2 Sickness and Healing: Embedded in the Symbol System of Culture 18
      2.3 Bridging the Hiatus between Cultural Symbols and Private Symbols 19
   3. METHODOLOGY OF THE STUDY 21
      3.1 General Issues 21
      3.2 "Objectivity" under Review 23
   4. LOGIC OF PRESENTATION 24
      4.1 Part One 24
      4.2 Part Two 25
      4.3 Part Three 25
      4.4 End Piece 26

CHAPTER 2 THE BEMBA IN ZAMBIA 27
   1. INTRODUCTION 27
   2. THE BEMBA: TRAVELLERS AND CONQUERORS 27
      2.1 Travellers in Time 27
      2.2 Conquerors of Space 35
   3. A CONCLUDING REFLECTION 40

PART I:
BODY AND ILLNESS:
AN ANTHROPOLOGICAL PERSPECTIVE 42

CHAPTER 3 AN OUTLINE OF THE CONCEPT OF BODY 42
   1. INTRODUCTION 42
   2. THE BODY: UMUBILI 44
   3. THE HEAD: UMUTWE 48
      3.1 Short Excursus on Hair 50
   4. THE SENSE ORGANS 50
      4.1 The Eye: Ilinso 51
      4.2 The Mouth: Akanwa 53

5. THE EXTERNAL AND INTERNAL CHEST REGION: PA CIFUBA AND MU CIFUBA 57
    5.1 The Lungs: BaPwapwa 58
    5.2 The Stomach: Icifu 58
    5.3 The Heart: Umutima 58
    5.4 A Definition of "Psyche" 59
6. UBUFYASHI: SEXUALITY - CULTURAL MANDATE TO PROCREATION 63
    6.1 Mbusa – The Sacred Emblems 63
    6.2 Ukufunda – Traditional Education 65
    6.3 'Hot' and 'Cold': Euphemisms for Sexuality and 'Access to the Divine' .. 66
    6.4 Other Euphemisms in Relation to Reproductive Biology 67
7. A CONCLUDING REFLECTION: SOME LINGUISTIC OBSERVATIONS 69
    7.1 From the Sense Organ to Sensitive Behavior 69
    7.2 From the Human Body to the Social Body 70

CHAPTER 4 AN OUTLINE OF THE CONCEPT OF ILLNESS 73

1. INTRODUCTION 73
2. DISEASES CAUSED BY VIOLATION OF TRADITIONAL LAWS: AMALWELE YA MAKOWESHA 74
    2.1 Ulunse leading to Cifimba (Acute Malnutrition): Kwashiorkor 75
    2.2 Ulunse leading to Ukondoloka (Acute Malnutrition): Merasmus 76
    2.3 Imililo/Amakowesha leading to Cifimba (Acute Malnutrition): Kwashiorkor 77
    2.4 Ulunse and Ukondoloka (Malnutrition) in Adults 78
    2.5 Chronic Malnutrition (Stunting) 79
    2.6 Conclusion 80
3. DISEASES CAUSED BY WITCHCRAFT (UBULOSHI): AMALWELE YA KULOWEKWA 81
    3.1 The Sickness Icuulu 82
    3.2 The Sickness Ulusuku 86
    3.3 The Sickness Intifu 87
4. DISEASES CAUSED BY SPIRITS/SPIRITUAL BEINGS: AMALWELE YA MIPASHI 88
    4.1 The Sickness Umusamfu 88
5. "SPIRIT SICKNESS": UBULWELE BWA NGULU 91
6. A CONCLUDING REFLECTION: SICKNESS IN BEMBA CULTURE – A KNOWLEDGE SYSTEM BASED ON PARADOX CREATING CULTURAL AMBIVALENCE 94
    6.1 'Disease Compartmentalization': Dialectical Conflict – "Education-Knowledge" vs. "Culture-Knowledge" 94
    6.2 Malnutrition: Dialectical Conflict - "Fertility/Sexual-Capacity-Ideal" vs. "Sanctioned/Sacralized-Sex-Ideal" 96
    6.3 'Compartmentalization' and Malnutrition: What keeps Paradoxes in Place? 96

PART II: NGULU SPIRIT POSSESSION – CULTURAL AND PERSONAL RELIGIOUS SYMBOLS: A SOCIAL HERMENEUTICAL PERSPECTIVE 100

CHAPTER 5 THE PHENOMENON OF NGULU SPIRIT POSSESSION .. 101
1. INTRODUCTION 101
2. HISTORIC APPROACH TO NGULU SPIRIT POSSESSION 101
   2.1 Introducing the 'Hut-Tax-System' 101
   2.2 Abolishing the 'Chitemene-Mitanda-System' 102
   2.3 The Upsurge of Ngulu Possession in the Year 1907 103
   2.4 The Upsurge of Ngulu Possession during the early 1960s ... 106
   2.5 Conclusion 107
3. LINGUISTIC APPROACH TO THE TERM NGULU 109
   3.1 The Term Ngulu 109
   3.2 The Verb Ukuwa 116
   3.3 Stages of Ngulu Spirit Possession 117
   3.4 Conclusion 119
4. SOCIAL APPROACH TO ILLNESS AND NGULU SPIRIT POSSESSION: A CASE STUDY 119
   4.1 G. Chewe P.: A Brief Account of his Life 119
5. A CONCLUDING REFLECTION 129

CHAPTER 6 THE PHENOMENON CULTURE – PUBLIC AND PRIVATE: A THEORY OF PERSONAL SYMBOLS ACCORDING TO GANANATH OBEYESEKERE 131
1. INTRODUCTION 131
   1.1 Early Paradigms of "Culture-Definitions" 131
   1.2 Recent Paradigms of "Culture-Definitions" 132
2. GANANATH OBEYESEKERE'S THEORY OF PERSONAL SYMBOLS ... 135
   2.1 Cultural Context: Human Agency – Giving Meaning to Existence 135
   2.2 Psychological Context: Deep Motivation – Symbolic Representation .. 136
   2.3 Social Context: Family Structure and the Oedipus Complex ... 137
   2.4 Thesis on Personal Symbols 141
   2.5 The Work of Culture 144
   2.6 "Objectification" and "Subjectification" 150
3. A CONCLUDING REFLECTION 152

CHAPTER 7 IDENTIFICATION AND INTERPRETATION OF PERSONAL SYMBOLS IN REFERENCE TO THE CASE STUDY 154
1. INTRODUCTION 154
2. THREE TRAUMATIC EXPERIENCES: 1978-1988 154
   2.1 "I Never Got the Cattle!" 155
   2.2 "I Never Got the Gun!" 155

    2.3 "I Never Got Education!" 156
    2.4 Interim Interview 157
    2.5 The Years between 1978 and 1988 158
  3. THREE LIFE CRISES: 1991-2000 159
    3.1 Prelude: The Ntenda Symbol 159
    3.2 1991: Role Resolution Crisis – A Change of Symbols 161
    3.3 1994: Endurance Crisis – Confirmation of Role Resolution 168
    3.4 2000: Existential Crisis – Inner Breakdown and Recovery 169
    3.5 The Terminal Point: Chewe's Death 180
  4. A CONCLUDING REFLECTION: OBJECTIFICATION - YES BUT
     SUBJECTIFICATION - NO 184

PART III:
THREE "C'S" – COMMUNICATION, CONVERSION, COUNSELLING – THE CASE STUDY APPLIED: A MISSIOLOGICAL PERSPECTIVE 189

CHAPTER 8 A FIRST MISSIOLOGICAL "C": COMMUNICATION... 192
  1. INTRODUCTION 192
  2. THE NEGLECTED DIMENSION IN COMMUNICATION THEORIES 192
    2.1 Five Constant Basic Structures of God's Communication 194
    2.2 Missiology and Communication: Three Dimensions 195
  3. TRANS-CULTURAL COMMUNICATION: MISSIO DEI – THE "CHRIST
     INCARNATE MODEL" 196
    3.1 Missio Dei: Scriptural Grand Theme 196
    3.2 Missio Dei: Missiological Grand Model 198
    3.3 Missio Dei: Outdated or Validated? 199
  4. ADORATIO DEI: MAN IN COMMUNICATION WITH GOD 202
    4.1 Prayer: Conquest or Dialogue? 202
    4.2 The Christian "Overcoat" Creates Cultural Ambivalence 204
  5. INTER-CULTURAL COMMUNICATION: IMAGO DEI AND THE
     'NIDA MODEL' 205
    5.1 Kraft: REALITY vs. reality 205
    5.2 Nida: "Bible Culture," "Missionary Culture," "Host Culture" 207
  6. A CONCLUDING REFLECTION 213

CHAPTER 9 A SECOND MISSIOLOGICAL "C": CONVERSION 216
  1. INTRODUCTION 216
  2. CONVERSION: REVIEW OF SELECT RELEVANT LITERATURE 217
    2.1 General Theory on Conversion in Anthropology 217
    2.2 A Sociocultural Theory on Conversion 218
    2.3 Introductory Entry Point 221
  3. CONVERSION: A READING ON CHARLES KRAFT 222
    3.1 Biblical Absolutes or Biblical Principles/Constants? 222

- 4. CONVERSION: A PSYCHOLOGICAL MODEL 227
  - 4.1 Moment or Process? 227
  - 4.2 Individual or Corporate? 230
- 5. CONVERSION: NEW CONTEXT – NEW VALUES AND NEW PERSPECTIVES .. 231
  - 5.1 Chewe and New Values 232
  - 5.2 Chewe and New Perspectives 233
  - 5.3 A Word to Missionary Workers 234
- 6. A CONCLUDING REFLECTION 235

CHAPTER 10 A THIRD MISSIOLOGICAL "C": COUNSELLING 237

- 1. INTRODUCTION 237
  - 1.1 Setting the Stage 238
  - 1.2 Demarcating the Field 238
- 2. A CALL FOR THEOLOGICAL ETHICS 239
  - 2.1 "Shepherd-Attitude": A Basic Structure of Counselling 239
  - 2.2 "Shepherd-Service": Mandate of the Church 239
- 3. WALKING FRONTIERS: COUNSELLING ACROSS CULTURES 240
  - 3.1 The Quest: What are the Points of References? 241
  - 3.2 Common Human Properties – Expressed in Unique Ways 241
- 4. A THEORY ON UNDERSTANDING PEOPLE 242
  - 4.1 To Know and To Understand: Related and Yet of a Different Kind 243
  - 4.2 A Call to Move from Know-ing towards Understand-ing 244
  - 4.3 Theories on Empathy 246
  - 4.4 "What Happens to Verstehen when Einfühlen Disappears?" 247
  - 4.5 Two Reasons for Failing to Understand a Person 249
  - 4.6 Afterthought 250
  - 4.7 Aftermath 251
- 5. A CONCLUDING REFLECTION 251

CHAPTER 11 CONCLUSION AND OUTLOOK 253

- 1. CONCLUSION 253
  - 1.1 Man in Context 254
  - 1.2 Man in Conflict 255
  - 1.3 What's in for Missiology? 256
- 2. OUTLOOK 257
  - 2.1 Imago Dei – Metatheory for Missiology, Anthropology and the Social Sciences 258
  - 2.2 Personal Final Comment 259

APPENDIX 1 261
APPENDIX 2 262
APPENDIX 3 263
ABBREVIATIONS 266
BIBLIOGRAPHY 267

TABLE OF FIGURES

FIGURE 1: *UMUBILI* TAXONOMY OF CREATURES 45
FIGURE 2: *UMUBILI* TAXONOMY OF HUMAN BEINGS 47
FIGURE 3: THE DIALECTIC OF PARADOX IN BEMBA SEXUALITY 99
FIGURE 4: OBJECTIFICATION ILLUSTRATED 151
FIGURE 5: SUBJECTIFICATION ILLUSTRATED 151
FIGURE 6: INTERACTION OF PERSONALITY, CULTURE AND SOCIETY 187
FIGURE 7: "FOUR-CULTURE-COMMUNICATION MODEL" 212
FIGURE 8: THE DYNAMIC SEQUENCE OF EVENTS IN CONVERSION 228

Foreword

As a rule, missionaries at work on their mission fields are not very research-minded. Many cannot afford to be because they are too busy with other work, or they are simply not research type of people. Robert Badenberg is different. Not only is he a dedicated missionary, during the many years he has spent on his mission field in Zambia he has become a dedicated anthropologist as well.

His book, which is also his doctoral dissertation, deals with a subject rarely chosen for study in either Missiology or Anthropology. By combining new research methods from cognitive anthropology with older methods of the culture-and-personality school, it describes and analyzes the life history of an African individual. Thus, it finally draws conclusions of a more missiological character.

Centering his study around the life of his informant Chewe, Robert Badenberg analyzes procedures of personal crisis (sickness) management in a setting of Bemba culture. This central subject is embedded in the wider context of a central African (animistic) world view. The concepts of body and sickness are described through the linguistic data he has collected during his long-term study of the Bemba language (the language of this particular Zambian ethnic group).

The most interesting and original part of his thesis is the comparison of his findings with the theory of cultural and personal symbols developed by Gananath Obeyesekere, a non-western anthropologist (Sri Lanka). Badenberg comes to the conclusion that Obeyesekere is right when he propounds that cultural symbols are chosen by individuals as a means of personal crisis management. These become personal symbols.

What Robert Badenberg has successfully brought to light is one important aspect of the dialectic between culture and the individual. His argumentation is consistent and easy to follow. It begins with the general concept of body and sickness, followed by discussion of Ngulu sickness (Ngulu is a special concept of sickness in Bemba society, dealing with altered states of consciousness and Vulgo spirit possession). The second part of his writing begins with the quest for healing, focusing on personal and cultural concepts. This is followed by Chewes life history and the dialectic between culture and the individual. It ends with missiological conclusions about the individual in his cultural context: communication, conversion, counselling.

In his thesis the author is breaking new ground, thus contributing decidedly to more knowledge of the subject. A cognitive study of the Bemba concept of the body, for instance, has never been done before. Moreover, research procedures and techniques are described in detail, literature has been explored widely, data is presented and analyzed thoroughly, and the content is structured and logically developed. To missionaries and anthropologists alike the book provides a wealth of information and models to be used in follow-up research. It is my hope that many may feel encouraged to follow in Robert Badenberg's footsteps.

Lothar Käser, Schallstadt, March 2002

Acknowledgments

This book was originally prepared as a thesis for the degree of Doctor of Theology in the subject Missiology of the University of South Africa (UNISA) and is published in substantially unchanged though now revised form.

I am particularly indebted to *Prof. N. A. Botha*, Head of the Department of Missiology at the University of South Africa (UNISA) and promoter of the thesis. I truly enjoyed his open-mindedness, the - I think unusual liberty in the discipline of Missiology he granted me in proposing ideas and concepts derived from other disciplines as well as freedom to proceed with presenting material to his desk as my schedule allowed.

Similarly, I would also like to sincerely thank the joint promoter, *Prof. Dr. L. Käser* from the Albert-Ludwigs-University Freiburg i. Br., Germany, for his constant advice and encouragement, speedy replies to cultural and anthropological issues that crept up while sifting and sorting research material. Thank you for having taught me the rudiments of cultural anthropology and the constant encouragement I received when "poking my nose" into other life worlds.

At UNISA, I owe special thanks to *Mrs. Natalie Thirion* (Subject Librarian), who was ever ready to help me out to locate books, articles, and the like. It would have been impossible to have enjoyed the benefits from the many sources she made available to me, had it not been for her willingness to search the library shelves as well as browsing the Internet on my behalf and forward material to Zambia. Thank you very much Natalie!

Dr. F. LeBacq contributed to this work by his valuable advice on medical issues and his willingness to share with me some of the insights of his own work when he filled the post of District Medical Officer in Kasama District from 1994 to 2000. The many informal discussions we had on numerous subjects helped me gain clarification on material that sprang up while researching. But most of all, I truly thank him for his personal commitment during the four months of Chewe's sickness.

Dr. M. Piennisch gave support in providing necessary details and material for the chapter on communication. For this I thank him duly.

Rev. Dr. R. Frey, a missionary colleague and co-worker in the Gospel over many years, provided me with stacks of books and articles from his own library. Had it not been for this kind provision, the collecting of the same materials in libraries and archives would have meant additional long trips, arduous work, and much time. Thank you for this gesture of companionship!

Among other people who contributed in certain ways to this thesis, I would like to acknowledge the help of *Mr. H. Simwanza* who traced and gathered some data on Bemba illness concepts.

A words of thanks goes to *Dr. M. S. Wolford*. His comments on parts of the thesis and his encouragement when the project had reached an advanced stage, is gladly acknowledged.

Furthermore, I would like to extend a special "thank you" to *Werner Schäfer*, a personal friend for many years. Though he had no direct input in the work, he accompanied me all the way from the initial stages of the study to its completion. His friendship, advice, and interest boosted the morale of the writer when things got tough at times.

I also thank all staff members of *Liebenzell Mission International*, who at the time of writing, resided in Zambia and prayerfully supported the project. I am indebted to colleagues who took extra effort to read and comment on some parts of the thesis.

In a very special way I want to express my gratitude toward the *Chewe family* for the many hours of hospitality, their openness to "intrude" upon their lives and making me feel at home in a different place of the globe. I warmly thank the Christian community of Chafwa and Andele among whom I have been allowed to live and move at liberty for many years.

I take special note of contributions made by *Gary R. Burlington* while himself very busy trying to finish his own Doctoral Dissertation. As a former colleague and personal friend, he drew my attention to specific parts of the study, namely, Gananath Obeyesekere's theory on personal symbols. A significant part of the thesis would have taken a different twist, had he not introduced me to the value of personal symbols and the dialectic of personality and culture.

Thank you Michelle for reading the text and improving on its quality for which I am deeply grateful!

Finally, I am greatly indebted to my wife *Rita*. She was a constant source of encouragement and inspiration. I fail to express in words what her input in this project was. She was ever ready to take on additional duties when things were tight and rendered comfort and encouragement to me during the stages of writing the chapters as time went on. I am aware of the fact that without her support and my childrens', *Ralph* and *Frank*, patience with their father writing in the office, this project could never have seen completion. In this respect, this work is as much theirs as it is mine.

Natotela Mukwai!

Robert G Badenberg, July 2008

Chapter 1
Introduction

1. Reason for the Study

I went to Zambia as a missionary in April 1989. During my years of residency in the country, I lived in the urban regions of the Copperbelt[1] and the rural areas of Northern Province. I mingled with highly skilled and well-educated people as well as with peasant farmers from village communities. In the course of time, I learned that sickness and healing are key categories and key concerns with many African people regardless of class, social background, or level of education. The Bemba, a once-powerful warrior tribe of the Northern Plateau of Zambia, look at both categories from their own unique perspective.

What are sickness and healing categories? How are they organized? What are the concerns in sickness and healing? What is being done about them? And who is doing it? The present thesis is concerned with showing the differences between African – or, more precisely, Bemba – and European perceptions of sickness and healing, curative measures, as well as the representation of the motivational force needed to achieve healing. These divergences create tensions, challenges and opportunities for the missionary.

1.1 General Injunctions

Tensions emerge due to the reality of two differing cultural concepts: the cultural bias of the messenger (missionary) and that of the recipient (host). Challenges develop the moment a person learns the concepts of the host culture because the messenger is forced to reflect on, even scrutinize, his own cultural biases. Reflection is an inevitable part of the learning process and will hopefully lead to an awareness of the trap of ethnocentrism. A willingness to learn and efforts to understand foreign concepts create opportunities to meaningfully share the Gospel of Jesus Christ.

However, it is not enough to learn about the culture of one's host.[2] It is equally important to understand *what culture does to the individual and what the individual does to culture*. This understanding is crucial – first, because it makes possible an understanding of how sickness affects the individual and how healing is achieved. Second, it causes the messenger to look at sickness and healing from the recipient's vantage point and brings an awareness of the

---

[1] Copperbelt is a province bordering the Democratic Republic of the Congo. The main feature, as the name suggests, is the mining of copper. The name is also used collectively for all the towns within the provincial area.

[2] Learning about the host's culture is, however, of utmost importance in relating one's behavior in categories that make sense to the general public.

creativity of the human mind and how it acts in this particular context. An understanding that encompasses these two viewpoints has missiological implications in that it creates opportunities to communicate the Gospel with relevance.

I attempt to focus on illness and the quest for healing seeking to understand how a cultural insider dealt with it. The main actor of this study is G. Chewe P.[3] of Bemba ethnicity, though I am equally interested in taking up my own position in the story. Our life-paths crossed sometime in 1989. The initial acquaintance grew into a real friendship that lasted more than a decade and was sadly ended with Chewe's death on 3 July 2000. He died after four months of extreme inner turmoil and severe physical pain from a bleeding stomach ulcer (the scientific, western medical explanation-viewpoint!).

1.2 Scope of Problem

Initially, the contact point of our lives was our common profession of the Christian faith. Apart from this fact, we knew very little about one another. There was no obvious reason why there should have been a bond of friendship developing between the two of us. It just happened. Yet we were both willing to feed this relationship with personal data from our lives.

As time went on, I wanted to learn more about Chewe the person and about his life. This interest opened doors to many other avenues: Bemba culture in general with specifics of beliefs, values and customs, social structures and roles, family life, as well as personal struggles.

A main concern was his *permanent* ill health. The Bemba classification for this kind of physical condition is *ntenda* or *uwalwalilila*. What was the specific *ntenda* history buried in his past? How did his physical condition shape the person Chewe? Was he a passive victim of his "fate"? Was he content with cultural explanations of his condition or did he act upon his context? How did his history of ill health influence and affect Chewe as a Christian? These are some of the most pertinent questions that I address in this study.

To understand Chewe as a man, a Christian, a Christian leader and a person ridden by illness, one must take into account his personality, his life experience, and the socio-cultural context in which the events of his life occurred. The in-depth study of a person's life is essential to understanding their personal psychological dynamics in relation to social-cultural dynamics. I consider this to be an important approach because it allows for a more accurate presentation of Chewe's emotions and customs.

---

[3] I refrain from using the full name out of courtesy to the family. The middle name is, however, the person's real name. I would have used a full pseudonym had certain specifics not made it necessary to use the original name.

2. Significance of the Study

Sickness and healing experience is universal but the context in which they are perceived and dealt with is particular. This thesis, particularistic by intention, is an interdisciplinary approach focusing on the person Chewe in his context rather than an approach centered in an individual field of research.

2.1 Sickness and Healing: Context Variables

Sickness and healing are significant in three contexts:

Sickness and healing constitute a *cultural problem*. In this study, I make use of tools developed in the field of cultural anthropology to bring to light how Bemba culture deals with issues such as the concept of the body and classification of illnesses. Among the issues that arise are the problem of "compartmentalization" (Carey 1986: viii-ix) of sickness due to the presence of western scientific models, and the validity of traditional concepts based on worldview values. Another problem faced is the dialectic of conflicting cultural ideals as one of the root causes of Sexually Transmitted Diseases (STD's) and the pandemic of HIV/AIDS.

Sickness and healing constitute a *personal problem*. It is individuals who fall sick. Consequently, it is the individual who takes ameliorative action. Sickness always has an individual character because no two people experience the same sickness in exactly the same way. Sickness and healing must be viewed in the context of a person's personal life situation. How Chewe dealt with chronic ill health requires more than just listing and telling his life story and noting at what times he had suffered from what illness. The all-important issue is how he reacted to his chronic ill health context at various stages in his life. Further, which cultural givens provided the motivation to attain healing? To understand and attempt to explain Chewe in this context takes more than a simple, one-faceted tool. Rather, it requires a social hermeneutical approach.

Sickness and healing constitute a *missiological problem*. The primary concern of mission is to reach people. To understand them, we need to realize that people are not "unformatted matter," as one might say in computer language, but rather are entirely and thoroughly primed by their culture, including that culture's perception of sickness and how to deal with it. Further, people are molded by their personal life experience of sickness within that culture. Thirdly, we should look at how people act upon their culture in their efforts to deal with illness within the given cultural parameters. Mission therefore needs to take into account a person's individual history with sickness as a part of that whole history. With this in mind, the missionary can then attempt to introduce the Bible context into the person's specific cultural context. The primary biblical concern is communicating the Gospel with the aim of leading people to see the reality of God, and to accept His authority over their lives in sickness or in health – in other words, to experience conversion. Another aim is to see individuals progress in the Christian life through counselling, enabling them to bring the past, present and future into the proper focus. We must not, however, concentrate only on those who are receptive to the Gospel. The missionary is just as much a person in context as are the people he is trying to reach; this factor also figures into the communication and discipling processes.

2.2 Sickness and Healing:
Embedded in the Symbol System of Culture

Chewe was *ntenda*, a chronically ill person. In the first instance, one approach could be to try and establish "the meaning" of sickness to "the group" or to "the individual." Componential Analysis or Cognitive Anthropology as a tool is strongly inclined to establish "the meaning" (of sickness) because of its methodology of collecting and analyzing primarily linguistic data. This particular approach seeks to elicit "the meaning" of the subject from the supposedly inherent "meaning or meanings" of the relevant linguistic material. While I have benefited greatly from using this theoretical tool in an earlier work (Badenberg 1999) and found some of its properties beneficial in parts of this study, I have since broadened my view of looking at sickness and healing.

The meaning of sickness is not in the vocabulary or the language in general. Both entities only reflect the cognitive dimensions in which people move and think as well as the diversity of cognitive possibilities of peoples around the globe. Meanings are in the people who use the symbol "language" – which is itself an array of symbols – to comment, state, describe, act, and so forth, on the symbol of "sickness." Looking at sickness as an integral part of a culture's symbol system leads to recognizing its dynamic twist.

Therefore, to research sickness, and in particular to understand Chewe the *ntenda* person, is to take note of the dynamics of meaning ascription. People ascribe meaning to their existence in various ways and at various times. This holds true for people who enjoy health or those who suffer from sickness, for people with riches or those in want. Every person ascribes meaning to his existence in his own particular context.

In the second instance, symbols occur or are embedded in the context of culture. In other words, culture hosts a vast reservoir of symbols with more or less assigned historical meanings. But symbols are transformed (and are even newly created if certain factors fall into place) through individual agency as individuals mediate them through consciousness and life experience. Taking this second argument further, there must be a link between the public and the private, between cultural (public) symbols and private (personal) symbols. Bruner counters the notion that individuals might be merely pushed along cultural avenues. Cultural changes or personal experiences like sickness create conflicts in a person. But individuals are actors, Bruner maintains. They act as "creative agents interpreting the changing world in which they live" (1976:241) and, one could easily add, interpreting the personal dilemmas they undergo. Chronic ill health is a profound dilemma of the most certain terms.

2.3 Bridging the Hiatus between Cultural Symbols and Private Symbols

How did the illness-ridden Chewe act upon his life context, taking into account socio-cultural and cultural givens? His *ntenda* status had separated him, first from his family, and second from the people he lived with in the community. This estrangement from the family and the wider social group caused intrapsychic conflicts in Chewe. In order to cope with his situation – with estrangement, his *ntenda* condition, and the tension this caused in relationships with significant others – Chewe symbolized his travail in the *umupashi* symbol.

In traditional Bemba culture, *umupashi* is the being that survives the death of the body. As a Mupashi Mukankala, a rich and generous ancestral spirit, it is waiting to dispense its properties (individual characteristics of the forbearer of its name) to a next-generation child of the family. In short, *umupashi* is the *spirit double of a living person*.[4] Chewe's *spirit double* was a famous and reputed hunter of his mother's family line who was also *ntenda* during his lifetime! *Umupashi* became a personal symbol. Deep motivation provided the inner urge toward the *umupashi* symbol causing it to attain a profound personal meaning.

After Chewe turned to God in a personal commitment, his need to ascribe meaning to his *ntenda* situation did not fall into oblivion. Quite to the contrary, he was still a sick person and greatly hampered by being *ntenda*. Chewe shifted to another symbol, *ngulu* spirit mediumship, to objectify his travail. He, however, failed to make full use of the symbol to attain healing. Instead, he exchanged *ngulu* spirit mediumship with *intungulushi*, that is, spiritual leadership in the church.

Culture, and more specifically its provision of symbols, gives healing to people as "symbolic forms existing on the cultural level get created and recreated through the minds of people" (Obeyesekere 1990:xix). Chewe experienced inner healing after the failed *ngulu* episode because he effectively substituted it with spiritual leadership. However, on two occasions, in 1994 and in 2000, Chewe suffered prolonged periods of sickness. The six months of frailty and weakness in 1994 confirmed the *intungulushi* spiritual leadership symbol by causing him to experience God's intervention and healing. Things were different when his life was thrown into turmoil by a period of sickness that lasted from April to July 2000. Chewe was greatly challenged when, on these two

---

[4] I have written on this subject elsewhere (Badenberg 1999).

occasions, his life was at stake more than ever before. This crisis triggered conflicts on various levels: within himself, with his immediate family, with his brothers and sisters, with the home church, with his missionary friend and with the home village community.

2.3.1 Symbols – Public or Personal – A Review

Much research has been done by anthropologists studying cultural symbol systems or personal symbols. Unfortunately, these studies have been mostly concerned with either cultural symbols *or* personal symbols. Further, the social sciences have dealt with this field of study by concentrating on the social aspects of symbols. But little has been done to bring public culture (public symbol systems) and individual emotion (the deployment of personal symbols) together.

Gananath Obeyesekere, a Sri Lankan anthropologist and social scientist, bemoans this situation and has significantly diverted from this approach. In his two books *Medusa's Hair: An Essay on Personal Symbols and Religious Experience* (1981/84) and *The Work of Culture: Symbolic Transformation in Psychoanalysis and Anthropology* (1990), Obeyesekere convincingly shows that symbols can indeed work in the private and public domain at the same time.

2.3.2 Symbols – Dialectic between Culture and Personality

The failure to link the symbol system to personal experience and life application merely highlights the researchers' aptitude and "professionalism" in scientific research. Thus, the study suppresses the second main actor, the informant, as an active participant in the process of investigation. There is a real danger in viewing the informant as a "research object" *per se*. The informant needs to be seen as an individual who communicates himself to the outside world, and not only as a person who delivers scientific data for scrutiny. People do impose meaning on every aspect of their existence, says Weber (in Obeyesekere 1984:1). Just how much "civilization" or what degree of civilization does a given culture require to produce intellectual discourse and insights? And how much "education" does an individual of a given culture require in order to engage in rational self-reflection?

This study is concerned with showing how personality is shaped by a person's context, how a person acts upon that context through reflection, and how contextual factors relate to personal conflicts. In this way, emphasis will be placed on the dialectic between context (culture) and personality (life history). Obeyesekere will provide the theoretical tools to gain insight into how the public and the private intertwine. We will see how Chewe dealt with the dialectic between the social context and his individual personality which coaxed him into appropriating the symbols available to him from the public culture in order to objectify his inner conflicts and experience healing.

3. Methodology of the Study

The data for the research culminating in this thesis was collected over a period of six years. However, a fraction of the data was collected prior to the systematic research which began in January 1995. This collection process dates back to the early years of my stay in Zambia and my work there as a missionary.

3.1 General Issues

The project was self-funded, solely self-initiated, and purely motivated by my desire to learn more about the people with whom I worked as missionary and their social and cultural environment. The relationship that developed with G. Chewe P. over many years initiated that interest and kept it aflame when I was confronted time and again with the reality of the life world of Chewe and with the Bemba people in general.

The collection and gathering of empirical data alone is, however, not enough. We must also try and understand what they mean. This raises the questions, "How can we come to an understanding? What methods facilitate understanding?" The complexity of these questions includes such matters as informants, language, the use of interpreters, time, the personal circumstances of the researcher, "objectivity," and the theoretical tools necessary for this work, which I will deal with in the subsequent section.

Informants are indispensable to the researcher in order to obtain data with which to work. Spradley (1979) has extensively dealt with the advantages of engaging an informant and the ethical principles related to their engagement. Hence, I will not elaborate on this topic except for commenting on the ethnographer's problem in applying scientific principles and the crucial problem of his rapport with informants.

3.1.1 The Ethnographer and Science

When the informant simultaneously becomes the subject of study, empirical study as practiced by the "reality science" (Vendler 1984:200), will not work. Vendler remarks that, although "human beings too belong to the physical world," they are not "merely objects but also subjects of experience" (1984:200). This dual "reality" puts human beings clearly out of reach of "reality science." The second part of this thesis, which features the main actor G. Chewe P., therefore requires a way of collecting data *on* him and a way of interpreting this data *about* him. To do so, the researcher cannot go about this task by treating the research as an objective project of social science, but must rather treat it as a subjective exercise in social hermeneutics. Obeyesekere says, "Hermeneutics is no longer a novelty and is now part of the anthropological lexicon" (1990:xvii). Data on Chewe was collected in countless formal and informal interviews over more than five years (during which we lived in near vicinity of each other meeting frequently and regularly), although interaction with him covered a whole decade. Apart from these means of obtaining data, I have made use of participant observation and collected and incorporated autobiographical accounts I have been given.

3.1.2 The Ethnographer and the Informant/s

A general problem that ethnographers face is establishing rapport with their informants. I was in an advantageous position because I had already known Chewe for some years before I became engaged with serious and systematic research. There was already the firmly established relationship so essential to studying a person's life. We had a good, solid base from which to stage enquiries into very personal and sensitive areas and matters of human life.

3.1.3 The Ethnographer and Language

Another problem that ethnographers face is language. Often the researcher has to engage and rely on interpreters to collect his information. The medium of communication Chewe and I used was either English (more often used in the early stages of the research) or CiBemba (mostly used in the latter stages of the research). Many interviews and all autobiographical material were in the mother tongue of the informant. I participated in many events, gatherings and activities where Chewe functioned in an entirely Bemba-speaking environment. At no time was an interpreter used. (Issues on the interpreter effect are discussed in Obeyesekere 1984:11). All questions were posed directly to Chewe and drafted by me personally. Answers, explanations, accounts etc. were recorded in both English and CiBemba. I translated all texts from Ci-Bemba into English myself. Records of the day were almost always transcribed, rewritten, and organized during the evening of the same day to take advantage of fresh recollections of events.

3.1.4 The Ethnographer and Time

A further problem an ethnographer has to come to terms with is time. In studying a person's life and personal symbols, two factors weigh heavily on the articulation of a theory: time and reflection. Without a long-standing friendship, researching personal symbols is impossible.

First, time pressure while engaged in fieldwork severely limits, and to some degree diminishes, the openness of the informant(s) to speak about personal experience. This, however, was not the case here. I was under no time pressure because I lived where I worked and recorded while I worked. Second, having only limited time logically affects and severely restricts reflection on the personal relationship with the informant and on the data gathered. It goes without saying that a relationship that has to produce good, primary and original material under time-pressure affects the ethnographer as much as the informant. This is so because the subject matter concerns human experience that affects both researcher and informant, albeit in various ways and to varying degrees.

3.1.5 The Ethnographer and Human Factors

Next to time limitations, other human factors influence the ethnographer, for example loneliness. It is one thing to record customs, myths, linguistic data and the like, and it is another to engage in discussions of profound human problems of a rather personal nature. The ethnographer will, at one time or another, most certainly find in himself what he unlocks in the other. He is not simply a recording machine, but a human being "constituted of the same 'essence' (their human nature)" (Obeyesekere 1984:9) and will react to what he has encountered. But where to go with the memories, questions, anxieties, emotions, and problems, if he is alone in a strange and at times difficult world? Do such human conditions not truly and deeply influence the ethnographer?!

I count it an enormous advantage to have had my family with me during the entire time of the research. I not only researched there. We *lived* there! My wife was not only a helpful secretary, but also somebody with whom I could share whatever transpired during the interaction with Chewe, and somebody who also had her *own* personal rapport with him and his family. We had so many precious hours of discussing issues with one another and reflecting on our own lives, relationships, and our marriage. Mental fatigue, frustrations and loneliness were oftentimes balanced by the safe haven of my family. It would be a formidable task and unmerciful endeavour to accomplish anything while in the field if one were to face these human problems all by oneself.

3.2 "Objectivity" under Review

M. A. Jeeves, in his otherwise commendable article "The Psychology of Conversion," makes a plea for the psychologist (or any other scientist or serious investigator for that matter) to be a faithful "mapmaker of the territory he has set out to explore" (1988:185). What is the researcher's task or aim in making the map? Jeeves replies, "In principle, his aim is to give an account which is objective and value-free" (Jeeves 1988:185). Undoubtedly, this is a noble goal and many members of the academic fraternity would pledge their full support of this approach. But how does one produce an "objective and value-free" account when the psychologist, scientist, anthropologist, missionary and all the rest of them, are – by nature of being human – object and subject at the same time? There is no way one can escape the influence of the data one collects, at least not in the social sciences and cultural anthropology.[5] We must face up to the reality of what the research does to the researcher.[6]

---

[5] Lienhardt, in summarizing Lévy-Bruhl, says, "but when we study man in society we are still, as it were, *both subject and object of inquiry* (italics mine), and it is within the logic of social anthropology itself that we should finally examine some of the ideas we use and have used to represent the ideas of others" (Lienhardt 1966:151).

[6] Melissa Parker, in her article "Rethinking Female Circumcision," provides a brilliant example of the object-subject situation of the researcher. Briefly, Parker is concerned to show that a researcher's feelings, in her case on female circumcision as practiced in northern Sudan, under-

It was Obeyesekere who raised this issue (1984:8-9) and actually put into words what had loomed in my mind as unconnected, non-verbalized fractions of thoughts, namely, what is the impact of the research on the researcher? In fact, I was more inclined to banish reactions, impressions and emotions that were triggered within me while I was engaged in the fieldwork, especially during the months between March and July 2000, because I felt restraint to do so. It seemed to be outside of the scope of the research. Also, I was under the impression that it was not befitting a certain norm of professionalism called "objectivity" that one has to adopt when engaged in academic research. Then, when I read Obeyesekere and his ideas on this subject, I was encouraged to change my stance and to let myself be part of the study. This is to positively counter Obeyesekere's criticism of the absence of this element in so many ethnographies in which the ethnographer chips in as a person while doing ethnographic work.

4. Logic of Presentation

Along with two introductory chapters dealing with preliminary matters, this thesis consists of three parts.

4.1 Part One

Part One presents an outline of the concepts of body and illness from an anthropological perspective.

In chapter three, I establish an outline of the concept of body, since this is where sickness manifests. The chapter mainly deals with linguistic data. I concentrate on the head and the heart in order to show that the common Western notion of assigning intellect to the "head" and emotion to the "heart" does not hold true in Bemba thinking. Rather, intellect and emotion as well as character traits are tied to one organ only, the heart (*umutima*) for which the term *psyche*, and to be more precise SEIC,[7] is proposed.

It is *mu mutima*, in the psyche, where intrapsychic conflicts have their beginning and where conflicting desires operate. Other internal organs, the reproductive parts, and ideas on reproductive biology also come under investigation. In a closing section, injunctions from the physical body to the social body based on linguistic observations are made.

---

lie one's own interest and concern. A common Western opinion on this subject includes terms describing this act as "barbaric, futile and illogical" (1995:516). Thus, when researching and discussing this area of human life, "intense emotions often underlie popular scholarly discussion of female circumcision" (1995:518) in the above mentioned categories. Parker concludes by saying "that greater attention should be paid to understanding the source of these emotions and the way they influence fieldwork and data analysis" (1995:523).

[7] SEIC is an acronym meaning: **S**eat of **E**motions, **I**ntellect and **C**haracter. SEIC was coined by L. Käser and first introduced in his textbook *Animismus* (2004) and incorporated into my work *Das Menschenbild in fremden Kulturen* (2007), a manual on how to research the concept of man.

Chapter four contains an outline of the concept of illness, presenting select classifications under which Bemba culture views illnesses. These illnesses are conceived and dealt with in different categories based on assumptions derived from worldview values. The sickness *Icuulu,* so relevant for the case study that follows in chapter six and seven, is therefore presented in more detail.

4.2 Part Two

Part Two focuses on *Ngulu* possession, a specific category of illness. In a case study it will be shown that *Ngulu* possession has a twofold dimension: it operates on the level of culture and of personality. In other words, it functions as a cultural symbol as well as a personal (religious) symbol. To explain the interaction of cultural symbols and personal symbols, I invoke Gananath Obeyesekere's theory of personal religious symbols demonstrating that, in order to explain this interaction, a social hermeneutical perspective is required.

In chapter five, sickness is interlinked with possession because *ngulu* is distinctly connected with a specific sickness. A historic, linguistic, and social approach to *ngulu* possession is presented. A major part of the social approach will be that part of Chewe's life that related to the *ngulu* spirit mediumship episode in 1991.

Chapter six develops the theoretical tools required to show the dialectic between the public and the private domain and to extract the dynamics of dealing with sickness and healing from Chewe's life. The concept of culture consisting of dialectic forces competing with one another is investigated by leaning on Charles W. Nuckolls and his work *The Cultural Dialectics of Knowledge and Desire* (1996). I make use of Gananath Obeyesekere's two previously mentioned books to show how he demonstrates these dialectics in his theory on personal symbols.

In continuation of Chewe's life account, chapter seven identifies and interprets those personal symbols that were operational in his life. For example, why incorporate *ngulu* possession rituals in 1991 next to the *umupashi* symbol? Why did this happen three years after he had made a personal commitment to God and had joined the local church? Why could *Ngulu* status (spirit mediumship) not be achieved? Also, the interplay of other symbols in Chewe's life are identified and interpreted. The relationship we had is the source of good, primary, and personal information.

4.3 Part Three

Part Three develops the missiological perspective of this thesis by concentrating on three missiological "C's": Communication, Conversion and Counselling.

Missiology is an interdisciplinary enterprise, integrating and exploiting the insights of other disciplines within the realms of anthropology and the social sciences. Not to do so would not only be unwise, but would deprive missiology of a powerful thrust. As Tippet points out, Missiology "draws (not merely borrows, insertion mine) from all the social and human sciences and if the interaction is genuine something methodologically new will be born and Missiology will expand" (1987:xv). The case study of G. Chewe P. as presented in Part Two will be applied to these three missiological "C's."

Chapter eight looks at the communication of the Gospel as a major concern of the Christian mission. In this chapter, the notion of the sufficiency of cybernetic communication models concerning the Christian mission is questioned. Communications theories need the inner-trinitarian communication of "love, spirit, word, deed and life," as their base (Piennisch 1995:55, 212). How does God communicate with man? Is *missio Dei* still relevant? How does man communicate with God? How prominent is *adoratio Dei* in man's liturgical service? And how does man communicate with man? How important is the concept of *imago Dei* in this process? Discussions of these questions form the main parts of this chapter. E. Nida's three-culture-communication model is also reviewed and expanded upon.

Conversion is a next major concern of missiology. In chapter nine, attention is given to the fact that conversion is no longer unique to the Christian mission. Disciplines like anthropology and psychology have made conversion an integral part of their respective disciplines. At the same time, conversion is in danger of being swept from the missiological agenda. Relevant literature on both issues is presented and critiqued.

Missiological models on conversion by Kraft, Tippet and Johnson & Malony make up an essential part of this chapter. A major argument is that Christian mission, with a prime interest in conversion, must focus on people in context. A supplementary case study of Simon Peter, the apostle and author of some of the New Testament books, as well as the case study of G. Chewe P. will supply the data for this argument.

Chapter ten contains the third missiological "C" – counselling. The last four months of Chewe's life are at the heart of this chapter. The interaction between the counsellor (author) and counsellee (Chewe) is shown. Issues like theological ethics and matters pertaining to the cultural gap between the counsellor and the counsellee come under review. Of significant interest is Zeno Vendler's theory on understanding people as being especially critical in intercultural exchange (1984).

Conclusions and findings of this study are summarized in chapter eleven.

4.4 End Piece

The thesis ends with appendices, a glossary containing foreign words or technical terms, and a bibliography of all publications cited such as books, articles in magazines or periodicals.

Chapter 2
The Bemba in Zambia

1. Introduction

This chapter does not seek to reconstruct a romantic past or heroic history of the Bemba people in Northern Zambia. Nor does it attempt to facilitate a missionary call for indigenization. Instead, it is an intentional and researched presentation of data. Although basically historical in nature, it demonstrates its relevance to the concepts of space and time in order to bring to light some specific elements of Bemba traditional culture (e.g. the transcendence, *umupashi* as *"spirit double"* of a person) that will play into the discussion at a later stage.

2. The Bemba: Travellers and Conquerors

The Bemba occupy an area of approximately 20,000 square miles on the North Eastern plateau, between the latitudes 9°-12° south and longitudes 29°-32° east, in the Northern Province of Zambia. This vast surface area, Whitely writes, "includes virtually the whole of Kasama administrative district and much of Mpika, Chinsali, Luwingu and Mporokoso" (1950:1). How the Bemba came to settle into this vast expanse of the Northern plateau is part of their own tribal history as well as part of the migratory history of the Central Bantu tribes in general.

Carey's (1986) overview of the historical literature on the Bemba encompasses scholars from various fields. He acknowledges the works and writings by missionaries, (Garrec, 1917; Labrecque, 1931; Etienne 1948; Tanguy, 1954; Oger, 1972); colonial administrators (Gouldsbury and Sheane, 1911; Brelsford, 1942; 1944); an anthropologist (Richards, 1939; 1940); and a professional historian (Roberts, 1973) (1986:ix). The works of two linguists (Guthrie, 1962; Werner, 1971; 1979/1999) and the books of two educationists (Snelson, 1974 and Ipenburg, 1992) compliment the list of scholars as presented by Carey. Hence, there is no genuine need to undertake a comprehensive study of Bemba history, considering the bulk of the readily available data. I will therefore limit the scope of study by treating two features of Bemba history and Bemba culture: space and time.

2.1 Travellers in Time

The Bemba belong to the large group of Bantu tribes that migrated into North Eastern Zambia from the Lunda-Luba empires between the Lualaba and Kasai rivers in the present-day Shaba province of the Democratic Republic of Congo (Carey 1986:31). In light of the available data, it appears that the

Bemba did not emigrate[1] from their place of origin as a whole tribe at one particular time, but were rather organized in the form of clans (Roberts 1973:67-85) who moved out of their original habitat in successive waves of emigration. Roberts' reconstruction of oral and written accounts of the Bemba royal Chitimukulu dynasty proposes a *"terminus ante quem* for the settlement of the Bemba royals in Bembaland" c. 1700 (1970:232. See also Tanguy 1996:9). This chronology leaves approximately two hundred years of immigration, settlement and establishment of harsh and powerful Bemba rule (Hinfelaar 1994:21)[2] and domination of the Northern plateau before they had to submit to the colonial powers in 1899.[3] The span of approximately two centuries of Bemba reign is preserved in oral tradition, albeit interspersed with gaps and inconclusive data.[4]

Missionaries and colonial personnel were the first persons who compiled written records of Bemba history, extracted from and constructed of Bemba oral accounts beginning at the turn of the twentieth century. The few written documents by early travellers and explorers,[5] the absence of more accurate written information prior to the colonial and missionary era, and the disparity of oral data pose problems for the science of history[6] in which historical events are presented in linear time sequences. However precarious the historical data may be, there is a history to tell, history that is grounded in language, a history that receives validity in real life events within the oral community. As Ki-Zerbo observes, for African societies "history is seen less as a science and more as a form of wisdom, as an art of living given substance through speech" (1990:89). A Bemba proverb aptly attests to the previously mentioned: *umweo wa muntu waba mu kutwi,* "the life of someone is in the ear." Obviously, the proverb does not speak about biological life and its origin in the ear. The proverb reiterates that life, and, more precisely, wisdom to act, emanates from speech and its content of past events preserved in language

---

[1] Also known as the "Luba-Lunda dispersion" (Carey 1986:31).

[2] Hinfelaar says that Bemba women speak of the Bemba chiefs of former times as "the *Bashamfumu ba ku Lubemba* (paramounts from Bemba-land) ... [to have] been *Nkakashi* (mean) and *Bakali* (cruel)" (1994:21).

[3] For more detail on the Bemba surrender to colonial rule, see Part Two, "Historic Approach to *Ngulu* Possession."

[4] Snelson remarks that "there are many gaps in the recorded history of Zambia" (1990:v).

[5] "Lacerda, Father Pinto, Gamitto and Livingstone are the most well-known of the early explorers and missionaries who have written in this area" (Werner 1971:3). See also Coxhead 1914 (in Whitely 1950:8).

[6] That, of course, does not imply that written accounts are inherently accurate, nor does it mean that oral accounts are to be treated with a note of caution per se. Rather, both modes of preserving history can contain an element of fake, manipulated, partial, incomplete, etc. data. Either way, the whole question of accuracy hinges on the human factor, that is, the person who writes or speaks history.

(e.g. historical records, proverbs, riddles, parables etc.) rather than the facts preserved in the impersonal medium of paper and ink.[7]

"Language as a system and tool of communication is a historical phenomenon" because "history is a product of language on two accounts: as discourse and as historical evidence" (Ki-Zerbo 1990:89). It is the sound of words conveyed from the mouth of the speaker to the ear of the listener that creates a bond – and thus life – between the two in space and time.[8]

The travelling episodes of the bands of Bemba clusters from the forfeited West to the hopeful East over periods of migratory movements into North Eastern Zambia are deeply engrained into the worldview of the Bemba. For example, during the initiation rite of Bemba girls (*Cisungu*), the east-west axis is a central theme for the initiates, says Hinfelaar, an acknowledged Catholic scholar (1994:3-6).[9] The West signifies the place of origin but also the place of turmoil, darkness, night and death.[10] In sharp contrast, the East represents "the future, hope and expectation, light and happiness."[11] Even after the settling of the earliest immigrants from the East had taken place in the land, perpetual travelling did not cease. The first settlers had to give way to subsequent waves of "conquistadors" pressing in from the West. Moreover, the country was infested with the tsetse fly, and the poor fertility of the soil kept people on the move to even greener pastures (Hinfelaar 1994:2). This historical experience made a deep imprint on peoples' life. Thus, the perpetual travelling of their past experience permeated Bemba worldview.

---

[7] Wendland, investigating sermons of the Malawian Evangelist Wame, speaks of the Malawian people as "still predominantly oral-aural, rather than print/script oriented, by nature" (2000:43-44). I take it that this would be also the general situation in Zambia and even more so among the Bemba people in the Northern Province. Maxwell too explicitly characterizes the Bemba "as an oral people" (1983:26).

[8] The major difference between the narrator of history and the writer of history lies in the fact that literate technology makes a person's mind withdraw into self-consciousness apart from tribal consciousness. Maxwell adds that "a writer works alone dissociating words from the total situation of the original dialogue" (1983:153). Ong says that a writer does not merely write words but analyzes elusive sounds into spatial components which are abstract. This in turn makes processes of greater analysis possible (in Maxwell 1983:153).

[9] The Bemba girl undergoing the *Cisungu* ceremony is called *nacisungu* (pl. *banacisungu*). "*Na*" is a female prefix. Because of the practice of teknonymy, women are called by the names of their daughters or sons. For example, *banaChanda* means "the mother of Chanda." The prefix "*ba*" is a second person plural personal pronoun and frequently used as an honorific.

[10] The Bemba Royal Charter tells of the three sons of Chief Mukulumpe Mubemba in the land of Kola whose anger was aroused against them when one of the three was held responsible for the death of many tribespeople. Katongo, the culprit son, was punished and blinded by his father. The two other sons, Chiti and Nkole, evaded punishment and escaped with their followers on a journey to the East, fleeing their father's wrath (see Maxwell 1983:37).

[11] In the East, the Bemba migrants found a place of refuge and a homeland for future generations (Hinfelaar 1994:3). The west-east axis also comes to light at death. Graves are aligned with the West-east axis. The head will always face the East.

Histroy as a form of wisdom is, however, not derived from the reiteration of the linear sequence of historical events, but is recalled in cyclic intervals, reaffirming their relevance for the present condition. The abstract idea of linear time (and its finite boundaries!) is effectively substituted with the concept of cyclic sequences upholding the perpetuity of life. Within the realm of the Immanent, perpetuity of life is maintained through the rites of passage which usher the individual from one level to the next higher and more important sphere of perpetuity.

For example, the first crucial passage of entering the world of the living is birth. But in Bemba belief, this merely underlines the biological event. A newborn baby has not yet entered into the state of being human. **The birth-event must be completed by the *name-event,* that is, *human-identity* is achieved by *name-identity.*** Before this can happen, the infant must first dispose of the umbilical cord, the physical evidence of its former attachment to the mother. Thereafter, the child is ready to receive its name. It is the ritual at the name-giving ceremony (*kwinika ishina*) that transforms the human like creature, *katuutu*,[12] into a fully recognized human being, *umuntu*.[13] But the naming of a child is not just an affair of random choice. To many Bemba people, the choosing of a name involves careful consideration. It is an act of guided and directed choice.[14] Direction in the choice of the name comes from the Transcendence via dreams given to the parents or other close family members of the child by *umupashi*. By definition *umupashi* is "*the being that survives the death of the body and retains the personality of a person.*"[15] In short, at death a person turns into *umupashi*[16] (pl. *imipashi*) and becomes the "*spirit double*" of another living person.[17]

---

[12] A newborn baby is called *katuutu*. The word consists of the preposition "*ka*" and places the term into the diminutive class of nouns and not into the specific class of nouns for human beings. The stem *-tuutu* contains the elements of *white or transparent* and *emptiness*. Thus, *katuutu* signifies a "little, white/transparent" and "empty living *thing*." This term is exclusively used for newborn babies. A newborn baby is *not* a human being until it receives its name. Similar beliefs also exist among other African people. For example, in Lugbara thought, a mature adult is "distinct from an infant who is referred to as a 'thing'" (Middleton 1973:495).

[13] *Umuntu*, meaning "a member of the Bantu race in particular and person, human being in general." The plural form is *abantu*.

[14] I have written on this subject elsewhere (Badenberg 1999:75-77).

[15] I proposed this definition in an earlier discourse (Badenberg 1999:90).

[16] There are exceptions to the rule. Mad people, witches and wizards, and persons who have committed suicide are disqualified.

[17] In an earlier work (see above), I used the term "*spiritual double*" as a definition of *umupashi*, but here I revise this definition and use instead the term "*spirit double.*" A. E. Crawley (1909; 1911) in his book *The Idea of the Soul* (1909) and his article "Double" (1911) first coined the term "*spiritual double.*" I kindly acknowledge this information provided by Prof. Käser: Private correspondence, June 13, 2000.

2.1.1 Definitions of *"Umupashi"* in the Relevant Literature

Barnes (1922) was of the opinion that *umupashi* cannot be associated with a living person (1922:41). He was, however, restrained in his observation in as far as he tried to establish the meaning of *umupashi* according to the English concept of "spirit" or the Greek term *"pneuma."* Moreover, his article on the subject is rather short to say the least. His information is too vague to arrive at conclusive ideas on the concept of *umupashi* – a fact, which Hochegger (1965), in his overview of soul concepts in Africa considering data from 1881 to 1961, rightly bemoans (1965:319).

Audrey I. Richards worked in Bembaland as the first anthropologist in the early 1930s. In her book *Mother-Right among the Central Bantu* (1934/1970), she remarks and specifically acknowledges the "unusually complete"[18] identification that takes place between the deceased person and his or her heir. Richards interpreted this interaction of *umupashi* and a living person to mean that the former becomes the *"guardian spirit"* of the latter.[19]

Tanguy (1954) writes that in Bemba thought the composition of a human being is twofold: the body (*umubili*) and the spirit (*umweo*). At death, *umweo* leaves the body and is called *umupashi*. Tanguy calls the *imipashi* (pl. of *umupashi*) the *"ghosts of the dead"* (1954/1983:106).

For Werner (1971), the worship of the *imipashi* forms the "most significant personal commitment among the Bemba" (1971:7). His definition of *umupashi "tutelary spirit,"*[20] is in essence a guardian or protector (of a living human being), following Richards' line of thinking.

More in line with Tanguy's definition of *imipashi* is Oger's (1972) who speaks of them as the *"souls of the ordinary departed"* (1972:27), while pointing out that there are exceptions like the nature of death or the mental state of a person during his lifetime.

Maxwell's position (1983) on *imipashi* takes on a forceful human twist. Though they are *"ancestral spirits,"* they undoubtedly have a human matrix. "They were humans once and may be born human again" (1983:23). Despite the superior powers of *imipashi*, which are obvious to and acknowledged by the community, the Bemba extricate themselves from their innate powers by "religious finesse" (1983:23).

---

[18] Every Bemba must be succeeded at death. The heir takes, next to his name, status, and social obligation, his *mupashi*. "In this case the identification between the dead man and his heir seems to me unusually complete" (Richards 1970:269).

[19] See also Richards 1982:28-29.

[20] I am not entirely satisfied with the term "tutelary spirit" in relation to *umupashi*, because, as Schoffeleers remarks, the term carries a wide range of meanings. He says, "Tutelary spirits appear to be of a great variety. There are snake deities, High Gods, prophet-like figures, deceased chiefs, priests and other persons of fame" (1999:11).

Carey (1986) agrees with Maxwell, referring to *imipashi* as *"ancestral spirits"* (1986:32). However, Carey is less elaborate on how the human mode comes into play, but is more concerned in commenting on the rituals for *imipashi* such as veneration (*kupala*), ritual beer drinking after the funeral (*bwalwa bwa lupopo*), succession (*ubupyani*), and so on (see 1986:32-39).

Ipenburg (1992) only briefly touches on the subject in a reference to the Bible Translation by Lubwa protestant missionaries into the vernacular Bemba. He claims the Bemba word *umupashi* is "a word that originally meant *an ancestor who had passed on* [italics mine]" (1992:23).

Hinfelaar (1994) takes a distinguished position insofar as he draws attention to a Bemba person's ultimate strife in life during his earthly days. For example, during the girls" initiation rites (*Cisungu*) emphasis is laid on teaching the neophytes that perfect Transcendence is achieved through the acquisition of the opposite gender. (1994:6). "One is created here on earth in order to become a *Mupashi Mukankala*, a rich and generous spirit/forbearer." (1994:6) It is in this regard that *umupashi* is to be understood as a *""twin-gender shade,"* that grants life and health to the next generation" (1994:6). From what has been said above, the outstanding feature of perpetuity in Bemba tradition, thought and belief is evident. Perpetuity ingrained in the Bemba worldview assigns the human being his rightful place in the realm of the Immanent; but the spirit being is to render his services in the realm of the Transcendent.

2.1.2 A New Definition Proposed

The reason why I proposed the definition of *umupashi* as the *"spirit double of a living person"* stems from research I did in the years 1995 to 1998. The linguistic data I collected revealed that the concept of *"spirit double"* is an important addition to what earlier research (as roughly sketched above) had previously brought to light. The concept of *"spirit double"* is thouroughly documented in Käser's dissertation (1977), a linguistic documentation of the concept of "soul" among the islanders of Truk (today Chuuk), a tiny island in the Pacific Ocean belonging to the Federated States of Micronesia.

In the Truk (Chuuk) language there is the term *ngúún* which carries various characteristics. *Ngúún* is the shadow of an object when the outer shape of the object is at least recognizable. Also, the mirror image of an object or a person is called *ngúún*. A third aspect of *ngúún* is the conception that all things in this world, next to their material, physical existence, also exist in an immaterial, spiritual form. These two forms are so meticulously identical that one can easily be mistaken for the other (1977:119-121). The *ngúún* of a human person, however, outweighs the *ngúún* of the above-mentioned contexts.

First, a human being possesses two *"spirit doubles"* at the same time: a benevolent *"spirit double"* (*ngúnúyééch*) and a malevolent *"spirit double"* (*ngúnúnngaw*) (1977:229).

Second, the *"spirit double"* of a human being has features that are exclusively his. The *ngúnúyééch* (benevolent *"spirit double"*) of a person can be seen in a person's dreams but, while he is awake, can only be seen by persons who qualify as medium or seer.

Above all, a *ngúnúyééch* possesses human-like features such as body attributes, speech and senses.

But most importantly, the *ngúnúyééch* possesses a psyche of its own. In times of trouble, a *ngúnúyééch* moans, might be frightened or feel homesick. Its permanent psychical disposition is positive and the *ngúnúyééch* is endowed with exceptional intelligence. In short, a *ngúnúyééch* resembles his human counterpart in detail, is intelligent and friendly, has a positive permanent psychical disposition, and has strongly-attached emotions toward the physical body of a person (1977:232-237, 290). [21]

Käser's definition of *"spirit double"* is fitting for the Bemba context. *Umupashi* resembles the human companion in detail (*umupashi* may appear in human-like form in a dream, but his[22] existence does not require a body). *Umupashi* is conceived to be a good and beneficiary being, that is, he possesses a positive permanent psychical disposition – *imibele isuma* (despite some disciplinary actions – like sickness – dealt out at times to his human counterpart). Furthermore, *umupashi* possesses a psyche or *SEIC* of his own:[23] he is capable of intellectual processes like thinking, wanting, and remembering, but also undergoes psychical changes like feelings of anger and discontent. Moreover, *umupashi* is the decisive agent in affecting the transformation of a "little, empty/transparent thing" (*katuutu*) into a human being (*umuntu*) at the reception of a child's name. The "emptiness" or "transparency" is replaced by *umupashi* depositing *imibele* (permanent psychical dispositions or charac-

---

[21] For more information on *ngúnúyééch* see pages 238-291.

[22] Though *umupashi* is of neither male nor female sex, I prefer to use the personal pronoun "my/he/his" in order to reflect Bemba language characteristics. For example, *umupashi wandi wacimpela icimonwa ku tulo*, means 'my *umupashi* (*spirit double*) gave me a vision while asleep.' The genderlessness of *umupashi* is also the reason why both boys and girls can receive the same name. One cannot distinguish the sex of a person by only the name. For example, *Chilufya, Mutale, Bwalya,* and *Mubanga* are typical Bemba names given to boys and girls alike.

[23] There is evidence to support this assumption. *Umupashi*, "the being that survives the death of the body," the *"spirit double,"* carries with it the *umutima* (heart), that is, psyche of person. A specific aspect of *umutima* is the reference for personality or character traits (*imibele*). It is the "good *imibele*" which qualify *umutima* to be "good." Musonda says of the Bisa, a Bemba speaking people: "*umutima* survives after death and the *umupashi* continues to have it. If an individual had a good *umutima* then his or her *umupashi* would have a good *umutima* too" (1996:126). The idea of *umupashi* possessing a psyche himself is clearly expressed here. Other aspects of *umutima* include the seat of emotions (*imyumfwikile ya mutima*) and the center of intellectual processes: *ukufwaya* means "to want," *ukutontonkanya*, "to think, to ponder," *ukubukisha*, "to cause to come back to life," or "to remember," etc. (see Badenberg 1999:70-71).

ter traits) into the *SEIC* (*umutima*) of the child. *Imibele* stem from the forbearer of the name of the child and are, so to speak, revitalized or made tangible again in another person. From that moment on, the child has left the sphere of things and has entered the community of human beings.[24]

2.1.3 "Reincarnation?"

At this point, the issue of "reincarnation" might arise. In my own understanding, this term is only partly suitable for describing the revitalization of the "incorporeal dimension" (Klass 1995) of *umupashi*, as it may include the notion of fate and the inescapability of a person's destiny. This is not the case, at least not in the Bemba context. A person in his or her lifetime is indeed capable of effectively breaking the cycle of perpetuity ('multiple incarnations') through careless living. The life-style and *imibele* of a person correspond in a reciprocal manner. Bad morals and permanent evil as well as an individual's unacceptable behavior do not only affect his or her own psyche, but also qualitatively alter the *SEIC* of one's *umupashi* and turn the benevolent *"spirit double"* (*umupashi*) into a malevolent *"spirit double"* (*icibanda*). Such a person most certainly forfeits his potential of becoming a *"Mupashi Mukankala."* In the event of that person's death while in this unreformed state, the name would most probably be erased from the potential repertoire of family names. Therefore, the term "reincarnation" is used at best as an auxiliary term, for lack of a better definition.

2.1.4 The Concept of "Spirit Double" in other African Cultures

The concept of *"spirit double"* in the African context is a field of research that has so far been rather neglected.[25] Nevertheless, this concept has not gone unnoticed, and African scholars like Ikenga-Metuh (1991a and 1991b) and Ogunboye (2000)[26] have reinforced this area by documenting the thought-world of the Igbo and the Yoruba in West Africa. As Ikenga-Metuh puts it,

---

[24] For more details see Badenberg (1999) chapters 4 to 6.

[25] "Until recently, Western scholars have failed to appreciate the extent to which African religions are founded upon a systematic anthropology and ethics," says Ray (in Ikenga-Metuh 1991:51).

[26] In Igbo context, "the *chi*...is a sort of spirit double or guardian genius associated with the person from the moment of conception...but *eke* is believed to be an ancestral shade incarnate in each new baby. The baby takes after the *eke* in appearance and/or character." Yoruba thought conceives of *ori* as a guardian spirit of the person (Ogunboye with Lois Fuller 2000:77-78). The Lugbara of Uganda also have the term *ori* and may be defined as "the being that survives the death of the body." *Orindi* (the essence of the spirit being *ori*), is the seat of the emotions, or, as I have suggested above in the Bemba context, the psyche of a person. If and to what extent the two terms have a common root could be a worthwhile subject of investigation. Especially in the light of the geographical distance between the Yoruba of Nigeria and the Lugbara of Uganda! The interplay between *ori* and *orindi* is not just a linguistic accident, but has specific bearings on the concept of person in Lugbara thought. For more details see Middleton 1973: 493-494.

"to understand Igbo religious beliefs as the Igbo understand them."[27] The concept of *umupashi* as the *"spirit double"* of a person should not be understood as universalistic or normative for every Bemba person to the same degree.[28] But despite the dynamics that operate in culture and the variations of people's personal views on this subject, the validity and the relevance of *umupashi* as the *"spirit double"* of a person is not diminished. Finally, I mainly consider Bemba rural village communities, which tend to be far more traditional and conservative, opposed to Bemba communities of metropolitan background.

Pell suggests that time in the Zambian/African context carries the basic notion of event rather than the concept of time in linear fashion (Pell 1993:54). Time dimension in Bemba culture switches effortlessly back and forth from the past to the present, from past event(s) to present event(s), from the Immanent to the Transcendent. The Bemba employ the historical resources of the past for their services and requirements in the present. The nexus that holds the perpetuity of life together is solely placed into the hands of the human agent. It is man who encompasses the Immanent and the Transcendent and conquers both by infusing historical events into present situations in cyclic fashions generation after generation.

2.2 Conquerors of Space

The vast expanse of the Northern plateau was not devoid of peoples when the Bemba first pressed into their territories. Geographical space was a pertinent issue that had to be settled with the earlier, original inhabitants and earlier immigrants. The immigrating Bemba used predominantly force and only limited negotiation and diplomacy to decide the matter. Their immigration was a successive wave of conquest and subjugation of previous immigrants[29] and

---

[27] Quoted in "BookNotes for Africa: Notes on Recent Africa-related Publications of Potential Interest for Theological Educators and Libraries in Africa." Theological College of Central Africa (TCCA), Zambia and Harare Theological College, Zimbabwe, no. 4 (October 1997): 1-21, 11. The Book review is signed with the letters LKF (the full name could not be traced).

[28] In the quest for understanding human culture, the history of studying culture and cultural themes has experienced a great many different approaches and opinions like, for example, the Durkheimian view. For Obeyesekere, Durkheim's early view of culture ("culture exists independent of and before the individual" (1984:111) led anthropologists to belief that "shared culture must produce shared behavior – or, to be more exact, behavioral regularity" (1984:111). A view Obeyesekere calls a "horrendous fallacy" (1984:111). He further says that "collectively held knowledge may vary with individuals and groups within a larger society (1984:111). The emphasis clearly is on "the same degree per se." The concept of *umupashi* as the "spirit double" of a person is knowledge held by members of Bemba culture. This knowledge is, however, held collectively as well as individually. "Collectively held knowledge" is the smelter from which individuals draw the substances to form and construct individual ideas/concepts, which in turn will eventually be infused into the smelter again and become part of the "collectively held knowledge" as the individual ideas/concepts circulate and permeate other members of society.

[29] Such as the Lungu, Tabwe, and the Fiba. See O'Shea 1986:25-26.

the original inhabitants.[30] At the peak of their quest for land, they had penetrated deep into the territories of the Tabwa, Lungu, Bisa,[31] and Lala and, through the incessant wars with these peoples, had established firm control over them. The original inhabitants, the *Bashimatongwa*[32] and their presence in this part of Central Africa have become history.[33] They were either completely absorbed by intermarriage with the Bemba Bantu people, or driven out and forced to migrate to the south, or even both.

But the matter of claiming and controlling physical space was but one side of the ambitious and cruel war episodes of the marauding Bemba. Such successes of conquest could never have rested on the bravery of the Bemba warriors. Nor can it be ascribed to the shrewd tactics of their commanders alone. Conquered space was more than vast expanses of soil. It was land that was richly endowed with rivers, trees, mountains, waterfalls, caves, and watersources – in short, habitats of spiritual powers. Also, the remnants of abandoned villages were strong reminders of forces that could not easily be subdued by bravery and tactics (Maxwell 1983:83). All these geographical features and places once full with human activities were "sacralized by the spirits of former chiefs and fixed in memory by the stories told about them" (Maxwell 1983:83). Thus, the other side of the Bemba conquest is an episode of geographical space versus transcendental territory. The invasion by Bemba forces into occupied geographical space was simultaneously an invasion into the realm of the spirits of the land. While the matter of geographical space was confronted forcefully, the issue of conquering transcendental space had to be settled with an attitude of compromise.

2.2.1 Hypothesis: The *"Shimwalule"* Compromise

Van Binsbergen (1979/1999) hypothesizes that the Bemba *Bena Ng'andu* royal clan immigrants had little interest in strengthening their relationship with earlier Luba immigrants and making them priest-councillors. There was minimal to nil benefit from this union. The *Bena Ng'andu* interest lay clearly in the control over land to which the pre-Luba priests "possessed the key to ultimate legitimacy: ritual control over extended land areas" (van Binsbergen 1999:70). A compromise was therefore not an option but an act of forced necessity. One

---

[30] Ipenburg notes that the Bemba were "dreaded" by their neighbours. As an example of their reputation, he recounts an incidence that happened to Rev Dewar who tried to reach the Bemba in 1896. "In that year the Dewars had an encounter with a raiding party of Bemba, who had put human heads on poles to terrify them" (1992:30).

[31] Hinfelaar says that around 1830 the Bisa peoples were forcefully separated, as the Bemba drove a deep wedge into their territory stretching as far as the Chinama area of Mpika (1994:24).

[32] They were people of Khoisan extraction, and were called the *Bashimatongwa*, the aborigines. (Hinfelaar 1994:2).

[33] About three kilometers East of Kasama, on the road to Isoka, cave paintings of "bushmen" origin can be visited.

way to achieve full control over the land was to encapsulate the pre-Luba territorial priests into the *Bena Ng'andu* system. Van Binsbergen further suggests, though admittedly hypothetically, that the *Bena Ng'andu*, for example, moved swiftly and made *Shimwalule*, a local original priest, "the most senior non-royal Bemba authority" (1999:71).[34] Subsequent *Shimwalule* attained authority to oversee the burial of the Chitimukulu, the Bemba Paramount chief "who has important "ecological" functions" (van Binsbergen 1999:71).

The hierarchical leadership style of the *Bena Ng'andu* achieved dominance by holding political power in a twofold manner: by commanding service[35] and by controlling resources. Conquests of earlier inhabitants and their territories, was established by enforcing a tributary system upon the conquered peoples. Thus, they effectively were at the service of their overlords. The latter came about by encapsulating the earlier territorial priests into the *Bena Ng'andu* system (as it might have been the case with *Shimwalule*). In doing so, they placed a firm hand on the control of ecological power and natural resources. In effect, they consequently became the owners of the land. A successful political system like the Bemba exercised is highly dependent on at least these two factors: defining and controlling the power structure, and maintaining control over all available ecological resources.

2.2.2 Hypothesis: The *"Mwine wa Mushi"* Compromise

Hinfelaar (1994) points out that the *Bena Ng'andu*, for example, resorted to yet another compromise.[36] Before the Bemba conquest, villages had a *Mwine Mushi*, a local priest, "often the son of a secondary wife and regarded as a *mwine calo* (owner of the land)" (Hinfelaar 1994:21). After the conquest, the villages and their *Mwine Mushi* were complimented by the appointment of the *Mwine wa Mushi* (Headman).[37] His installation was decreed by central appointment (chiefs and/or Paramount chief Chitimukulu) and his function was political rather than spiritual. His function was that of a governor answerable to the chief and responsible to see to it "that royal ritual was observed" (Hinfelaar 1994:21). The Bemba were resourceful enough to seek a best possible solution to the problem of placating the spirit guardians of the land for them-

---

[34] Maxwell refers to *Shimwalule* as the "priest and royal undertaker" (1983:44).

[35] Compare Richards 1970:269.

[36] It was compromise exclusively from the Bemba point of view, but certainly not one for the original inhabitants.

[37] Interestingly enough, the history of the Luapula valley depicts an almost identical case. The original or earliest remembered inhabitants of a piece of land, the *Bwilile*, were remembered as *mwine wa mpanga* or *mushi wa calo*, "the owners of the forest/land." When the *Shila* and later the *Lunda* pressed in and imposed themselves, they would provide a *"mwine wa mpanga* in a political sense for every piece of country" from their own ranks. The *mwine wa mpanga*, the original settler, was the owner by the fact of being there first, and his ritual authority. The *mwine wa mpanga* imposed by the conquerors became the political owner "by right and might, or cunning or duplicity" (Cunnison 1951:14, 16).

selves. They were in dire need of the blessings of the *mwine calo*, the "owners of the land." A total abolition of original guardians of geographical space (*mwine mushi*) and their mediating role as guardians of transcendental space would have resulted in a cosmic catastrophe with serious repercussions for the intruders as well as the whole country. This was prevented by the cunning move of incorporating the exit and introducing the alternative under the guise of the *Mwine wa Mushi*. In terms of language, the adaptation was minimal but in terms of societal impact, it carried maximum effect. An effective substitution might eventually come to mean an effective abolition.

2.2.3 Transcendence and Immanence: Cultural Ambivalence

As far as the Bemba are concerned, their cosmic view of the Transcendence reaching out into the Immanent constitutes cultural ambivalence. People must find ways and means of coping with the two. Acts committed against *imipashi* (familial ancestral spirits), such as negligence, attract their vengeance. Sickness and other calamities might befall the family or village community. In times of drought, famine or other disaster of magnitude, man and society are compelled to seek and obtain "mercy" from *imipashi*. But the critical point is that this situation is not without remedy. It is not a cultural one-way street with a dead end. Long-established rituals handed down over generations not only help in approaching the *imipashi*, but also in achieving *mipashi's* compliance with human requests. An illustration shall make the issue clearer.

2.2.4 Ritual in Word and Deed: Conquering Transcendental Space

The correct or appropriate ritual in *word* and *deed* compels the spirits to render their services to the receptive earthly community. For example, the concept of *umupashi* as the *"spirit double"* of a living person is a potential element in the upbringing of a child to Bemba communities. At a certain stage, above the age of five or six years, a child's recurring misbehavior against communal laws and values cannot be tolerated or left unattended. Misbehavior is the outward manifestation of the kind of *imibele* (character traits) that dwell *mu mutima* (inside the heart, the *SEIC*) of the child. In other words, bad behavior of the child might also reflect the temporal psychical disposition of its *umupashi*. *Umupashi* might be angered by some careless actions and might signal his displeasure via non-conformity in the child's behavior. Measures of reprimand and/or discipline of the child are not really thought to correct this situation. It is the ritual in *word* – the sound that is released in immanent space and penetrating transcendental space – and *deed* that can ameliorate this precarious situation. In the example of the behavior of a child found to have been involved in repeated stealing, the family elders gather to confront *umupashi* of the child in *word* and *deed*. According to the seriousness of the matter, the deed could involve the death of a chicken with its blood being poured onto the ground. In accompaniment of the *deed*, the following *words* might be said.

> *Twamipeele nkoko iyi pakuti mutubeleleko uluse uyu mwana aleke ubupupu.* "We present to you [*umupashi*] this chicken seeking mercy and pleading with you to forgive us so that this child desists from theft in the future."

The concern that is felt over the child who is showing a tendency of developing bad habits (e.g., stealing) and nourishing bad character traits (*imibele iibi*) is brought before *umupashi*. The *deed* in the sacrifice is meant to sooth the psyche (prevent *umupashi* from further withdrawing from the child) whereas the accompanying *words* are thought to sooth the "ear" of *umupashi* (to arouse positive emotions in his psyche/*SEIC*).

The request for intervention brought before *umupashi* already carries the expectation of potential change of the child's behavior in future. Noticeable positive changes in the child's way of life are readily welcomed and acknowledged in a statement like:

> *Umupashi ulelungamika imibele ya mu mutima. Umupashi* (usually the name is also mentioned) is straightening out *imibele* (character traits) in the heart.[38]

By calling on *umupashi* to "straighten out" *imibele* of a child, man is *ipso facto* conquering transcendental territory. The chicken that is given in the sacrifice is not the demand of *umupashi*, but the choice made by the human agent(s). The crux of the matter, the ambivalence of total reliance on and total command over *imipashi*, has, in the final analysis, not only been balanced through the ritual, but has in fact made the pendulum swing wholly in man's favor. "Religious finesse," to borrow Maxwell's words (1983:23) – indeed.

Again, Maxwell aptly comments:

> All Bemba religious practices seek to establish and maintain the central and regulative human place in the whole formed by the spiritual and physical universe. The Bemba are tenaciously terrestrial, and their vision of themselves-their life, their world and divinity-is determined by their earthly fixation. They are at once the image, the model and the integral part of the universe in whose cyclical life they are powerfully engaged but not overwhelmed (1983:22).

---

[38] The metaphor of "straightening out" implies that something was "bent, or "crooked." The perception is that bad character traits (*imibele iibi*) are due to a "bent" or "crooked" *SEIC*.

3. A Concluding Reflection

MacGaffey asserts that the Europeans and the BaKongo understand the organization of the world in their own ways. Each presupposes its own cosmology. Western culture defines the dimensions of space and time by history and geography. The BaKongo express their cosmology by myth and beliefs about life, death or race (1983:18-19).

What MacGaffey establishes for the BaKongo is also a valid observation for the BaBemba. Earlier in the discussion, it was shown that the travelling history of the Bemba has left a definite and deep imprint on Bemba worldview. Time is not channelled and squeezed into linear chronological sequences ("western cosmology") and logical subjection to finite borderlines. Time and again, oral history draws from infinite time, recounting past events in order to extract life from the historical load infusing it into the present context of personal and societal experience.[39] Says Mbiti about African societies in general "...time is a composition of events, people...do not reckon it in a vacuum" (1969:19). Infinite time in oral history is thus transferred via the oral community onto the life history of the clan, family and individual.

Life itself is not finite; rather, death is a transition from one mode of existence (*umuntu*) into another mode of existence (*umupashi*).[40] Although history-time and life-time derive their meaning and power from cyclical intervals, both are far from being a closed circuit. Oral history is recounted and reconstructed by both the narrator and the listener. Life history is the account of events describing and characterizing the relationship between a human being and his *"spirit double."* To sum up, man is the main protagonist in oral time as well as in oral history, which is broken down into clan, family, and personal history.

It was also shown that geographical space vs. transcendental space was the other side of the Bemba conquest. In conclusion, I concur with Maxwell when he says that, in *both realms,* man takes on a regulative position in the universe. Maxwell also singles out five "basic characteristics of Bemba religion" of which one is "anthropocentric."[41] Bemba worldview is 'anthropocentric': at

---

[39] Wendland in a section entitled "The Indigenous Model of African Oral Tradition," highlights three important features in "oral tradition." First, "they are firmly grounded in the real life experiences and environmental setting of the audience, ... secondly, they are strongly participatory in presentation, ...and finally, these varied instances of oral literature (e.g. proverbs, riddles, dramatic narratives, dilemma tale myths, legends etc.), are clearly functional in nature" (2000:39-41).

[40] Maxwell says: "Death is an interlude, a fall back position, a higher rank from which the Bemba regroup their human resources for a new assault on terrestrial life" (1983:23).

[41] The other four basic characteristics of Bemba religion are: "traditional," "communal," "vitally dynamic," and "cosmically holistic" (Maxwell 1983:20).

its center is man indeed.[42] It is exactly for this reason that the concept of person "is central to any conceptualization and understanding of social relations" (Middleton 1973:492).

But the concept of person is not only central to understanding social relations, it is also central for a better understanding of the person in his species-conditioned mode of physical and psychical existence. In order to comprehend a person in his physical existence, a linguistic description – that is, the names describing the human body – has to be researched and recorded. The Bemba language provides material for such an investigation, as there is ample vocabulary for the different parts of the body. The collection and the recording of linguistic data are indispensable elements in formulating a theoretical framework of the concept of body for any culture.

Therefore, the following chapter shall provide specific and select linguistic data on the parts of the body forming a basis for a closer description of man and in particular a Bemba concept of body.

---

[42] "The spirits have to give us what we request from them. If they are approached in the morning, it is expected that they will respond positively in the afternoon." This statement underlines the fact that it is man indeed who sets the conditionalities of action. Private conversation with Gabriel Pitiloshi, Kasama, June 13, 2000.

PART I:
BODY AND ILLNESS:
AN ANTHROPOLOGICAL PERSPECTIVE

Chapter 3
An Outline of the Concept of Body

1. Introduction

Lothar Käser's (1983/1989) detailed linguistic documentation on the concept of body of the Islanders of Truk (today Chuuk) has made important contributions toward attempting to fill the historical gaps that exist in the migration theory of peoples of the islands of Micronesia.[1] Next to physical objects of the existing material culture and artefacts of the archaic material culture, language, in particular the terms for the parts of the body, consists of extremely important keys to unravelling, for example, the migratory history of peoples. The methodology of collecting and presenting linguistic data of the body in Käser's study of the Truk concept of body furnish the basis for this chapter on the Bemba concept of body. Considering the limitations of this study, I will limit my scope of investigation on this concept to the Bemba of Zambia. I am aware that this restriction poses a deficiency insofar as I have to focus on select linguistic material for select parts or functions of the body in Bemba thinking.

With regards to the theoretical framework of this chapter, I will make use of the tools cognitive anthropology provides for this particular field of research. Cognitive anthropology operates by applying qualitative methods. Taylor and Bogdan write that "participant observation, in-depth interviewing, and others that yield descriptive data" (1984:2) inform qualitative methods. Taylor and Bogdan further note that the above elements of qualitative methods were first applied in anthropology by Boas (1911) and Malinowski (1932) whose work helped to make fieldwork a "legitimate anthropological endeavor" (Taylor & Bogdan 1984:3).

Cognitive Anthropology, also known as Componential Analysis (see Goodenough 1956), became very popular with anthropologists as a qualitative method in the study of cultures from the 1950s onwards. Tyler recognizes cognitive anthropology as a tool that "attempts to understand the *organizing principles underlying* (italics in the original) behavior" (1969:3) because, as Spradley points out, culture is knowledge people have learned. It is knowl-

---

[1] For more information see Käser 1997:9-15.

edge that exists in the minds of people and the challenge is to find out in what categories this knowledge is stored in their minds (1979:8).

Though the critique that Cognitive Anthropology tends to be "universalistic," (tries to pin-down cultural knowledge to one universal meaning applicable to practically all cultural insiders) is justified, cognitive anthropology nevertheless seeks to strive for an understanding of cultural concepts or to grasp the "motives and beliefs behind people's actions" (Taylor & Bogdan 1984:2). The ball, so to speak, is in the court of the one doing cognitive anthropology. The researcher has to make a decision whether one will solely seek and satisfy oneself with "the" or "but one meaning search" of the elements under scrutiny, or whether one will set out in a quest for understanding, which Weber (1968/69) called *verstehen* (Taylor & Bogdan 1984:2).

Such a quest for understanding appreciates the meaning(s) of cultural elements identified by componential analysis, but does so knowing that meanings vary depending on where the meanings hold true (e.g. urban, rural, social group), or who assigns such meanings to those elements (e.g. men, women, social status). Tools developed by cognitive anthropology in this chapter are used with an awareness of the "universal" bias of this tool. Nevertheless, the research should not suffer because the data is genuine linguistic data of those people who were able and willing to share their views with me.

It is not necessary to give much consideration to the development of Cognitive Anthropology as a scientific discipline as I have done so elsewhere (Badenberg 1999:29-34) where I extracted from Roy D'Andrade's comprehensive book *The Development of Cognitive Anthropology* (1995).[2] The basic technique of Cognitive Anthropology may be summed up in three guiding questions in order to form a basis of the acquisition of data and their relationship to one another. (1) What is the word/term of this thing/part, this action, this attribute, or this condition? (2) What else does this word/term/phrase mean? (3) What kind of thing/part, action, attribute, or condition is this?[3]

As pointed out above, I will be unable to present a more comprehensive linguistic description of the body, much as I would have liked to do so, but this study demands limitations. After a brief introduction to the term *umubili* (body), two key domains – *umutwe* (head) and *cifuba* (chest/chest region), with special reference to the most important internal organ *umutima* (heart) – will follow.

The reason for dwelling on the domain of the head and chest/internal organs is, firstly, that the head in Bemba understanding is primarily the focal point of the sense organs, and not the seat of the faculty of thinking. Second, intellec-

---

[2] In this book D'Andrade describes the development of Cognitive Anthropology as a scientific discipline in length and depth.

[3] This kind of questioning is also known as "eliciting" (Käser 1997:304; also Käser 1989:77).

tual processes are not really associated with the brain, but with the heart. *Umutima* (heart) is the major body organ but it also encompasses the seat of emotions, the faculty of intellectual processes, as well as the center of personality (character traits), all of which I combine in the term Psyche, or as I have already pointed pointed out – **SEIC**. However, the Bemba language provides more than one term to speak of the innermost, the *SEIC* of a person. All these terms are related to a particular part or region of the body. Differences between the various terms will be presented.

A major segment of the Bemba concept of body is reproductive biology. Bemba culture is highly concerned with fertility and sexual capacity. A brief outline on this subject will therefore be featured in this study.

In a concluding reflection, I will present some linguistic observations linking the human body to the social body.

2. The Body: *Umubili*

The most general term with which the Bemba language qualifies the human body in its entirety is the word *umubili*. However, *umubili* only refers to the body of living persons. A dead body is classified as *citumbi* (pl. *fitumbi*), a corpse.

Also, all living animals have *umubili* and are divided into several groups. There are *inama* – also the word for meat – that is, animals with four legs. Then there is the category of *ifisenya*, insects, and the category of *ifyuni*, birds or animals that fly. There are two distinct sub-groups in the *inama* group: *inama sha mpanga*, that is, wild animals and game, and *ifitekwa*, domestic animals (literally, "the things that are ruled/governed"). Five sub-groups belong to the category of *ifisenya*, while the category of *ifyuni* includes two sub-groups. The incomplete graphs below (table 1 and table 2) merely serve as illustrations and provide examples for the categories mentioned above.

Chapter 3: An Outline of the Concept of Body

FIGURE 1: *UMUBILI* TAXONOMY OF CREATURES

***Inama* (animals)**

Inama sha mpanga

wild animals
game

Ifitekwa
(domestic animals)

imbushi/goat,
nkumba/pig,
ng'ombe/cow, *imbwa*/dog
etc.

***Ifisenya* (insects)**

| *Ifikulaika* (creeping insects) snakes *mealipede*/ snail | *Ifishishi* (tree/plant insects) caterpillars | *Ifipaso* (jumping insects) grasshoppers/ *palala*/ red locusts/ *amakanta*/ cricket/ *inyense* | *Balunshi* (flying insects) *utushembele*/ tse tse fly *ifipowe*/ kind of housefly *bamung'wing'wi*/ mosquito *inshinge*/ flying ants | *Isabi* (fish) |

***Ifyuni ifipupuka* (birds, animals that fly)**

Domestic birds
Inkoko/chicken
Imbata/spurwing goose
Kalukuluku/turkey
Amakanga/guinea fowl
Inkunda/dove

Birds of prey
Cembe/fish eagle
Nkwale/red-necked francolin
Cipungu/bateleur eagle
Mukanga/marabou stork

Plants and trees do not possess *umubili*. The latter are often named after their characteristics. In general, things or objects (like bottles or tins) also do not possess *umubili* but are sometimes referred to as *umubili* when a part of an object is described. For example, *pa mubili wa cilimba,* lit. "at the body of the guitar", means "the neck of the guitar." This example is interesting because *umubili* does not refer to the "body", the hollow part of the guitar, nor does it mean the neck itself. Rather, it describes a specific feature of the neck: its thickness, the rounded back part of the guitar neck – in other words, its shape. The "*umubili* metaphor" is applied to the longish and rounded back part, the particular shape of the guitar's neck.

All spirit beings are without *umubili*. They are disqualified due to their nature (*Wesenhaftigkeit*). Their mode of existence prohibits physical properties. Only beings that allow physical contact have *imibili* (pl. of *umubili*). However, spirit beings possess the ability to appear in physical form such as in the shape of a snake, a streak of lightning or bright light, or in the form of a human being, an apparition a person sees in a dream.

The human body forms a domain[4] that incorporates all other parts of the body. Consequently, the term *umubili* forms a domain that incorporates all other terms that may themselves form a domain of their own. *Umubili* is subdivided into eight categories or domains: *umutwe* (head), *umukoshi* (neck), *ifipea/amabea* and *amaboko* (shoulders and arms), *icitimbatimba* (chest), *ulufumo* (abdomen), *inuma* (back), *umusana* (waist), and *amolu* (legs). Each of these eight domains forms its own hierarchical structure or taxonomy. Terms of the lowest hierarchical level belong to the next highest level; and terms of that level again belong to the next highest level and so forth, until the top of the taxonomy, *umubili*, is reached. Despite the taxonomical order from top to bottom, term-inclusiveness applies from bottom to top but not vice versa.

---

[4] "A domain is an area of conceptualization like space, color, the human body, kinship, pronouns, etc." (D'Andrade 1995:34).

Chapter 3: An Outline of the Concept of Body

FIGURE 2: *UMUBILI* TAXONOMY OF HUMAN BEINGS

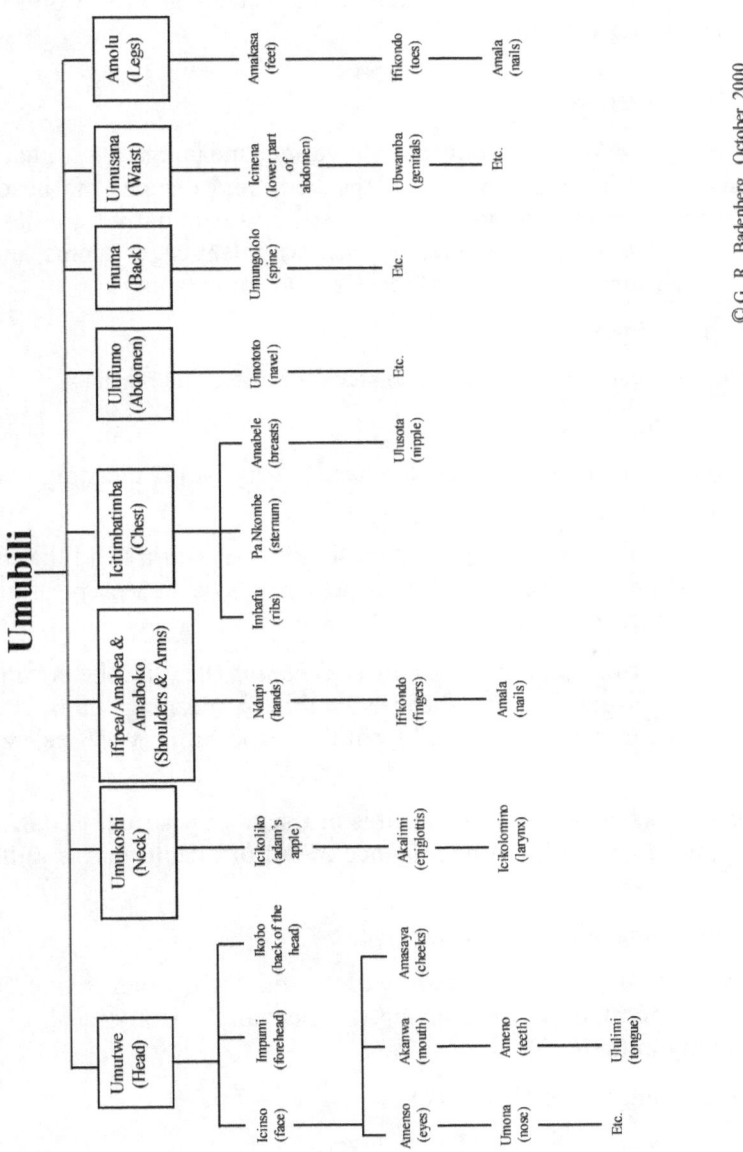

The order from left to right reflects the hierarchical structures of the terms in the cognitive perception of Bemba people in general. This cognitive process is expressed by saying *ukufuma pa mushishi ukufika pa fikondo*, "from the hair to the toes," that is, "from top to bottom." For example, to look at the feet of a person for a long time is considered an act of improper behavior. The above phrase is used in several contexts: (1) It is used to describe someone you know very well; (2) it is used to describe a stranger of whom only details are known for the purpose of finding out more about that person; and (3) it is used in the case of men eyeing women.

3. The Head: *Umutwe*

The word *umutwe* (pl. *imitwe*) is endowed with various meanings. Its primary meaning is associated with the anatomy of the body and denotes the head. Other meanings range from hair, intelligence, will-power/initiative, to sickness (fever or headache). Also, *umutwe* is used with language idioms and proverbs. I will give examples for each of these strands of meanings.

(1) *Umutwe* meaning Hair:

- *asomo lusengo mu mutwe*, he/she stuck a horn in his/her hair.

(2) *Umutwe* meaning Intelligence:

- *ifwe mutwe walikosa*, lit., "us, the head is very hard", meaning 'we are very dull.'
- *ukuba no mutwe ubi nangu usuma*, lit., "to be with a head that is bad or good", which is said of a person whose bad or pleasant dreams/aspirations come true.
- *aliba no mutwe wa mano* or *umutwe ulebomba,* lit., "he/she is with a head of wisdom" or "the head is working", meaning 'he or she has brains, is clever'. Said of a child that performs very well at school.
- *umutwe walionaika,* lit., "the head is in a state of destruction/ruin", meaning 'a person lacks intelligence'. Said of a child that is dull, performs poorly at school.

(3) *Umutwe* meaning Will-power/Initiative:

- *ico naasosa ni pa mutwe wandi naasosa*, lit., "what I am saying, it comes from my head, I am saying it", meaning 'it is my idea, it is due to my initiative.'

(4) *Umutwe* meaning Fever/Headache:

- *ukulwala umutwe,* to be sick with fever.
- *ndi no mutwe*, lit., "I am with a head", to have a headache.
- *umutwe ulekalipa*, to have a light headache.
- *umutwe naulepuka*, lit., "the head is in a state of shaking or refusal", meaning 'to suffer from severe headache.'

Chapter 3: An Outline of the Concept of Body

(5) *Umutwe* in the Context of Idioms:

- *umutwe we lyashi* or *umutwe wa lisambililo ili,* 'the headline,' or 'the headline of this particular lesson.'
- *umutwe wa lukasu,* the knob of the hoe.
- *ku mitwe ya busanshi,* at the ends of the bed; the end where the people put their heads.
- *ku mutwe wa luputa,* at the end of the grave; the end where the head is.
- *ulutwe ulu wa ntampo,* the end of a rope at either side.
- *umutwe wa ng'anda,* the head of the house; the one who controls the family affairs.
- *umutwe wa cilye,* chairperson (male or female).
- *umutwe we bumba,* a group leader.
- *umutwe wa cilonganino,* a church leader or leader of a political party.
- *umutwe we spoke,* the nut of a spoke of a bicycle rim.
- *umutwe wa nsunga,* the head of a nail.
- *ulutwe lwe sumbu,* the ends of a fishing net.
- *Mutwe wa museke,* the egde or the top of a basket.
- *ali ku lutwi,* the first person of a queue.
- *nseke ishituntulu mu mutwe,* the full grain in the ear of corn.
- *umutwe,* the ear of corn.
- *ukukusho muntu umutwe,* lit., "to enlarge, make a person's head bigger", meaning 'to shame, disgrace a person.'
- *Uyu mulandu wa mutwe wa ng'ombe,* lit., "this case is like the head of a bull," meaning 'this is an endless affair like a bull's head.'
- *ukukalifya umutwe,* to wear one out, to give one a headache.

(6) *Umutwe* in the Context of Proverbs:

- *amano tayekala mu mutwe umo,* lit., "wisdom/intelligence does not live in one head only"; used when a person undertakes a project without consulting others and fails miserably.

- *munshipingulwa: amano tayafula mu mutwe,* lit., "the one who is not advised does not have a lot of wisdom in his head"; used on a person who denounced advice from others and then fell into trouble because of his stubbornness.

- *uushili noko: takutonya mutwe,* lit., "the one who is not your mother does not feel your head", meaning 'only a mother has genuine concern and will not delay her help.'

The domain head includes various sub-domains such as *icinso* (face), *impumi* (forehead), and *ikobo* (back of the head).

3.1 Short Excursus on Hair

The Bemba language has a range of vocabulary on hair. For example, while the German language generally qualifies hair by a specific location (e.g., *Kopf-haare* [hair on the head], *Bart-haare* [beard], *Brust-haare* [hair on the chest], *Nacken-haare* [hair in the neck], *Scham-haare* [pubic hair] or qualification like *graues Haar* [gray hair]), the Bemba language employs distinct words for hair at distinct locations.

- *Inkopyo,* only used for hair on eyebrows and eyelashes.
- *Imishishi,* hair on the head.
- *imishishi ya mu matwi,* hair in the ears.
- *imishishi ya mu kwapa,* hair under the arm.
- *imishishi ya pa cifuba,* hair on the breast.
- *imyefu,* beard, moustache and the hair in the nose.
- *amapipi ya ku molu,* hair on the legs.
- *amapipi ya ku maboko,* hair on the arms.
- *amapipi ya kunuma,* hair on the back.
- *amaso,* pubic hair.
- *mfwi (*sg. *lufwi),* gray hair.

4. The Sense Organs[5]

The majority of the sense organs (four out of five) are attached to the head. A closer look at the sense organs is therefore appropriate. The Bemba language has no term that could define the "five senses". Hearing, feeling, and tasting

---

[5] I have made use of expressions pertaining to the verbs *ukumfwa, ukumona,* and *ukununsha* from the White Fathers Dictionary (1991 s.v. "*-umfwa*"; "*-mona*"; "*-nunsha*").

are all packed into but one word, *ukumfwa*! Other terms to denote the two remaining senses are *ukumona*, to see (vision), and *ukununsha*, to smell (smell).

The role of the "nervous system" and the brain with regard to the origin and perception of physical and emotional feelings is not known. A term for "nerve(s)" is non-existent. An approximation of "nerve" is "blood." Blood is thought to convey sensations like itching or the feeling of pain. All blood is pooled in and distributed from the heart. Information of pain or other sensations are then transferred via the blood and eventually registered with the brain. The brain operates like a command center receiving and sorting all incoming information. After processing the data, it issues directives of action.

4.1 The Eye: *Ilinso*

Ilinso is the word for the eye of a human being. Animals too possess *ilinso* (pl. *amenso*).

(1) The parts that belong to *Ilinso*:
- *inkopyo sha pamulu we linso,* the upper eyelashes.
- *inkopyo sha panshi we linso,* the lower eyelashes.
- *icikumbi ca pamulu we linso,* the upper lid.
- *icikumbi ca panshi we linso,* the lower lid.
- *amanongo,* eye pus.
- *ifilamba,* tears.

(2) *Ilinso* in the Context of Expressions:
- *ukushibata amenso,* to close the eyes.
- *ukutumbula amenso,* staring with wide open eyes.
- *ukushibashiba,* blinking with the two eyes.
- *ukutoteka,* to squint.
- *ukufinya pa menso/ukukaka pa menso,* to frown (wrinkles on the forehead – a sign of disagreement).
- *akulebeleba kwa linso,* "frantic movement with the eye." *Alelebaleba*, said of somebody who is a suspected thief; one who moves his head vigorously in order to observe everything that is going on.

(3) *Ilinso* in the Context of Idioms and Figurative Speech:
- *pa linso lya lukasa,* the middle of the sole of the foot.

- *ilinso lye taba/amenso ya mataba*, the maize corn itself.
- *ilinso lya mushi*, the headman (one who keeps watch over the village).
- *ilinso lya nshindano*, the eye of the needle.
- *ukupima na menso*, to measure with the eyes.
- *pa linso lya cishilwa*, the center point of a circle.
- *amenso ya sefya*, the holes of a sieve.
- *amenso ya mucetekanya*, a good judgment; someone who is usually right with his observations, judgments or explanations.
- *ukulufyanya pa menso,* lit., "to do wrong at the eyes," meaning 'to look angry.'

4.1.1 Sense of Vision: The Verb *ukumona*

Ukumona is both a transitive and intransitive verb. Three principal meanings as well as some verb extensions are given below.

(1) to see:
- *namumona ku menso,* I saw him with my own eyes.
- *ifyo mfwaya ukumumona mwe,* how I desired to see you.
- *nshilamona,* that is not enough; it's not what the thing is worth.
- *mona mulelu,* to have a glimpse of... .

(2) to perceive, notice:
- *ulucelo namona isembe lyasendwa,* in the morning I noticed the axe had been taken.

(3) to see, to find, to have, to see a way out:
- to find:
  nga fwaka ndemumona kwi?, where shall I find some tobacco?
- to have:
  Mwapoleni! ati: nshimona mutende, meaning 'how are you?' He said: 'I have not seen health/I am not well.'
- to see a way out:
  Ntensha mundu wandi, nshimona ukuti nyende, I am taking care of a sick relative, I cannot see a way of getting out.

(4) to be in affliction, grief:
- *namone inshiku,* "I see days," meaning 'I am in affliction.'

(5) conjunction : when (synonym: *ukumfwa*)
(6) *ukumonwa* (passive extension of *ukumona*):
- to be seen, visible:
  ici cintu tacimonwa, this thing is not visible.
(7) *ukumonana/ukumoneshanya* (reciprocal extension of *ukumona*):
- to see or visit each other; to face each other:
  amayanda yamonana minshi, the huts are facing each other.
(8) *ukuimona* (reflexive extension of *ukumona*):
- *baimona fye ni filya fine cali na kale,* meaning 'they saw for themselves; they perceived that nothing had changed from former times.'

4.2 The Mouth: *Akanwa*

Etymologically, the noun *akanwa* has its root in the transitive as well as intransitive verb *ukunwa,* to drink. This etymological link signifies the primary task of *akanwa* (pl. *utunwa*); to be the agent facilitating the satisfaction of an elementary human need. The mouth as the organ from which thoughts proceed as sounds appears to be of secondary importance. That which enters the body via the mouth takes precedence over that which exits the body via the mouth. In other words, before one can speak, one has to live.

(1) The parts that belong to *Akanwa*:
- *umulomo* (pl. *imilomo*) *wa pamulu,* the lip and the part between the upper lip and the nose.
- *umulomo wa panshi,* the lower lip.
- *mumbali ya kanwa,* the corners of the mouth. (*Ifulo* – foam at the mouth).
- *ululimi (pl. indimi),* the tongue.
- *kalimba (pl. tulimba),* the frenum of the tongue.
- *amate,* saliva.
- *ifiponshi,* the gums.
- *ameno (sg. Ilino),* the teeth.

(2) Other contexts in which *akanwa* is used:
- *akanwa ka mupini,* the hole of a hoe where the blade is inserted.
- *pa kanwa ke botolo,* the opening of a bottle.

- *pa kanwa ka mpoto/ umupika*, the opening of a cooking-pot.
- *pa kanwa ka cilindi/ pa milomo ya cilindi*, the edges of a grave.
- *pa kanwa ka mbukuli*, the opening of a bag (term for all bags that can be closed).
- *pa kanwa ka museke*, the opening of a basket.
- *pa kanwa ka lukombo*, the opening of a gourd used as a drinking cup.

(3) *Kanwa* in Proverbs:
- *Icilya icibiye cikula umutwe*, lit., "that which eats the other should have a big head" (e.g. the pot which cooks the pumpkin should be bigger than the same) meaning 'one who is a leader must be wiser than others.'
- *Akanwa ka mwefu takabepa*, lit., "a bearded mouth does not lie," meaning 'a wise person does not lie; he has wisdom and maturity instead.' Also, 'the advice of an elderly person should not be neglected.'

4.2.1 The Teeth: *Ameno*

The teeth may further be qualified either according to the task they perform or the condition they are in:

- *insongwa*, the cutting teeth.
- *banaboya*, the molars.
- *imishila ye lino*, "the roots of a tooth." There is another word, *cabo* (pl. *fyabo*), which also carries the notion of roots in a variety of contexts (e.g. *ifyabo fya meno*, the roots of teeth, *cabo fya ngala*, the root of a fingernail).
- *icipunda ce lino*, a hole in a tooth.
- *umucene*, the space between teeth.
- *umwangashima*, the space between the two upper big front teeth.
- *umuca*, toothache and swelling of the cheek (*ukufimba kwe saya*).
- *ubulwele bwa meno*, lit,. "sickness of the teeth", meaning 'the loss of a tooth or teeth.'
- *ukusenganya na meno*, gnashing teeth.

4.2.2 The Tongue: *Ululimi*

Not only is the tongue, *ululimi* (pl. *indimi*), an important body part, it also appears in many different contexts. The tongue is an ambivalent organ because of its powers to build and to destroy. *Ululimi* turns thoughts into sounds and words. Words either build and confirm relationships or denounce and destroy personal and communal bonds. Bemba knows no word for "language" but uses instead *ululimi* to mean a different language. For some church communities, *ululimi* forms a key word in their sacrosanct vocabulary; *ukulanda mu ndimi ishalekana lekana,* "speaking in tongues," has become an object of much debate among churches of various denominations.

Below I will give still other meanings of *ululimi*.

(1) *Ululimi* as metaphor for cognitive associations:

- *ululimi lwe sembe,* the blade of the axe.
- *ululimi lwe lukasu / icilimi ca lukasu,* the blade of a hoe.
- *ululimi lwa mwele,* the blade of a knife.
- *ululimi lwa citenge / ululimi lwa citambala,* the piece/tongue of cloth which hangs loose after the knot.
- *ululime lwa supuni,* the part of a spoon to scoop with.
- *ululimi lwa cibampa,* the part of a ladle to scoop with.

(2) Other proper meanings of *ululimi*:

- *ululimi,* language.
- *ululimi,* a single flame.
- *ululimi lwa mulilo,* the flame/tongue of a fire. The whole fire is called: *ulubingu lwa mulilo.*

(3) *Ululimi* describing the character of a person:

- *uwa ndimi shibili,* is a negative term! This expression is used on someone who has a "split tongue." A person who cannot be trusted. His words say one thing but in his heart, in his thinking he means otherwise. Such a negative character trait is in Bemba called *umubele ubi,* a permanent negative psychological disposition.

4.2.3 Senses of Hearing, Feeling and Tasting: The Verb *ukumfwa*[6]

The verb *ukumfwa* is a very interesting word. Its meanings are manifold. *Ukumfwa* denotes *three* senses! It is a transitive and intransitive verb. Below I will present the three main meanings of *ukumfwa* as well as some of its extensions.

(1) to hear/listen, to understand, to take notice, to listen to advice

- *umfwa nkwebe ifyo natesha*, listen that I will tell you what I heard.
- *toomfwa*, he or she does not listen or hear.
- *ulya alomfwa*, this one, this person listens.
- *waumfwa?* do you understand?
- *ukumfwa mu menso*, to stare without listening.
- *tuumfwe!*, silence that we may hear!
- *umfweni!*, listen to that now! (sometimes expressing contempt).

(2) to feel, to perceive, to realize

- *icikalipa cumfwa umwine*, what hurts, is felt or realized by oneself.

(3) to taste

- *icakulya caumfwika shani?* The food, how does it taste?
- *umucele tauumfwika iyoo*, the salt doesn't taste at all.

(4) *ukumfwana* (reciprocal extension of *ukumfwa*)

- to hear one another
  abapalamene mu mitanda balomfwana, those whose gardens are close together can hear one another.
- to agree, come to an understanding, to be on good terms
  balomfwana no mukashi, he is on good terms with his wife.

(5) *ukumfwanya* (verb transitive; causative extension of *ukumfwana*)

- *abalekumfwanya*, he is causing them to live on good terms.

(6) *ukumfwika*

- to be heard, understood, perceived
  mulandu waumfwika, the case was heard.
  Ishiwi lyaumfwika, the voice/ word was heard or understood.

---

[6] The verb *ukumfwa* is transitive and intransitive. The double *"uu"* is due to the infinitive prefix *uku* and the verb stem *-umfwa*. Though vowels fuse in certain circumstances, the double *"uu"* indicates a stress in pronouncing the verb.

- to be known, make known to
  mulandu waumfwika, the case/affair was made known.
- to hear of
  baya kale no kumfwika, iyo; they went away a long time ago and have not been heard of (since).

(7) *ukumfwikika* (verb intranisitve; intensive extension of *ukumfwika*)

- to be well understood
  amashiwi yaumfwikika, the voices/words are well understood.

(8) *ukumfwikisha* (verb transitive; intensive extension of *ukumfwa*)

- *aumfwikisha umulandu*, he understood the case perfectly well.

4.2.4 Sense of Smell: The Verb *ukununsha*

The sense of smell appears to be of lesser importance than the previous sense of vision and certainly inferior to the senses of hearing, feeling and tasting. *Ukununsha* is a transitive as well as intransitive verb and has two principle meanings: (1) "to smell" indicating sniffing or scenting and (2) "to stink" with the meaning of annoying with an offensive smell.

(1) to smell, to scent:

- *ndenunsha ifyakulya ifisuma filenunka mu kitchen,* I am smelling good food in the kitchen.
- *alenunsha bwema bwatula ku maluba,* he/she smells the scent coming from the flowers.

(2) to stink:

- *fumako, witununsha,* go away (get out of here), do not stink us out.

(3) figurative expression:

- *amununsha lya ikofi kumununsha,* he made him smell his fist; he beat, thrashed him.

5. The External and Internal Chest Region: *Pa Cifuba* and *Mu Cifuba*

Pa cifuba denotes the external region of the chest starting from the top of the breastbone down to the bottom of the sternum (*pa nkombe*). Major features of this external region are the two breasts (*amabele;* a term that is used on females and males alike. Even animals possess *amabele*). The word *cifuba* alone refers to sickness, rather than the chest as such, like *ukuba ne cifuba,* which literally says "to be with a chest" but actually means "to have a chest cold," or "cough." A synonym is *ukulwala cifuba* literally "to be chest sick" which also means "to have a chest cold," or "cough."

Changing the locative preposition *pa cifuba* into *mu cifuba*, "in the chest," different meanings evolve. *Mu cifuba* in a very general way refers to the internal chest region or the internal organs of that region. In a narrow and specific sense, *mu cifuba* is a synonym of *mutima* (heart) or *mu mutima* "in the heart," for which I proposed the term psyche (Badenberg 1999:58), but which I want to substitute now with the acronym *SEIC* (see above).

5.1 The Lungs: *BaPwapwa*

The word *bapwapwa* (sg. *pwapwa*) is an onomatopoeia derived from the sound generated when breathing in and out. The task of *bapwapwa* is to act as an instrument pulling and trapping air (*ukutinta kola mwela; ukutinta* means 'to pull' and *ukukola* 'to trap'). The idea of "trapping" air is a concept that appears to exist in African as well as in Indo-Germanic languages. For example, in English the expression "to catch one's breath" expresses the same idea.

The lungs "pull" and "trap" air and push it on into the liver (*ilibu*). There it undergoes a cleansing or washing process (*ukusamfya umwela*). From the liver the cleaned air goes to the heart which sets the breathing process into motion by pumping blood through the body.

5.2 The Stomach: *Icifu*

The stomach (*icifu*) acts like a storage chamber for the food entering the body. The gall bladder (*ndusha*) "melts" the food (*ukusungulula ifyakulya*).[7] This leaves the stomach with the task to separate and sort out (*ukusobolola*) the good (*ifisuma*) ingredients from the bad (*ifibi*). The residue (*ifiseekwa*) leaves the body via the bowels (*amala*). The blood (*umulopa*) is responsible for taking (*ukusenda twala*) the digested food to all parts of the body. The primary task of this process is to strengthen the heart in order for it to perform its work well (*no kupela amaka ku mutima pakuti ulebomba bwino*).

5.3 The Heart: *Umutima*

Umutima (heart) is the noun proper for the most important of all internal organs of the body. It is charged with two principle tasks: to set the breathing process into motion and, thereby, to pump the blood to all parts of the body. In other contexts, *umutima* takes on a variety of meanings: the intestines; a character trait; conscience; intention, inclination, tendency; presentiment; will; and attention.

---

[7] *Ukusungulula*, a transitive verb meaning "to melt, to dissolve, to digest (food). *White Fathers, Dictionary* 1991, s.v. "*-sungulula.*"

Chapter 3: An Outline of the Concept of Body

There are three locative prepositions used with *umutima*: *pa*, *ku*, and *mu*. Each of these prepositions denotes a difference in meaning.

(1) *Pa mutima* is often an expression that refers to a body function that is in disorder and felt pain (e.g. *alwala pa mutima*, "he has diarrhea;" *pa mutima palekalipa*, "at the heart there is pain," meaning 'I have a colic').

(2) *Ku mutima* describes actions of external origin done or placed toward the "heart." *Cinshi ico musosela ku mutima wandi?* meaning 'why do you talk to me?'
Ine kwali ku mutima wandi, meaning 'I had it upon my heart.'
Mucibike na ku mutima yenu, lit., "place it toward your heart," meaning 'take it to heart.'

(3) *Mu mutima* is the place where emotions form and manifest, and where intellectual processes occur.
Wilapata munonko mu mutima obe, meaning 'do not hate your brother in your heart.'
Ilyo amwene, amusuulile mu mutima wakwe, meaning 'when he saw him, he despised him in his heart.'
Alepanga ifibi mu mutima, meaning 'he is devising evil, malicious things in his heart.'
Alesosela mu mutima wakwe, meaning 'he spoke, thought, contemplated in his heart.'

The *ku* and *mu* locatives concern the "heart" either in terms of what is done *to*, or what happens *in/inside* the psyche/SEIC. Following is a more comprehensive definition of psyche.

5.4 A Definition of "Psyche"

The Bemba language furnishes three terms to denote the psyche: *mu cifuba*, *mu nda* (*mukati ka mu nda*), and *mu mutima*. Despite their formal differences, all three terms mean the same in certain circumstances and are differentiated when it comes to highlight certain aspects of the psyche. However, contexts including *mutima* are by far the most numerous.

The term *mukati ka mu nda* or just *mu nda* characterizes the psyche as a "spot inside the belly, in the middle" and could be rendered as "the innermost."

- *na mu nda ya bawelewele muli ukufulungana*, meaning 'the innermost of fools is scattered, confused and full of chaos.'
- *Moneni, icishinka ca mu fya mu nda eco mubwekelamo*, lit., "behold, the truth which dwells inmost of you, you should return to it," meaning 'watch out for the truth; return to its principles, return to your convictions.'

The term *mukati* consists of two words; the preposition *mu* (*in*) and the word *kati* (*inside, into, in the middle of*). It denotes the "center core of a thing", "the middle between two points", or could mean "among" when used as preposition.

Mu is a locative preposition, which can be used with various word constructions. It alters the terms for things in such a way that they appear as a place in space or time.

5.4.1 The Term *Mu Cifuba*

Mu cifuba is an alternative to both other terms but is not very much in common use. It focuses on the locality, on a concrete part or area of the body, and is associated with the psyche in its ability to desire or to have intentions, but in a less differentiated way than *mu mutima*.

> *Ankumbwa mu cifuba,* he desires me in his heart, he loves me.
> *Nshishibe ico waba naco mu cifuba,* I don't know what you are and what is in your heart, meaning 'I don't know what is on your mind.'

Due to the minor role the term *mu cifuba* plays where the psyche is concerned, and the fact that it has become a relatively rare term for expressing psychical motions, it will be dropped from further discussion.

5.4.2 The Term *Mu nda*

The word *Mu nda* carries various meanings depending on the context in which it is used.

(1) *Mu nda* is a compound noun prefixed with the locative preposition *mu*. *Nda* without the preposition *mu* is a noun and means 'a louse (pl. lice).' The etymological link between the prefixed locative preposition and the noun proper is not clear.

(2) *Mu nda* as a generic term denotes the whole internal region of the chest and abdomen. This assertion is confirmed by the expression: *Ishina lya mu nda lipilibula ifyaba mukati ka mubili onse,* meaning 'the word *mu nda* can also stand in place for the entire interior of the body.'

(3) More specifically, *Mu nda* refers first to the organs *icifu*, stomach, and *amala*, bowels, intestines. But *mu nda* itself is not a body organ.

- Certain *imyumfwikile ya mubili* (lit., "feelings of the body") can be associated with *mu nda*.

  Imyumfwikile ya mu nda are 'stomach pains', and *ukulwala mu nda* is "to be sick in the stomach, to have diarrhoea."
  To be with hunger is packed into the phrase *ndeumfwa insala mu nda*, "I feel hunger inside"; or, *mu nda muli lubebeelu*, "my stomach is empty", meaning 'I feel hungry.'

  To gather strength through eating can be expressed by using the verb – noun construction *-ikasha mu nda*, lit., "to strengthen the stomach", meaning 'to strengthen oneself by eating food (e.g. *ukuya ku milimo kano naikasha mu nda)*, meaning 'I can't go for work unless I eat).

- *ndeumfwa ukwikuta mu nda*, is the equivalent of *ndeumfwa ukwikuta mu mala*, meaning, 'I feel satisfied in my stomach/bowels; I am full, have had sufficient food.'

- *Mu nda mulecita macololo,* lit., "my stomach is doing *'cololo'* (the word *macololo* is onomatopoeic, an imitation of the sound when belching) meaning 'my stomach belches, eructates.'

(4) *Mu nda* as a euphemenism for the maternal womb

- *twafyelwe mu nda imo,* we were born from the same womb/mother.
- *wa mu nda nkalamba,* lit., "one of a great womb", meaning 'a person of royal blood.'
- *akabufi kaba mu nda,* lit., "the lie is in your womb", meaning 'the proof of your adultery is in your womb.'

5.4.3 The Term *Mu Mutima*

Mu mutima characterizes the psyche as the center of those psychical-intellectual appearances, which primarily focus on the origin of intentions, exercising of will-power, thinking, the seat of character attributes (permanent psychical dispositions, *imibele*), the acts (*imicitile*) and attitudes of a person, and, finally, the seat of emotions (temporal psychical dispositions, *imyumfwikile ya mutima*).

> *Mu* (in), as outlined above, is a locative preposition causing a thing to appear as a place in space or time. *Mu mutima* pin-points the place where permanent psychical dispositions (character traits), temporal psychical dispositions (emotions), and intellectual processes take place.

5.4.4 *Mu nda* and *Mu Mutima*: Collectivism vs. Particularity

Despite the fact that *mu nda* stands for thinking, thoughts, making plans, having intentions, character attributes, actions, etc., the usage of *mu nda* in connection with these appearances of the psyche is collective.

Mu nda: Collective Aspect of the Psyche

Whenever a certain aspect of the psyche is expressed in a collective manner then *mu nda* **is** a synonym to *mu mutima*. For example, *amatontonkanyo*, thoughts; *amapange*, plans, intentions; *imibele*, character attributes; *imicitile*, actions, deeds. All these collective categories can be associated with *mu nda*.

(1) Examples where *mu nda* is a synonym of *mu mutima*:

- *ndetontonkanya amatontonkanyo mu nda* is equivalent to saying *ndetontonkanya amatontonkanyo mu mutima*, lit., "I think the thoughts in my psyche," meaning 'I am thinking.'

- *ndepanga amapange mu nda* is the is equivalent to saying *ndepanga amapange mu mutima*, lit., "I am making plans in my psyche," meaning 'I am planning.'

- *mu mutima yabo batila abati: ico tucitile taciweme*, is equivalent to saying *mu nda shabo batila abati: ico tucitile taciweme*, lit., "in their psyche they said, saying: what we did was not good," meaning, 'when contemplating about the matter they realized what they did was not good.'

Mu Mutima: Particular Characteristics or Motions of the Psyche

Specific characteristics or motions of the psyche/*SEIC* are localized and associated with the heart, or to be more precise *mu mutima*, in the heart/psyche (*SEIC*). For example:

- *Insansa*, joy, happiness and anger, *icipyu*, are specific emotions. One is positive and the other negative. *Ukupeela*, to give, being generous, is regarded as *umubele usuma*, a good character attribute; *ukwiba*, to steal, is regarded as *umucitile wibi*, a bad action, or bad deed. Emotions, character attributes, and deeds have their origin *mu mutima*, in the heart (*SEIC*).

(2) Examples were *mu nda cannot* be used as a synonym of *mu mutima*:

- *ndeumfwa insansa mu mutima*, I feel joy in my heart, I am joyful, happy cannot be substituted by saying: *ndeumfwa insansa mu nda*.

- *ndeumfwa icipyu mu mutima*, I feel anger in my heart, I am angry cannot be substituted by saying: *ndeumfwa icipyu mu nda*.

- *ndeumfwa ulupato mu mutima,* I feel hate in my heart, I am hating cannot be substituted by saying: *ndeumfwa ulupato mu nda.*
- *ndeumfwa ukutemwa mu mutima,* I feel love in my heart, I am loving cannot be substituted by saying: *ndeumfwa ukutemwa mu nda.*
- *Alikwata umutima wa kupeela,* he/she has a heart of giving, meaning 'he/she is a giving, generous person' cannot be substituted by saying: *alikwata mu nda ya kupeela.*
- *Aba no mutima wa cikuuku,* he/she is with a psyche (*SEIC*) of mercy, kindness, tenderness, meaning 'he/she is a kind, merciful, tender person' cannot be substituted with *aba no mu nda ya cikuuku.*

6. *Ubufyashi*: Sexuality – Cultural Mandate to Procreation

Bemba vocabulary for parts and functions concerning the reproductive realm of human life is rather basic. Names for external parts exceed the number of names for internal parts or organs. Up to today, biological processes and functions of reproductive organs remain a subject of speculation or compose a "blank" in the knowledge system of many Bemba speakers.[8] The absence or "basic set" of vocabulary, however, does not suggest that this area of life is given less interest than other areas which do abound in vocabulary. The contrary might be true.[9]

"The focus on sexual capacity in both male and female in African societies is considered to be of crucial importance" (Dillon-Malone 1988:1167). Frankenberg and Leeson, commenting on African societies, observe that, "in terms of body openings, western medicine is focused on mouth and anus – nutrition and hygiene, and traditional medicine on genitals – impotence and birth" (in Dillon-Malone 1988:1167).

6.1 Mbusa – The Sacred Emblems

The Bemba focus on fertility and sexual capacity, for example, surfaces in the rich symbol system (*Mbusa,* the sacred emblems) apparent in the initiation ceremony (*Cisungu*) of girls and also in sanctioned and expected sexual practice within wedlock.

---

[8] Says LeBacq, Technical Advisor Health/ District Medical Officer of Kasama District from June 1994 to June 2000: "Traditional midwives expressed a strong need for knowledge about anatomy and physiology of external and internal genitalia" [1998:47].

[9] I just refer to Kambole's book, *Ukufunda Umwana Kufikapo.* Kambole is of Bemba ethnicity. The book abounds in descriptions of the richness of traditional Bemba life, in particular stressing fertility and sexual capacity as areas of prime concern and prime attention (1980:16-112).

Mbusa: Sacred Emblems of the Bemba is the title of Corbeil's book (1982). His rich collection of more than two hundred pottery *Mbusa* models and one-hundred-and-seventeen initiation songs reflect the rich traditions of Bemba family life, marriage and sexuality, although the collection is admittedly far from exhaustive. In an attempt to bring to light the richness of the *Mbusa* sacred emblems, he classified them into ten groups. Some groups in his classificatory system, such as "wife's obligations", "domestic duties" and "agricultural duties," specifically relate to sexuality and proper marital relations. For example, in the group of "agriculture duties" there appears the *Kalonde, the Little Hoe* pottery model. One alternative song[10] attached to the *Kalonde, the Little Hoe* model pottery compares the man to a hoe and the girl, his future wife, to a garden. The "hoe" and the "garden" sustain and guarantee life, that is, both husband and wife are charged with the responsibility to use their sexual capacity to give children to the clan.[11]

Richards (1956/1982) in her book *Chisungu: A Girls Initiation Ceremony among the Bemba of Northern Rhodesia* writes that, among the various emphases and meanings of the *Cisungu*[12] rite, features pertaining to sex and fertility (pottery figures and models, paintings and songs) scored second behind the "social obligations of husband and wife" (1982:140). Marital duties between husband and wife are performed under the initiative of the husband. A woman is taught to "yield herself to her husband" whenever he desires her (1982:91). Among other emblems, the *mputa* or "garden mound" *mbusa* emblem stresses that the *mputa* represents a garden that is owned. "Trespassing on the land" shows lack of respect. Likewise, the woman is owned by her husband and should only be "cultivated" by him. Conjugal relations are supposed to take place nightly except for the period when the woman is set apart due to her menstrual cycle.

---

[10] "*Nimpa kalonde, Nsebaule kongwe, Mulume wamona,*" literally says "Give me my little hoe. I will clean '*Kongwe.*' You have seen my husband." The meaning is "the initiated girl wants to be given to her husband" (Corbeil 1982:105). Richards' translation of the song is as follows: "Give me my little hoe, So that I can make ready the hymen. You have seen my husband." Richards explains, alongside other rational explanations, "the girl would be hoed up by her husband as the ground is ... (this) has a frankly sexual meaning: the girl wants to be given to her husband" (1982:206).

[11] "The bridegroom in a matrilineal society of the Bemba type is honoured as a *genitor*, not as *pater* (italics in the original). The bride belongs to her own matrilineage and the bridegroom is allowed access to her to make her fertile. He is welcomed in the village as a *procreator* (italics mine), and honoured as such. The bride's family is indebted to the bridegroom for the "gift" of a child" (Richards 1982:158).

[12] "*Cisungu* is sometimes spelt *Chisungu* to approximate more nearly the pronunciation of the word. The initial 'c' is pronounced as 'ch'" (Corbeil 1982:8).

6.2 *Ukufunda* – Traditional Education

R. Kambole[13] in his effort to preserve traditional knowledge for future generations also emphasizes the prominence of maturity, fertility/sexual capacity in Bemba culture. In his book *Ukufunda Umwana Kufikapo*,[14] he elaborates on these topics extensively in Bemba.[15] The Bemba text below[16] contains some teaching about traditional practice and perception of marriage and conjugal relations of man and woman (Kambole 1980:96).

Kabili umbi ayipusha ati:	Then another [elder] would ask; he would say:
Nga umwana apangwa shani?	A child, how is it formed?
Umubiye ayasuka ati:	The fellow elder would answer and say:
Imwe mwebo tufishe, tamwakulayikala fye iyo.	You, whom we have wedded, you are not here on earth to merely live. No!
Mwakulabombo milimo uwacila pa milimo yonse ukucindama.	You are continuously to engage into the work/task that is beyond all tasks of honour.
Mwakulapanga icupo, kashita-kashita cila bushiku, mpaka uyu mwanakashi akemite.	You are continuously to engage in the marriage act (have sexual intercourse) a little while and again each night, until this woman conceives.
Ninshi aleka no kulaaba ku mpepo.	This is the time when she ceases to be "cold."
Baleeti fye ico bapombosa, Bayeba shibwinga na nabwinga.	Whatever they [the elders] wanted to say, they would say it to the bridegroom and the bride.
Babwekeshapo umo bacilandile umo umo.	They repeated it as the first one said it; one by one, they said it.

---

[13] Kambole makes a strong plea for traditions being preserved. Otherwise, he says, there will be darkness over the land and forest; darkness over Zambia (*Pafiita ninshi, Pafiitila imiti-ikula, Pafiitila impanga yonse, Pafiitila Zambia*) (1980:vii).

[14] Joel L. Makopa translates *Ukufunda Umwana Kufikapo* to mean "Providing Complete Traditional Education to a Young Person." Handwritten notes, Chinsali, 1998.

[15] For example, Kambole says: *Icisungu calicindeme mu Lubemba; Embusa ikalamba yalimo, Entulo yabwanakashi; Ebwanakashi bwine,* meaning, "Maturity, female puberty [fertility] is the most significant, honourable, respectable tradition to the Bemba; indeed it is the greatest sacred emblem there is; indeed it is the source of womanhood (fertility); indeed it is womanhood (fertility) itself" (1980:17-18).

[16] The translation into English is my own. However, I have counter-checked the text with Makopa's English translation of the same passage.

Kabili umbi ayipusha ati:	Again another (elder) said:
Bushe umwanakashi nga ali ku mpepo, kuti mwapilibuka nankwe?	When a woman is in the month (menstruating), can you turn round with her (can you have sexual relations with her)?
Iyoo, tecakwesha, kuti mwaikowesha.	No, never! That is not a thing to be attempted; you could cause yourself to become "contaminated" (become lean or sick).
Mwalwala icifuba ca makowesha.	You will contract the "cough of contamination" (technical term: tuberculosis).
We mwanakashi lyonse ilyo uli ku mweshi,	You woman every time when you are in the month (menstruating),
tauli nakufutatila umulume pa kusendama;	you are not in the position to be wetted (made wet by the sperm) when you sleep with your husband;
tauli nakwisalako iciibi;	you are not in the position to close the door (of your hut);
tauli nakwikata pe shiko;	you are not in the position to touch the studs of the fireplace (where you cook);
tauli nakwipika	you are not in a position to cook
no kulunga mu munani tecakwesha.	and to season (put salt in) the relish; that is not a thing to be attempted.

6.3 "Hot" and "Cold": Euphemisms for Sexuality and "Access to the Divine"

In Kambole's teaching on cultural issues pertaining to sexuality, he makes mention of the woman to be in a state of "coldness." The opposite correlating metaphor would be "hot" or to be in a state of "hotness."

Hinfelaar (1994) relates the state of "coldness" and the state of "hotness" to the three seasons of the Northern plateau. During the months of May to August is harvest time; these months are cold and dry and symbolize the Feminine. August to November is the time of the hot season, which is more like the Masculine. The rainy season runs from November to April. These are the fertile months and characterize perfection as hot and cold merge. In the same way, sexual intercourse is seen as symbolizing the interaction of these three seasons. The perception of the cold state of the woman and her ultimate task of "receiving the divine gift of parenthood" needs the complementation of the "hot influence of the husband" (1994:7-8).[17] In merging "cold" and "hot" in marital intercourse, "Access to the Divine" is achieved (1994:8).

Maxwell (1983) sees water, blood, sex, fire and life as "root metaphors" of Bemba culture as they "set in motion their most sacred values" (1983:28). As regards sex (*icupo*), husband and wife can be potential threats to the family and the community at large. In fact, unsanctioned or non-sacralized sex is the cause of diseases and social tension within the community (cf. chapter four: "malnutrition"). Sex and fire constitute powers, which need utmost care and control. Once let on the loose, they can destroy the very life they are supposed to grant. The pollution of the fire on which sexually active persons who are not purified cook food, affects the life of the group that eats together (1983:31).

Richards (1956/1982) speaks of sex and fire as the "*idée maîtresse* behind most of the ritual behavior of the Bemba" (1982:30). Like the heat of the fire that poses danger if not carefully handled, so do sexual relations which make husband and wife "hot." This state can only be relieved of its danger by the purifying element of water. For this rite a miniature pot, the possession of the wife, is filled with water and put on the fire. The washing of hands with warm water from the pot "removes the condition of hotness from the body of man and wife" (1982:31). They are now free to touch the fire on which food is cooked without imposing ill effects on others, especially small children. The connection between fire, "hotness," and sickness in children will be dealt with in chapter four.

6.4 Other Euphemisms in Relation to Reproductive Biology

Bemba culture is very discreet about matters pertaining to sex within public settings. Despite the terrible effects of HIV/Aids in the communities, there is still great reluctance to speak on these issues in public, especially in rural areas. People want these issues to be discussed in a proper forum that includes age separation and is gender sensitive. One way this discreetness concerning sex or sexual matters becomes apparent is in the many euphemisms that are used to refer to sex, sexual parts, or reproductive biology as a whole.

6.4.1 Reproductive Parts

- *Bwamba* means nakedness but is also a euphemism for the sex organs (Richards 1982:188); a generic term for the sexual parts of human beings.

---

[17] Among the Bisa, a kindred group of the Bemba, the same idea of "hot" exists. Musonda writes that being in a "hot" condition is a dangerous condition since there is a "link between life and 'blood'" (1996:58).

- *U/bwanakashi,* womanhood, derived from the noun *mwanakashi* (pl. *banakashi*) meaning "woman"; by implication the "female sexual organs."

- *U/bwaume,* manhood, derived from the noun *mwaume* (pl. *baume*) meaning "man"; by implication the "male sexual organs."

- *U/bufyashi,* parenthood; by implication (1) "offspring, progeny", and (2) "procreation."

- *Ulufumo,* the maternal womb. *Ulufumo* is derived from the verb *ukufuma,* "to come out". It also designates the trunk of a tree. A tree has three major parts. *Imishila,* the roots, *ulufumo,* the trunk, and *fibuula,* the branches.

- *Mu nda,* the maternal womb. *Twafyele mu nda umo,* we were born of the same womb.

- *Ubula,* the maternal womb. (pl. *amala,* primarily "the bowels").

- *Mfwalo,* the private parts, nudity. The etymological meaning is "the parts that must remain clothed."

6.4.2 Menstruation

- *Ukuwa cisungu,* to fall into maturity/puberty, meaning 'to have first menstruation.'

- *Akuba na mpepo,* being in a state of coldness, meaning 'to pass through the monthly period.'

- *Atiina mulilo,* fearing fire, meaning 'to pass through the monthly period'.

- *Ukuba mu mitanda,* to be in a shelter outside the village, to be in a liminal state, meaning, 'a woman during her monthly period.'(Hinfelaar 1994:10)

- *Ukutaba,* "to move away (from the village)" (Hinfelaar 1994:10).

- *Ali mu minwe,* or *ukuba mu minwe,* "she is or to be in the hands (of the forebears)" (Hinfelaar 1994:10), meaning 'a woman passing through her monthly period.'

- *Ali mu mwenshi,* she is in a state of moving about, meaning 'a woman passing through her monthly period.'

- *Ali ku mweshi,* she is at the month, meaning 'to pass through the monthly period.'

6.4.3 Pregnancy

- *Muli pa bukulu,* lit., "you are at greatness, largeness" (physically) meaning "you are pregnant." *Kapiye ku cipatala no kupimwa lintu lyonse nga mwaishiba ukuti muli pa bukulu,* "Go to the clinic to be weighed regularly when you know you are pregnant."

- *Naimita umusuku,* I have conceived a fetus, I am pregnant.

- *Aba no musuku,* she is with a fetus", she is pregnant.

- *Ali ne fumo,* the term *l/ifumo* carries a number of meanings. In a general way it denotes the abdomen or belly. It also means womb, pregnancy or foetus. Hence the expression *ali ne fumo* means: she is pregnant.

7. A Concluding Reflection: Some Linguistic Observations

I return to the word *ukumfwa* which is so tightly linked with the three senses of hearing, feeling and taste! As regards *ukumfwa* and hearing (sound), the notion of listening (understanding) is strongly implied.

7.1 From the Sense Organ to Sensitive Behavior

Not heeding advice, an unwillingness to hear what others say, could end disastrously. It could mean a person's "social death," that is, alienation from the community. To listen to one another builds and unifies communal bonds. A lack of mutual understanding could lead to the loss of communal peace and stability. *Ukumfwana,* a reciprocal extension of *ukumfwa,* means "to hear one another; to come to mutual understanding." Where *ukumfwana* does not form the basis of building a community, living in peace with one another is not possible. So, in a very real sense, where the "ear" is neglected, social consequences or the "death" of a peaceful community can result.

The concept of listening has attained such high status in the value system of Bemba communities that it has found its way into language that reflects the interplay between "ear", "peace" and "death". The hierarchical power structure, *imfumu* to *mwine mushi* (chief to village headman etc.) functions on this very premise. Disobedience and the punishment of perpetrators who have violated cultural norms result in the intervention of those who hold power. The *abakalamba-umucinshi* (age-respect) structure operates on the same axis. Neglect of elderly advice, *toomfwa,*[18] "he/she does not listen or hear," is a strong verdict pronounced over an individual. Such a verdict stresses the shortcomings in a person's socializing abilities, perhaps even his intention to

---

[18] *taumfwa,* the "a" and "u" fuse to "o".

wilfully destroy communal norms.[19] Investigations of a possible etymological link between *ukumfwa* and *ukufwa* (to die) or *imfwa* (death) could yield interesting results. Linguists might find it an interesting topic for study.

7.2 From the Human Body to the Social Body

In this section, I would like to take some linguistic excursions. These may seem obscure to Western people (as they did to me when I first thought about them), but they really just highlight the diversity of cognitive possibilities. For example, the phrase *ndi no mutwe* literally translates as "I am with (a) head." But the meaning of this phrase is quite different from what the literal translation suggests. The words explicitly mean "I have (a) headache." Another phrase is *ndi no cifuba,* literally translated "I am with (a) chest." Again, the literal meaning is far from what the phrase actually means, namely, "I have (a) chest cold." There are further examples to furnish the same line of cognitive diversity. But these two already reveal interesting features.

First, the focus is squarely on the object noun, and not on an action done to the head or a condition to which it is subjected. It is the self that is subjected to a particular condition. In other words, like in the former phrase, emphasis is not on the pain (as in English), but on the object that is affected, the head. It is the emphasis on the object proper which singles out the head from all other parts of the body drawing attention to a disrupted wholeness. The phrase *ndi no cifuba,* "I am with (a) chest", puts stress on the malfunction of body functions (breathing problems, coughing, fever etc.) rather than descriptively refering to the anatomy of the body.

Dorothy Lee in *Freedom of Culture* (1959) says of the Wintu Indians in Northern California that their self is inseparably linked with the physical aspect of the individual. The Wintu have no word for body (!), but instead use and speak of the whole person (*kot wintu*). Consequently, there are no specific terms for the parts of the body; body parts "are aspects or locations" (1959:134). She furnishes the following example, among others: "I broke my arm" is expressed in Wintu by saying *"arm-broke-I."* The English language *separates* the person from the activity (the person's own action that is), putting emphasis on the verb in conjunction with a second personal pronoun highlighting an action. The Wintu draws attention to him as a *whole* person and qualifies a specific aspect or place/part of him (one could say *I-* the-*broke-arm*) thus highlighting a condition. Lee says Wintu only separate or delineate the self from the part when a part of the body no longer is a physical

---

[19] Musonda, referring to the neighbouring Bisa whose language is closely related to Bemba, points out that *ukumfwa* "is used to express respect for the source of the word of instruction. It further expresses attentiveness to the speaker. Since the word is intrinsically linked to the one who speaks it, to listen to what is said is a sign of respect for the speaker. Not attending to what is said is a clear sign of disrespect" (1996:104).

Chapter 3: An Outline of the Concept of Body

part of a person (e.g. "this is *his* arm" means "the arm which was cut off, it is his") (1959:135).

The Bemba self, too, is holistic. But the Bemba have yet another way of contrasting the self. While the Wintu highlight a specific aspect or place/part of the self when, for example, an arm is broken, the Bemba do not. They stress the self to be in company "with" a specific part ("I am *with* head"). In so doing, a Bemba speaker particularizes the self, but – and this is important – he thereby indicates a *negative* disruption of the whole.[20] The explicit reference to the head at a particular time and in a particular situation does not mean a Bemba person lacks awareness of his head as being part of himself outside this situation. With the Bemba, the self assumes a separate self-awareness when the whole (health, well-being) undergoes *negative* influences or changes. When the self is "with" a particular part (head or chest) of the whole (body), then wholeness (health) is faced with a boundary. *Particularization threatens the whole*. To single out a specific body part and placing it in the accompaniment of a particular part/location indicates a worrisome disruption of *Mutuntulu*.[21] *Mutuntulu* means to be whole, to be in good health, reflecting harmony, and is a highly treasured human condition in Bemba thinking.[22]

Now, connecting the human body to the social body is not really far-fetched. Bemba culture ascribes high value to communal bonds. Individualism – here I mean "independence" from the group – equals *particularization that threatens the whole* (social body). Individualism means that a person sticks out from the rest of the community by, for example, putting in hard work and reaping a bumper harvest. Such situations upset communal norms and might create tensions among members of the community, such as envy. Does this mean the "low value" for particularization and the "high value" for group conformity lead to an absence of, or a minimal degree of individuality, personality, or individual agency? No, not really.

---

[20] An alternative phrase to *ndi no mutwe* is *ndeumfwa mutwe*, lit., "I feel head", meaning "I have (a) headache." The latter phrase underlines the assumptions made above.

[21] *Mutuntulu* is a compound adjective. *Mu* is a locative particle but its value is prepositional and adverbial; *mu* may mean "in, inside, within, on" etc. The adjective ... *tuntulu*, means "whole, living, complete." The extension *Mutuntulu* means therefore "to be complete, to be whole, to be in good health, to be in a state of completeness and health." See also the discourse on *ubutuntulu* in Hinfelaar 1994:108.

[22] The *Mutuntulu* maxim does not exist in isolation from other ideas expressing wholeness and health. For example, the greeting *mwapoleni*, "how are you, how do you do" is a predominant or common Bemba greeting. It specifically stresses the idea of wholeness. Clearly, the interest is in one's physical condition. The intransitive verb *-pola*, from which *mwapoleni* is derived, expresses a specific and much desired state of existence, that is, good health. It is the state of *mutuntulu* (wholeness, completeness, health) that one wishes another person to enjoy in the *mwapoleni* greeting (if the greeting is meant to really communicate an individual's desire for someone else is, of course, not a matter of vocabulary alone).

On the contrary, one focal point of this study is to show that an individual is not only acted upon by culture – subscribing to stereotyped behavior – but that individual agency also acts on the cultural context, that is, actively moves toward particularization. It will also be seen that particularization does not necessarily mean a threat to the whole. Such a move toward particularization, however, is dependent on how that particularization succeeds in the process of integration. That is, how personality succeeds in integrating creativity and particularity into one's social group and society at large.

Illness, too, particularizes, and also poses a threat to the whole. Illness disrupts *Mutuntulu*. Illness threatens health. Not only this new condition of incomplete, disrupted *Mutuntulu* – that is the condition of ill health – but also the cause(s) of illness or ailments must be investigated. This is where the following chapter attempts to connect. With its outline of the Bemba concept of illness and illnesses, the chapter focuses on the different classificatory systems as well as on the various origins and causes of illness or illnesses in the Bemba classificatory system.

Chapter 4
An Outline of the Concept of Illness

1. Introduction

The Bemba concept of illness is significantly from Western scientific models of illness.[1] The latter are built on precepts of a materialistic view of illness, healing and health, whereas the Bemba concept is mainly based on a transcendental spiritual view of illness, healing and health.[2] Consequently, to the Bemba, illnesses and their causes are subject to different patterns of categorization. Of course, the groups of sickness categories are not clean-cut entities, nor are they always rigorously followed. However, the group categories do exist. They guide cultural insiders in establishing the cause and treatment of sicknesses. Similarly, they help outsiders to translate ideas and perceptions of sickness and healing in Bemba culture into something understandable. Bemba culture recognizes at least eight distinguishable sickness categories which include sicknesses due to immanent causal factors as well as sicknesses whose causal factors must be attributed to transcendental, external forces.[3]

Aschwanden in his book *Symbols of Death* describes this aspect of the culture of the Karanga of Zimbabwe in similar manner. According to Aschwanden, the Karanga discern potential causes for sickness by distinguishing between three basic kinds of diseases: (1) Diseases sent by God; (2) diseases caused by the spirits; and (3) the most feared and treaded diseases which are contracted through witchcraft (1987:14-15). The intricate structure of this system is reflected in the classificatory names used for different categories of sicknesses, and the variety of specific names referring to their causes and the remedies for particular ailments or complaints.[4]

---

[1] Western medicine looks at the symptoms (of a sickness) and separates body and mind. Eastern and African medicine looks at the whole body. Dr. Robert Abel, ophthalmologist, in a radio interview on "Talk to America," a program of *Voice of America* broadcast on Sunday, April 2, 2000.

[2] Compare also LeBacq [1998]:18.

[3] Bate, leaning on Harriet Ngubane in *Body and Mind in Zulu Medicine*, reports of the Zulu that there are sicknesses of basically two kinds. (1) *Umkhuhlane* is a bodily sickness not attributed to external forces. "*Izifo zabantu* or *Ukufa kwabantu* lit. "sicknesses of the people" or "death of the people" are sicknesses "tied up with the idea of not living well and not being in harmony with one's environment especially in relationship to others both the people around and the ancestors." However, such distinguishing "is not normally distinguished within a traditional Zulu cultural paradigm and so both "sickness" and "healing" will not correspond with Western understandings" (Bate 1993:331).

[4] The classificatory system of names for different categories of medecines and their utilization as remedies for a variety of complaints is not unique to the Bemba only because it also "constitutes a basic, pan-Indonesian culture trait." The same mechanism is true for sicknesses, their

As was true in the previous chapter, a measure of constraint is exercised in both the selection and presentation of sicknesses and healing in this chapter. Not all classificatory groups of sicknesses can be dealt with here. A first focus will be on malnutrition with specific reference to children under five, because it represents a real and serious health problem needing to be tackled in the Kasama District.[5] At the same time, malnutrition is connected to a network of cultural factors which, at first glance, seem without apparent reason. However, these factors turn out to be the actual causes of this particular problem. Among the other sicknesses, the sickness *Icuulu* receives prime attention and is examined because of its perceived exclusive transcendental cause. *Icuulu* will also be seen to have a crucial bearing on the case study that will be presented later. *Ngulu* sickness will also receive attention because of its unexplainable nature and its implications for the case study.

In a closing section, I would like to treat sickness as an ambivalent element of Bemba culture. This ambivalence is due to worldview values operating within a dialectical relationship between ideal and practice, thus creating a cultural paradox.

2. Diseases Caused by Violation of Traditional Laws: *Amalwele ya Makowesha*

The World Bank's (1994) assessment of Zambia's malnutrition classified the disease as a serious and persistent problem in the country. The report stated that poverty is connected to the majority of people being "hungry (and being in a state of) undernourishment because they are poor."[6] The correlation between the two variables, however, is not always easily and clearly established, writes Nangawe (1998a:6). A comparison of Northern Province to the rest of Zambia revealed poor primary health care and abnormally high levels of malnutrition.[7] Contrary to the World Bank's assumption that the causes of malnutrition hinged on hunger and undernourishment because of poverty, the study by Nangawe and his team (1995 and 1996) was based on the researcher's assumption "that malnutrition in under-fives is probably influenced by deep-seated cultural factors beyond child feeding" (Nangawe et. al 1998a:2).[8]

---

causes and their treatment (Slikkerveer & Slikkerveer 1995:13). Also, the Jalari of South India apply various criteria in the identification of illnesses. For example, *Jabbu* illnesses are assumed to respond to curative measures of modern medical means. *Ammavari Jabbu* (goddess illness) requires specific diagnostics and curative strategies (Nuckolls 1996:215).

[5] Nangawe et. al., say that "malnutrition seems to be taken as a simple problem and is not viewed as seriously as it deserves" (1998a:6).

[6] World Bank, "Zambia Poverty Assessment," vol. 1, report no. 12985-ZA, Cap 7, 162-170, 1994 (in Nangawe et. al. 1998a:2-3).

[7] Chronic malnutrition in Under Five was at 57% in 1992 (Nangawe et. al. 1998a:3).

[8] The study revealed that cultural factors are indeed far more the cause of malnutrition than is known to the public. The abundance of rainfall and food production activities in the area only

Bemba causal theories of malnutrition revolve around two sets of explanatory models. The first model comprises the term *Ulunse* and the second model the concepts of *imililo* (fire) and *amakowesha* (contamination). I will first set out to describe the *Ulunse*[9] model and its variants and then continue to highlight the *imililo/amakowesha* complex and its variants.

2.1 *Ulunse* leading to *Cifimba*[10] (Acute Malnutrition): *Kwashiorkor*

A very general description of *Ulunse* is the perception that early resumption of sexual intercourse after delivery leading to early pregnancy will cause *Ulunse* in the infant.[11] At the first sign of a pregnancy during breast-feeding, the child is abruptly weaned. The abrupt weaning causes psychological[12] and physical problems in the child.

---

underlines the findings of the study. "In Kasama district malnutrition is highly prevalent even in areas with abundance of food (such as the Chambeshi flood plain)" (Nangawe et. al. 1998a:5).

[9] My own probing into this topic confirms the following section on *Ulunse*. The research was done in Andele village, east of Kasama in the first half of 2000.

[10] *Cifimba* is derived from the intransitive verb *ukufimba*, meaning "to swell, to be swollen." *The White Fathers Bemba-English Dictionary*, (1991) s.v. "-*fimba*."

[11] Frank LeBacq, interview by author, Kasama, Zambia, January 20, 2000. Dr. LeBacq was Technical Advisor Health/ District Medical Officer of Kasama District from June 1994 to June 2000.

[12] Ritchie attempted to theorize on the emotional effects of nursing (breast-feeding) and weaning on African children at length. His basic line of thinking was that the different modes of nursing and weaning exemplified on European babies and African babies will have a lasting effect on individuals of either culture for life-time. (I use the term culture here in a very general way). Ritchie's theory alleges that an infant subjected to a regulated measure of feeding intervals triggers in him or her anger and hatred (aroused by a momentary parting from the mother and her breast felt as a severe privation) as well as love and gladness (aroused by the return of the mother and her breast and felt as a condition of utmost pleasure). "This regularity of nursing establishes a keen time-sense," says Ritchie. The interrupted intervals of feeding cause the infant to learn to reconcile the "pain of privation" with the "joy of indulgence" giving compensation for having to wait. Therefore, Ritchie writes ..."the past provides a precedent for the future, and the child learns to wait with purpose." On the other hand, a child that enjoys the mother's breast at any given time and moment, as is the case in African cultures, keeps the child in the present. It instills in him or her the notion that the present is a state of perfect pleasure, or at least pleasure can be obtained at will if only demands for it are articulated. This state of timeless pleasure impacts the conscious of the suckling greatly as the duration of the nursing period, the time the infant has access to the mother's breast, extends at least from one year up to two years and even beyond (1968:9-19). Abrupt weaning, as is the case when *ulunse* prompts the mother's decisive action, constitutes the painful ending of the child's hitherto fully conscious pleasure. The magnitude of the emotional upheaval this situation creates (having to cope with a forced separation from a fully conscious pleasure and the ambivalence of hate and love towards the mother) is enormous. The situation is further aggravated by erratic food patterns (caused by poverty and/or the reaction of refusal toward the introduction of "new" or alternative eating habits as it means venturing out into the unknown) prevalent in so many village communities within Kasama District. The brutal reality of now regulated, though irregular, feeding patterns which are dependent on a great number of variables (water, firewood, type of food available, workload of women, access to primary health care facilities etc.) and the stereo-

There are three variants of *Ulunse* in connection with an early pregnancy of a woman still breastfeeding an infant.

(1) Early pregnancy[13] leads to abrupt stoppage of breastfeeding. The *lack of food* leads to *Cifimba (kwashiorkor)*, which eventually leads to death. *Cifimba* shows in edematous swellings in which children display swollen legs, swollen arms, or a swollen tummy.

(2) Early pregnancy leads to the abrupt stoppage of breastfeeding. The *introduction to new food* leads to infection which leads to diarrhoea, which leads to *Cifimba (kwashiorkor)* and eventually to death.

(3) In the event of an early pregnancy, the blood of the womb contaminates the breast milk of the mother.[14] This contamination leads to diarrhoea which leads to *Cifimba (kwashiorkor)* and eventually to death.

The perception of *Cifimba* is extremely strong and entails the assumption that such a condition means the certain death of the child. *Cifimba* is diagnosed or recognized as a hopeless case. There is no treatment for the child. It is almost the same as being dead.

A further variant of *Ulunse* is connected to the early resumption of sex after the delivery of a baby.

(1) Early resumption of sex leads to unclean hands of the mother which leads to diarrhoea, which leads to *Cifimba (kwashiorkor)* and eventually to death.

2.2 *Ulunse* leading to *Ukondoloka*[15] (Acute Malnutrition): *Merasmus*

During infancy, the child sleeps very close to the mother. In the event of a pregnancy, the mother's warmth (*icikabilila*) is deemed bad for the child. Her

---

typical diet according to months and seasons, greatly contribute to malnutrition in children under five. For statistics on malnutrition in children under five in Kasama District see Nangawe et. al. 1997. The psychological impact of abrupt weaning must not be taken lightly. There are strong emotional reactions to which the child is subjected. Mothers literally scare away their babies from the breast by applying hot pepper on the nipple, or wearing frightening objects underneath the brassiers, etc. (Nangawe et. al. 1998a:28).

[13] "Early pregnancy is defined as pregnancy within **the first six months after delivery** (bold script in the original)" (Nangawe et. al. 1998a:15).

[14] The breast-feeding child is "sucking the blood of the fetus in the womb." People say: *alionekela* meaning, "he/she (the child) has sucked the blood of the fetus." The fetus is thought of as consisting of blood. Since the blood circulates in the body, it also reaches the breast of the mother and is thus sucked through breast-feeding, which contaminates the milk and causes the breast-fed child to fall sick. Therefore, the child is weaned immediately. A recurring sickness of the weaned child, e.g., diarrhoea, is known as *alilwala ulunse* meaning, "he/she has the sickness of *ulunse*."

[15] *Ukondoloka* is an intransitive verb meaning: "to be emaciated, to be wasted."

"warmth" "is considered to have deleterious effects (fevers)" (Nangawe et. al. 1998a:28) on the child. These effects lead to *Ukondoloka* (*merasmus*). Malnutrition in children is further dramatized by the fact that the mother becomes the second victim. As shown above, malnutrition is related to a mother's (sexual) behavior, behavior not condoned by the community. The mother of the child is laughed at by the community, communicating to her that she has been "playing around" either with her husband or another man. Though it is understood that pregnancy takes two people, it is the woman who is blamed for an early pregnancy. The understanding is that she does not know how to behave. The man might be embarrassed but the blame is put on the woman. If abrupt weaning of the child is observed, people know there was a breach of a traditional norm, that is, the woman was not careful to avoid pregnancy before the proper time of weaning the child had come. The mother experiences a stigma of shame and contempt.[16]

The Nangawe study revealed a second set of the explanatory model of malnutrition in children which focuses on the wider complex of the *Imililo* (fire) or *amakowesha* (contamination) perceptions (Nangawe et. al. 1998a:17-20).

2.3 *Imililo/Amakowesha* leading to *Cifimba* (Acute Malnutrition): Kwashiorkor

(1) Intra-marital sex makes a person "hot, warm" (*icikabilila*). The child cannot be touched and fed before the bodies involved in the sex act have cooled down, or the hands have been washed. If this rule is not followed, the child may become *amakowesha* (that is, enter into the state of contamination when fed) which leads to *Cifimba* (*kwashiorkor*) and eventually to death.

(2) Extra-marital sex of either the wife or the husband makes her or him a potential threat to the health of the child. This can happen when such a person *touches the cooking*, or *the fireplace*, or *feeds the child*, or *holds the child* without having bathed or cleansed himself with herbs beforehand; the child may suffer from *amakowesha*. The state of "contamination" can cause the child to experience weight loss, loss of appetite, *ukondoloka* (wasting), fragility (*ukunyomboloka*),[17] chronic cough, or chronic diarrhoea, all of which lead to *Cifimba* (*kwashiorkor*) and eventually to death.

(3) *Ubupulumushi* (immorality, promiscuity) of other members of the household (men or women, girls or boys) poses a threat to the child's health if those members *touch the cooking*, or *the fireplace*, *cook*

---

[16] Private discussion with Dr. Frank LeBacq, Kasama, Zambia, January 20, 2000.

[17] *Ukunyomboloka* is an intransitive verb meaning "to be tall and slender, slim, lanky." It also means "to be emaciated." *The White Fathers, Dictionary*, (1991), s.v. "-*nyomboloka*."

food, *feed the child*, or *hold the child*. The child may suffer from *amakowesha* and experience weight loss, or loss of appetite, or *ukondoloka* (wasting), or chronic cough, or chronic diarrhoea, or fevers, all of which can lead to *Cifimba* (*kwashiorkor*) and eventually to death.

(4) A girl who is experiencing the initiation of menstruation (*Cisungu*) or her regular menses, and who *touches the cooking*, or *the fireplace*, or *adds salt to the food* being cooked either for the child or the family, may cause the child or the family to suffer from *amakowesha*. Again, this can lead to *Cifimba* (*kwashiorkor*) in the child and eventually cause its death.

(5) A girl who has lost her virginity through unsanctioned sex, and who *touches the cooking* or *the fireplace*, or *adds salt to the food* being cooked either for the child or the family, may cause the child or the family to suffer from *amakowesha*, which could lead to *Cifimba* (*kwashiorkor*) in the child and eventually cause its death.

(6) A woman or girl who has had an abortion, and who *touches the cooking*, or *the fireplace*, or *cooks food*, or *feeds the child*, or *holds the child*, may cause the child to suffer from *amakowesha*, which could lead to *Cifimba* (*kwashiorkor*) in the child and eventually cause its death.

2.4 *Ulunse* and *Ukondoloka* (Malnutrition) in Adults

Traditionally it is believed to be difficult for adult persons to suffer from *ulunse* unless there is *ukukowesha* involved, that is "contamination" cause by a breach of a traditional law. *Ukondoloka* is used on adults who show signs of weight loss and coughing.

Chewing leaves from the *Kunda* tree or soaking the roots of the *Kampembe wansha* tree in water and drinking the mixture are treatments for the ordinary cough. Often, it is the elderly people in the villages who have specialized in this field. Failure to cure coughing by the use of these two treatments and the worsening of the cough are explained by saying that the affected person is suffering from *cifuba ca makowesha*.[18] A constant, deep and persistent cough that continues over a prolonged period of time is no longer more treated and perceived as an ordinary cough. If a person has received proper treatment and there is still an absence of significant improvement, the person is suspected of having contracted *cifuba ca makowesha*. Traditional medical practice is left with very few options to treat *cifuba ca makowesha*.[19] Most of the time, con-

---

[18] Literally translated the phrase could mean, "the cough of contamination."

[19] My informant's father used to treat *cifuba ca makowesha*. But he has no specific knowledge of how his father prepared medicine for treating this sickness. He does remember that the patient had to bring a chicken: a cock when the patient was a man, and a hen when the patient was

traction of this particular kind of cough is attributed to the violation of sex norms. For example, promiscuity of a married man makes him "unclean"; he has disqualified himself from *ukukumya pe shiku*, "touching the three studs of the fireplace."[20] The ability to practice *ukukumya pe shiku* is a clear indication of the husband's unquestionable moral state, as he will not vomit the family food prepared on the family hearth. His refusal to conform to the traditional norm, however, is a clear signal to the wife that her husband has had extramarital relations. Such an act would cause harm/sickness to all persons eating food cooked on this fire.

The most common sickness contracted by "polluted fire" is constant coughing, *cifuba ca makowesha* or *cifuba ca ntanda bwanga*[21] leading to *ukondoloka*. This type of coughing is often related to tuberculosis.[22] Also, HIV/AIDS in the villages is understood as being *ntanda bwanga* (a lingering or incurable disease). As HIV/AIDS is often accompanied by coughing, people talk of *cifubu ca makowesha or ntanda bwanga* which relates to the breach of a sexual norm.

2.5 Chronic Malnutrition (Stunting)

Chronic malnutrition is still not identified as a serious problem within Bemba communities. Surveys indicate that 56% of Zambia's children suffer from chronic malnutrition also known as stunting (Nangawe et. al. 1998b:3). There is no Bemba term for chronic malnutrition until later stages of development when stunting can be clearly seen. A person suffering from chronic malnutri-

---

a woman. "The chicken was slaughtered but not cut into pieces – only the intestines were removed. Then the chicken was cooked in a pot together with medicine. When the chicken had been cooked, the patient was told to go to the rubbish place (*pa ciskala*) where he or she was told to eat the chicken on his or her own. An important instruction was not to chew any bone of the chicken because teeth touching the bone would render the medicine ineffective. Careful eating of the flesh had to be observed. After the patient finished eating the flesh of the chicken, my father would go and cut the patient's hair and shave the head bald. Then the leftover bones of the chicken and some of the hair from the patient's head were collected. What my father did with these items I do not know. But the remains of the chicken and the remainder of the hair were collected for a specific reason, which I was not told. I suspect they were buried."

[20] Maxwell states: "any promiscuous person, whose sex is not socialized and sacralized in the purification ceremonies possible only to married persons, are terribly dangerous contaminants of fire" (1983:31).

[21] *Ntanda bwanga* is an incurable disease and spreads like fire. *Ntanda bwanga* consists of two noun compounds *ntanda* (lit.: star) and *bwanga* (lit.: witchcraft, sorcery, spell). The concept of *bwanga* explains the futility in treating the disease, termed as incurable because its causes are attributed to forces outside human control. *Ntanda* carries the notion of vastness or multitude. The idea of vastness or multitude is found in the expression *Wa ntanda* meaning: "the father of a large family; his offspring is uncountable" like the stars. Compare *The White Fathers Dictionary*, (1991) s.v. "*lutanda.*"

[22] *Cifuba ca makowesha* and *cifuba ca ntanda bwanga* are considered as tuberculosis until proven otherwise (90% of the persons will be TB positive). Frank LeBacq, interview by author, Kasama, Zambia, March 21, 2000.

tion is called *Ntuse,* a dwarf or a short person. The only factor that indicates stunting in a child is the ratio between age and height. Stunted growth is acknowledged when the height of the child does not correspond to its age, even though the weight for that height may be satisfactory. Chronic malnutrition is not usually noticed until a medical person measures height in relation to age. Out of 296 children measured and weighed in Kasama District between 1995 and 1996, 155 children between the ages of three and fifty-nine months (three months to five years) showed stunted growth. This means that 52,3 % of all the children measured and weighed were seriously affected by stunting (Nangawe et. al. 1998a:3).

2.6 Conclusion

In the two sets of explanatory models presented above (*ulunse* and *imililo-fire/amakowesha-* "contamination"), it is evident that malnutrition in children under five is considered to be primarily caused and related to sexual behavior of persons. In only one instance is malnutrition directly linked to hunger/starvation (*insala*) leading to *ukondoloka* (merasmus) (Nangawe et. al. 1998a:29). The obvious disparity between the World Bank's report in 1994 and subsequent research by Nangawe and his team (1995 and 1996) is enlightening indeed. The conventional explanations of the causes of malnutrition (hunger, undernourishment, poverty) leave huge gaps in the reality of the malnutrition problem in Kasama District. What seem to be such obvious reasons on a surface level prove to be marginal and almost insignificant when contrasted with the deep-structure level of the cultural factors at work which reflect worldview values.

National health workers further compound the problem. Though they know of the cultural factors or concepts connected with malnutrition, they simply ignore them. Instead, they continue to hold a purely medical perception and adhere to "western" explanations of the disease. "Health workers are aware of the local taxonomies on malnutrition but could not construct the local explanatory models which the people incriminate," writes Nangawe (1998a:28). Malnutrition rooms of hospitals and clinics are often the most overcrowded wards. Traditionally, this is an indication that mothers with malnourished children have not had proper teaching during a girl's initiation ceremony (*Cisungu*). The presumption is that they were not taught how to look after children. In hospital, they are told off and scolded by medical personnel as being ignorant about feeding the child.[23] The mother experiences another stigma of shame and contempt. The "double stigma" (Nangawe et. al. 1998a:13) – shame and contempt from the community as well as from medical personnel – makes it even more difficult to overcome the serious problem of malnutrition in Kasama District (Nangawe et. al. 1998a:5). The "shame and

---

[23] Frank LeBacq, interview by author, Kasama, Zambia, March 21, 2000.

contempt" experience by mothers put them in a corner with little manoeuverability for change.

The ignorance of people regarding chronic malnutrition underlines the seriousness of the overall situation in Kasama District. As long as the community does not identify malnutrition *in all its variants* as a pertinent problem, and as long as medical personnel ignore cultural explanatory models in their efforts to provide health care, acute malnutrition will claim the lives of many more under-fives. And the cruel reality of stunting will impair the lives of significantly more children in the future.

The "contamination" (*ukukowesha*) of the fireplace has serious implications and consequences for virtually all members of Bemba society, as seen in the description of the complex of causes of malnutrition in children. The same holds true for sicknesses that are more commonly associated with adults. The most dangerous act in Bemba traditional life is participation in unsanctioned sex or sexual activities before marriage and within the bond of marriage. Traditions hold that, when a woman is discovered to have broken the rule of premarital sex before marriage, the chances of her getting married drop drastically. She is now referred to as *aliposa Cisungu*, "she has thrown away/discarded her *Cisungu*."[24] Also, extramarital sex of either the woman or the man is not a private affair of two individuals with her lover or his mistress, but rapidly becomes a public problem that touches the lives of many members of the community. Says Nangawe et. al., "an important cue from the *imililo/amakowesha* complex is its close agreement with what is conventionally known about dangers of exchange of body fluids," as it highlights "the desire of traditional societies to be clean and hygienic" (1998a:29). What remains, however, is the question: Can these perceptions affect the rapidly changing Zambian society that has been so badly hit by the HIV/AIDS pandemic?

3. Diseases Caused by Witchcraft (*Ubuloshi*): *Amalwele ya Kulowekwa*

Diseases and witchcraft are two inseparably linked realities in African societies. Parrinder writes that "witchcraft belief is an expression of social disease, and this time is a time of exceptional unrest" (1976:133). It is equally true that witchcraft belief is fuelled by the reality of physical sickness and ill health of members of society, a reality that cannot ordinarily be explained. But it is not enough to simply assume that the inseparable link between disease and witchcraft settles the whole spectrum of cause and effect. It is not enough to be content with witchcraft as a causal theory of illness per se. Witchcraft is sim-

---

[24] *Aliposa Cisungu* means a girl has neglected or discarded the teachings she received at the *Cisungu* ceremony performed for girls at the appearance of the first menstruation.

ply a medium through which *individuals* act upon *other individuals,* thereby causing "exceptional unrest" within the community. Therefore, as Obeyesekere rightly observes,

> ... it is also necessary to explain why hostile activity of witchcraft or sorcery is attributed to another individual. It is then that we can know why that particular idiom (language or symbol; addition mine) is chosen from a potential or actual large number of causal theories (1984:108).

Personal physical sickness and social disease form a vicious circle that is difficult to escape. For one, it provides an explanation of a specific condition of a particular individual that cannot otherwise be explained by culture – in scientific or biological explanatory models. Second, it is a culturally sanctioned avenue on wherein individuals act upon each other. Such action carries negative notions or emotions that cannot otherwise be expressed unless open conflict or physical confrontation takes place. The sickness *icuulu,* as the sample case will show, provides just such an example.

3.1 The Sickness *Icuulu*

The word *Icuulu* designating this sickness is derived from the anthill (also called *cuulu*). There are some three points of references: (1) *cuulu* (pl. *fyuulu*), is a symbol of endurance. The anthill is known for its solidity and sturdiness; (2) *cuulu* is also a swear word and may also symbolize death;[25] and (3) *cuulu,* the anthill, sticks out of its environment because of its conical shape. These three characteristics accompany a person who is *ukulwala icuulu,* "to suffer from" or "to be sick with *icuulu."* *Icuulu* is a swelling (at times rather big) on the body and resembles the shape of an anthill. The spot where *icuulu* manifests is usually very hard and often forms a solid lump.

However, indications are that this sickness takes a long time to ultimately cause the death of a person. Someone suffering from *icuulu* may initially feel pain in their whole body, but later experience pain at one particular part of the body. *Icuulu* is not locally bound to only one place, but may shift to other parts of the body, e.g., from the leg to the arm, from the leg to the abdomen and so forth. Importantly, when *icuulu* manifests itself as abdominal swelling,

---

[25] When taking an oath, the expression *ku cuulu*! can be heard. Compare *The White Fathers Bemba-English Dictionary* (1991) s.v. "*-cuulu.*" In a sample case of *Mutumwa Nchimi* diagnosis, the anthill was associated with a shining light that was moving towards a house at night. The majority of the family members occupying the house were struck with sicknesses and at one time the husband said that both he and his wife were going to die if the sicknesses continued. The shining light supposedly emanating from the anthill was the harbinger of ill-fate, continued sickness, and eventually death. For a complete account of the Sample Case see Dillon-Malone1988:1170-1172.

a person is faced with imminent death; the manifestation of *icuulu* in the stomach is a harbinger of death.

3.1.1 Context and *Icuulu* Explanatory Models

Earlier in this discussion (cf. chapter two: concept of *umupashi*), it was said that persons who share the same culture might assign different meanings to cultural elements or might have different views on a certain subject. As regards the sickness *icuulu*, data gathered from different persons underscore this assumption. My fieldnotes provide at least three different emphases on this kind of sickness, depending on the context.

"Appropriation-Context"

A woman was complaining of pain and swellings in her body. Small lumps would occur at different locations and cause her much discomfort and pain. She is not a Bemba by tribe but lives in a Bemba neighbourhood in the vicinity of a town in Bembaland. When she explained her problem, her neighbours and friends advised her to see *Shing'anga* (Healer). They identified her symptoms as being related to *icuulu* sickness and probably caused by witchcraft. Although she was not really inclined to accept the suggested explanation, she took her neighbours' and friends' advice to heart. She went to see a number of healers in order to get rid of *icuulu* sickness, which the healers also confirmed to be her problem. During the course of seeking relief from her ailment through the engagement of various healers, she spent a handsome amount of money on them. At times, the sickness would cause severe restrictions in her movements and daily routine. At at other times, she would feel better. But the *icuulu* symptoms never disappeared completely.

It must be noted that the ascribed meaning of her symptoms stemmed from others (neighbours, friends and healers) rather than from her own set of possible explanations. Not being a Bemba by tribe, she did not initially draw on Bemba cultural elements. But she also failed to draw on her own cultural elements and thus did not effectively counter these proposals by ascribing her own meaning to her sickness. Rather, because of her residence and ties of relationship developed within the predominant Bemba community, she bowed to the interpretation of others, probably "significant others." Symbols are not only assigned meanings by a person himself, but are also appropriated for oneself as a result of "outside forces," pressures, relational ties, or simply because of convenience.

"Professionalism-Context"

Healers also assign their own set(s) of meaning(s) to *icuulu*. Mr. Soandso, a healer,[26] emphasized the various kinds of treatments given when desperate

---

[26] For reasons of courtesy, I refrain from using the real name.

patients come to consult him about this sickness. Treatment of *icuulu* will, however, depend on its root cause. He identified two causes of *icuulu*: witchcraft (*ubuloshi*) or spirits that possess humans (*ngulu*). Treatment may involve the washing of the body with medicine (*ukusukwila umubili*), the drinking of medicine (*ukunwa umuti*), and making tattoos (*inembo*) around the area of pain and rubbing medicine inside the incisions. The medicine used in connection with tattoos involves ingredients from an animal, such as blood taken from cutting off the talon of a chicken. Medicine mixed with ingredients from an animal is called *icishimba* (pl. *ifishimba*, also referred to as "magical medicine") and only used on the outer parts of the body. Though the origin of *icuulu* is important and is specifically noted, *Shing'anga* clearly puts emphasis on the curative attempts of the sickness. In other words, the interest is in the symbol of healing (rather than on the symbol of origin) and in the symbol of the healer, that is, the upholding of the *Shing'anga* institution within society.

"Family-Context"

A third emphasis surfaces when *icuulu* is viewed from a patients (and family's) point of view as the root cause of deaths of family members. The traditional explanatory pattern of *Icuulu* is often exclusively related to witchcraft (*ubuloshi*) as the prime cause of the sickness. The "Family-Context" greatly determines the cause, the treatment, and the implications *icuulu* sickness creates. The cause and the treatment considered to effectively counter-attack the illness, along with family relationships, create a whole web of meanings and implications. The "Family-Context" of *icuulu* sickness is of utmost importance in this study because it was believed that *icuulu* was the cause of G. Chewe's father's death in 1978, as well as the death of one his sisters. Moreover, it was also believed to have played a significant part in Chewe's own death in July 2000.

3.1.2 A Sample Case

> Abraham P. (the father of Chewe) was bewitched (*ukulowekwa*) in 1945. He died in 1978. His family connected his sickness and death to *icuulu*. In the last stage of his sickness, he had a big lump protruding from the side of his belly. The lump had reached a considerable size. Abraham was taken to the hospital in order to have an X-ray done. The doctors said the lump might require an operation but they somehow failed to establish a plausible diagnosis of the sickness. (I suppose it is very possible the doctors had reached a diagnosis, but felt there was nothing else they could do.) Therefore, Abraham was discharged without having an operation and without being given any treatment at all. The only medication he received were tablets to reduce the pain. A short while later he died in the village.

One morning in the year 1945, Abraham woke up and went about his work. As a gun repairman, he kept guns in his house that people brought to him for repairs. Later that morning, a relative of the extended family (*ulupwa lwa patali*) called and greeted him with some beer he had brought in a small calabash. The man invited Abraham to join him in drinking an early morning drink. Abraham kindly declined the offer, replying that he could not now drink beer as he had drunk rather much beer the previous night. But the man was very persistent and insisted that Abraham drink the calabash of beer, saying it was out of love and friendship for him that he had brought this beer. Finally, Abraham succumbed to the man's persistence and drank the small calabash of beer. The relative then said goodbye to Abraham and left.

Within hours, Abraham fell sick. He felt like vomiting and he had pain in his stomach. Not long thereafter, he vomited and was overcome by severe stomach pain. The very same day, a *Shing'anga* (Healer) was passing through the village and happened to come by Abraham's house where he found him in ill health. Immediately he attended to him and, after doing his examination, explained to Abraham that the sickness was due to *ukulowekwa* (being bewitched). Furthermore, the healer said that a malicious person had intended to kill him through poison in the beer. This kind of poison was meant to kill him the very same day, he explained. The Healer gave Abraham medicine in order to make him vomit until his stomach had emptied itself. Abraham felt better and relieved after vomiting. *Shing'anga* administered more medicine to him in order to heal him completely. Abraham did feel better the same day, but a full recovery was not immediately possible, the *Shing'anga* said. The healer did not stay for long and left to continue on his journey. At his departure, *Shing'anga* promised Abraham he would return as soon as his duties allowed him to do so.

However, the Healer never returned. *Shing'anga* could not fulfill his pledge because he died at the place where he had gone for visitation. But, prior to the *Shing'anga's* death, he had not only provided the medication for the healing of Abraham's sudden sickness, but had also outlined the cause of the sickness. *Shing'anga* had established that the very relative who had come to see him in the morning to greet him with some beer was a *muloshi* (wizard). Before this incident with the beer, Abraham had enjoyed good relations with his relative. Now, after the bout of sickness, their relationship completely broke down. Abraham renounced his friendship with the alleged *muloshi*[27] and carefully avoided any further dealings with him.

3.1.3 *Icuulu* Treatment

Icuulu is a very difficult sickness to cure. In fact, this sickness cannot be cured completely according to a traditionally held view. Medicine may only suppress the sickness, sometimes even over long periods of time. For this reason, *Shing'anga* is required to deal with this sickness and prepare medicine for treatment. The treatment of *icuulu* may also involve the concept of *ukusukwila*.[28] This treatment is aimed at washing off the disease and transferring it to some other individual. Transferral of *icuulu* can mean to intentionally target a particular person or to make a random selection, that is, to choose anyone who happens to pass by the place where the washing has taken place. The latter is known as *ukusukwila kunyantapo* meaning "transferring the disease to anyone who happens to step on the place where the sickness was washed off."[29]

3.2 The Sickness *Ulusuku*

Another sickness that is attributed to the effects of witchcraft is *ulusuku*. The predominant symptom of *ulusuku* is an inflated stomach. The belly of a person grows inexplainably big even though the intake of food is normal and fairly moderate. When a woman suffers from this sickness, one might assume she is pregnant. *Ulusuku* sickness can affect all people.

The word *ulusuku* is derived from the intransitive verb *ukusuka* meaning, "to be bad, to turn sour." *Ukusuka* means (1) an egg, which has not developed into a chick. The egg is without yolk but contains whitish water or fluid. *Ilini*

---

[27] At one time in 1972, my informant's family attacked this man, Mr. Kapembe, because he allegedly bewitched the informant's elder brother E. Mr. Kapembe wanted his brother to become mad. (According to other people and even to himself, Mr. Kapembe was a fierce man). They went to his house and told him that they were going to kill him if he was not willing to give medicine to the brother to help him recover. He obliged and provided medicine and E. recovered. But because this man was a known and established *muloshi* (wizard), the whole village community approached the Chief, saying they want him to be chased from this area. Mr. Kapembe had a very bad funeral in the late 1980s. There were only a few people who attended his funeral and there was general happiness about his death.

[28] *Ukusukwila*, a transitive and intransitive verb, is the applicative extension of *ukusukula*, meaning: "to peel off, to pull off." The term acquires a special meaning when used in connection with a ceremonial washing. *Ukusukwila* means "to peel off" a disease by washing oneself with medicine at a crossroad to the west of the village.

[29] Information provided by H. Simwanza, Kasama, May 12, 2000.

nalisuka, "the egg is bad, has turned sour, the egg inside has become watery." (2) *Ukusuka* is also used on Mwango fruits, for example, *Mwango naisuka,* "the fleshy part of the Mwango has become watery." Furthermore, the verb *ukusuka* (3) appears in the context of milk, *uyu mukaka nausuka,* "the milk has turned sour." The abnormally big belly is due to great amounts of water or whitish fluid inside the stomach, like the whitish fluid in the analogy of the egg without a yolk.

There are instances when *ulusuku* is perceived as a normal sickness. In such cases, the belly is not extraordinarily big and is treated by people in the community or by medical personnel in clinics or hospitals. However, if a person's belly appears to be unusually and extraordinarily big, the sickness is diagnosed as *ulusuku lwa kulowekwa,* meaning: *ulusuku* due to bewitchment.

3.2.1 A Sample Case

> Mr. C., the late headman of A-village died of this problem. When the sickness reached an advanced stage, he was taken to hospital where the water was drained several times but to no avail. Therefore, he was discharged and taken home where he died the following day some time in 1995/96.
>
> The family, like most of the village community, attributed his sickness and death to *ukulowekwa,* "to be bewitched." Prior to the treatment the headman received at the hospital, the *Shing'anga* (healer) had already treated him. Though there was initial improvement in short intervals, the healer could not achieve a complete healing. In the case of Mr. C., a *kamucapi* (witch-finder, witch-cleanser) was also engaged when the signs of *ulusuku* first started. *Kamucapi* was able to identify the culprits who bewitched the late headman; he even disclosed their names to the family. My Informant happened to hear how some names were mentioned in connection with this case. The persons were all members of the Village Committee at that time.[30]

3.3 The Sickness *Intifu*

The *Intifu* sickness is diagnosed in the accompaniment of two signs. (1) *ukubyola,* "to belch" and (2) *ukutifula,* "persistent hiccups." It is understood that *ukubyola* and *ukutikula* are both natural body functions that occur after

---

[30] A headman has about 8 to 10 elderly men called *bacilolo ba mushi* (lit. "the witnesses of the village") around him. They always meet at the headman's *nsaka (pa nsaka)*. *Pa nsaka* is like the Council Administration in town.

eating. However, regular hiccups in short intervals with no signs of improvement, and side-pains (*utubali*) over a prolonged period of time even at night and during sleep are eventually related to *Intifu*. *Intifu* and *ubuloshi* (witchcraft) are interrelated. A common perception about this sickness is that it is untreatable by medical persons. Dillon-Malone comments that "the illnesses more specifically identified with the African psychiatrist are commonly known as "African diseases" as distinct from those which, it is believed, can be cured by western-type medicines. Wizardry falls into the former category" (1988:1160). The option of seeking medical advice and/or treatment from the hospital is almost ruled out.

Intifu requires special treatment by highly qualified *Shing'anga* who are *kamucapi* (witch-finder, witch-cleanser) and *Shing'anga wa miti* (herbalists) at the same time. My informant provided an example of *Intifu*: His son-in-law,[31] B. Bwalya, the husband of his niece, had once suffered from this sickness. Ordinary persons first treated him but could not help him. Then he was taken to the hospital but, even there, all efforts failed. Finally, back home in the village, a *Shing'anga* was consulted who treated him successfully so that he recovered.

4. Diseases Caused by Spirits/Spiritual Beings: *Amalwele ya Mipashi*

Sicknesses related to the agency of *mipashi* range from *impepo* (fever, shivers), *umutwe* (headache), *cifuba* (coughs, breathing problems), *inuma ukufina* (heavy shoulder-blades), to *ukupolomya* (diarrhoea) and *ukuluka* (vomiting). The sickness *umusamfu* has special significance among sicknesses that are attributed to *mipashi*. It will be treated in some detail in the following section.

4.1 The Sickness *Umusamfu*

Umusamfu is known to be a sudden, unexpected sickness. The description I was given emphasized the suddenness with which *umusamfu* takes hold of a person. In young children from the ages of one to five years, fever is also a symptom. The feverish condition causes shivers and nervous agitation. Also, at times, the whole body stiffens and *ifulo* (foaming from the mouth) appears. *Ifulo* is a sign of *umusamfu,* which only occurs in children. *Umusamfu* is predominantly found among infants and usually occurs only once. It can be cured as discussed below. Usually *umusamfu* is not preceded by history of illness. Such sudden sicknesses are related to *imipashi,* ancestral familial spirits who employ sicknesses like *umusamfu* to declare interest or express their dissatisfaction with family or communal affairs by targeting an individual person.

---

[31] In the Bemba family-taxonomy a niece (the daughter of one's sisters) is counted as a daughter, which makes her husband to become the son-in-law to his wife's maternal uncle.

Techinically speaking, *umusamfu* are fits or epileptic episodes. When *umusamfu* strikes a person, the suddenness and severity of the attack may leave a person unconscious. But usually the person recovers after a short time.

4.1.1 A Sample Case

> There was a boy who was struck by *umusamfu* in Milambo village. He was believed dead and people had already begun funeral arrangements, when the boy suddenly came back to life. He announced to the gathering that, while "dead", he had seen a man who gave him *Kapenta,* a kind of small fish which is a cherished relish in Zambia. Furthermore, he said, in his vision he saw a woman who was fighting with him. (*Comment*: I am not sure of the interpretation of the two episodes; there was no comment on that.) Thereafter he was taken to Mwamba clinic and given an injection. But on their way back, before they reached his home, he died on the back of his human carrier.

Sudden, unexpected sickness (fits) followed by a quick death is often diagnosed as *umusamfu*. A repetition of *umusamfu* is called *cipumputu,* "kind of fits, which also affects adults." Fits leave a person unconscious for a short time. When the fit is over, the person returns to a normal state. Some people explain the unconsciousness as a disruption between *umupashi,* the *"spirit double,"* and the person. Reoccurring *cipumputu* is perceived as an unstable or weak relationship between a person and his *"spirit double."* The names of persons suffering from *cipumputu* are will no longer be passed on in the family lineage.[32] During the lifetime of persons who are prone to *cipumputu,* they are referred to as *alikwata icipumputu,* "he/she has fits/epilepsy," or *alilwala icipumputu,* "he/she has the sickness of fits/epilepsy," and are not given responsibility within the community. In most cases such persons have to rely on the help of their families.

4.1.2 *Umusamfu* Treatment

Umusamfu can be treated by medicine made from a tree called *ndale.*[33] The leaves of this tree are chewed by the parents of a sick child or any other adult persons. Usually they are women. The following is a short description of the procedure employed.

---

[32] This is the ideal and also largely common practice. However, there might be exceptions, for example, when an ancestor was renowned for exceptional skills, displayed outstanding character attributes, or was praised for certain achievements during his lifetime.

[33] The scientific name for *ndale* is *Swartzia madagacahensis*. *Ndale* is also counted as a timber tree used for Carpentry (Hoch 1992:230).

The person while chewing the leaves performs *ukuputilisha*, "to blow air" to a certain part of the body. In this case, air is blown into the nose, into the ears, inside the palm of both hands, and on both foot-soles. After that, the leaves are spit out. Next, the *ndale* leaves and the *umusokolobe wafita*[34] leaves are mixed, that is, they are pounded in a mortar. Thereafter the mixture is soaked in water (*ukwabikila*). After soaking the mixture, the woman/person who blew the air takes some of the liquid (which has turned green) and sprinkles (*ukusansa*) the liquid mixture on the chest and the back of the patient. The remainder of the mixture is used to wash the whole body of the child. After the washing is finished, the child returns to a normal state.

4.1.3 Interpretation of *Umusamfu* Treatment

Because of the sudden appearance of *umusamfu*, *imipashi iibi* (malevolent ancestral familial *"spirit doubles"*) are suspected to have been the cause of this sickness. The blowing of air unto several parts or regions of the body is meant to drive out or drive away *imipashi iibi*. The sprinkling of medicated water supports or enforces the expulsion of *imipashi*. The washing of the body with the medicated water is thought to apply some sort of "protective shield" to the body of the child to guard it against further attacks. When *umusamfu* leads to death, *ubuloshi* (witchcraft) is very quickly implicated.

Several cases of *umusamfu* at once can cause a community considerable concern. In the community of A-village, about five *umusamfu* cases occurred at the same time. Community members attributed those *umusamfu* occurrences to a disturbance of the relationship between people and *imipashi* (*"spirit doubles"*) of particular families or *imipashi* "governing/controlling" a certain area. One hears an expression like *namulaba ku mipashi ya fikolwe*, "they (the family) have forgotten (to honour) the ancestral spirits of the family/forefathers." If, for example, out of the total number of *umusamfu* cases, two or three children belong to the same family line, focus will be directed toward the "family *imipashi*." Should the *umusamfu* cases be spread over the whole area/community, priority will be given to the "area *imipashi*."

Family *imipashi*, (*imipashi ya pa lupwa*), are believed to be responsible for *umusamfu* found in a number of children of the same family line. Such a situation demands action. First of all, it is necessary to establish if children with the same name are affected with *umusamfu* and whether it was in order to name them after a particular ancestor. If it turns out that several persons

---

[34] The scientific name is *Uapaca nitida Muell. Arg.*, and belongs to the family of fruit trees (Hoch 1992:231).

with the same name simultaneously suffer from *umusamfu,* and that one of the past bearers of the name had the same illness, this name will be erased from the repertoire of eligible family names.

Concerning the area *imipashi,* it was common practice in the past that elders of some villages (at least one *Shing'anga* was always part of this group) would gather at a particular place called *mpuubwa,* a place with stones around a water hole with fish in it. There, an offering such as Mealie meal, beer, or a white chicken was offered in order to approach the *imipashi* (*ukupupa imipashi*). The offering was meant as a remembrance of the presence of *imipashi* and to try to imitate their actions. That is, *imipashi* being approached were formerly notable men from the area such as hunters, brave warriors, clever fishermen, great *Shing'anga* and so forth. Approaching *imipashi* (*ukupupa imipashi*) through sacrifice and showing veneration to them secured *imipashi's* protection. At the same time, through the offerings and sacrifice, the elders were striving to attain the very skills of the persons whose *imipashi* were being approached at *mpuubwa.*

5. "Spirit Sickness": *Ubulwele bwa Ngulu*

Ubulwele bwa ngulu is distinguished from sicknesses that are caused by *imipashi* (familial *"spirit doubles"*) such as *umusamfu* as outlined in the section above. "Spirit sickness" (*ubulwele bwa ngulu*) takes a very special place within the array of sicknesses known to the Bemba. "Spirit sickness" has two characteristics: (1) It is not considered to be an ordinary ailment, and (2) it is not an illness that is caused by bewitching (*ubulwele bwa kulowekwa*).[35]

Ubulwele bwa ngulu is considered to be a mysterious illness, *ubulwele ubushilondolweke,* meaning, (1) "an affliction that cannot be explained;" an illness that is mysterious by its suddenness and its effects on the person. (2) "Something" has seized a person who had been enjoying good health and who was neither mentally deranged nor epileptic. This something – "it" – wanders in the body, disturbs the mind, and affects the behavior of a person (see Oger 1972a:3).

Sicknesses related to *ngulu* spirits can be expressed in two different ways: (1) *ngulu naimukumya* ("*ngulu* has/have touched him"), or (2) *ngulu shilemucusha* (*ngulu* cause/causes him suffering). Symptoms of *ubulwele bwa ngulu* can be treated. However, the range of medicine available is rather limited and mainly confined to *impemba* (white clay), which is given to the patient in small portions to eat. At times, patients may also ask for drums to be beaten, maybe for only five minutes, to which they dance. After the dance is finished, the fever (or whatever the symptom was) is gone, and the person is fine again.

---

[35] *Ukulowa* (active infinitive), meaning "to bewitch." *Ukulowekwa* (passive infinitive), meaning "to be bewitched."

Below is a list of symptoms that manifest with *ubulwele bwa ngulu*. One will note that the symptoms that are registered with women by far exceed the symptoms found with men. At the same time, the symptoms in women are described in much more detail than the symptoms that are ascribed to men. As will be shown later, women are and were the dominant group associated with *ngulu* spirit possession in Bembaland.

Symptoms of *Ubuwele bwa Ngulu* prominent with women

1. Oppression of the chest and aching of the back (as if loaded with a heavy stone)
2. Colics and nausea, heartburn and repeated vomiting. Feeling as if the heart is melting and developing confused speech pattern; feeling hot in the chest and the bowels.
3. Feeling as if something is travelling in the head; disturbance of the mind; if you try to speak, you become delirious, dizzy and your head is throbbing shu, shu, shu...; if you try to stand, you feel like falling; if you try to walk, you feel like floating and carried by the wind.
4. The eyes are sore and watery and your body is itching all over. When seated, your body sways back and forth as if being rocked; you feel a painful twitch all over the body, especially in the legs. You begin dreaming.
5. After beer drinking you feel dead tired as if you have been beaten. You tremble. If someone speaks to you, you become sour [hot] tempered and your eyes flare.
6. The back and the chest are aching. The "tummy" is hard, the heart beats fast, and the legs quiver. Eating is impos-

Symptoms of *Ubuwele bwa Ngulu* prominent with men

1. Repeated belching
2. Stiffness
3. Dizziness / headache
4. Shivering with cold (fever attacks)
5. Hiccups
6. Hard tummy
7. Painful sexual intercourse. It hates sexual union (*Capate cupo*).

sible; you can only drink water, but even then, your bowels hurt and rumble and you belch.
7. Below the navel (in the groin) it hurts. The navel is sunk deep like during pregnancy and it is painful. When menstruating, you feel like splitting, as if you have cut yourself with a wood splinter.
8. Feeling cold and numb in the back and a lot of pain between the ribs; a rumbling noise starts in the back and goes through your bowels; The lungs are "itching", fever goes to your head and you stretch yourself in the sun.
9. No strength. You have a burning head as if you were in a fire. Painful back as if you are menstruating. Inside you are burning as if you have cut yourself. The back is hot with fever and the flanks hurt as if you have pleurisy.
10. It is like having tuberculosis (*ntanda bwanga*). Feeling of dizziness; you start breaking household equipment and afterwards ask who did it.
11. It [the not yet identified spirit being] hates (*Capate cupo*) sexual union; that is the worst. If you are pregnant, you feel your life drained away from you.

In the 1960s and the beginning of the 1970s, Fr. Bonaventura Kapombole based the listed symptoms on a study of more than one hundred cases of *ngulu* possession among men and women. Louis Oger compiled them in the manner presented in the chart. I presume that Oger intentionally stuck to the "unstyled" English because he wanted to maintain Bemba "vocabulary and structure of thought" in the translation (Oger 1972a:3-4). Compare also Archdiocese of Kasama (1970:1).

6. A Concluding Reflection: Sickness in Bemba Culture – A Knowledge System Based on Paradox Creating Cultural Ambivalence

Carey (1986) attempted to advocate an improved curriculum for in-service Education of primary school teachers in Zambia (in particular Bemba teachers) that would give more attention to the beliefs and customs of Bemba traditional concepts. He points out that education[36] (health education) does not necessarily bring about a fusion or integration of the two kinds of knowledge systems:

> Bemba teachers compartmentalize their attitudes towards disease and healing. They use their knowledge derived from Health Education to explain cosmopolitan illness, and their beliefs derived from Bemba Traditional Religion to explain African sickness (1986:viii-ix).

6.1 "Disease Compartmentalization": Dialectical Conflict – "Education-Knowledge" vs. "Culture-Knowledge"

The reality of compartmentalizing attitudes towards disease and healing is bewildering because it constitutes a paradox. At its heart are conflicting desires and values. For one, teachers are being trained to teach biology, science and perhaps some basic health care, but their own compartmentalization of disease and healing profoundly contradicts that of their profession. Why does the compartmentalization of what I would term "Education-knowledge" vs. "Culture-knowledge" exercise a "paradoxical-dialectical relationship" (Nuckolls 1996:24-35)?

First of all, "Education-knowledge" is acquired through the process of information acquisition or *acculturation*, and therefore entails selectivity in both, i.e. the kind of information that becomes knowledge or forms a knowledge system, and the extent to which that knowledge or knowledge system is applied.

In contrast, "Culture-knowledge" is acquired through the process of *enculturation*, or early childhood socialization, and therefore is by definition knowledge which provides solutions to existential threats that can and will effectively take precedence over other knowledge systems in times of existential crises (e.g. sickness). The option of selectivity is suppressed because the inherent logic – and the strong emotional ties – that govern "Culture-knowl-

---

[36] By education I mean the broad spectrum of learning as the western approach imparts, for example, categorized learning, interrelated thinking etc.

Chapter 4: An Outline of the Concept of Illness 95

edge" are qualitatively and existentially conceived to be superior.[37] As long as both knowledge systems are locked in dialectical opposition, the paradox will continue to exist.

The two knowledge systems compete with one another.[38] The preference for one over the other lies in the motivational force[39] that the particular knowledge system generates in the individual resulting in an allegiance and, consequently, application of that system's inherent mechanism. Leach says, "emotion is aroused not by the appeal to the rational faculties but by some kind of trigger action on the subconscious elements of the human personality" (in Obeyesekere 1984:14). "Culture-knowledge" in the case of the Bemba teachers provides exactly this motivation, or, in Leach's terms, triggers emotion to pursue a solution (cure) for a particular illness. Especially in instances of existential magnitude, for example when sickness poses a real threat to life, the motivation to "take sides" for one or the other knowledge system often lies in the confidence the knowledge system bestows upon the individual or that the individual ascribes to it. The social group's approval of one syestem or the other, or support in "taking sides" further boosts the confidence-effect.

If the dialectic of "Education-knowledge" vs. "Culture-knowledge" does not produce a sufficiently deep or meaningful favor towards one or the other, the gap that exists between them will and cannot be bridged. That is, the paradox stays in place, and, according to Nuckolls, accounts for cultural continuity, at least in this cultural part.[40] Thus, the competing reality of disease and healing and its compartmentalization with reference to Bemba teachers will not likely experience a major shift in the near future. Nor will the existing paradox be erased. Rather, the opposition of the two knowledge systems will give rise to further debate back and forth between the two systems and perhaps the positions will be redefined.

Sicknesses (and their causes) and health are explained within the framework of worldview. As Pell has noted, "sickness is seen as the result of evil doing... while health is evidence of one's personal integrity and right living in the community" (Pell 1993:54). In this regard, a fusion of "Education-knowl-

---

[37] The "superiority feeling," I think, can be also termed "affective tone" or "emotional identity" and is what Gregory Bateson summed up in *ethos*. Nuckolls summarizes Bateson's *ethos* saying "*ethos* includes among its many possible meanings reference to a constellation of concepts that infuses 'culture' with affective tone or emotional identity. It refers to the standardization of a culture's affective and emotional aspects" (1996:49).

[38] Referring to L. Fallers, Bruner depicts the situation of an African chief. In his role of chief, he has to follow one set of ideology, but at the same time, he is also part of the modern system of civil service (1976:238-239).

[39] See Nuckolls 1996:65-66.

[40] See Nuckolls 1996:271.

edge" and "Culture-knowledge" must take place in order to generate a fundamental re-orientation of worldview.[41]

Healing, as Musonda points out for the Bisa, a kindred tribe of the Bemba, concerns the individual as much as the community of which a person is part. He continues by saying that healing has two functions: (1) revitalization of life of the patient and in extension also the life of the clan, and (2) fortifying "life against future dangers" (1996:98). The cause of the sickness matters because it determines the precise counter-attack in choosing the specific protective medicines from the repertoire of available medicines.

Traditional approach to sickness and healing is concerned with symptoms, diagnosis, and treatment. Western medicine also looks at the symptoms, diagnosis, and treatment, but envisages treatment that very often demands long-term therapy. The time factor is a crucial element in both approaches, except that traditional medicine looks for more or less instant success, whereas Western medicine looks at healing as a process over time.

6.2 Malnutrition: Dialectical Conflict – "Fertility/Sexual-Capacity-Ideal" vs. "Sanctioned/Sacralized-Sex-Ideal"

Another example of paradox in Bemba culture is connected to causal concepts and its variants of malnutrition as outlined earlier in this discussion. The local causal concepts of malnutrition in children center almost exclusively on sex and sexual behavior and not, as commonly suggested, on poor child feeding. The people have strong convictions concerning the devastating effects of "unsanctioned" or "non-sacralized" sex activities – of girls and boys, women and men alike – on children. Yet, communities find themselves trapped by their own sexual behavior (Nangawe et. al. 1998a:49). The upholding of the sacralized-sex-ideal is dealt a blow by the sexual practices of the very custodians of the ideal! From a rational point of view, paradoxes should not exist. The opposing elements can very often be clearly identified and exposing them should make them easy to eliminate. But this is not the case. Why then do such paradoxes continue to exist?

6.3 "Compartmentalization" and Malnutrition: What keeps Paradoxes in Place?

Charles W. Nuckolls (1996) writes that the "paradoxes that motivate cultural institutions are powerful" (1996:271). Motivational force operates behind the rational patterning. Nuckolls outlines three things on which this power is dependent.

First, it is the nature of the paradox itself that matters. A paradox must be based on "values that are fundamental but mutually contradictory" (Nuckolls

---

[41] Compare Pell 1993:54.

1996:271). This is exactly what happens in the context of sacralized sex and practiced sex. The cultural ideal of fertility and sexual capacity (cf. chapter three) is in competition with the other ideal of sanctioned or sacralized sex within wedlock. (Marriage facilitates and regulates the powers of procreation, averting its disastrous capacity.) Individuals, especially not yet married boys, are caught in between. Their sexual desire is partly fuelled by living up to the sexual-capacity-ideal. But they cannot live up to the one ideal without violating the other. Because their manhood comprises their social identity, the failure of boys to prove their manhood and thus live up to the ideal of sexual capacity can lead to the loss of self.[42] As a solution to this conflict, boys rationalize their sexual desires in argumentative dialog with girls. Boys tell the girls that they will "seal" or close up if they put off their sexual engagement indefinitely. And boys tell themselves they will fail to "perform," if they do not exercise their sexual organ.[43] Moreover, cultural discretion on sexuality[44] compounds the problem because it locks up information on sexual matters creating a nebulous terrain.[45] Boys exploit this situation and entice girls to cooperate.

---

[42] Nuckolls, revising Bateson's ethnography on the Iatmul ritual *Naven*, says that the matrilineal Iatmul are also faced with a paradox where values that are fundamental are mutually contradictory. The matrilineal system gives the mother's brother (*wau*) and the sister's son (*laua*) a special relationship. A dominant emotion of Iatmul men is the display of pride, "a constant emphasis on making oneself the center of attention, and thus in lessening or eliminating, through insult or mockery, the posturings of other men." The *Naven* ritual "recognizes the accomplishments of the *laua*" (e.g. primarily homicide, the first kill of an enemy or foreigner, next the assistance one renders in completing homicide, etc.). It is the *wau* who celebrates it with his nephew by giving all the credit to *laua*. But this compromises his very own position. He has to and wants to boast about his own achievements, but must also celebrate and recognize another mens' accomplishments. But "the male ethos does not make that kind of emotional response easy." Also, both, *wau* and *laua* "are now in a socially competitive relationship, competing with each other in words and deeds. ... The solution to both problems is male transvestitism." In the *Naven* ritual "the *wau* acts like a woman and, as a woman, can express admiration through subservience and self-abnegation toward the *laua*." The implicit strive in *Naven* is to maintain identity. *Laua* is celebrated acknowledging his social status as man and building up his emotion of pride. *Wau* takes on the role of a woman, and in doing so, retains his social status as man and secures his true self (1996:53, 63-65).

[43] My wife was involved in a nutrition program with a village women group. Time and again, the topic of sex, family planning etc. became the focal point of discussion. The dominance of this topic has to do with a value that emphasizes sexuality, but at the same time the women voice their concern over the fact that they simply can't handle one child after the other. Attempts to get their husbands' cooperation or understanding, especially during breast feeding time which might extend up to two years, is often met with them beating the wife or seeking sexual companionship elsewhere.

[44] The fact that traditional values, such as silence on sexual matters, prevent effective combat against HIV/AIDS was stressed by Dawson Lupunga, former Minister of Community Development & Social Services, in a speech read on Television (Zambia National Broadcasting Corporation [ZNBC], Lusaka) in "Commemoration of the International Day for the Eradication of Poverty" on the eve of Oct. 16, 2000.

[45] One major feature of *Chisungu*, the initiation rite of girls, is to "teach" them, to grant them access to secret knowledge (e.g. secret terms, *Chisungu* songs, secret language of marriage etc.). Uninitiated girls are thus "ignorant." See Richards 1982:125-129.

Second, a paradox cannot be changed as long as it exists in its present form. Nuckolls says that this means that such a paradox will stay in place for a long time "and constitute at least one important aspect of cultural continuity" (1996:271). As long as compartmentalization concerning illness and the dialectical relationship between the sexual-capacity-ideal and the sanction/sacralized-sex-ideal exist, these paradoxes will prevail and promote cultural continuity.

Third, a paradox creates "cultural ambivalence as the result of the desire to resolve them in pursuit of a culturally defined goal" (Nuckolls 1996:271).

The accompanying chart represents an attempt to illustrate a culturally defined goal and the cultural ambivalence this creates producing a paradox (see figure 3).

Nuckolls" understanding of dialectic is based on following assumptions (1996:25):

1. Dialectic begins with a standard/goal;
2. Dialectic totalizes the problem, that is, a dialectical system *embraces* the whole to which a problem (e.g. malnutrition and sexual behavior) belongs;

A dialectical system seeks to "characterize the relationship between disparate parts" (Nuckolls 1996:25) which is usually one of paradox.

FIGURE 3: THE DIALECTIC OF PARADOX IN BEMBA SEXUALITY

DIALECTIC "STANDARD"/GOAL:

Perfect Transcendence / "Access to the Divine"[46] or Butuntulu (Wholeness/Completeness)

Fertility/Sexual-Capacity-Ideal	Relationship between the two disparate parts constitutes a	*Sanctioned/Sacralized-Sex-Ideal*
<u>Everyone must exercise procreative power</u>	**PARADOX**	<u>Only Husband and Wife are entitled to exercise procreative power</u>
The full realization of the ideal **cannot** exercise **restraint; it must enjoy liberty.**	The fertility/sexual capacity-ideal is *restrained* by the sanctioned/sacralized-sex-ideal.	The full realization of the ideal <u>works</u> by **restraint; it cannot enjoy liberty.**
Every person is mandated to procreate: – male to "prove" manhood – female to "prove" fertility or/and – satisfaction of sexual desires	But the latter is *destroyed* by the *actual (liberal)* ***sexual behavior*** leading to: • MALNUTRITION Also to: • HIV/AIDS or STDs • Pre-marrital sex & pregnancies • Promiscuity • Prostitution • Abuse etc.	Sex – the act of procreation – is confined to the cultural institution of marriage, the formalized/sanctioned sexual relationship between one man and one woman. (Pregnancies outside marriages violate and disturb the sacralized-sex-ideal as it endangers community life.) Pursuit of complete Perfection (Transcendence, or *Butuntulu* or, "Access to the Divine") is sought by combining the Male and the Female; Perfection is "made possible by the fecund union of *husband* and *wife* (italics mine)."[47]

DIALECTIC

© G. R. Badenberg, June 2001

---

[46] Hinfelaar 1994:8.
[47] Hinfelaar 1994:6-8.

PART II:
NGULU SPIRIT POSSESSION – CULTURAL AND PERSONAL RELIGIOUS SYMBOLS: A SOCIAL HERMENEUTICAL PERSPECTIVE

Part Two is comprised of three chapters. In chapter five I will first treat *ngulu* spirit possession in a historical reflection. It will introduce the element of human agency in dealing with socio-economic factors and personal experience.

Secondly, the subject matter will be looked at from a linguistic viewpoint. Elements of *ngulu* spirit possession will be described in more detail.

Third, the two areas of investigation will be complimented by a case study. The person I studied, G. Chewe P. – a male person of Bemba ethnicity – was stricken with ill health for almost all his life. At one time, his poor physical condition was related to *ngulu* spirit possession. This person's history of illness is meant to demonstrate some of the dynamics that are at work: personal-psychological dynamics interacting with social-cultural dynamics.

To explain the relationship between personal-psychological dynamics and social-cultural dynamics, an integration of personality and culture must be established. I will do this in chapter six, introducing the theoretical tools that can describe the relationship between personality and culture. The culture concept of Charles W. Nuckolls is most suitable for this description since it brings to light the dialectical relationship between personality and culture.

The personality development theories of Wyatt MacGaffey, Talcot Parsons, and Gananath Obeyesekere receive attention in regard to the Oedipus complex as a significant part of this process – significant with respect to the role that deep motivation of the oedipal type plays in motivating symbolization, that is, appropriating and employing personal symbols.

This is where Obeyesekere's theory of personal symbols becomes operative. Personal symbols will be defined, their operational mode will be explained, and the "work of culture," that is, the conditions for success and failure of personal symbols in symbolic remove will be described. Also, the two processes of objectification and subjectification will be highlighted.

Part Two concludes with chapter seven, where I will present that part of Chewe's life where personal symbols are identified and interpreted.

Chapter 5
The Phenomenon of *Ngulu* Spirit Possession

1. Introduction

Ngulu spirit possession is connected to the concept of body and to illness because it is characterized by "a visible and specific sickness" (Carey 1986:49) (cf. chapter four) and food taboos. There are some three factors which, in my view, make *ngulu* possession a phenomenon.

(1) The historical events pertaining to Bemba history around the turn of the twentieth century, and the pre-independence years of Zambia in the late 1950s and early 1960s.
(2) Linguistic evidence and considerations.
(3) The prevalence of *ngulu* possession among mostly women, demonstrating the dialectic between cultural context and personal agency.

2. Historic Approach to *Ngulu* Spirit Possession

"The years between 1900 and 1940," writes Roberts, "...witnessed on an unprecedented scale, transformation in social identities, cognitive systems and means of communication" in Africa (1990:1). With regards to the transformation of cognitive systems among the Bemba, it will be seen that the causes of transformation must not only be attributed to outside influence. They were also aided by forces of dynamic change inside Bemba culture.

In principle, the changes that occurred were not merely signs that colonial Zambia had now also joined in the achievements of the technological era, but were rather clear signals that they would bring dramatic changes to the African lifestyle. There was a definite understanding on the side of the colonial administration of precisely how the African lifestyle had to change with regards to the Bemba people on the Northern plateau.

2.1 Introducing the "Hut-Tax-System"

The introduction of a hut tax in northeastern Rhodesia in 1901 was a definite milestone marking the arrival of the wind of change. This occured barely two years after the end of Bemba resistance to colonial intrusion[1] at the defeat of

---

[1] The Bemba paramountcy was one of several other paramountcies in Southern Africa (like the Zulu, Ndebele, Changanana, Yao and Nguni and others) that responded to the influx of European imperialism and colonialization by violent confrontation, rather than opting for protectorate or allegiance with the British as a model of response. For more details on this topic see Boahen ed. 1990:96.

Chief Ponde in early 1899, and later of Chief Mporokoso in April 1899.² Meebelo writes that "every adult African male person paid three shillings each year for his hut."³ The payments were initially made in cash – a system diametrically opposed to hunting, fighting wars, and raiding campaigns,⁴ agriculture, and the barter system – but at times the levy was also paid in kind. However, the administration did not accept payment in kind for long, and by 1905 "the payment of the hut tax in this way had ceased" (Meebelo 1971:86-87).

2.2 Abolishing the *"Chitemene-Mitanda*-System"

In a second development, an attack was made upon the *chitemene* (slash and burn) system of agriculture and on the further practice of residing in *mitanda* huts (temporary residency in huts built near the gardens). At a meeting of Bemba chiefs in August 1905, Justice Beaufort, the then-acting administrator for the eastern half of Zambia, made it very clear to the chiefs that the *chitemene* system had to stop as it was a "wasteful method of cultivation" (Musambachime 1992:11). The issue was even more complicated by the chiefs being told that the building and occupation of *mitanda* huts during the crop season would have to be abandoned without fail.⁵ These harsh measures of imposing colonial rule not only surprised the Bemba chiefs, but also brought great disturbance to age-old traditional agricultural practice (Musambachime 1992:11). An appeal by the paramount chief Chitimukulu made on behalf of the Bemba people for the suspension of the prohibitions was met with a dismissal.⁶ The forceful imposition of the measures on *chitemene* and

---

² An extensive account of the years prior to the victory of the colonial administration in 1899 and the different developments which took place, especially in Bemba polity, is given by Meebelo. For instance, the death of Nkula Mutale Shichansa at the end of 1895 and the death of Chitimukulu Sampa Kapalakasha in May 1896, gave rise to a "leadership crisis" among other Bemba chiefs (Meebelo 1971:34-78).

³ The hut tax system was designed without allowing for loopholes. Each male person was also liable to pay the taxes of other adults who were his dependents occupying their own huts, increasing the burden of finding means of acquiring the demanded cash (Meebelo 1971:86). The hut tax system, and with it a money economy, was soon extended to other parts of Northern Rhodesia. Carmody states: "The introduction of a hut tax by the British South Africa Company in 1904 exacerbated the need for cash" (1988:194). See also Gann 1964:101-105, 112-113 and Dixon-Fyle 1976:33.

⁴ Meebelo states that "the Bemba had been engaged in incessant wars of conquest with other tribes of the Northern Province," and that "raiding became an established way of life of the Bemba" (1971:2-3). He, however, attributes these renowned features of the Bemba not solely to their warlike tradition. Instead, he argues, it was the infertile soils of most of the heartland of Bembaland, and the land being infested with tse-tse fly, that also impacted their lifestyle (see Meebelo 1971:3-10).

⁵ The abolition of *mitanda* and *chitemene* was finally enacted in 1906. Chibonga [probably Chilonga] Mission Diary, 16 August 1906. Referred to in Meebelo 1971:130, Footnote 126.

⁶ The dismissal followed "severe warnings and advice to grow crops other than millet" (Musambachime 1992:12).

mitanda led to a drastic shortage of food. Turner states that "the results were a massive discontent and passive resistance and a serious famine" (in Oger 1972a:1).[7] Apart from the economic hardships this development brought to the Bemba village communities, the psychological impact was even more forceful.[8] "Passive resistance"[9] was a reflection of the "anxiety and fears of imminent unrest" (Musambachime 1992:12) so strongly felt among the Bemba population.

The developments that took place during the first decade of the twentieth century in Bembaland, and the way they affected traditional Bemba lifestyle, depict vividly the kind of challenges that had to be faced. How could a people react toward the foreign agents of change when the means of military resistance was out of question? The retreat into "passive resistance" was an option (perhaps the only one) left in order to cope psychologically with pressure and frustration. It is in these times of utmost suppression of values when people exploit traditional avenues.

2.3 The Upsurge of *Ngulu* Possession in the Year 1907

Passive resistance exercised toward the administration was but one way to deal with the fears and frustrations that had permeated all levels of Bemba society. The psychological pressures captivating Bemba communities had to be dealt with on a much deeper level. Although the verdict of 1906 (the abolishment of *mitanda* and *chitemene*) affected each and every member of society at all levels, the velocity with which it penetrated the different social groups varied. It is therefore especially interesting to investigate the link between passive resistance after the 1906 verdict, and the upsurge of *ngulu* pos-

---

[7] The Chilonga Mission Diary, 16 August 1906, makes mention of reduced food production due to the abolition of *mitanda* and speaks of a famine, though a partial one (see Meebelo 1971:130, Footnote 128). The situation, however, must have worsened in the subsequent years, especially in the Chilonga area where Fr. Eugen Pueth talks of a severe famine, which he witnessed when touring the District (Pueth 1910/11:177-179).

[8] The aim of the abolition of the *mitanda* and *chitemene* practices was to make people settle into bigger settlements in order to enhance the Administration's control over the people "using the enhanced authority of the chiefs resulting from such regroupings" (Meebelo 1971:105). As much as this move brought obvious advantages in terms of a centralized administration on the side of the Authorities, the social implications on the side of the Bemba communities in grouping together hitherto small settlement units were enormous. Meebelo writes that these large communities "lacked the unifying bonds of consanguinity and affinity," were stricken with a "high mortality rate" due to the absence of "modern health facilities," and harbored "suspicion, hatred and witchcraft ... just as adultery was rampant" (1971:105).

[9] The passive resistance was a systematically organized boycott of villagers to deny the Native Commissioners on their visitation tours in the Districts the customary gifts of welcoming visitors so readily offered prior to 1906. "Things had dramatically changed," comments Meebelo (1971:107). For further details see "Report on the Attitude of the Awemba in the Mpika Division, 1908", KSD7/4/2, referred to in Meebelo 1971:130, Footnote 138.

session so prominent in the year 1907.[10] Moreover, it is of interest to establish the reason why the women (of mainly remote villages) of the Bemba heartland were the main actors in cases of *ngulu* spirit possession.

2.3.1 Pre-Colonial Upheavals Affecting Bemba Women

In adressing the issues described above, more than a casual glance at the situation of the women within Bemba society during the first decade of the twentieth century is necessary.

The Bemba societal structure is based upon matrilineal descent, in which women are regarded "as the appointed persons to approach the Transcendent" (Hinfelaar 1994:xi).[11] Also, Bemba-speaking peoples traditionally adhered to a House-Religion, writes Hinfelaar, where the married women had access to the Divine. They also passed on the community's religious heritage and guidelines for worshipping the Transcendent during the ceremonies of Initiation (1994:xi). Hinfelaar further states that it was the women who had embraced the new Christian teaching more enthusiastically than any other group of Bemba society when the first missionaries arrived in Bemba country in the 1880s and 1890s (1994:xi). What did the women hope to find in the new religion that was brought to them by mainly male "missionaries of the West" (1994:xi)?

Hinfelaar sees the answer as lying in a major shift of the original House-Religion that had already taken place a long time before the arrival of the missionaries and the agents of colonial imperialism. It was the ascendancy of the Bemba paramountcy, the exaltation of the *Bena Ng'andu* royal line, and the claim of divine authority for the Paramount Chief Chitimukulu (see Badenberg 1999:43) which initiated the shift from the traditional House-shrine cult to the Court Cult, where the royal relics[12] became the supreme objects of veneration (Hinfelaar 1994:xi). The women were eventually and radically deprived of their role as mediators between the Immanent and the Transcendent.

---

[10] Oger took up the phenomenon of *ngulu* possession as a workshop topic in 1972. He particularly mentions the year 1907 as the year of intense cases of *ngulu* possession. He based this date on the reports of two informants, Alfonsho Sokoni, born in 1888, and Musa Kandete, born in 1895. The former emphatically claimed that since 1907, there had not been such an upsurge of *ngulu* possession until the early 1960s (1972a:1).

[11] Hinfelaar's prime interest is to illustrate the reasons why Bemba women were, and still are, the main active members of the mission-churches, though they were "less motivated by material advancement" than the men (1994:ix).

[12] The Bemba term is *Ababenye*. The *Abanenye* "are the most important possession of any chief," writes Doucette ([1997]:125-126).

2.3.2 Christianity Affecting Bemba Women

The arrival of Christianity was perceived as a new avenue of reviving the women's spiritual role because the biblical teaching emphasized the equality of male and female. After a long time of suppressing their traditional spiritual role, the "women found new roles and respect," writes Gray (1990:152).[13] The newly defined boundaries between male and female pried open the "psychological enclosure" in which the women had been "held prisoner" for many generations.[14] Their hopes, however, where daunted when the missionaries of both faiths, Roman Catholic and Protestant, could not put equality of male and female into practice. They were not able to see to it that the women be put on a par with their male counterparts. The neglect of women was (1) visible in the general practice of the Roman Catholic Church to Christianize the Bemba by trying to instill the Christian faith through the hierarchical power structures of Bemba chieftain and eldership.[15] (2) Similarly, the neglect of the women was visible in the general approach of Protestant Missions. Here, emphasis was placed on the younger generation who were both trained and incorporated into the clerical and leadership ranks (this privilege was solely reserved for the men) according to their gifting and qualification.[16] (3) To a lesser degree, the women's disadvantaged position also surfaced as the colonial office was only interested in the ***"man*-power"** of Bembaland to meet demands for supplying and reinforcing the much-needed workforce for the copper mines in the distant Copperbelt province.

---

[13] The impact of Christianity in regard to women's status and role affected many African tribal societies. Bemba society was therefore no exception to the influence of Christian teaching, but may have compounded a specifically unique situation within the historical setting as described.

[14] Hinfelaar writes that already "starting from around 1700 A.D.", the Bemba paramountcy had begun to alter the "original House-Religion" (1994:xi). This timeframe is confirmed by Robert's chronology of Chitimukulu paramountcies, which substantiates the settlement of Bemba royals in Bembaland c. 1700 (1970:232).

[15] Oger compares the Roman Catholic situation with a pyramid and says that, "in the eyes of the people, the clerical pyramid greatly resembled the Bemba traditional one from local village headman with their councillors to the local chief and ultimately to the paramount chief" (in Pell 1993:12). Ipenburg writes: "The White Fathers, however, concentrated on the 'real' Bemba, on the *bena Ng'andu*, on the elite" (1992:284).

[16] In Snelson's opinion the Lubwa Mission School (a Protestant Mission Station) in the Chinsali District, Northern Province, might have been the "outstanding educational institution of the 1930's." For many years, promising young men were sent there to receive advanced training primarily to stock up teachers for new central village schools (1990:204). Ipenburg stresses this point by saying that young boys and girls entered the school system. Later, "the incorporation into the mission and church structure" would follow (1992:282). Employment as a teacher, evangelist, catechist or medical assistant would await successful school graduates. "Mission employees, products of Lubwa's educational system, were dominant in the church structure as church elders and deacons." Naturally, these posts were reserved solely for men. Ipenburg continues to say: "Evangelists and teachers, *all male* (italics mine), who were in paid employment by the mission, dominated in Lubwa Church and in the church council" (1992:227).

2.4 The Upsurge of *Ngulu* Possession during the early 1960s

So far, nothing has been said about Zambia's pre-independence years and the political and social environment at the verge of a new era. This new era of independence had already dawned in the 1930s when the majority of white settlers of Zambia and Zimbabwe pushed for the amalgamation of the two countries. This demand loomed large in the minds of the Zambian Africans (then North Rhodesians) as they were seen "as a big native reserve of cheap labour" (Needham 1991:173).

2.4.1 Political Developments Affecting Bemba Women

Amalgamation, however, was not carried out, partly because the Hilton Young Commission of 1938 was more inclined to see Zambia joined with Malawi. The amalgamation also failed because it was met with opposition by the British government (Needham 1991:173). The end of World War II also brought about drastic changes. The war had put a heavy burden on many colonial economies. This situation made it imperative for colonial administrations to seek economic expansion in their colonies and it meant "the entry of Africans into the market to fill technical roles," says Keller (1986:143). A new social class emerged. The training of African elites "increased opportunities for formal education" and eventually influenced "the development of the national movements which emerged after the war" (Keller 1986:143).

If the cry in the 1930s was for amalgamation, in the 1950s it became one in favor of the formation of a federation between Zimbabwe, Zambia and Malawi. So forceful was this cry for Federation by white settlers and their government in Zimbabwe that "the British government finally agreed to federation" (Needham 1991:178). Despite the fierce African resistance toward federation through the newly formed Anti-Federation Committee of Zambia, and the Nyassaland African Congress of Malawi, the federation was imposed in October 1953 (Needham 1991:176, 178-179). But the federation did not work because it further strengthened European dominance, seen in the election of Godfrey Huggins as Federal Prime Minister of the Central African Federation. Further, growing African resistance, especially in Zambia, "through various nationalist groups" caused the "Federation (to come) to an end in 1963" (Kemp 1987:14).

Despite the victory of independence for Zambia, it was mainly the Zambian men on whom the new "situation" poured lavish care. Offices, ministries, industry, and commerce were the domain of the men. Women were left wondering what the changes were for, if they were not meant to better their lot, too. Especially Bemba women who allied themselves to the Lenshina Movement[17] in the Northern Province, where soon made to realize and feel the in-

---

[17] The movement is named after Alice Lenshina (Regina) Mulenga Lubusha, the woman founder of the Lumpa Church that was started in the Chinsali District of Northern Province, Zambia, in the mid 1950s (Mulenga 1998:2).

tention of the new political reality that took root in Zambia. The Lumpa Church, as it was also known, was perceived as a dangerous threat to the newly established government of Kenneth Kaunda's United National Independence Party (UNIP).[18]

2.4.2 Upsetting Traditional Society Affecting Bemba Women

Oger attributes the revival of *ngulu* possession in the early 1960s to these pre-independence years, which brought "a certain amount of insecurity, uncertainty, and changes to traditional society" (1972a:1). The upsurge of *ngulu* possession during 1907 and the pre-independence years were manifestations of acute symptoms of the ill health of the Bemba social body. For many Bemba people meant the difficult times a need to be apprehensive of traditions and triggered a return to ancestral values.

Hinfelaar states that, despite the period of dialogue during the pre-independence period emphasizing "the need to have the Christian message expressed in the religious concepts of the Domestic Cult," little was contributed to the cause of women: They were "hardly accepted as equal partners in this process" (1994:xii). The conclusion Hinfelaar draws – "the women reacted by claiming the protection of the guardian spirits" (1994:xii) – underscores the fact that *ngulu* possession in the early 1960s was a symptom and indication that both individual bodies and the social body, especially the women, were seriously ill.

Oger summarizes the events of the early 1960s saying that the Bemba rediscovered their spirits (1972a:1).[19] For Maxwell, spirit *(ngulu)* possession brings to light the religious reality of the spirit world. Such a powerful reminder serves as a warning signal to negligent individuals "to reorder their lives according to ancestral tradition" (1983:137-138).

2.5 Conclusion

To explain in retrospect the phenomenon of *ngulu* possession as it erupted to the surface in 1907, and similarly in the early 1960s, it is necessary to take several factors into account.

First, the psychological state of Bemba society at all levels must be considered. This state included a sense of frustration due to the loss of age-old cultivation practices, *mitanda* and *chitemene,* and the fear of a constant shortage of

---

[18] Mulenga leaves no "stone unturned" to expose the wrongful approach and the atrocities committed against the Lumpa Church by the hands of UNIP (1998:ii-ix; 190-243).

[19] Maxwell follows this argument saying that, "contemporary increased phenomena (he refers to *ngulu* possession) are related to hard economic times (as prevalent in 1907) and an anxious sense that modernity (as independence appeared on the horizon) will not deliver on its promises" (1983:139).

food leading to famine and poverty (which proved true in 1906 and subsequent years).

Second, the social upheavals emerging within the large village communities, disrupting the social equilibrium, and the plight of the women triggered a hitherto unseen reaction. The women had been losers before the dawn of Christianity[20] and the colonial administration, and became losers once again when they were sidelined by the two mainstream Christian churches, the Roman Catholic Church and the Protestants, despite the new roles and respect, they had been given. If van Binsbergen was right about the encapsulating politics of the *Bena Ng'andu* (the royal clan) by incorporating the *Shimwalule* priest, the highest non-Bemba office holder, into the royal clan (van Binsbergen 1999:71) (cf. chapter two), then there would be further circumstantial evidence of how great the loss of status and role for the women was. Traditional priests, the owners of the land, were elevated into new spheres of mediating services. But the women, the owners of parenthood, were pushed out of their traditional roles as house priests, the "Enabler of the Domestic Cult," the "Initiator of Worship," and the "Transmittor of the Sacred Heritage" (Hinfelaar 1994:1). The women lost their role as keepers and and facilitators of a house religion.

Third, on the cultural level, *ngulu* possession sparked a deeper realization of ancestral values among a wider range of Bemba people. The return to the spirits came as no surprise to the women, because they were re-claiming their age-old right of mediating with the Transcendence.

Moreover, the broad scale *ngulu* manifestations provoked a broader awareness of the society for a particular cultural element or social institution within the whole of the cultural context.

Furthermore, on a personal level it catapulted *ngulu*-possessed women (and, in exceptional cases, men) right up to the same level as the Royal clan, the *Bena Ng'andu*, and allowed them to enjoy "royal etiquette"[21] as a commoner.

Finally, the *ngulu* cult was a way of political protests against Bemba rule – more specifically against the *Bena Ng'andu* royal clan – "who imposed the cult of their royal ancestors on conquered peoples" (Maxwell 1983:139). The conquered peoples resented the harsh manners of the political machinery of Chitimukulu and his chief vassals, and even more rejected the hierarchically organized *imipashi* beliefs (veneration of the royal ancestors) as the tenets of religious practices.

---

[20] See also Hinfelaar (1994:x).
[21] Compare also Maxwell 1983:139.

3. Linguistic Approach to the Term *Ngulu*

The term *ngulu* poses some difficulty in establishing a clear-cut definition. It is impossible to pin down the meaning of *ngulu* to a dictionary definition, because the meaning is more accurately determined by the context in which it is used.

3.1 The Term *Ngulu*

Carey highlights four such contexts.

(1) The **spirit context** (the *ngulu* kind of spirits as distinguished from other spirits).

(2) The **geographical context** (a specific place associated with the *ngulu* spirit).

(3) The **person context** (*ngulu* as the term describing a person who is possessed by such a spirit).

(4) The **sickness context** (a specific sickness caused by *ngulu*[22] indicating their intention to come and possess a person) (1986:46).

3.1.1 A Linguistic-Historic Viewpoint

From a linguistic-historic point of view, Werner (1971) showed that spirit possession was unknown to the earlier, original inhabitants[23] of the Northern Plateau. In fact, spirit possession as it became known in Bembaland, came into existence some time after Chitimukulu's arrival there (1971:6). Werner further states that, by establishing an isogloss, the "process of dialect differentiation can be reasonably outlined" (1971:8). Applied to the three words *Lesa*, (God) *-pashi*, (spirit) and *ngulu*, he concludes that *ngulu* came into use by the Bemba at a more recent time than *Lesa* or *-pashi*.

Etienne (1937/38) implies that the root *-ulu* of the word *ngulu* is pre-Bemba.[24] Cunnison (1959) supports this view on the grounds of oral tradition he gathered in the Luapula valley. He concludes that *ngulu* pre-dates the Bemba

---

[22] *Ngulu* is a Class three noun where the singular and the plural carry the same prefix.

[23] The original inhabitants were "people of Khoisan extraction ... These "bushmen" were called the *Bashimatongwa*, the aborigines" (Hinfelaar 1994:2).

[24] Etienne's investigation of the term *ngulu* in the years 1937-1938 led him to this conclusion. His two main informants, John Kafumbuka, a member of the Lungu tribe, and Gabriel Kawimbe, stressed that *ngulu* was a pre-Bemba term (in Oger 1972a:14). Interestingly enough, the stem *-ulu* also appears in other Bantu languages. MacGaffe's chart on ancient and modern cults among the BaKongo of former Lower Zaire, presents the KiKongo word *y-ulu* [separation mine] meaning, "sky". The Bemba word for "sky" is *umulu*, or de-linking it from the class prefix *umu* it would read *umu-ulu* (the "u" of the prefix and the "u" of the stem fuse to form just one "u"). The striking identical word-stem of both words most surely warms the heart of linguists. For more on the KiKongo word *yulu* see MacGaffey 1983:182.

groups in the area (Cunnison 1959:223).[25] Of further interest, says Werner, is the absence of other words meaning nature spirits in all the other dialects which use the word *ngulu*. (*Ngulu* are associated with natural phenomena like waterfalls, big trees or stones, or recognized extraordinary natural features.)[26] This absence also testifies to pre-Bemba existence (1971:12).

Oger (1972) follows this line of thinking, pointing out, that *ngulu* are spirits that never had a part in the lineage of the Bemba. They were legendary persons who attained a degree of fame; persons who were associated with natural phenomena, or were perceived as "divinities," that is, "ministering spirits" (1972a:13) of God.

The consensus on the root *-ulu* as being pre-Bemba might have yet another ally in the names by which *ngulu* spirits are known.[27] These names designate either persons of renown of times long ago before the Bemba established themselves as a tribe on the plateau, or they refer to "secondary divinities" (Oger 1972b:23) of the tribes the Bemba subjugated. Also, they are names that the waves of Bemba immigrants brought with them from BaLuba (Oger 1972b:23), the country of the Luba and Lunda states in Katanga (Roberts 1970:221).

3.1.2 Possible Inferences from Linguistic-Historic Data

From what was said above and other evidence presented below, the following outline of the phenomenon of *ngulu* possession could be constructed.

(1) The word *ngulu* is pre-Bemba, but *ngulu* spirit possession is a post-Bemba phenomenon.[28]

(2) *Ngulu* spirit possession was a cultural importation brought by *later* waves of Bemba immigrants from the West (Werner 1971:6).

(3) In order for the Bemba to settle in alien territories and to cope with the religious threat of the "owners of the land", (the *Bashimatongwa* and their veneration of regional spirits), spirit possession took root by appropriating regional *ngulu* for the aim of establishing Bemba supremacy over conquered territories and its people (Maxwell 1983:96).

(4) The reason for spirit possession was to transport the Bemba "indigenous spirits into the alien area by means of spirit possession" (Maxwell 1983:96).

---

[25] Compare also Werner 1971:11.
[26] Compare Louis Oger 1972b:23
[27] Such as *Kabwe, Chishimba, Chyanga, Kapongolo*. See Oger 1972b:23.
[28] See Werner 1971:8; Etienne and Oger 1972a:14 and Oger 1972b:23; Cunnison 1959:223.

(5) Spirit possession, however, was limited in occurrence and had "a role to play in society" (Oger 1972a:1).[29]

(6) *Ngulu* spirit possession (the *ngulu* cult) was dealt a severe blow by the hands of Paramount Chief Chitapankwa in the mid-nineteenth century.[30] "Chitapankwa was known among the women as *Kaluba Ngulu* and *Mukungula Mfuba* ('Destroyer of the Landspirits' and 'Suppressor of the Spirit-shrines'" (familial *mipashi* shrines) (Hinfelaar 1994:26-27).

This rough draft of the historic and linguistic elements of *ngulu* spirit possession sheds some light on its development within Bemba culture, but also poses a number of questions that beg for answers. Some of the questions that arise from the brief outline above are as follows:

(1) If *ngulu* was pre-Bemba, that is, if the term existed before Bemba became the *lingua franca*, why was it incorporated into Bemba usage in the context of spirit possession at a later stage among Bemba speakers?

(2) Who were the main protagonists (men/women, shrine priests/commoners) of the initial emergence of *ngulu* possession before the turn of the twentieth century?

(3) Were efforts to establish political supremacy over the original inhabitants and other subjugated tribes really aided by religious means such as *ngulu* spirit possession?

(4) Was this reason the only reason for *ngulu* spirit possession as it emerged among the Bemba people?

(5) The Bemba immigrants, probably the Bemba royalty, introduced the *ngulu* spirit possession themselves, for reasons outlined above. Why would a paramount Chief Chitimukulu, as seen in the particular case of Chitapankwa, earn himself a reputation as "destroyer" of the *ngulu* cult?

(6) And why would Chitapankwa become a person of such profound negative renown, especially among the women?

It may be very difficult, if not altogether impossible, to provide satisfactory answers to all of these questions and many more not raised in this discussion. I will, however, try to provide possible answers for a select number of the

---

[29] Oger states that in the early written monographs and notes, [those predating the 1880s and 1890s when an influx of Catholic and Protestant mission activities started], a confirmed "*ngulu* person" was often times an itinerant wanderer or someone to whom people came to seek help in times of "epidemics or for fertility (*ubufyashi*) medicines" ([1987 or later]:2).

[30] Chitapankwa died in 1883 (Roberts 1970:224).

questions raised, especially the latter two. First, why did Paramount Chief Chitapankwa react so strongly against the *ngulu* cult, when initially it was an element that strengthened the Bemba royal line and reign?

The answer was partly given earlier in the discussion. The latter parts of the nineteenth century and the first decade of the twentieth century brought enormous changes to the peoples of the Northern Plateau. The Bemba became a homogeneous unit – contrary to the royal clan, the *Bena N'gandu* which was always of the same kind – as a result of absorption, fusion, and incorporation of earlier inhabitants by constant waves of conquering Bemba immigrants from the West. The conclusion that *ngulu* spirit possession became "predominantly a cult of affliction" (Oger [1987 or later]:3)[31] or a means by which resentful non-Bemba people could exercise a "religious alternative" (Maxwell 1983:139) appears to be a rather appropriate one.

From what was said, however, one could easily deduce that *ngulu* possession came into existence as a result of a mere coincidence of specific, historic constellations: the climax of non-Bemba resenting the Court Cult, the Bemba fighting the encroachment of colonialism, Bemba traditional beliefs coming to grips with new religious beliefs, and practices brought by missionaries. The phenomenon could be interpreted as an act of utter desperation fighting against historical events, an act that was not accompanied by intelligent deliberations. I am inclined to think otherwise. The phenomenon of *ngulu* possession was rather devised, than accidentally constructed; it was more the result of intelligently re-organizing and molding cultural substance (of whatever origin and time reference), than the result of an improvised, frantic re-assembly of a cultural relict.

3.1.3 *Mumbi Makasa Liulu*: Founder Queen of the *Bena Ng'andu* Dynasty

Maxwell, in the third "paragraph" (1983:36-38) of his exegesis of the Bemba Charter Myth, mentions the woman *Mumbi Makasa Liulu* ("Mumbi, steps from heaven") (Hinfelaar 1994:22). She is the first woman to receive a mention in the oral accounts of Bemba history. According to the narrative, she "fell from the sky/stepped down from heaven" and married *Imfumu Mukulumpe* (the Great and everlasting Chief) *Mubemba* (Hinfelaar 1994:22).[32] Together they had three sons, Katongo, Nkole, and Chiti, and one daughter, Chilufya Mulenga. Through their mother, the three noble sons could claim divine descent. Chiti became the first king of the migrating Bemba people and all subsequent kings were called *Chiti-mukulu*, "the great tree," after their first

---

[31] MacGaffey shows that in the case of the BaKongo, *Kimfumu* "as 'chiefship,' is political, but as an 'affliction cult' it is religious" (1983:18-19).

[32] The name of the Bemba tribe is supposed to derive from this very chief Mukulumpe Mubemba. Compare Oger 1972b:7.

ruler. *Mumbi Makasa Liulu* belonged to the crocodile clan *Ng'andu*[33] hence, the Royal Clan of the Bemba was established as the *Bena Ng'andu* dynasty among the *Bashimatongwa* (original inhabitants) and other subjugated tribes on the periphery of Bembaland.

The striking resemblance to royal etiquette and protocol witnessed in the phenomenon of *ngulu* possession[34] is no mere coincidence. Weber's (1969) theory of culture implies that "culture is the result of the human tendency to impose meaning on every dimension of existence" (in Obeyesekere 1984:1).[35] And MacGaffey asserts that, for the BaKongo, one institution can have a different meaning on different levels (1983:178). The Bemba *Imfumu* institution (chiefship) and its royal etiquette operate on the political level, and the *Imfumu* etiquette in the *Ngulu* cult acquires a religious role. The logical sequel of Weber's proposition leads to dynamic processes taking place within culture, rather than culture maintaining a status quo; a static conglomerate of elements, ideas and values, so to speak. Such is not the case. "The reason is that each culture is a combination of characteristics but never static or uniformly consistent," says Nuckolls (1996:xliii), a position that Boas had already taken in the 1940s (in Nuckolls 1996:xlii-xliii). For Boas, dynamic processes contain contradictory elements and the task is to determine how they influence each other in dynamic combination. The influence contradictory elements exercise on each other can, however, only be understood historically (Nuckolls 1996:xliii). This is precisely the case with the phenomenon of *ngulu* possession. The activation of *ngulu* elements, as outlined within its historical and contradictory context, testifies to the creativeness of the human mind and its potential for making changes – changes that are either consciously or unconsciously desired and deliberate, made in an effort to cope with and make sense of life.

3.1.4 *Mumbi Makasa Liulu*: "The Queen who Steps from Heaven"

In consideration of the persuit of meaning, the assumption that *ngulu* possession, as an alternative to the Court Cult, appropriated the stem *-ulu* from the noun *um-ulu* ("that above," "sky," "heaven")[36] *as well* as *Li-ulu,* gains in

---

[33] This word is not of Bemba but of Luba origin and is maintained in the Bemba language up to date. The Bemba word for crocodile is *Ng'wena*.

[34] Oger writes that possessed persons, after having revealed the name of the *ngulu* spirit/s, are given an appropriate chiefly welcome. Such an event is further stressed by language and expressed with two verbs, *kutotela* ("to pay respect, usually by clapping hands") and *kucindila ngulu*, (dancing) (1972a:15). Both symbols are explicit royal etiquette reserved for chiefs, and in particular, the paramount chief Chitimukulu. The revelation of the *ngulu* spirit causes person to become *uwa ngulu* (a person of *Ngulu* status) and the person is henceforth treated as a royal personage. Tanguy describes in more detail the royal regalia such a person wears and the status he enjoys among the people (1954:108).

[35] Obeyesekere makes reference to Weber "Objectivity in Social Science" (1969).

[36] David Livingstone, in his travels through present-day Zambia in the mid 1860s, translated the word *Gulu* into "Deity above, from heaven above" (in Hinfelaar 1994:34).

strength and momentum. At this point, one is lead to ask the question: why was it the women, who so emphatically expressed their feeling of dislike and their opposition to the centralized Court Cult personified in the paramountcy of Chitapankwa? *There was reason and resource for the women to do so.*

The women could effectively counterbalance the imposed divine authority attributed to chief Chitimukulu and transfer divine authority back to the commoner. It was the women, as a select and afflicted social group, who were in dire need of divine intervention. *Ngulu* possession provided just that intervention, as it became known as an experience that was primarily and explicitly related to "that from above" (Archdiocese of Kasama 1970:3; also Oger 1972a:10). The "heaven-metaphor" provided the women with the legitimate ground from which to stage their battle! It also made it more difficult for the opposing fraction to challenge the women, because *ngulu* origin and legitimacy lay outside the opposition's immediate jurisdiction. How could they dare to oppose the Transcendence?

Interlinking *ng-ulu* with *Li-ulu*, the heavenly woman and queen, would cast a distinguishing light on *Mumbi Makasa Li-ulu,* "the queen who steps from heaven". As the protagonist of Bemba mythology, Li-ulu's predominant significance as the founder-woman of the Chitimukulu *Bena Ng'andu* dynasty – which is exclusively male dominated and vested with the privilege of mediating with the Divine – does have considerable potential to ascribe to *Li-ulu* a totally new role. In her archaic role of bridging the Divine with the Earthly, *Mumbi Makasa Li-ulu* now emerges out of the dark, distant past of myth, steps down from heavenly realms, and unites with her female kith and kin by assuming the role of women's liberator in the present crises of social and personal upheavals. In her new role, she becomes a powerful ally of the women's cause in general, and the *ngulu* women in particular.

In a certain way, the phenomenon of *ngulu* spirit possession exposes something extraordinary: the creativity of the human mind. It might also be an indication of the women's shrewdness in counter-attacking the "enemy" (male dominance and royal elite) with the devices of his own making!

Ngulu: Phenomenon, Possession, and Symbol

Ngulu as phenomenon must be understood as a product of the historical events that molded it into a cultural symbol that was initially conferred on only a few select individuals. But, at a later stage, the symbol became infused with cultural life and meaning as increasingly more persons, mainly women, made use of this cultural symbol through possession.

In contrast, *ngulu* as a state of possession must be understood as a cultural symbol that was molded into a personal symbol by individuals in times of deep cultural, social, and, most probably, personal crises mediated through personal experience. In light of this fact, *Mumbi Makasa Liulu* is depicted as a group model for a whole social group (women in the majority) as well as a personal model of individuals (to a much lesser degree also of deprived and marginalized men).

Parsons, as summarized by Obeyesekere, says,

> "...that there are situations in human life where the problem of meaning become especially acute: when there is a sharp disjunction between expectation and experience (actuality) – for example, when a group is hit by sudden flood or earthquake..." (1984:114).

The socio-economic situation as described in the previous section (e.g. abolition of the *chitemene* and *mitanda* system leading to a severe famine in 1907), their loss of religious status and role under the rule of the *Bena Ng'andu* dynasty, and the somewhat dashed hopes of the women with the dawn of Christianity, is just another form of calamity that befell Bemba women.

This "sharp disjunction between expectation and experience (actuality)" must be seen as one of the major causes of *Ngulu* as a phenomenon (mostly with women), and *Ngulu* as possession (the "problem of meaning" with individuals and their particular life experience).

Ngulu: The Imfumu Etiquette

The *imfumu* element within the *ngulu* context intentionally draws elements from the cultural *imfumu* etiquette. On the one hand, *Ngulu* status works on a personal level as a personal religious symbol by releasing personal experience into culture; an abreaction of frustration and social deprivation. Successful mediation of personal conflicts and successful appropriation of the *ngulu* cultural symbol provides for a successful integration into the public culture, as is evidenced by the respect such a state attracts from society. It also returns self-esteem to estranged individuals and provides a way to again make sense of life.

On the other hand, *Ngulu* status and *imfumu* etiquette work on the social level as a cultural symbol because they are recognized as cultural constituents. This recognition is real, as *Ngulu* status attracts gifts that articulate and acknowledge high status and power to commoners, gifts otherwise rendered only to royal personages. Also, in economic terms, a person's welfare experiences a noticeable upgrade with the accompaniment of aristocratic privileges.

To sum up, I would say that women were as much active agents acting upon their socio-cultural context in the upsurge of *ngulu* possession as they were acted upon by their context (personal life experience and/or the socio-cultural situation).

3.2 The Verb *Ukuwa*

The verb *ukuwilwa* is the passive applicative extension of the intransitive verb *ukuwa*[37] with the primary meaning "to fall," which in the passive extension means "to be fallen upon." The term *uwawilwa* denotes a person "who is befallen upon," or, to put it differently, a possessed person.

What comes into a human being in the initial stage of possession is a "thing." *Camwikata*, "**it** seizes him or her." At that stage this thing has no identity and is called *mwela*, meaning "wind." The noun *mwela* is also used in connection with a sudden stroke of illness. Expressions used are: (1) *napamwa*, "he/she has been struck," and (2) *camupama*, "it strikes him or her." Usually these verbs refer to special diseases like epilepsy (*umusamfu*), delirium or madness (*lushilu*), that is, diseases which are not considered as *kuwilwa*, spirit-possession. There is, however, a clear distinction between the two terms *camupama* and *kuwilwa* (see Oger 1972a:3).

Kuwilwa spirit possession, says Oger, is tied to *ngulu*, whereas the symptoms of sickness are distinguished from diseases like *umusamfu*, (fits, epilepsy) or *lushilu*, (madness), which are usually linked to *imipashi*, familial, ancestral or royal "*spirit doubles*." Only when the symptoms point to possession, the neuter designation *camwikata* changes to "*kuwilwa*," "to become possessed." In conclusion, I summarize Oger (1972a:2-5).

(1) *Camupama* describes a spirit possession experience at the very initial stage when possession is a mere possibility.

(2) *Kuwilwa*, in contrast, explicitly refers to "be fallen upon, to be possessed." *Kuwilwa* also denotes the suddenness and the totally unexpected arrival of the event. Such an experience is unintentional, and a person is involuntarily seized.[38]

(3) *Uwawilwa* is a person who unintentionally experiences seizure by something invisible, mysterious, – something external.[39] That "something" is free to move from place to place and manifests itself wherever it wishes.

(4) Oftentimes this event is described as *kufumfuma mu muntu*, "creeping into a human being" (like wind penetrating a house).

---

[37] *The White Fathers Bemba Dictionary* (1991) s.v. "*-wa*."

[38] In a discussion on this topic the sudden experience of seizure was explicitly emphasized. It was also stressed that *ukuwilwa* is temporary and is accompanied by certain behavioral patterns (e.g. shaking, wriggling on the ground, glossalia, etc.). Workshop for the Bemba Bible Translation Project held in Kasama, 10 October to 12 October 2000. I was a participant in all discussions during these days.

[39] At the same Workshop (10-12 October 2000), it was pointed out that *uwawilwa* ("a person who is fallen upon, seized, possessed") or *aliwilwa* (a certain person seized or possessed) describes a person, who is under constant influence of possessing spirits (e.g. *ngulu*) though acts of possessions only occur periodically at times with long spells (sometimes years) in between seizures.

3.3 Stages of *Ngulu* Spirit Possession

Symptoms, physical ailments, that is, certain symptoms of sickness, as well as dreams and visions (such as apparitions of persons dressed in bright white clothes) create a strong presumption of *ngulu* possession, the first preliminary stage. But to attain full *Ngulu* status, a person has to undergo sequential preliminary stages, each of which requires successful completion before one moves on to the next stage.

3.3 1 First Preliminary Stage: Initiation – *"Kutundule Ngulu"*

The transitive verb *ukutundula* means "to clear, uncork/unplug, clean out." The perception of *kutundule ngulu* is therefore to "unplug" the *ngulu* spirit(s), that is, to reveal the name(s) of the male or female spirit(s). This initiation session marks the first preliminary stage and requires the presence of a person who is an expert or pre-eminent *Ngulu*. The audience is comprised of family members, members of the *ngulu* entourage, and members of the public. Drums, dancing, and singing are essential elements of this ritual. The following is based on the personal account of my informant Chewe who underwent *"kutundule ngulu"* in 1991.

The initiate is seated in the middle of a circle that is drawn with white clay (*mpemba*, "clay or white soil from the riverbed").[40] Then, when seated (seating position: legs stretched with the arms stretched out touching the knees), the patient is given tobacco medicine, tobacco rolled into a paper (*ibange*: see Chanda 1982:39). Alternatively, a drug that is drunk may be given for inhalation. Also, the patient is instructed to lick (*ukumyanga*) white clay (*mpemba*). Other portions of clay are used to anoint or rub a small spot on the center of the person's forehead. When this is done, the *abangulu* (the expert-*Ngulu*'s assistants) start beating the drum and sing songs. The public is not permitted to join them. The initiate falls into a trance. Failure to stage a trance condition means the end of the ritual. The case is dismissed.

When possession has been established, the person falls sideways or backwards to the ground, rolling and wriggling on the ground while the drums are beaten and the singers sing. In trance, the person struggles and kicks, heralding the arrival of *ngulu* until finally he/she discloses or designates the name(s) (*ukulumbula*) of the *ngulu* spirits present. All names that are uttered are carefully memorized. When the person has finished speaking/designating the names, the expert-*Ngulu* helps the patient to resume the former seating position. The person is still with *ngulu,* and they give him a song to sing. Drums are beaten to accompany his song. The initiate gets up and dances until he/she stops singing. Dancing stops and the person sits down again. The expert-*Ngulu* approaches the candidate and speaks to the *ngulu* spirits in order to find

---

[40] The meaning of the circle is to show that the demarcated area is sacred (Chanda 1982:39).

out what they want and why they have come to this person. A very common answer would be: *twaisa mukundapa,* "we have come to help and to give medicine to sick people."

The whole procedure is conducted at night. Then, at dawn, the initiate is given uncooked broth or gruel (*mufuba,* made of *mwangwe,* "white millet"). This mixture is supposed to have a purifying effect. The "gruel breakfast" signals the end of the *kutundule ngulu* ritual. A relationship with the spirits, disclosing their names and identities, has been established.[41]

3.3.2 Second Preliminary Stage: Confirmation – *"Kukushe Ngulu"*

At a later stage, some weeks later, the patient is introduced to a special *Shing'anga* (Healer) who is a specialist in *ngulu* spirits. Oger says that, in modern days, the period between the first and the second ritual depends on how quickly the demanded amount of money is secured. It appears that there is a variation in the way this ritual is carried out (1972a:5).

Oger alludes to the fact that the specialist *ngulu Shing'anga* affirms the patient's possession through divination. A confirmation of possession ushers the initiate into *"kukushe Ngulu"* status, that is, "to make the person who is with a spirit grow." The initiate has now fallen back to the status of a child who, according to traditional Bemba culture, needs special food cooked on a new fire (the ritual performed for a newborn baby is called *kukusho mwana.* Note the terminology: *kukushe ngulu* and *kukusho mwana*). Thereafter, a ritual hunt is staged. This hunt is the center stage of the ritual. Two animals (duiker), a female and a male, have to be killed. The order female-male is absolutely essential. If the first kill is a male, the interpretation is no possession, no *Ngulu status.* A female duiker represents a successful hunt. The initiate has to drink the blood of the animal from the jugular vein while it is still alive. A person is then officially recognized as *uwa-ngulu,* a person of *Ngulu status.*[42]

My own research yielded another version of the *kukushe ngulu* ritual which is mainly concerned with establishing sanctioned food regulations. On an appointed day, perhaps one month after the *kutundule ngulu* ritual, *BaShing'anga* (healer) and *abangulu* (persons of confirmed *Ngulu status*) are begun in the same way as in the first preliminary ritual.

The major burden in terms of expenses is now on the patient. All the food the patient was forbidden to eat by the *ngulu* spirits (e.g., bubble fish, fresh chicken, cassava leaves, small mushrooms (*samfwe*) etc.) has to be bought by the candidate. Once everything is prepared, the drums are beaten and the per-

---

[41] For another detailed account of the *-tuntuula* initiation ceremony as performed among the Lungu (some 160 km north of Kasama on the southern shore of Lake Tanganyika, see Willis 1999:92-101!

[42] For this section see Oger 1972a:5-6).

son sits in the middle of the circle. Then he falls into a trance, announces the arrival of *ngulu*, and mentions their names. A short while later, the patient again resumes consciousness. Meanwhile, others start cooking the various foods that have been brought, and medicine for purification is added. Of each dish, one piece after the other is given to the patient. Whatever dish the patient manages to eat without rejection, is interpreted as a sign that *ngulu* have given consent to the inclusion of this dish in the future diet of the patient. Refusal to eat certain dishes is interpreted as *ngulu* indicating their disapproval of inclusion of those particular food items in the patient's future diet.

An *ngulu* candidate will have to observe strict eating restrictions in the future. After *BaShing'anga* and *abangulu* have finished with the list of permissible diet items they give the patient medicine intended to be an addition each time the *Ngulu* person cooks food. Once a person has achieved an officially recognized *Ngulu* status, the individual has also attained spirit-medium status.

3.4 Conclusion

In the two preceding sections, I have tried to illuminate the phenomenon of *ngulu* possession from two angles. First, the available historical facts and circumstances of the phenomenon of *ngulu* possession were highlighted. In a second step, linguistic evidence on the subject matter was referenced. There is, however, a need to link both elements to real life implications. This will be attempted in in a case study described in the following section.

4. Social Approach to Illness and *Ngulu* Spirit Possession: A Case Study

The upsurge of *ngulu* possession in 1907 and the early 1960s occured in a broad context of history and was a movement among anonymous persons, mostly women. In the following section, I want to intentionally narrow the research context to particulars. The section is particularistic insofar as I present a specific history – the life history of one person, a male individual who at one time related his life and the history of his sickness to *ngulu* spirits.

4.1 G. Chewe P.: A Brief Account of his Life

Chewe was born in August 1959, as the seventh of nine children. His father, Abraham P., was a very active man and pursued several work engagements to make a living. For many years, he was the village Headman of M-village, west of Kasama town. He had a good knowledge of bricklaying work, knew carpentry, was engaged in small business enterprises including a small shop in M-village, and also owned a sewing machine with which he earned some money. But, above all, he was a skilled repairer of guns and this earned him a good and wide reputation among gun-holders near and far. Chewe's father was married twice and had five children from his first wife.

Two of his four sisters have died. His four brothers are all married and his two immediate younger brothers live in the neighbourhood in the village. He and his family made a living as small-scale farmers, usually growing maize, cassava, finger-millet, and various other crops. Apart from being involved in this cultivation activity, Chewe was a founding member and a key leader of a local Christian Church for many years.

Chewe was a highly skilled man. Like his father, he was a gun repairer, a trade he had learned from him. Further, he repaired bicycles, sewed, and mended clothes as the occasion arose. Sometimes he did bricklaying work; he was also a self-taught guitar player. He possessed a fair command of English and, naturally, spoke his mother tongue Bemba extremely well. I am not aware of any other languages he might have spoken.

Chewe died in July 2000. Up to his death, he lived with his family in A-village, some 15km east of Kasama, the provincial capital of the Northern Province. He had moved there in 1980. The shift from M-village, where he was born, was necessitated by his father's death in 1978. The interim time he spent in Lusaka, the Capital City, first staying with his immediate elder brother, and then seeking shelter with his sister and brother-in-law in Luangwa, Eastern Province.

In October of 1999, Chewe travelled to the Copperbelt for his *first time ever*. He had not travelled to Lusaka, the capital city, since his return from Luangwa in 1980! This is most unusual, as most Zambians travel widely and often.

Chewe was married to Grace. They married in 1988. Their marriage produced five children, four girls and one boy. His first, European name Gabriel was given to him at his Baptism (both his parents were adherents to the Roman Catholic faith) as an infant in honor of the archangel Gabriel. His second, African name Chewe was given to him by his mother to continue an old family lineage. Most of the time, he was addressed by his African name. (I will have more to say about this name later.) Following this brief introduction to Chewe's life, particular attention shall be given to him as one who struggled with sickness for most of his life.

4.1.1 Early Childhood and Family Relations

I know very little of Chewe's very early childhood. When I realized the importance of that part of his life, he was already on his deathbed and I was not able to engage him in a more enlightening journey into his past. However, I have tried to piece together what came up during some formal and many informal discussions during the many years of our friendship.

Early Childhood

Chewe enjoyed good relationships with both of his parents.

[*Comment*: This, despite the fact that his father was married to two women who, for some time, lived together. The reality of two brothers and three sisters from the first wife, and four sisters and two brothers from the second wife, "was quite tough," as Chewe put it. However, they did not starve because his father was village headman, gun repairer, and a good hunter].

When I asked him whom he had loved more, his mother or his father, he did not commit himself to a quick answer. After contemplating a short while, he settled on a compromise, saying, "both." "I do not know why they loved and why they favored me so much." (The emphasis is on "favored ... so much"!)

At one time, I asked him about the earliest memory he had of his father. Again, Chewe was quick to point out the good relationship he had had with his father. He depicted him as a "loving father," but one who "was also very disciplinary." He said: "He (Father) used to give harsh beatings or punished misbehavior by withdrawing food for a whole day." When asked whether his father ever beat him when he was a boy, he answered straight away. "Yes, one time. I was making a catapult and used mother's shoe to cut a piece of leather to finish the catapult. When father found out, he didn't do anything at the first moment. Only after we had had supper, he got hold of me. He beat me with a whip until it broke into pieces. Then he kicked me. It was only because of my mother's intervention that I was spared more punishment. This was the first time I remember that Father beat me. After that, he never beat me again."

Then Chewe made an interesting injunction. He related his father's restraint in following disciplinarian principles in his upbringing to his poor physical condition. "My sickly state may have contributed to (his) showing favor to me. From this incident, I learned a lesson. I realized that beating comes as a result of doing wrong. I tried to be more careful in doing wrong things thereafter." He has no recollection of his mother beating him. "Maybe when I was very young," he said.

Family Relations

Relationships with his siblings varied in closeness and affection. His favorite and closest sibling among his sisters was his elder sister, Elisabeth. She died in 1998.

[*Comment*: The Brother-Sister relationship (*Ndume ne Nkashi*) is very important in matrilineal societies (Hinfelaar 1994:23). Especially the Bemba *Muntunse* narratives of the "choric tragedy category called *Nshimi*, which are told by the women in the yard near their home" (Hinfelaar 1994:22),[43] deal with the Brother-Sister relationship. A major theme that threads through the *Nshimi* narratives is of the younger boy who, when got into trouble, gets helped by his elder sister who comes to his aid and saves him. (Hinfelaar 1994:23.]

---

[43] See especially Frost 1977.

Richards notes:

> Most Bemba delight in describing the brother-sister relationship which is such a pivot of the matrilineal system. They refer to it in proverb and folk-tale, and adopt a specially sentimental tone in speaking of it in daily life (1982:83).

Chewe also enjoyed close relations with Rose, another elder sister: "We were at good terms with one another," he claimed. Rose stood at his side in 1991 when he was in a difficult situation to establish *Ngulu status*. In a way, she "got him out of trouble," because she solicited and defended his stand of discontinuing the attempt of establishing *Ngulu status*. Chewe could always lean on her.

Their relationship was a special bond. After Chewe's father's death in 1978, Chewe first went to Lusaka to stay with his immediate elder brother Abraham and then moved on to Luangwa (a town on the Zambezi river bordering Mozambique) where his sister Rose lived. He stayed with her family until a dreadful accident involving his brother-in-law occurred. He was killed by gunshots while on duty as a Police officer. This incident happened while Chewe was staying with them. Chewe was forced to go back to Lusaka and later, finally, to return home to the village. Eventually, his sister Rose, too, came back to the village. When Rose fell terminally ill, her mother looked after her. But Chewe went to see her every day in the morning and in the evening until her death.[44]

Then, he stressed, he was very close with his youngest brother J. Chota K. He "has been my closest (brother) from childhood," Chewe emphasized.

[*Comment*: K. had been mute since childhood and both had developed their own system and means of communication by signs].

Strained relations existed with his immediate young brother. Chewe frankly mentioned his name. He said that Marvin[45] seemed to be different from the rest of the family. Apparently, Marvin also had problems relating to other siblings. Chewe said about this brother that Marvin "has problems with this one and that one. He has been in trouble with all my siblings. Even with my mother, he had problems. He stole items from her house and her fields. He never showed much willingness to help her in her work. When drunk, he used bad language on her when she was still alive. She never entrusted things into his care. Sometimes she gave him money to go to town and buy some relish. When he came back, he had used the money on something else, mostly beer."

---

[44] I was present at the funeral in 1996.

[45] Not the person's real name. I use an appropriate pseudonym.

I was curious about their relationship and probed deeper. So, I asked Chewe.

Robert: When Marvin was a boy, was he like this? (Chewe answered by travelling back into childhood days).
Chewe: My father had a "Walkers License."[46] Marvin would at times steal biscuits and sweets from the shop. Father was very disciplinary. He beat him after discovering he had been stealing. But it did not help. Marvin stole in large quantities. Each and every time we got to know about him stealing, either my younger brother J. Chota or I went and reported this to our father. For the two of us father had words of praise, but Marvin got the beating.

Not being content with the account, I pressed on and posed another question.

R: Do you think your brother still remembers those times?
C: Yes, I am sure he does.

Now, the ultimate question was hanging in the air and I asked it.

R: Do the stealing incidents still matter in your relationship with him?
C: Not really. He is stubborn and has been like this since he was young. Even now, I cannot trust him with money. So, too, my elder brother does not entrust him with money.
[*Comment:* Here I had the impression he was reluctant to put his "real" thoughts into harsh words. But I am quite positive there were strong feelings he had toward his brother. This was confirmed to me during the prolonged sickness of Chewe from April to July 2000. Only on rare occasions would I meet Marvin visiting his sick brother. I think their relationship was deeply affected by the events of childhood days].

4.1.2 Sickness: Chewe's "Life Companion"

Chewe suffered from recurring illness (severe headaches, stomach pain, and fever). Most of the time when he went through bouts of sickness, especially stomach pains, he was confined to his house. The mentioned ailments impaired his living and well-being for almost all his life. In the Bemba context such a person is known as *ntenda*, or *uwalwalilila*, "a sickly person."

In 1968, Chewe developed extreme bouts of headache accompanied with nose bleeding (*impongwe*) especially during the months of August to November. Around this time his father tried to cure him by cutting a line of hair in the middle of his head and making small incisions in which he rubbed some medicine to cure the headache. This treatment was given to him only once.

---

[46] A system that allowed him to buy merchandize directly from Wholesale agents and sell the goods at home in his own little shop.

In 1971, Chewe began suffering from stomach pains. They were very severe. The attack happened on his way back from school. The pain was so severe that he was forced to stop walking and sit down on the ground. An elderly passer-by took him home where he was given local medicine. He recovered.

In 1972, the problem reappeared with the same severity. The parents diagnosed Chewe's ailment as a special kind of stomach pain called *ikando* (*ikando* designates the most severe form of stomach pain. Chewe described it, saying "one feels like dying"). A number of incisions (*inembo*) just below the navel area were done and medicine was rubbed inside. This was done because it was feared that *ikando* would also cause *ubuumba* (impotency), a highly feared and treated affair in Bemba traditional culture. Additional oral medicine was prepared to supplement the incision treatment. He remembered that some groundnut butter (*icikonko*) was mixed with other ingredients that he could not recollect. He was instructed to eat the peanut mixture at once in order to experience a quick recovery from the sickness. His mother said if the medicine was not taken as directed, the sickness would not go away. He obliged and his health improved; the stomach pains disappeared completely. However, he was not rid of the headache.

In 1973, Chewe again developed severe *impongwe*, "nose bleeding." He would experience nose bleeding whenever he bent forward with his head facing the ground. At school, his teacher was very understanding about Chewe's particular situation and gave him much support. The teacher's successor, too, was an understanding man so that Chewe was helped to finish Grade 7 in 1974.

In 1980 (two years after his father's death in 1978), his family moved from M-village to A-village. This move was initiated through the traditional law of *ubupyani* (the late husband is succeeded by a male from the family). Usually this is a younger brother of the deceased. Chewe's late father was to be succeeded by his younger brother, who took his mother Maria B. as his second wife. There, in A-village, his mother consulted other people in the village concerning Chewe's illness problems. She was advised to use *isako lya cinungi*, medicine made from an animal called *cinungi* (porcupine). Chewe was told to take some *cinungi* quills, burn the tips of them in fire, and smell the scent of the burnt ends. The instructions said that he was to inhale the scent deeply. He followed this procedure for a few days and *impongwe* (severe nose bleeding) was cured, not to occur again until his death in 2000.

4.1.3 Encounter with "*Ngulu*-Spirit-Mediumship"

Sometime in 1991, his sickly state began to trouble him very much. An arrangement to see an expert *Ngulu Shing'anga* (Healer) was made. According to cultural rationale, Chewe showed signs of *ngulu* spirits who might want to take possession of him.

[*Comment*: his poor health – frequent fever attacks, headaches, and stomach pains – were seen as signs of *ngulu* spirits wanting to establish a relationship with him. Cf. chapter four].

However, possession status could not be achieved. He failed to complete the first preliminary stage of *ngulu* possession, the *kutundule ngulu* ritual. Hence, he could not be confirmed of having attained *Ngulu* status, of having become *uwa-ngulu*.

Robert: How did Shing'anga Shimpala interpret your sickness?
Chewe: He said I was *"ali naba shamfumu"* (to be with spirit beings which are not yet identified). The *Shing'anga* wanted to help me to identify the name(s) of *ngulu* (he had a suspicion of *ngulu* possession). These kinds of *Shing'anga* are called: *BaShing'anga ba myela,* "wind (spirit) healers."

R: What else made you relate your sickness to Ngulu?
C: The *Shing'anga* are always very particular about one's sickness history. They have a questioning pattern to extract information and interpret your sickness. His questioning me lead him to diagnose me of being in contact with *ngulu*. That's why he wanted me to undergo *kutundule ngulu*. (*Ukutundula* literally means "to unplug." *Kutundule ngulu* means to "uncork, unplug," that is, to identify or designate (*ukulumbula*) the name/s of *ngulu* spirits.

A person who undergoes a successful *kutundule ngulu* ritual is called *umwana ng'anga,* "the child of the healer." In fact, all those called *abana ng'anga* (pl. "the children of the healer"), become a special group of people. They become apprentices to *Shing'anga,* some sort of disciples. The very committed ones would even try to become a *Shing'anga* themselves and are helped by their *Shing'anga* (they call him *Tata,* "Father") to become like him. The relationship between the *Shing'anga* and his disciple is like father child, *Tata-Mwana*. Most of the *Shing'anga ba myela* are men. A woman *Shing'anga* is called *Nang'anga*. Her "children" too would call her mother, *Mayo*. Even in instances where there is a considerable age difference (e.g., is *umwana* much older, the person still calls his/her instructors *tata/mayo* respectively).

Chewe pointed out that, in his case, *kutundule ngulu* did not work out. *Ngulu* could not be identified. This was in 1991. After the failure of *kutundule ngulu*, *Shing'anga* Shimpala told him to buy the following items: (1) *Insalu ya buuta* (a white piece of cloth; (2) *ubulungu* (beads) and other items he could not remember. Shimpala also told him that maybe *ngulu* do not "like the way I presented myself without any gifts for them. If I bought the things mentioned, *ngulu* would see my seriousness in wanting to honour and to live with them."

[*Comment*: My view is that the initial positive assertion of Shimpala on Chewe's possible *ngulu* spirit relationship declined as he proceeded with the rituals. He begun shifting attention to his "candidate's shortcomings" in order to manoeuver himself out of focus. Probably, he also sensed Chewe's inhibition and foresaw the impossibility of ever establishing genuine *Ngulu status*. People like Shimpala are experts in their own right. Their special work with people gives them great powers of discernment and skill in handling people].

It was then, after the failure of the "*Kutundula* ritual," that Chewe asked himself why he was committing himself to these sessions. His retreat and self-reflection were strongly related to his Christian life and belief that he had begun not too long before. Since it was already his second attempt to receive help from Shimpala, he came to the conclusion that continuing the sessions would not help him any further. *Shing'anga* Shimpala had told him to come back the following day. But the night before, as he was going to bed, "I knelt down and prayed. This night I slept soundly, I had no dreams. When I woke up in the morning, I felt refreshed and did not go with my sister (Rose) to see *Shing'anga* as per arrangement. My strength picked up during the day and the following day, I spoke openly to my sister that I felt no desire anymore to see *Shing'anga*. Seeing my improvement, she understood my decision."

4.1.4 Journey into the Past

In 1994, Chewe was again tormented with stomach pains. It was bad. His mother moved in strongly to help him during this time as she had before. At this point, we have to refer back to some earlier events.

After the family had moved to A-village in the early 1980s, his mother suggested to Chewe that his constant health problems were surely related to an ancestor of her family line. She again told him how a certain ancestor, Chewe Shimfwamba was connected to his particular condition. This man was the forebearer of Chewe's name. His mother was one of his fourth generation offspring (*icishikulula*).

According to family history, this man was a valiant hunter. His skill and fame had earned him great renown in Chief Munkonge's area (to the West of Kasama) where he lived in Shimkumbula's village. He, too, had been a continuously sick person (*ntenda*) and had been given the nickname *cikuni camfita,* "a burnt tree stump," or "a totally charred log of wood." In explaining this link to his past to Chewe, his mother also called Chewe *cikuni camfita* as people had called this ancestor. She would say: **Cikuni camfita icishisenda umbi kano uwacibelela,** "a fire stick that is burnt black cannot be carried by someone else, except by the one who is accustomed to doing so."

People shun a *cikuni camfita,* because it makes a person's clothes black when they are carrying it. In the same way, other persons shy away from a *ntenda* person, they cannot handle a *cikuni camfita* person, except when there is willingness to accept the situation. Only a person who is willing to handle the personal circumstances of his life could live with him. His mother, though, knew how to handle him.

When in 1994 severe stomach pains manifested again, his mother would prepare medicine (*umusunga wa male,* thin millet porridge) and herbs. After cooking the mixture, she would feed him with the blade of an ax (*ululimi we sembe*), considered to be part of the medicine itself). There was some success and relief through the treatment until 1996, when the stomach pains recurred even more severely than before. From that time, he suffered bouts of stomach pains particularly during the rainy season.

During an unusually long period of sickness from February to November in 1994, his condition was related to witchcraft. His mother encouraged him to take his stand and not to submit to the pressure. She said that, when he was a young boy, she and his father had wanted him to be involved in God's work, maybe by becoming a priest (both his parents followed the Catholic faith). But seeing his health problems during adolescence, they realized he would not be able to continue his education in that direction.

Later, when Chewe became involved in taking on the responsibility of spearheading church work in A-village area, his mother said that she could now see that her former wish had become true: *he had become a recognized leader of a Christian Church.*[47] Then, some time in November 1994, Chewe was unexpectedly healed.

In 1997/98, Chewe also had chest pains and was afraid of participating in working the fields because of breathing problems. Sometime in 1998, he was given a course of chest medicine at Lukupa clinic. The sickness was diagnosed as bronchitis. He recovered and no relapse occurred. Before Chewe got married, his mother used to talk to his wife-to-be about his particular health problems, also reminding them that Chewe's physical condition must be related to the said ancestor Chewe Shimfwamba. She wanted her daughter-in-law to become an understanding person concerning Chewe being an *ntenda* (chronically ill) person and to learn to deal with a *cikuni camfita,* "a charred log of firewood."

4.1.5 A Preliminary Interview

Robert: When you were young, did you ever compare yourself with others?
Chewe: No, not really. I started comparing myself with others in the late 1980s and early 1990s. I was worried because of the sufferings the sickness caused me.

[*Comment*: From 1994 onwards – after his recovery from the most difficult period of sickness in his life up to that time – he saw his sickness as a deficiency of his body.]

---

[47] But herself adhered to the Catholic faith until her death in 1999.

I understand my sickness as a condition that is related to a deficiency of the body. Now, I have come to see my illness as not being caused by spirits. It is true, however, I am not fit enough to lift heavy things. When I have to do hard work, I have to set my own pace.

But before 1994, my sickness was related to spirits and *ubuloshi* (witchcraft). When you inherit the name of one who was sick, like the forebearer of my name, then you relate your sickness to the sickness of your ancestor. From the late 1980s to the early 1990s, there was much talk about *ubuloshi* believed to be the cause of my sicknesses. That's why I also began to connect my illness to *ubuloshi*. But my mother used to tell me about my *umupashi* name and I came to accept it to be the way it was.

R: *Did you want your umupashi ("spirit double") to improve your health?*
C: Because of my mother's talk, I endured the way *umupashi* was dealing with me. Only in time of severe bouts of sicknesses, my mother would plead with *umupashi* to help in my health. Especially before I got married, she would plead with *umupashi* because she thought *umupashi* was not fully aware of my sickness. She wanted me to be a healthy person before I entered into marriage. If she could achieve an awareness of his son's sickness, *umupashi* would have to help to improve his health.

R: *Was there a time when you wanted to change your name?*
C: No, because the forebearer of my name was a famous hunter and I also have a strong inclination to hunting. That's why I did not want to change my name. Mother also said my name had a great family tradition and she would not want to lose the name. That is why she gave my firstborn child the name Chewe in order to continue the name in the family.

[*Comment*: Chewe's firstborn child is a girl who was born in 1989].

R: *Were there others in the family who suggested changing your name?*
C: No, no one.

R: *Was your sickness handled as a family problem?*
C: They all knew about my sickness and tried to adjust to it. They always gave me light work to do. The family elders did not gather to plead with *umupashi* to take the sickness away, because it was a known fact that this *umupashi* was like this. There was no cause to be overly concerned.

R: *After moving to A-village and living with your stepbrothers and stepsister how was it?*
C: In the beginning, when I was very ill, they said that I was bewitched. Later on, they suggested I might have contracted AIDS. They did not talk to me directly but to others. I heard from other people what they talked about me.

R: *How did you feel about it?*
C: Well, I did not bother much because I knew my life [*Comment*: he meant his life history and how he perceived of it] and was confident that they, too, would come to understand.

R: *When you became a Christian did you express the wish to God to be healed?*
C: Yes, very much! I also used to find remedy by consulting *Shing'anga* about this problem (health). From 1994 onward, this changed. The Sunday-power-experience made me see and understand that God cares for me.

5. A Concluding Reflection

In this chapter, I have focused on illness and *ngulu* spirit mediumship, first giving consideration to the historical events of *ngulu* possession. Then, linguistic material was sifted and investigated, followed by the presentation of a case study.

A main theme of the first section was the investigation of historical events around the turn of the twentieth century. Colonial rule brought drastic changes (e.g. the hut-tax-system and the abolition of the *chitemene-mitanda*-system) in terms of socio-economic implications like the famine in 1907/08 in Bembaland.

The advent of Christianity collided with the Bemba coming under British rule. Women experienced an uplift of recognition: Christian teaching regards both men and women as equally unique before God and man. However, church practice (Catholic and Protestant) did not always reflect and value this truth, and, more often than not, women were not put on equal par with men. For women, the situation was even more vexing. Neither the Colonial Administration nor the two mainstream churches could wholly compensate for the loss of status the women had suffered through the hands of the *Bena Ng'andu* dynasty long before either colonial officials or missionaries had really set foot in Bembaland. Women had previously been in charge of a House-Religion with a threefold role: (1) "Enabler of the Domestic Cult;" (2) the "Initiator of Worship;" and (3) the "Transmittor of the Sacred Heritage" (Hinfelaar 1994:1). The upsurge of *ngulu* spirit possession in the year 1907, whose main actors were women, must be attributed to these developments.

In the same vein, it was argued that historical events, culminating in Zambia's Independence from Britain in 1964, and socio-economic developments in the pre-independence years, caused another upsurge of *ngulu* spirit possession in the early 1960s, again mostly among women. In this time of crisis, women remembered ancestral traditions, returned to traditional values, and reacted in a culturally acceptable mode of behavior expressing inner conflict.

The linguistic section focused on the term *ngulu* and invoked the works of scholars familiar with the topic (Carey, [1986], Werner [1971], Etienne

[1937/38], and Oger [1972]). The consensus was that the term *ngulu* is pre-Bemba. Bemba immigrants from the West, however, introduced *ngulu* spirit possession into Bemba culture at a later stage. Bemba culture became a mix of original cultural elements and adopted cultural elements of earlier inhabitants of conquered territories. Most likely, it was the Bemba royal elite (*Bena Ng'andu*) who initiated possession, appropriating regional *ngulu* spirits in order to establish supremacy.

However, over time, *ngulu* spirit possession developed into a counterforce to the harsh political regiment of the *Bena Ng'andu* and their vassals. *Ngulu* spirit possession became "predominantly a cult of affliction" (Oger [1987 or later]:3). As Hinfelaar established, it was the women who were cultural losers and *ngulu* spirit possession, commonly found with them, reflected that loss on a grand scale. The *Bena Ng'andu* dynasty perceived of *ngulu* spirit possession to constitute a threat to their power and fought it vehemently; Paramount Chief Chitapankwa in particular. This happened shortly before Colonialism and Christianity took root in Bembaland in the 1890s.

It was proposed that the women had *reason* and *resource* to turn to *ngulu* possession to communicate their disagreement with the suffered loss of role and status and, also, to express the inner conflicts this loss inflicted on them. The Bemba Royal Charter Myth provided them with the resource in *Mumbi Makasa Liulu*, "*Mumbi* who steps from heaven," the founder mother of the *Bena Ng'andu*. As the main female protagonist of the myth, she became an ally to the suffering women.

Moreover, the striking resemblence of the *imfumu* element vested in a recognized person of *Ngulu status*, is a further hint that *ngulu* spirit-mediumship could have acted as a deliberate resemblance to official *imfumu* etiquette and protocol of the royal court cult.

Then followed a linguistic investigation of the verb *ukuwa* and *ukuwilwa*, "to be fallen upon, to be possessed." Further, two descriptions of the preliminary stages necessary to attain full, recognized *Ngulu status* were given.

The third main section comprised a case study. G. Chewe was introduced to the reader. A brief account of his life, with a focus on his family, his hishory of illness, his encounter with *ngulu* spirit-mediumship, and his special relationship with his *umupashi* ("*spirit double*"), was presented. The section closed with a preliminary interview with Chewe relevant to a later stage of this study.

This chapter has merely touched on the relationship between culture and personality. The subsequent chapter shall give much consideration to culture as shared values, versus culture as individual agency or action on one's experience within culture. In other words, the necessary position of culture as a dialectic of public and private will be defined.

Chapter 6
The Phenomenon Culture – Public and Private: A Theory of Personal Symbols According to Gananath Obeyesekere

1. Introduction

There has been – and still is much debate on the phenomenon of culture. As Nuckolls aptly puts it, "One of the easiest ways to get into trouble in anthropology is to define a term, and the most difficult term of all is 'culture'" (1996:xxiii). The debate itself, and the complexity of the subject under study, has caused culture to become or to be understood as a phenomenon. If it was – and had been – easy to produce a formula or definition in which all aspects of culture could fit comfortably, culture's characteristic as phenomenon would not play into this discussion.

1.1 Early Paradigms of "Culture-Definitions"

The fact that by 1950 some 164 definitions of the term culture were formulated (Kroeber and Kluckhohn: 1952) (see Käser 1997:29-30) attests to culture being a phenomenon. The problem of pinpointing one overall definition for culture for all times is a complex task indeed and might be altogether impossible.[1]

1.1.1 The "Behavior" Paradigm

D'Andrade notes that, before 1957, the emphasis on the definition of culture was primarily on behavior. The focus was on "patterns of behavior, actions, and customs" (in Shweder 1984:7). Emile Durkheim heavily influenced this one-sided view. The Durkheimian view, as summarized by Obeyesekere, holds that "culture exists independent of and before the individual," which led to the rule that "shared culture must produce shared behavior" (1984:111).[2]

1.1.2 The "Idea" Paradigm

The Durkheimian position was met with severe opposition – rightly so, I believe – starting from the late 1950s. D'Andrade argues that, in psychology,

---

[1] Shweder comments: "I don't think our goal is to arrive at a standard version of culture theory. Indeed, I doubt it would be possible to arrive at a standard version, even over a long run." [Because] there will always be divisions between evolutionists, universalists, and relativists" (1984:7).

[2] Freund summarized Durkheim by saying: "He mistakenly interpreted "collective consciousness" as an ascertainable fact, whereas it is no more than a hypothesis ..." (1970:11).

papers, by Bruner and Miller, for example; in linguistics by Chomsky (1957) and others; and by Goodenough (1957) and others in anthropology, shifted that emphasis and proposed a paradigm shift from describing behavior to looking at ideas (Shweder 1984:7).

D'Andrade, leaning on Goodenough (1957), stressed that "knowledge typically consists of rules – rules by which one decides where to live, how kin are to be classified, how deference is to be expressed and so on" (in Shweder 1984:7).[3]

Tyler (1969), Spradley (1979), Kraft (1996), and others are advocates for an understanding of culture as knowledge that has to be learned.

1.2 Recent Paradigms of "Culture-Definitions"

Whatever the emphasis is, ideas (and knowledge) exist in the minds of people. The task is, as it was argued, to access these ideas via language in order to elicit knowledge. But even this proved to be a problem of its own kind. Language, it was realized, does not only consist of vocabulary.

1.2.1 The "Idea-Knowledge-Meaning" Paradigm

Though it is possible, theoretically, to analyze language "without reference to the person, society, or culture in which it is embedded" (Obeyesekere 1984:20), such an exercise would be one of paperwork only. What would it accomplish? What would we gain? The insights such an exercise might produce would still not link me to another person. One would be denied an essential part of communication. Language, that is vocabulary, conveys messages. But the meaning of messages is dependent on the context. Context is more than the grammar and syntax of a language. Context is also the internal world (the internal state, e.g. emotions and conflicting desires) of the language speaker[4] broadening the "function of language to include the directive, emotive, and constitutive functions of language" (Shweder 1984:20-21).

Here we have, it seems, two opposing elements. How can culture as a system or institution (or behavior) be reconciled to the individual who learns culture (by imitation), who acquires cultural knowledge (vastly through the medium of language), and who makes culture tick (individual agency)? Can language (vocabulary, grammar, and syntax) comprehensively bring together the "language-context" with the "internal-world-context" of the speaker? Is language the only way to transmit messages pertaining to the "internal-world-context"? And, does language really adequately and comprehensively represent the state

---

[3] Also D'Andrade 1984:88-89.

[4] Berlo asks: "What are messages?" Messages are "behavioral events that are related to the internal states of people." He goes on to say: "Meanings are not in messages ... meanings are in people" (1960:168-169, 175).

of affairs in the speaker's "internal-world-context"? The answer is no. This is a theme we will take up again later when personal symbols come under review.

1.2.2 The Dialectic – "Human Mind vs. Culture" – Paradigm

Charles W. Nuckolls suggests a way out of the dilemma of culture as institution vs. individual agency. He proposes that culture as a system "is larger than any of its constituent members" (1996:xxx). As an illustration, he takes the human body. Nuckolls says,

> We do not encounter the human body as a collection of discrete and independent organs, with the option of viewing it from the perspective of the pancreas or the bladder. But that is exactly the way in which we normally encounter culture, as individual human beings with different roles and obligations which are socially defined. Such roles and obligations index the social whole and refer to a system which is larger than any of its constituent members. This provides the only basis for the inference that "culture" actually exists (1996:xxx).

That being the case, Nuckolls says, the larger extent of the system exercises autonomy from the individual and vice versa. The larger system embraces the individual because of the "deeply shared and institutionally embedded values people who are members of the same culture seem to possess" (1996:xxxi). On the other hand, the individual exercises autonomy from the cultural system, because he can "creatively shape" his "own experience" (1996:xxxi), that is, he can act on, influence, change, or manipulate the larger context of the cultural system. The autonomy of the cultural system and the autonomy of individual agency necessarily produce dialectical implications. Hence, Nuckolls argues, culture poses a "problem that cannot be solved" (1996:xvii, 270).

If cultures were only a network of neat structures (structuralism) or a set of highly defined functions (functionalism), then culture would not be an insoluble problem.[5] Structures and functions – as their labels imply – are governed by laws or logical sequences that tend to treat the "personal part of the culture-person interaction"... as part of culture itself"(Kraft 1996:133).[6] Such a

---

[5] In regard to structuralism, Ganoczy comments: "Lévi-Strauss, the father of structuralism, has insisted that his structural analysis begins, like psychoanalysis, with the "unconscious structures" underlying such diverse phenomena as morals, cultures and linguistics systems" (1973:81). Obeyesekere's main critique on structuralism is that it "analyzes signs without reference to context" (1984:20).

[6] Kraft argues that the forms, functions, meanings, and usage – the four constituents of culture proposed by Ralph Linton (1936) and others – are inadequate if separated from the actor. It is

position would mean that conflict and opposition – manifest within every culture – would both be predictable and thereby open for easy elimination, or both would simply be insignificant. But, as both Nuckolls and Obeyesekere convincingly argue, culture is profoundly dynamic. What accounts for the dynamic operating in culture? Nuckolls writes:

> As I understand it, culture is a set of emergent properties, organized systematically and at three levels, all dialectically structured. At the lowest level it consists of individuals whose conflicted desires provide some of the motivation for internalizing cultural symbols. The second level is the psychosocial, and refers to the dialectics, both "objectifying" and "subjectifying," which connect individuals and cultures, making them mutually interdependent. The third level is the level of cultural dialectics, of symbols and their relationships to each other. ...What all share is the property of dynamic opposition. It is the motivational force which keeps them from becoming static or unchanging (1996:xxxiv).

The common "property of dynamic opposition" occurs on three levels which Nuckolls identifies as:

(1) a dialectic within individuals due to "dynamic opposition between conflicting desires" (1996:xxxiv).

(2) "a dialectic operating between living individuals and the cultural system that informs them, providing integrations or resolutions in the form of cultural symbols" (1996:xxxiv). Integration or resolution occurs in the form of cultural symbols. Obeyesekere calls this dialectic *"objectification"* [italics in the original] (in Nuckolls 1996:xxxiv). Conflict resolution also occurs when individuals achieve compromise by constructing their own symbols and "these achieve social acceptance,"... which then become "collectively shared symbols" (1996:xxxiv). This process Obeyesekere calls *"subjectification"* [italics in the original] (in Nuckolls 1996:xxxiv).

(3) a dialectic "which operates in and through cultural symbols themselves ... the level of *cultural dialectics* [italics in the original]" (1996:xxxiv).

Having dealt with the culture concept relevant for this study (the dialectical relationship between culture and individual agency/personality or custom and emotion), I will now move on to Obeyesekere and his theory of personal symbols.

---

people who develop forms, determine function, give meaning, and make use of cultural elements (1996:132-147).

2. Gananath Obeyesekere's Theory of Personal Symbols

Obeyesekere introduces his theory of personal symbols in two of his books. In *Medusa's Hair: An Essay on Personal Symbols and Religious Experience* (1981/1984) he solely focuses on personal symbols. His other book *The Work of Culture: Symbolic Transformation in Psychoanalysis and Anthropology* (1990) develops a progression away from a person's deep motivation toward public meanings. He calls this act "symbolic remove" (1990:56-68).

Obeyesekere's new approach to personal symbols is based upon the statement that the social sciences fail to link unconscious or deep motivation to public culture.[7] Obeyesekere sees the reason for this position in the strong bias prevalent in the social sciences "that culture must deal exclusively with group processes rather than with individual motivation" (1984:1). He says this is wrong. Symbol systems, he argues, must be studied with reference to context, that is, the cultural, social, and psychological dimension of the existence of subjects (1984:1). The following sections will treat each dimension of symbols with respect to their cultural, social, and psychological context.

2.1 Cultural Context: Human Agency – Giving Meaning to Existence

Regarding the cultural dimension, Obeyesekere takes the view of culture stemming from Weber that says that "culture is the result of the human tendency to impose meaning on every dimension of existence" (1984:1). Again leaning on Weber, Obeyesekere stresses that culture consists of collectively held ideas created in the minds of people mediated via consciousness (1984:1, 109-114).

The Weberian view of culture moves far beyond Durkheim. The Durkheimian view, as Obeyesekere sees it, holds that "cultural norms and collective representations act directly on the *passive* [italics Obeyesekere] person, constraining him to perform." Thus, "culture exists independent of and before the individual" (1984:11).[8] This view of constraint, says Obeyesekere, "has also produced, in my opinion, the horrendous fallacy that shared culture must produce shared behavior – or, to be more exact, behavioral regularity" (1984:111).

---

[7] MacGaffey comments on the same issue saying: "In a tradition of social sciences whose philosophical roots reach back to Hobbes, Locke, and the Social Contract debates of the eighteenth century, "the individual," studied by the psychologist, and "society," studied by sociologists, are treated as *separate systems* [italics mine]" (1983:213).

[8] Obeyesekere is referring to Durkheim and his *Rules of the Sociological Method* (1984:111). Lienhardt says that in *Rules of the Sociological Method*, Durkheim set out to establish several principles of investigation. One of it is "his insistence that since social life is not the product of any individual's psychology, it cannot be adequately understood by reference to the consciousness and motivation of individuals only" (1966:30).

Obeyesekere further argues that culture cannot be studied by exclusively dealing with group processes rather than with individual motivation. "Certain cultural symbols are articulated with individual experience" (1984:2).

Despite his respect for the Weberian view of culture, he exercises critique in saying that "Weber neglected one area of human existence: those critical experiences that lie outside conscious awareness" (1984:1). It is at this point where psychoanalysis comes into play.

2.2 Psychological Context: Deep Motivation – Symbolic Representation

Concerning the psychological dimension – "those critical experiences that lie outside conscious awareness" – Obeyesekere falls back on Freud and his "theory of unconscious or deep motivation" (1984:1) which links motives with symbols or images.

Obeyesekere demonstrates that the public and private meanings of some symbols must be linked, if one wants to understand the resolution of intrapsychic conflict in individuals.[9] In doing so, Obeyesekere departs from Edmond Leach's position, articulated in his influential article *Magical Hair*, that "public cultural symbols have no unconscious motivational significance for the individual or the group" (1984:13). On the other hand, Leach says, as summarized by Obeyesekere, that, "private symbols may involve deep motivation, but they have no cultural significance" (1984:13). Obeyesekere takes this position regarding symbols as the "standard social anthropological position" (1984:13) and criticizes this view as inadequate, because it "introduces a radical hiatus between public and private symbols...between culture and emotion" (1984:15).[10] This "radical hiatus" is the reason why Leach cannot explain how a private symbol is transformed into a public symbol (1984:15, 17).

To prove the point that some symbols operate on both a public and a personal level, Obeyesekere selects one personal symbol, the matted hair of south Asian ascetics, and relates that symbol (a public cultural symbol) to critical

---

[9] Obeyesekere sees the reason for a radical distinction between private and public as "the operative ideology of modern industrial man." The private "is shut off ... from public culture." He argues that this hiatus must in no ways be assumed to be nomological for other cultures. On the contrary, in other cultures, like South Asian cultures [I would also include African cultures], dreams or religious symbols function as conduits "between the public and the private" ... and what matters is to take note of "the movement back and forth between private and public" (1990:xviii-xix).

[10] Also Obeyesekere 1990:xviii. MacGaffey, commenting on Leach's article *Magical Hair*, has this to say. "He [Leach] accepts the conventional distinction between private symbols, studied by psychoanalysts, and public symbols, studied by anthropologists, attempting only to bridge the gap between the two presumptively independent systems with the Darwinian suggestion that public symbols are effective because they happen to engage repressed libidinal energies; public and private meanings then coincide" (1983:213).

personal life crises of ascetics. On the public level, "matted locks act as a marker to set aside their bearer as a special and redoubtable being" (1984:37). On the personal level, matted hair carries an emotional message of intrapsychic conflicts and their genesis lies in early childhood experiences of the Oedipal type.

2.3 Social Context: Family Structure and the Oedipus Complex

The employment of a symbol that expresses intrapsychic conflict in an adult person is not the work of a present mood. Intrapsychic conflicts have their root in the structure of relationships in early childhood. The structure of relationships that is developed in early childhood is directly related to the structure of the family in which one grows up. Though family is a universal reality, it does not mean that a universal family model exists, even though all families share a common human nature (Obeyesekere 1990:95). A logical consequence of this insight is simply the fact that there cannot be a universally uniform Oedipus complex. At this junction, one departs from the Freudian Oedipal path. Relevant literature on this subject, though, shows considerable differences of opinion.

2.3.1 Malinowski: Oedipus Complex is Culture-Bound

Bronislaw Malinowski, the well-known anthropologist, first questioned Freud's model of the Oedipus complex. According to Malinowski, the classical model according to Freud – the son develops hostility towards the father and harbors sexual feelings towards the mother – cannot be understood as universally uniform on account of the matrilineal family structure of the Trobriands. He argued that the Oedipus complex "varies with the type of family structure, especially in relation to the allocation of authority" (Obeyesekere 1990:71). In the case of the Trobriands, as in other matrilineal societies, authority lies with the mother's brother. In that case, the male child develops hostility towards the maternal uncle while the sister takes the place of the mother (Obeyesekere 1990:71).

2.3.2 Spiro: Oedipus Complex is Universal and Uniform

Melford Spiro (1982), a prominent psychoanalytic anthropologist, countered this view with Malinowski's own data, trying to show that in Trobriand society the classic Freudian Oedipus complex does exist and is central to Trobriand social life (Obeyesekere 1990:71). He substantiated his argument by pointing out that during the first five years, "when the Oedipus complex is formed and resolved" (Obeyesekere 1990:71), the Trobriand family stays together in a single household. Therefore, the mother's brother, as authority figure to the nephew, comes on the scene long after the Oedipus complex has been resolved (Obeyesekere 1990:71). Therefore, contrary to Malinowski's Oedipus in the Trobriand family that is based on authority, Spiro wants to recognize the Freudian Oedipus complex based on sexual feelings.

2.3.3 Obeyesekere: Oedipus Complex is Complex

Obeyesekere takes a different position from both Malinowski and Spiro, and, in a certain way, from Freud. The Oedipus complex as advanced by Freud in his sexual thesis (and transferred cross-culturally by Spiro), and by Malinowski in his domination thesis, are both too narrowly defined.[11] There is no universal and uniform Oedipus complex "on the basis of a universal form of a human family life" (Obeyesekere 1990:95). Obeyesekere argues that

> ...there is no nuclear Oedipus complex ... there are several, possible finite, forms of the complex showing family resemblance to one another. One might even want to recognize the likelihood of different forms of the Oedipus complex within a single group, especially in complex societies...." (1990:75).[12]

Obeyesekere further substantiates his argument by drawing attention to at least four universal family conditions to which each child, regardless of its cultural background, is exposed. These conditions play heavily into the discussion of the Oedipus complex:

> a) the existence of the incest taboo among family members, excluding the parental pair; b) the sexuality that all members possess, including infants, stimulated by the diffuse affection, body contact, and care by the parents, and especially the mother; c) the coexistence of complex feelings of pity, love, fear among the members that produces a fundamental feature of familial relations – ambivalence or multivalence; d) the continual frustration that is implied in all these relationships, such as the impossibility of a sibling or parent being a love object and the moral difficulty of retaliation against those who dominate you (1990:95-96).

Considering all these elements of family life, Obeyesekere concludes that there is "no way one can escape from ambivalence and the desirability of *all* [italics in the original] intimate familial persons" (1990:96). To sum up, one can say of the Oedipus complex that its formation and resolution follow pat-

---

[11] From the Trobriand matrilineal kin system, Obeyesekere speaks of the matrilineal Oedipus in which four crucial relationships exist: "... father, mother, sister, and mother's brother" (Obeyesekere 1990:71, 75).

[12] Elsewhere in the same book Obeyesekere writes: "The Oedipus complex is much more complex than the simple triangular relationship where the son hates the father and loves the mother" (1990:86)!

terns that are variable across cultures and are based on the "context of varying familial relationships" (1990:76).[13]

2.3.4 Oedipus, Personality and Society

Ambivalence and tension during early childhood are inescapable in any given family model and do influence and shape personality structure. As Obeyesekere pointed out, ambivalence of feelings and erotically charged relationships with significant others are culturally and socially configured.

How then does Oedipus formation and resolution interrelate with personality development?

The Ortigues say

> that the Oedipus complex describes the fundamental structures according to which the dialectic of desire and demand, of evil and suffering, takes shape in the society as well as in the individual. The Oedipus complex cannot be reduced to a description of the child's attitude to his father and mother; it is a semantic problem, as much social as psychological (summarized in MacGaffey, 1983:215).

The important issue the Ortigues raise is that the Oedipus complex cannot be locked into a description of the attitude to one's father and mother. Similarly, the oedipal conflict **cannot be locked into a specific timeframe**. In the investigation of a possible view on the above-raised question, I turn to Wyatt MacGaffey and Talcott Parsons (1964), as summarized by MacGaffey.

MacGaffey, drawing from Talcott Parsons, writes that the structure of personality and society is continuous (1983:215).[14] MacGaffey then also highlights the convergence between Freud's view and those of Durkheim and G. H. Mead, who both hold to the "idea of internalization" (1983:215). Parsons, summarizing Mead and followed up by MacGaffey, continues to say that "the development of the personality through the internalization of object-relations continues into adult life" (1983:215).[15] If this is the case, then the Oedipus conflict is not finally resolved during childhood.

---

[13] See also Obeyesekere's discussion on the Indian Oedipal conflict. In short, he concludes that, for example, the son in *replacing* the father solves the Western Oedipal conflict, whereas the son in *duplicating* the father solves the Indian Oedipal conflict (1990:75-84).

[14] MacGaffey charges Lewis" summary on the psychology of shamans with the fault that he (and others) "presuppose that personality is something the individual brings with him ready-made in his encounter with society and that its normality or lack of it can be assessed independently of his engagement in any institutional context" (1983:215). MacGaffey refers to Lewis' *Ecstatic Religion: An Anthropological Study of Spirit Possession and Shamanism* (1971).

[15] MacGaffey summarizes Parsons 1964:80. This assumption, says MacGaffey, is contrary to the general psychoanalytic theory that there is no serious modification of personality structure after the age of about seven (1983:215).

Continued internalization of object-relations, especially after adolescence, occur when the individual adopts "adult roles in the political and economic institutions of his society, all of which presuppose a basic personality formation" (MacGaffey 1983:217). Parsons identifies two key areas which shape basic childhood personality formation: gender and generation.

Parsons writes,

> Two of the subsidiary identifications within the family, by sex and generation, are to become structurally constitutive for [the child's–insertion by MacGaffey] status in the wider society, and these are cross-cutting (in MacGaffey 1983:217).

Oedipus and Gender

Sex (gender) and generation, writes MacGaffey, "contribute to the child's basic personality, which is the matrix for the development of subsequent object-relations through the adoption of more specific roles in extra-familial social systems" (1983:217). In all societies, an actor's role presupposes the sex of a person, which in turn influences to a great extent what role and position a person takes on in society.

Oedipus and Generation

In regard to generation, basic personality formation is heavily informed by the fact that people occupy different statuses. Already at a very early age, children learn that family and the society at large are hierarchically organized. MacGaffey writes: "The cross-cutting principle of differentiation is that of generation, which is a relationship of both authority and (diachronically) of succession" (1983:217).

Oedipus and Personality

Earlier, Obeyesekere advanced a view of four conditions which are prevalent in all family models. One element was the ambivalence produced by the coexistence of complex feelings such as pity, love, hate, and fear that exist among family members. Another element was the fact that these feelings give rise to continual frustrations, as those feelings cannot be satisfactorily expressed. The only way to deal with such continual frustrations instigated by significant others is repression. But repression cannot be maintained into adulthood as a continuous conscious exercise. As a child grows out of infancy, relations to significant others assume different meanings. The early responses to frustrations are repressed, that is, they are placed into the unconscious. Oedipus has reached a phase of latency. All oedipal experiences are assigned to the unconscious and are technically known as archaic or deep motivations.

Oedipus and Society

It was noted that the Oedipus cannot be locked into a timeframe, or, in other words, that the Oedipus conflict is not finally resolved during childhood. MacGaffey states that, "the current social situation of the adult is more than a trigger or a facilitating circumstance revealing some deep-seated flaw" (1983:215). The final resolve of the Oedipus conflict hinges on the successful integration of an individual into society with respect to gender and generation (especially in regard to authority and succession). MacGaffey says,

> In psychological terms, "failure" in confrontation with authority and the rules of succession means that the internalization of the authoritative other does not take place; the relationship with "father" (or in matrilineal societies with the maternal uncle) remains problematic, and the final resolution does not occur (1983:226).

Failure to integrate can cause oedipal experiences to resurface in **symbolic disguise**. Therefore, directly related is the question: Why do individuals employ cultural symbols and mold them into personal symbols? Because deep motivations – oedipal experiences – resurface and manifest in images or motivate symbolization.

2.4 Thesis on Personal Symbols

Obeyesekere states that personal symbols "form an identifiable set within the larger class of psychological symbols, not all of which have motivational significance" (1984:2). But those symbols that do have "motivational significance" are linked to the life history of a person. However, the past of a person is "often constituted of 'filtered memories'" (1984:22). That does not mean that they are irrelevant to the study. Obeyesekere argues that these memories have to be taken seriously, "since they are the existentially real ones for the informants and are critical to their identity" (1984:22).

2.4.1 A Necessary Distinction with Regard to Personal Symbols

According to Obeyesekere, psychological symbols appear in a "minimum of two types: personal symbols where deep motivation is involved, and psychogenetic symbols where deep motivation does not occur" (1984:13). Both types of symbols might simultaneously be operative in a culture.

Personal Symbols

Personal symbols are "cultural symbols operating on the levels of personality and culture at the same time" (1984:2). How can they operate on those two levels? Personal symbols are invested with deep motivation and the symbols chosen allow for the expression of personal trauma without disrupting the social life of the group. What is the significance of personal symbols? Their "primary significance and meaning lie in the personal life and experience of individuals," says Obeyesekere (1984:44). A personal symbol is "locked into an emotional experience, which can be unraveled only through our knowledge" (1984:21) of the person himself.

The most decisive element in studying symbols in general and personal symbols in particular, is context. With personal symbols, the context of a triangular relationship must be kept in view: (1) the person himself (personality/his life history); (2) the group in which he lives (society/the relevant group); and (3) the people among whom he moves (culture) (1984:20, 91, 123).

Psychogenetic Symbols

Psychogenetic symbols derive from the unconscious, but they are not "recreated anew (lack of choice, no manipulation)" and therefore lack "unconscious personal meaning" (1984:46). That is, psychogenetic symbols lack "ongoing operational significance" (1984:14). Their "current meaning of the imagery is unrelated to its origin in the dream reservoir" (1984:47).

The determinant of a symbol is its "institutional context" (e.g. myth or ritual), which in turn is "decisive in determining whether the symbol is personal or psychogenetic" (1984:50). The difference between the two symbols is important to the ethnographer. It is important in the sense that the researcher cannot operate from the same plane as the informant. His position as outsider, due to cultural, language, and other reasons, of necessity causes him to work from a distance.

The wider the gap to the subject, the more difficult it is to confirm a symbol as either personal or psychogenetic. It is therefore essential to narrow down the "gap" as much as possible as to positively identify a personal symbol. And in a second step, it is necessary to understand how personal symbols operate.

2.4.2 How Personal Symbols Operate

Personal Symbols Require the Context of Personal Experience

"Personal symbols ... are cultural symbols that are related to individual motivation and make sense only in relation to the life history of the individual," says Obeyesekere (1990:24). At the root of personal symbols are traumatic experiences of individuals with significant others, mostly family members. Complex personal experiences of the individual are crystallized in the public symbol. Thus, **symbols become vehicles of communicating inner states, primarily those which caused and continue to cause inner conflict in the individual.**

Personal Symbols Require the Larger Institutional Context

"Personal symbols must be related to the life experience of the individual *and* [italics mine] the larger institutional context in which they are embedded" (1984:13). In the case of the South Asian ascetics, Obeyesekere selects one symbol, matted hair, and argues that the symbol encompasses three interrelated problems: (1) origin and genesis of the symbol; (2) its personal meaning for the individual or the group; (3) and the social-cultural message it communicates to the group (1984:33).

(1) the origin and genesis of the symbol:

Matted hair is a public symbol, "but it is *recreated* [italics in the original] each time by individuals ... on the anvil of their personal anguish" (1984:33). The symbol would cease to exist if individuals did not create it. The genesis or recreation of the symbol by individuals "is linked with painful emotional experience" (1984:33).

(2) personal meaning for the individual or group:

To the person, matted locks are like "beauty marks" (*hada palu*, the proper Sinhala public term) despite the smell and dirt, and discomfort. But when asked, matted hair triggers revulsion in members of the public, and people say the locks contain a fleshly growth: "buds of flesh," or "tender fleshly growths" (*mas dalu*) (1984:35).

(3) the socio-cultural message it communicates to the group:

Symbols vary in their meaning, that is, the message they convey. The formal meaning of matted hair is chastity. Why? This meaning is laid down in texts. The public meaning or message that the symbol relays is emotional: fear, horror, disgust, and revulsion. Why negative emotions? The symbol belongs to a larger class of polluted objects (exuviae) and/or castration anxiety (1984:35-36).

Matted hair of South Asian ascetics operate as a personal and a cultural symbol. Though the symbol means different things to the individual and to the public, there is no radical gap between custom and emotion (compare Obeyesekere 1984:20).

Personal Symbols must not be Interpreted as Symptoms

Coming back to Obeyesekere's criticism of Leach and the gap between personal and public symbol, Obeyesekere advances his argument on the strict separation of symbol and symptom with the same example of matted air. Leach says matted hair is a symptom not a symbol. Obeyesekere argues that matted hair is *not* a symptom *but* a symbol. Why? Because "a symptom is a somatic manifestation of a psychic or physical malady" (1984:37). And matted hair of ascetics must not be confused with matted hair of beggars, because with them "they are simply dirty locks matted together through neglect" (1984:37). In other words, matted hair with beggars is an idiosyncratic somatic sign and therefore non-communicative. Obeyesekere places the non-communicativeness of the symbol "under the domination of motive"

(1990:12).[16] No interpersonal communication can take place. But matted hair as a symbol is different. It is "under the rule of meaning" (1990:12). It is a public *and* private symbol and therefore has communicative power.

Personal Symbols are open to Manipulation

A personal symbol is, on one level, a cultural symbol with a more or less fixed meaning. But on the private level, the same symbol does not exercise its recognized meaning on the individual; rather, it is the individual who appropriates the symbol and invests it with personal meaning. Obeyesekere remarks:

> Even when symbols that have primary social and interpersonal significance are manipulated by individuals (in religious rituals, trance, and other emotional contexts), they become invested with personal experiential significance ((1984:45).

Where does the reason behind manipulation of symbols lie? Personal symbols are characterized by "looseness and ambiguity" which are critical characteristics "since they facilitate manipulation" (1984:45). If symbols are open to manipulation, then the degree to and the time at which this is done lie totally within the individual's own resolution. This fact presupposes a last feature of personal symbols.

Personal Symbols Require Option, Voluntariness or Choice

"Another feature of a personal symbol is option – choice or voluntariness involved in its use or manipulation" (1984:45). Cultural symbols can attain personal meaning when a person appropriates this symbol and gives it its own specific meaning that is based on deep motivation. In the context of South Asian ascetics, Obeyesekere remarks that there is absolutely no obligation or statutory rule that force ascetics to have matted hair. Their hair option is one of choice and is based on deep motivation (1984:45).

2.5 The Work of Culture

Obeyesekere's studies of ascetics in Sri Lanka, lead him to develop a distinguished and unconventional view of culture.

> Neither observables nor behavioral regularities are directly relevant – more important are the nonobservables and behavioral irregularities. Sharing a common culture does not

---

[16] Obeyesekere acknowledges that symbol and symptom both contain motive and meaning," but as indicated above "a symbol is under the rule of meaning" and "a symptom is under the domination of motive." "Domination of motive" means that a symptom "is fully dominated by the archaic motivations of childhood, rather than a surplus of meaning" (1990:12).

> imply that X and Y act in an identical or similar manner, but rather implies that they can express their dissimilar behavior in relation to shared values. Thus the existence of behavioral regularity may often indicate the existence of shared culture, but the absence of behavioral regularity or shared behavior does not entail its absence. Culture refers to collectively held ideas, and ideas are phenomena of the mind, not things on the ground (1984:112).

"Behavioral irregularities" come about through the creative work of people and have motivation at its base. "For irrespective of cultural differences or similarities," Obeyesekere asserts that, as human beings, we are all "culture creators, and symbol makers, though the content of our symbol systems may differ" (1984:9). There is reason or motive behind the irregular ways people behave. The reasons or motives are unresolved tensions due to personal experiences, often traumatic in nature, with significant others. The "work of culture" (1990:xix) is now to help people find solutions when caught in motivated irregular behavior through symbolic forms, that is, symbols that operate on the public and the personal level. In other words, the work done by culture is the engaging of the individual in the creation and recreation of symbolic forms that exist as cultural symbols. The formation and transformation of symbolic forms is not a detached intellectual task of the mind, but requires a person's life experience as a medium. Secondly, the work of culture is more than Freudian confinement to deep motivation, as this would mean a person is locked into regressing into archaic psychic conflicts (1990:xix).

How do religious symbols help people find solutions to their psychic conflicts? First, when a system of symbols moves in a regressive direction, it has defensive potential, protecting individual integrity. In a more serious manner, it prevents a person from experiencing inner breakdown. Second, personal symbols possess progressive potential, that is, they dissolve tension and inner conflict and eventually bringing healing.

2.5.1 Regression, Repression and "Defense Mechanism"

Personal symbols send taproots into unresolved tensions with significant others. These unresolved tensions create problems in the individual, "problems of guilt, alienation, betrayal, and despair" (1990:24), which lie buried in the unconscious as deep motivation. How to deal with guilt, alienation, betrayal, and despair, if these feelings are operating outside conscious awareness? The answer is regression. By regressing into the archaic origin of psychic conflict, Nuckolls writes,

> Unconscious conflict motivates behavior in ways that are inaccessible to consciousness due to the operation of defensive mechanisms, such as repression (Nuckolls 1996:18).

Does the unconscious exist and how does it operate? Nuckolls continues to say:

> The unconscious exists; its conflicts are motivating; and its mechanisms – repression, compromise formation, and transference – have consequences for what we say, think, and feel (1996:20).

Personal symbols allow a person to regress and to deal with repressed unconscious conflicts. In other words, repression occurs by displacement and projection, which act as mechanisms of defense. By acting out the symbols, various elements of these mechanisms of defense help a person to maintain inner order.

Personal Symbols Protect Integrity

Personal symbols help a person to come to terms with disruptive feelings because they protect personal integrity. Technically, this is known as "compromise formation." How does compromise formation work? According to Nuckolls,

> A compromise formation is a thought, feeling or action that represents an accommodation of some kind among multiple motives, such as the desire to maintain self-esteem, to obtain gratification, and to respond to moral imperatives (1996:18-19).

Personal Symbols Prevent Alienation

Psychic conflict leading to the breakdown of relationships with significant others, is the most painful of all emotions. It inevitably leads to estrangement (*Entfremdung*) from oneself, one's culture, and one's society (Obeyesekere 1984:104). Obeyesekere, summarizing Spiro (1965), provides two characteristics of estrangement:

(1) The individual's feelings, emotions, and affects are different in their quality and intensity from those of others in the society; the patient suffers from affective disorientation (1984:104).

(2) The individual's thoughts are private, incommunicable, or a fantasy; he suffers from cognitive disorientation (1984:104).

A person in such a condition cannot perform social roles and consequently becomes a stranger to himself, his culture, and his group. A communication breakdown has occurred. Personal symbols can alleviate alienation and estrangement – and consequently an inner breakdown – because they allow for the expression of personal conflicts in a publicly recognized idiom.

Personal Symbols Provide a Channel of Communication

When a person appropriates a cultural symbol to mold it into a personal symbol, he in fact employs a shared idiom. "The primary significance of a shared idiom is that the cognitive disorientation of the sufferer is ameliorated"

(Obeyesekere 1984:104). As a result, the patient has successfully re-entered reality, a cultural reality that is shared with others. Hence, the channel of communication is re-established and reinforced, as others may be able to share the "range of experience likely to be encoded by the symbolic idiom" (1984:104-105).

Personal Symbols are more than "Defense Mechanisms"

Obeyesekere, however, advances beyond the regressive potential of personal symbols and emphasizes the progressive character and potential of personal symbols. The progressive potential of personal symbols is the junction where he departs from Spiro. To only advocate the defense mechanism of personal symbols would eventually mean religion is the product of psychotics. But this is clearly not the case. Ascetics, as Obeyesekere describes them in Sri Lanka, or as individuals who have attained *Ngulu status* in Bembaland, are not psychotics. Persons of both categories would not describe themselves in that way, and neither would the public label them in this way.

Supposing we put regression on one pole of a continuum and progression at the opposite pole of the continuum, personal symbols can help a person to progress from the regressive pole to the progressive pole of the continuum. The more a person moves away from the motivation of the symbol, the more he is able to achieve healing from the inner turmoil that was involved in the initial symbol, because the symbol bestows meaning upon his life. Through symbolic remove, a personal symbol can move an individual progressively toward healing.

2.5.2 From Regression to Progression – Symbolic Remove

The work of culture is not just to help a person to regress into the past, into the realm of the unconscious and deep motivation, but also to move a person effectively and progressively away from psychological motivation toward public meaning. How can progressing toward public meaning be achieved? The process of transforming ideational representations (symbols, images) into culturally constituted symbolic forms through symbolic remove is the work of culture (Obeyesekere 1990:289). This movement from regression toward progression is dialectical and may be encoded in "numinous religious symbols" (1990:xviii, 51).

For a person to move from the regressive, symptomatic pole of the continuum to the progressive, symbolized pole of the continuum, there are at least three areas that determine a successful progression toward healing.

Performance vs. Leisure

What has been said so far about personal symbols might cause a problem to Western cultures in some respect. Deep motivation and its representation in symbolic idioms are not given the same liberty in every culture (or no liberty at all in some cultures). For example, the ascetics and their behavior that Obeyesekere describes in detail would most probably be labelled differently in Western societies. Can we realistically imagine an individual of a Western society behaving in a South Asian ascetic manner (like hanging on hooks) and still receiving a place in public culture? Would such a person not be diagnosed with psychosis and fantasies and be locked up in a special mental institution *away* from public culture? **Fantasy deals with symbols which lack the approval or acknowledgement of cultural meaning.** "Psychotic fantasy is a private, incommunicable set of images. ... Fantasy has no cultural meaning" (1984:102-103). What could be an explanation that similar behavior in one culture receives public "recognition," whereas in the other culture the same behavior receives public "denunciation"?

Obeyesekere suggests that recognition or denunciation is due to the social structure of a culture. Industrial societies do not allow for the public expression of cultural symbols in the personal life of individuals because the symbol system has been secularized (1984:165). Leaning on Marcuse (1955), Obeyesekere advances a view that Western societies, or modern industrial civilization, are governed by a specific reality principle, the "*performance principle* [italics in the original]" (1984:166).[17] This situation does not allow for the free expression of fantasy, but denigrates it to an infantile level (1984:166). "In a society where the performance principle does not operate," Obeyesekere asks, "is (there) greater freedom given to drive gratification and the expression of fantasy" (1984:166-167)? Obeyesekere answers this question by saying that

> In societies dominated by the performance principle, fantasy is uniquely associated with infantile and psychotic behavior. It seems obvious that a high premium on performance must necessarily devalue fantasy and curb its expression. By contrast, where other forms of the reality principle operate – as in traditional South Asian societies – there is a high value on leisure and a greater tolerance for fantasy. ... Furthermore, and this is most important, fantasy itself is further given indirect and symbolic representation in the various idioms (of personal symbols). In fact, fantasy itself may be rendered redundant, since it is often converted into subjective imagery or personal symbols (1984:167).

To sum up, personal symbols, which are heavily informed by religious ideas and concepts, prosper in an environment – or reality – (e.g. South Asian or

---

[17] The performance principle "places a high premium on domination of man and nature by man, a compulsive work ethic, and a low premium on leisure" (Obeyesekere 1984:166).

African cultures) where there is a high value on leisure, providing the freedom of expression of deep motivation in symbolization even to the extent of achieving healing

In contrast, in societies (e.g. Anglo Western cultures), which are governed by performance, personal religious symbols wither away as they are not publicly recognized idioms for the expression and communication of deep motivation.

Cultural Background

A second area of concern, says Obeyesekere, is the "cultural background of the person, (since this) is crucial in assessing the *potential* [italics in the original] for the "progressive" development of the symbol" (1990:20). Even in cultures permeated with religious pluralism such as Sri Lanka where Buddhist, Hindu and Muslim traditions abound, the specific social context of the individual either restrains or favors the progressive development of the symbol. Obeyesekere's case studies show individuals using multi-religious elements in their use of symbols. However, a constellation of Buddhist and Hindu elements poses far fewer problems than the constellation that appropriates Muslim and Hindu elements. The monotheistic tradition of Islam cannot entertain deities of Hindu origin or any other religion. This in turn constrains a Muslim from acting out his psychic conflicts in personal symbols in Hindu elements.

In contrast, in Sri Lanka, Buddhism has always integrated Hindu deities and beliefs, giving considerably more freedom of symbolic maneuver to individuals (1990:20). To utilize the potential of progression, a person is effectively constrained by his cultural background, mainly by the package of "his childhood religious enculturation" (1990:20). The more constraint is operative, the more manipulation of the symbol is limited. The less manipulation is possible, the less a person is able to move from the symptomatic pole away toward the symbolistic pole. Psychic conflicts acted out at the symptom level are usually under "repetition compulsion" (1990:10) in a ritual. In contrast, psychic conflicts that are overcome by the symbol system achieve healing, because the deep motivation that triggered the symbol in the first place is transformed into a spiritual experience (1990:8-13).

Self-Reflexivity

Lastly, Obeyesekere takes position against a view that he ascribes to most psychoanalytic anthropologists. This view proposes that personal symbols "may provide adjustment but not introspective self-awareness" (1990:21), or "curative insight" as George Devereux puts it (in Obeyesekere 1990:21). True insight, as advanced by this kind of psychoanalysis, "can occur only in the analytic session" (1990:21). Consequently, a patient would always need the help of an expert psychologist to interpret unconscious motivation.

Obeyesekere objects strongly to this view. With the support of Habermas (1971), he says a person struggling with unconscious motivation speaks a "privatized language" (in Obeyesekere 1990:21) which prohibits him from communicating his privatized thoughts in everyday language (1990:22). Personal symbols, however, enable a person to communicate privatized thoughts because,

> The symbol is both personal *and* (italics in the original) cultural, and insofar as this is the case it provides a basis for self-reflection (the personal dimension) as well as for communication with others (the cultural dimension) (Obeyesekere 1990:22).

Obeyesekere continues to say that,

> personal symbols ... are public symbols that permit the expression of the unconscious thoughts of the individual; but since they make sense to others, they also permit communication with others in the language of everyday discourse (1990:22-23).

In summary, the degree of self-reflexivity and self-awareness of one's existence influences the extent to which symbolic remove occurs. To limit healing of psychic conflicts to analytical sessions would seriously impair the potential of symbols. But, as established earlier, because cultural symbols are open to everyone, a culture rich with symbols "permits Everyman to reflect on the nature of experience, (which) is especially so for introspective individuals" (1990:23). Symbolization of psychic conflicts has "a double thrust of personal self-reflection and public communication" (1990:23).

2.6 "Objectification" and "Subjectification"

By "objectification," Obeyesekere means "the expression (projection and externalization) of private emotions in a public idiom" (1984:77). Or, in other words, intrapersonal conflicts experience culturally provided resolutions.

In regard to "subjectification," Obeyesekere says,

> Subjectification is the reverse of objectification: cultural ideas are used to justify the introduction of innovative acts and meanings. Subjective imagery is to subjectification what personal symbols are to objectification. The former help externalize (but to not objectify) internal psychic states; yet such subjective externalizations do not, and cannot, constitute a part of the publicly accepted culture (1984:123-124).

And elsewhere he defines subjectification as

> cultural ideas [that] are used to produce, and thereafter justify, innovative acts, meanings, or images that help express

the personal needs and fantasies of individuals. The vehicles that help canalize fantasies ... are *subjective images* [italics in the original] and meanings (1984:137).

Thus, intrapersonal conflicts are subjectified and resolved by applying new individually created symbols, which find acceptance with the social group. Both processes, subjectification and objectification, are illustrated in the graphs below (figure 4 and 5).

FIGURE 4: OBJECTIFICATION ILLUSTRATED

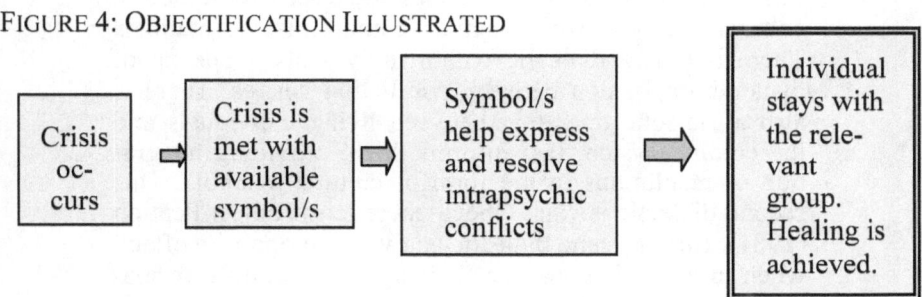

Objectification is the process by which personal meanings **and** deep motivations (personal trauma) are channeled into public culture via cultural symbols (1984:136).

FIGURE 5: SUBJECTIFICATION ILLUSTRATED

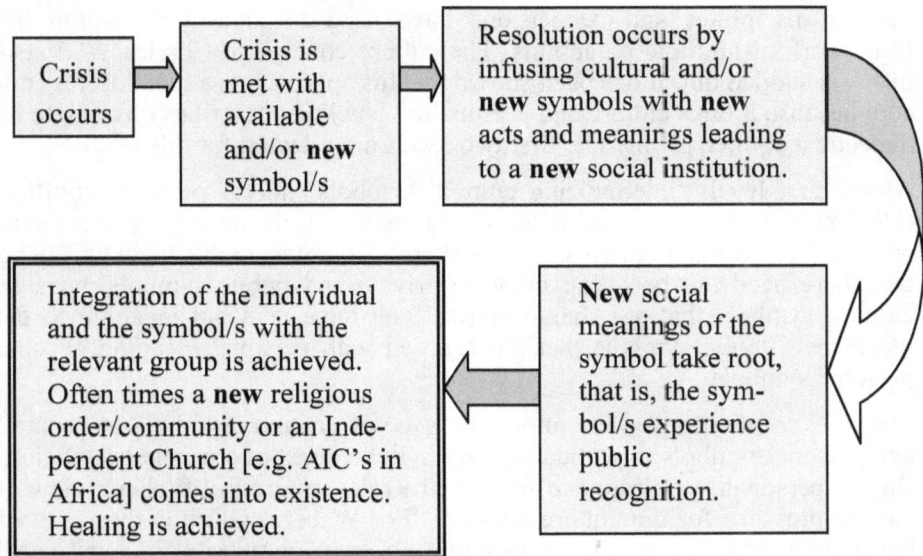

The graphs illustrate how both processes, objectification and subjectification, achieve the same result, though they affect an individual and society to varying degrees.

Nuckolls, summarizing Obeyesekere, says:

> "Culture is an emergent system, dependent on individual psychological conflicts for its motivation. The only way to represent this relationship analytically is by way of the concept of dialectic. Just how broadly can it be applied? Conflicting desires within the individual seek resolution in cultural symbols which act as compromise formations. There is thus a dialectic within individuals, made up of dynamic opposition between conflicting desires. There is also a dialectic operating between living individuals and the cultural system that informs them, providing integration or resolutions in the form of cultural symbols. This second dialectic is what Obeyesekere terms objectification (1981). But the same dialectic can work to opposite effect, when individuals construct their own compromise formations and these achieve social acceptance, becoming collectively shared symbols. Obeyesekere calls this subjectification and identifies it as one of the mechanisms through which new cultural symbols are created (1996:xxxiv).

3. A Concluding Reflection

I began this chapter by describing culture as a phenomenon that scholars of various disciplines and persuasions have tried to investigate within the framework of multiple paradigms. The culture concept of Charles W. Nuckolls was singled out. It has been shown that his approach is a most useful concept because it links culture and personality. Nuckolls describes this link to be dialectical at three levels. The first two levels are relevant for this study.

At the first level, "internalizing cultural symbols" solves personal conflicts (1996:xxxiv). At the second level, the internalizing of cultural symbols connects individuals and cultures. Obeyesekere elaborates on this view by saying that there need not be a gap between private and public symbols, because cultural symbols that are shared can as well have personal meaning to the individual. Public symbols that are charged with personal meaning become personal symbols.

Obeyesekere then raised the important issue of context. Symbols in general, and personal symbols in particular, require the context of a triangular relationship of personality, culture and society (the relevant group). Weber's view of culture provides for the culture context. "For Weber, culture is the result of the human tendency to impose meaning on every dimension of existence," (Obeyesekere 1984:1).

The unconscious and deep motivation represented in symbolic form with personal and public meaning, constitute a further context. A major argument is that life is more than conscious experience. There is also the dark side of human existence: those emotionally charged experiences that lie outside conscious awareness (Obeyesekere 1984:1).

Concerning the third context of society (the relevant group), it was proposed that early childhood socialization, especially relationships with significant others, cause problems of the oedipal type. First, it was noted that the Oedipus complex cannot be reduced to a triangular relationship of father, mother, and male child, but instead, is culture bound and highly complex. Second, it was argued that the Oedipus complex is not finally resolved in childhood, but continues into adulthood as the internalization of cultural symbols is also a continuous process.

Then, Obeyesekere's theory of personal symbols was introduced and the characteristics and operational context of these symbols were outlined. Next, attention was given to the work of culture. The work of culture was described as helping an individual suffering from intrapsychic conflict to move from the symptomatic pole (governed by motivation) toward the symbolic pole (governed by meaning). Personal symbols help a person to regress into repressed emotional experiences and thereby protect integrity, prevent estrangement, and provide a channel of communication.

Obeyesekere, however, introduces a second dimension and potential of personal symbols: symbolic remove. Personal symbols are more than defense mechanisms; a successful remove from deep motivation via the symbolic idiom may eventually achieve psychic healing! However, success is dependent on at least three factors: (1) the kind of reality a culture assumes (e.g. performance versus leisure); (2) the specific cultural background of the individual; and (3) the degree of self-reflection a person may be able to exercise.

Finally, two means of symbolic remove, objectification and subjectification, came under review. Some individuals are able to achieve healing from personal trauma by objectifying their inner state in an available cultural symbol. Others find that existing symbols are not flexible enough for manipulation to suit their needs and therefore they create their own symbols. Subjectification occurs "when individuals construct their own compromise formation and these achieve social acceptance, becoming collectively shared symbols" (Nuckolls 1996:xxxiv). This is the case when new institutions emerge. Grand examples of this kind are religious orders/communities or institutions like African Independent Churches (AIC's).

In chapter seven, I will show that Chewe objectified his psychic travails. There was no need for subjectification or the establishment of his own religious order, church or even institution, since he was able to integrate himself into an already existing social (Christian) body, albeit one that had just taken root in his area and in which he played a leading role.

Chapter 7
Identification and Interpretation of Personal Symbols in Reference to the Case Study

1. Introduction

As discussed in the previous chapter, Obeyesekere argues that personal symbols are cultural symbols operating on the levels of *personality* and *culture* at the same time. On the level of personality, an individual's life experience must be considered. Therefore, identification of personal symbols requires the study of a person's life. I will outline major events in Chewe's life so as to expose the prominent symbols he employed in order to achieve some degree of understanding of the person and Christian Chewe.

But first, let me briefly recount major events of Chewe's life before 1978.

1. Born in 1959. Lived in M-village with his many siblings and stepsiblings.
2. Handicapped by chronic poor health. Cannot perform work-duties as others. Brothers and sisters have to treat him with much consideration.
3. Impaired in his education by his physical condition.
4. Great love for his father, which the father reciprocates. Is treated with favor by both parents. Father shows his favor by teaching him various skills but, above all, training him in repairing guns.
5. Problems of relating to his immediate young brother. Special bonds to his youngest deaf-mute brother, and to two of his elder sisters.

Up to the year 1978, the reality of his sickly condition and the restrictions and tensions this condition produced, was probably greatly balanced by the emotional und material support he received from his father. This situation changed dramatically with his father's death in the same year. Before Chewe converted to Christianity in 1988, he underwent three traumatic experiences.

2. Three Traumatic Experiences: 1978-1988

In the late 1970s, his father owned a herd of cattle. This was the result of a deal his father had made exchanging a sewing machine for two head of cattle in the early 1970s. The cattle had multiplied greatly in the care of his business associate. Unfortunately, his father never collected them. Neither the original two, nor any other cattle were ever collected. They were left with the caretaker for reasons Chewe explained.

2.1 "I Never Got the Cattle!"

The deal – a sewing machine in exchange for two head of cattle – had been made prior to his father falling sick in 1974, probably some two years earlier. His father, though, had never been able to collect the two head of cattle. Apparently, his business associate was a very honest man. He looked after them faithfully and, above all, they multiplied greatly. Despite regular notification by the caretaker to come and collect all of them, Chewe's father failed to do so. Since his sons had no part in the deal, they were unable to assist their father. The last time, Chewe said, the business associate sent word to collect the animals was in 1979 (this was a year after Chewe's father's death!). The only person of the family who had ever seen the cattle was Chewe's brother-in-law. This is how it happened.

Chewe's brother-in-law, the husband of his sister Elisabeth, was working as a driver for a certain meat processing company in Kasama town. His job took him to places near and far. One day, on a buying trip, he accidentally came upon these cattle. The man from whom he wanted to buy told him that these cattle were not up for sale as he was not the owner. Instead, the owner was a certain Mr. P. of M-village near town. Struck by this unexpected encounter, the brother-in-law did a head-count. There were about eighty head of cattle his father-in-law actually owned!

Chewe's father was a very well-known and respected man in the nearby town and the areas beyond. This reputation might have been the reason why this man did not tamper with the livestock. When the brother-in-law came to see his father-in-law about the cattle, he suggested that his company could easily buy the cattle and the money realized from the sale, could be given to him. However, Mr. P. resisted and said the matter should wait. He first wanted to write a letter to his business associate telling him his son-in-law would buy the cattle on behalf of his company. Unfortunately, this never happened as Mr. P. did not recover from ill health and eventually died in 1978. The matter was not resolved. As proven, the business associate was a very honest person. Even a year after of Mr. P's death he was still sending messages asking for the collection of the animals. However, it could not happen. At that time, Chewe was the only son around. Others had left for the far cities. He had no experience in dealing with this kind of situation. "I was only 19 years old," Chewe said. With some regret, Chewe noted that his father never involved him in resolving this issue. With even greater regret he stated: **"I never got any cattle!"**

2.2 "I Never Got the Gun!"

Some time in 1973, a man brought a gun which was in need of repair to Chewe's father.

Chewe: My father trained me to work with guns and it was me who repaired this very gun. I used this gun when going hunting. One day, I inquired of my father the name of the owner of the weapon. Nevertheless, he could not locate the paper on which he had written his name. My father was a registered gun repairer who was entitled to repair guns and charge money for work done. That is why he had to write down the names of people. Because of his work with guns, my father was well known in our area. The man who brought the gun was from the Chambeshi Area. At least this is what he had claimed. So, we fixed a small piece of paper to the gun reading "Chambeshi K 40." [Comment: K 40 means 40 Zambian Kwacha, the official Currency of Zambia].

The arrangement was that after three months the client would come back and collect his gun. The man never came. In fact, he never returned even after the death of my father. We didn't know what had become of him. When father died, I was left in charge of the gun. I was still very young. At the family gathering after my father's death, the young brother of my father decided that the gun be taken to Kasama Police Station. So it was done. When police tried to trace the owner of the gun, they identified a possible candidate. The registration number of the gun had given a hint on the man. Police contacted the alleged gun owner. But the man said he had no knowledge of this gun. In fact, he never owned one! This man was from Mungwi. The police pursued the matter further but failed to solve it.

In December 1978, I moved to Lusaka to live with my immediate elder brother Abraham. While in Lusaka, my half-brother James tried to get the gun from the police. But he was told that he could not be given the item, since it was me who knew the particulars about the weapon. So, the matter stayed like that. James informed me on the status of the gun. But because I was in Lusaka, I quit on following up the matter any further. The police also called me – and from what I heard – were prepared to give me back the gun. By this time, 1979, I had returned from Lusaka and lived in Mungwi. But I was told I was too young to be a gun-holder. The police further told me I had to be 32 years of age or above to qualify as an eligible gun-holder. **I never got the gun!** When looking back until a few years ago, I felt very bad about it.

2.3 "I Never Got Education!"

Chewe attended Primary School and did what was known as Form I, and Form II (Grade 10 in the modern school curriculum) from the beginning of 1975 to the end of 1977. He failed the Grade 7 exams in 1974. When speaking about it, he said, "we were unlucky." (I think, however, this statement is far too soft. The emotional pain was far more extensive and deep).

By "we," Chewe was referring to the other fifty or so fellow pupils who also failed in their exams. "We just didn't know what happened," he said. In 1977, he had a similar experience. He attended Form II classes at Night School first at Chiba Night School and later at Kasenda Primary School. He passed all the subjects except for one: Mathematics. (When he spoke about this part of his educational life there was still a tone of great regret mixed into the recollection of these particular past events).

The death of Chewe's father in 1978 also meant the discontinuation of his educational aspirations because he was the sole provider of the needed finances. After his return from Lusaka in 1979, Chewe moved back to the village. In June 1980, the family moved to A-village where he built himself a house. He had no job apart from repairing bicycles and guns as the occasion arose. Farming was not to his liking and he spent all his money on beverage. He was drinking heavily. But in 1983, an old desire awoke in him again. He wanted to further his education. Fortunately, an opportunity opened up and he was able to pursue studies in mechanics at Lukasha Trade School from 1983 to 1985. After successfully completing the two years of mechanical training, he suffered another trauma. He was unable to sit for the exams for lack of funds! During the many discourses we had, his failed educational experiences surfaced time and again. The recurring message was: "**I never got education!**" His financial situation denied him the fulfillment of a deep desire.

2.4 Interim Interview

Robert: Did you harbor any ill feelings against your father because of the cattle issue?
Chewe: Not immediately. But during the 1980s, especially the late 1980's, I very much regretted that the "golden opportunity" of 1979 was gone.

[Comment: There was a common feeling among the siblings about their father: *balitulekeleshe*, that is, "he neglected us" they said. The neglect they felt was in connection to the letter their father did not write in order to go and collect the animals. But Chewe immediately qualified his statement stressing *he* had no "strong feeling of hate" against his father as he had always provided for him during his lifetime. He made this clear by saying that his father bequeathed him **all** the tools he had: two bicycles, a sewing machine, four air guns of which one was in disrepair. "So in one way, I was very comforted by these items"].

R: What did your brothers and sisters get/inherit?
C: My oldest brother (step-brother) got Father's personal gun.[1] All the rest was left to me (Chewe said this without hesitation). My sisters were given some ducks and chicken, but all my other brothers got nothing! Asked about

---

[1] Note the prominence of guns in Chewe's life. It was the first item to be named!

this, Chewe said: "My perspective is that he loved me more than the others. Father and I were always together and he would send me to town to do business for him. He taught me basics of carpentry and bricklaying, but most of all to repair guns."

When his father's death drew near, Chewe was singled out again.

Chewe: Father talked to my mother saying that I was going to take care of her. Father told her: *Nakushile Chewe akakusunga*, meaning "I leave Chewe to look after you." I was still young by then and even my mother wondered how I could possibly do this. During my bachelor time, I was the sole provider for my mother. My younger brothers did not care very much. My mother also liked and loved me very much.

2.5 The Years between 1978 and 1988

Let me now briefly sketch the years between 1978 and 1988.

1. No cattle. No gun. No education. But, he is the major stakeholder of his father's heritage. Relations to his elder and especially to his immediate young brother are strained. His favored status is even more stressed when told to take care of his mother. His mother also loves him very much.

2. Has to leave home. Stays with his immediate elder brother in Lusaka but only for a brief stint. Moves to his elder and beloved sister in Luangwa (near the border to Mozambique). But the brutal death of his sister's husband forces him to return to the village.

3. The family (his mother and his two younger brothers) have to shift from the home village to the village of his mother's new husband (the younger brother of his late father). Their marriage was a *ubupyani* union (marriage by succession; there were no children born to this marriage). Moves to Mungwi to stay with a relative for some time. No job. No education. Starts drinking.

4. Takes hold of the opportunity to study mechanics at Lukasha Trade School. Completes course, but can't sit for exams for lack of funds! Continues drinking. No regular work. No interest in farming. Spends his days loafing and drinking.

5. Gets married to Grace Mulenga in 1988. Is brought into contact with a newly established church in his area. Makes an initial commitment to God. Stops drinking. Within a short time, he is put in charge of the small church group.

3. Three Life Crises: 1991-2000

Deep motivations of the oedipal type motivate symbolization (cf. chapter six), or in other words, help "create" personal symbols. In order to cope with difficult life experiences, the engagement in a process of self-reflection must take place. This self-reflexion process is embedded into historical events (personal and socio-economic). The governing factor of this process is culturally mandated logic guided by the array of available cultural elements. To begin with, I shall explore the essential historical events making up the ground for symbolization.

The death of Chewe's father posed at least three major psychological challenges to him. More precisely, they deepened intrapsychic conflicts. It will be recalled that

1. his ancestor namesake Chewe Shimfwamba (cf. chapter five) who was, like himself, a *ntenda* person, was a praised and powerful hunter. A satisfying identification with the "hunter-image" was dealt a blow: "I never had a gun!" That is to say, he never was the *legal owner* of a *real* gun. He owned a set of air guns, and also made use, at times extensively, of guns which were brought to him for repair. But truly speaking, a *real* hunter needs his *own* weapon! Second choice or minor calibre weaponry hardly benefits a hunter's status and passion. Unfortunately, he never had (owned) a (real) gun.

2. his prospects of a future of wealth were dealt a blow: "I never had cattle!"

3. a promising career accessible only through education was dealt a blow: "I never got education! I did not have the money." The psychological impact the latter trauma posed to him was still evident in 1998. Chewe referred to the lost education episode as "my biggest disappointment in life."

I would guess that these three traumas were main contributors to his becoming a drunkard and remaining in this state until he was brought into contact with a Christian church.

3.1 Prelude: The *Ntenda* Symbol

A person who is stricken with chronic illness, who suffers from a chronic condition of poor health, is known as *uwantenda,* or *uwalwalilila* or *ntenda* (a sickly person). For this reason, *ntenda* is a negatively loaded symbol.

Ntenda fulfils two criteria of Obeyesekere's study of symbols. According to Obeyesekere's differentiation between psychogenetic symbols – "lack of unconscious meaning" (1984:46), no "ongoing operational significance" (1984:14) – and personal symbols – whose "primary significance and meaning lie in the personal life and experience of individuals" (1984:44), "locked into an emotional experience ..." (1984:21) – *ntenda* qualifies as a personal symbol. The symbol has "operational significance" because it carries meaning in the personal life of Chewe, and at the same time is "locked into an emotional experience."

A second criterion Obeyesekere establishes is that a personal symbol belongs to a larger set of symbols. The *ntenda* symbol meets this criterion since it is part of a larger set of cultural symbols (see Obeyesekere 1984:13): witchcraft (*Ubuloshi*), lack of harmony between a person and his *umupashi* ("*spirit double*") or unattainable *ubutuntulu* (wholeness), *ngulu* spirit possession (*ukulwilwa ngulu*), and leadership (*intungulushi*). The various symbols evolved at different times in Chewe's life. I will start off by concentrating on *ntenda* in reference to *ubuloshi* and *umupashi*, and in a second step, show how Chewe manipulated (another feature of personal religious symbols!) the symbol.

3.1.1 *Ntenda*: *Buloshi* (Witchcraft) Implied

Sickness is almost never attributed to natural/biological causes. Someone or "some force" is acting out harmful influence upon an individual. The issue of witchcraft becomes even more pressing when chronic sickness encroaches upon a person's life. Thus the public meaning of *ubuloshi* being responsible for Chewe's condition determined to a large extent the public behavior toward him: fear, aloofness, pressure to combat *ubuloshi* by employing the help of *Shing'anga* (Healer) to stage a counter-attack on *ubuloshi* activities, which obviously were being carried out against him.

3.1.2 *Ntenda*: *Butuntulu* (Wholeness) in Question

Another explanatory model intertwined with that of *ntenda* is the belief that a chronically sick person is maintaining poor harmony with his *umupashi* ("*spirit double*"). Such disharmony would show up during intervals of poor health as in the case of Chewe (headaches over prolonged times, stomach pains, and fever). However, it would not result into prolonged serious sicknesses. Such would be the case when there is real disharmony between *umupashi* and the human companion. Chronic ill health is more or less attributed to the human who neglects his *umupashi (alilekelesha umupashi wakwe)*. Positively expressed, a harmonious relationship with one's *umupashi* is reflected in good health (*Mutuntulu)*, or wholeness (*Butuntulu*). But Chewe was far from being whole.

3.1.3 *Ntenda*: Symbol Manipulated

Now, what happened in Chewe's case? The public meaning of *ntenda* triggers repulsive reactions by the social group due to witchcraft associations. Moreover, the symbol implied a lack of wholeness (*ubutuntulu*), of a lack of harmony with his *umupashi*.

Being *uwantenda* produced ambivalence in Chewe's life. On the one hand, he was physically handicapped which imposed severe restrictions upon his life. Also, the social group set him apart by sending him signals of fear, aloofness and pressure. On the other hand, the attention and favor, especially that which his father lavished on him, also set him apart. But this time the message was one of acceptance and love. These complex personal experiences of Chewe are crystallized in the public *ntenda* symbol. Chewe turned the *negative public connotations* of the *ntenda* symbol into attaining a *positive personal meaning*! How did Chewe achieve a positive personal meaning of a symbol with negative connotations?

He compensated his *ntenda* status by way of assigning a personal meaning to the *umupashi* symbol: His name connected him directly to his ancestor, the renowned and powerful hunter (*Kalunga*) Chewe Shimfwamba (his *"spirit double"*) who also was *uwantenda*! Then, Chewe's skill in repairing guns and his own preoccupation with hunting reinforced that tie.

But that is not enough. The *umupashi* symbol, in the personal application of *cikuni camfita,* "a charred log of firewood," also carried a strong message. One will remember that his mother told him: **Cikuni camfita icishisenda umbi kano uwacibelela, "a fire stick that is burnt black cannot be carried by someone else, except the one who is accustomed or acclimatized"** (to the situation).

The *umupashi/cikuni camfita* symbol not only helped him psychologically to cope with his *ntenda* status, but also extrapolated responsibility to his social environment to handle him appropriately. If his *ntenda* state would cause problems for others, then the social group itself was to blame for its failure to "acclimatize" and/or for their exhibited "ignorance" to relate properly to him and his situation! Psychologically, Chewe would decisively move out of the socially assigned "corner" with more freedom to manoeuver. And, in turn, he was able to find much needed relief from inner tension in his peculiar life situation.

Moreover, though Chewe was *uwalwalilila* or *uwantenda* (a chronically sick person) and the social group showed fear, aloofness and exercised pressure on him (because of witchcraft implications), they were also dependent on his skills. For Chewe had to offer services to them: He repaired guns, repaired bicycles; sewed and mended clothes, and successful hunting trips on his part supplied others with much cherished game meat.

3.2 1991: Role Resolution Crisis – A Change of Symbols

The year 1988 became a significant year to Chewe. As stated earlier, he came in contact with a Christian church. In fact, his affiliation with the church would dramatically influence his later life in many ways. But – what about his poor physical health? Would his new faith in God also solve his physical needs, immediately and once and for all?

His sickly state first caused a crisis in his Christian life in 1991. This crisis occurred three years *after* he became involved with the new church that had come into existence within his immediate geographical area and within his social context. Even after three years of demonstrating sincerity and commitment to God, he was still a sick person, *uwantenda*. It appears that the "1991-crisis" could have been caused by his assumed leadership-role in the church, that is, after he had acquired a new role in his life. Chewe made this clear at one time by saying, "in September 1988, he (Paul, his Christian mentor and leader of the church at that time) went away and I became his *immediate successor*." Chewe had a strong urge to lead the small group. This urge to lead, he perceived as having come from God. A later event on a Wednesday afternoon further shaped this leadership idea.

When the small group gathered for Bible study, there was no one to lead. He said, "I felt that some words were calling me to start preaching to my fellow members. So, I started from that day [and] since this day, I have been the leader and preacher in this congregation."[2]

3.2.1 The *Ngulu*-Spirit-Mediumship Episode

Despite his commitment to God and his seriousness in his faith, Chewe was afflicted with bouts of sicknesses. More precisely, he showed the initial symptoms – hiccups, stomach pains, shivering with cold (fever; cf. chapter four: *"ubulwele bwa ngulu"*) – of *ngulu* spirits.[3]

In order to establish a link between his physical condition, the prevalent symptoms, *ngulu* spirits and spirit mediumship, he had to engage a professional healer, an expert *Ngulu Shing'anga* to help him. Nevertheless, despite the engagement of this expert, he could not establish "possession" and therefore Chewe was never able to attain full *Ngulu* status. The question of why he fell back on *ngulu* spirit possession, an institutionalized symbol, after he had allied himself with the new church, and after he had made a personal commitment to God, begs for an answer. Also, why did this happen in 1991? The answers to these questions, I will try to give on his behalf. I can only guess what the motive might have been. However, from his personal life history and

---

[2] His "leadership-role" was very prominent in his recollections of his past life. Being a leader and leadership strongly features in my notes taken in June 1995 as well as in May 1998.

[3] He even named some symptoms which the list of most recurrent *ngulu* symptoms in men did not mention, namely, *umutwe*, headache; *mu cifuba*, coughing, breathing problems, *inuma ukufina*, heavy shoulder-blades; *ukupolomya*, diarrhoea; *ukuluka*, vomiting. The additional symptoms were more frequently found with women. It appears that there is considerable leeway in attributing symptoms to *ngulu* sickness symptoms. It shows that sickness symptoms are not automatically put into marked slots, but that there is individual agency determining what certain symptoms are supposed to mean and to what larger context they can be ascribed.

what I can discern from what he told me during the many informal sessions we had, I cautiously suggest the following.

When Chewe came into contact with the new church in his area in 1988, he had a personal experience with God. "Significant others" (Spiro & Spiro 1975:414-416), especially Paul who was his first mentor, helped him to establish a relationship with God. Chewe stopped drinking[4] never to be caught in this vicious circle again (drinking had been an escape from life's reality and a way to cope with the three traumatic experiences "no cattle", "no gun", and "no education"). His attachment to the new group and his inner commitment to God made him one who could be depended upon for the cause of the new church. When Paul, his most influential significant other, had moved out of the area, Chewe was on his own.

During the latter part of 1989, I got to know Chewe. We developed a relationship that lasted for more than a decade. Coming back to 1989, together with my Zambian colleague we had regular mid-week meetings in Chewe's home village until the end of 1990.[5] By then, Chewe and I had a firmly established relationship. I believe I too, had become a significant other to him. Then, both my colleague and I were transferred and left the area. Chewe was again cast on his own.

Considering his *ntenda* status and the restrictions this situation imposed on him, he experienced another inner conflict. How could he commit himself fully to the work of God, when he was physically incapacitated? He was not always available when he was needed. Also, he was restricted in his movements due to his physical inability to walk long distances or ride his bicycle. There was so much work to be done but he was just on his own. In addition, he was not able to satisfactorily fill the gap and fulfil his assumed leadership role. When we talked about this situation, Chewe mentioned on several occasions that he had expressed a strong desire for God to heal him, that God lift from him this physical impairment. I believe Chewe was focusing on a near-future intervention of God, as he believed his motive for acquiring good health was justified. Good health would profoundly improve his performance as a leader (*intungulushi*)! However, God did not grant this request in the manner expected.

---

[4] The Bible study group met at his house and on one of these days (a Wednesday afternoon), a text from the book of Zephaniah (chapter three) was read and discussed. The meeting left a deep impression on his heart. It was "like a voice of someone saying: "today you should become a Christian." ... I was troubled the whole night." When he woke up in the morning he announced to his wife: "From today on I have stopped drinking beer, I want to be a Christian." Recorded in May 1998. The impact the Zephaniah scripture had on him is confirmed in an interview taken by Rev. R. Frey in September 1998 (2000:14).

[5] I was transferred to the Copperbelt to take up other responsibilities in January 1991. My family and I returned to Kasama in January 1995 and have been here ever since.

Whether Chewe pursued healing by *ngulu* spirits because of "frustration" caused by God's "leniency" to intervene, or because he felt that God would work the "miracle" through *ngulu* possession procedures, remains in the dark. Also, it is difficult to say how much outside pressure from the family (those who did not follow Christian precepts the way he did) and inner drive on his side coaxed him into this decision-making process and caused him to finally commit himself to a personal appropriation of the *ngulu* symbol. Nevertheless, motivation of symbolization of his inner travail **must** have been at work.

However, the link between available cultural symbol and the appropriation to his personal life making it a personal religious symbol (*ngulu* possession and *Ngulu status*) could, however, not be accomplished. At least two questions surface:

- Was the failure to do so due to the supervisor's, the healer's incapability to "reveal the spirits?" (Cf. chapter five).

- Was the failure due to Chewe's inner restraint from fully subscribing to the power of the *ngulu* spirit, a restraint caused by unconcious fear of, or anxiety concerning, the performing of an act contrary to his Christian convictions?

3.2.2 Interpretation of the *Ngulu* Failure

At this point of interpreting the failed *ngulu* spirit-mediumship episode, it is necessary to fall back on Obeyesekere. He argues that symbols must be dealt with by looking at three interrelated problems: (1) origin and genesis of the symbol; (2) its personal meaning for the individual or the group; (3) and the social-cultural message it communicates to the group (1984:33).

Origin and Genesis of the Ngulu Symbol

Ngulu possession, like matted hair with South Asian ascetics, is a public symbol, "but it is *recreated* [italics in the original] each time by individuals ... on the anvil of their personal anguish" (Obeyesekere 1984:33). The symbol would cease to exist if individual did not create it each time. *Ngulu* spirit possession would have vanished from Bemba culture long ago, had individuals not recreated it time and again. The genesis or recreation of the symbol by individuals "is linked with painful emotional experience" (1984:33).

The reason why Chewe tried to "override" his *ntenda* status with *Ngulu* status happened against the background of painful and traumatic experiences with significant others. The fact that he opted (note this marker of personal symbols as discussed in chapter six) for, and tried to recreate (!), this symbol shows that his *ntenda* condition had caused him inner travail. My guess is that his lifelong *ntenda* state, the ambivalence and painful emotions that this condition brought about in his life were further compounded by his Christian beliefs. Why?

Personal Meaning of the Ngulu Symbol

To Chewe, *ngulu* spirit possession could have meant several things. First, *Ngulu* status, in a traditional context, could have ended or at least diminished the bothering *ntenda* condition. Second, his social status could have experienced a significant uplift (e.g. *Imfumu*, royal etiquette. Cf. chapter five) once *Ngulu* status was achieved (compensation for the lost wealth of the cattle?!). People would no longer signal fear, aloofness and pressure, but treat him with respect and deference. The medical advice and service he would be able to render to the community as confirmed *Ngulu*, would bestow upon him an aura of knowledge and expertise (compensation for the forlorn education?!). Third, *Ngulu* status would essentially mean seeking residence in the feared forest.[6] Medicinal plants, herbs and other amelioratives can only be obtained in the forest and this requires the assistance of the spirits. The forest is also the domain of the hunter. Collection of plants in a certain way relates to "hunting" (a boost to his hunter image and compensation for the lost gun?!).

But the Christian values Chewe had aligned himself with and which operated on a conscious level prevented him from fully subscribing to the "possession-experience."[7]

> Chewe made this clear by saying that while being engaged with *Shing'anga* Shimpala[8] he became conscious of his Christian stand and felt it to constitute an apparent contradiction. Also, the very night before he was to go back to Shimpala for yet another session, he "slept sound" and had no "dream"; two elements that significantly influenced the decision-making process to discontinue on the *ngulu* path. It has to be noted that "sound sleep" as well as "dreams," are two important elements in Bemba traditional culture.
>
> "Sound sleep" signals the close presence of *umupashi*, one's personal *"spirit double"*, and the harmonious relationship between the two. Dreams are either harbingers of ill-omen causing fear, or are the re-collection of experiences that one's *"spirit double"* has had during sleep, or they contain messages from other potential spirit beings

---

[6] Hinfelaar in his illustration of the "Traditional Concept of Transcendency" designates the forest (*mu mpanga*) to be the "domain of the spirits (*imipashi*)" as well as the "domain of the ancestors (*ifikolwe*)" (1994: 8). Security is only in the community of the living, *mu mushi* (in the village).

[7] One must remember that by 1991, he had already had three years of exposure to Christian teaching and three years of experience and active involvement in church affairs.

[8] *Shing'anga* Shimpala died several years ago.

such as *ngulu* to convey particular messages or expressing desire to establish a relationship with a living person. Both, "sound sleep" and the absence of a "dream" were ascribed to his prayer to God this very night. The former element "sound sleep" stands for harmony, whereas the latter element "dream" stands for peace (absence of fear). Hence, he had intellectual reason and emotional strength to sever relations with *Shing'anga* Shimpala.

The Socio-Cultural Message of the Ngulu Symbol

Symbols vary in their meaning or the message they convey. It is the institutional context that frames the message. In Zambia, the common interpretation of *ngulu* is demon possession. And demon possession occurs in the institutional context of the church. Thus, "*ngulu* possession-experience" constitutes too severe a contradiction to church practice and biblical teaching. The reason why the appropriation of a cultural symbol (*Ngulu* status) to become a personal symbol failed might be due to his inhibition to fully commit himself to the attainment of *Ngulu* status.

The inner blockade to merge *ngulu* possession and to retain his Christian identity was too strong to allow the two horizons to be fused in his person. The institutional context of the symbol did not allow such a situation. *Ngulu* possession functions on negotiation terms. The spirits approach, the person responds. The person complies; the spirits respond and take possession. Within this scenario, a person has an active part in influencing the outcome of the process. Although public culture allows the use of this idiom, church culture is primarily concerned with *delivering* people (through exorcism sessions) *from* this state. Furthermore, the church would rather not encourage its members to engage in *ngulu* spirit possession and eventually attain *Ngulu* status. There was no way he could have escaped from the ambivalence *ngulu* possession posed to him.

The "peaceful night" helped him resolve this conflict. Chewe forsook his desire to resolve his intrapsychic state by relinquishing *spirit mediumship* (the *ngulu* symbol) and substituting it satisfactorily with *spiritual leadership* (the *intungulushi* symbol) in the church. For one cannot act as spirit medium, that is, enjoy *Ngulu* status and with it *imfumu* royal etiquette, and simultaneously be a spiritual leader of a church, which regards leadership as servanthood! God had made him a leader (*intungulushi or kapyunga,* leader, preacher, teacher) right from the beginning of his Christian life. This was a fact that was underscored by Chewe being a founding member and having been coaxed into assuming responsibility in the church by the "untimely" transfer of his mentor and initiator Paul into his new role, as well as by the transfers of my colleague and myself a little later.

Intrapsychic conflicts have their root in early childhood experiences with significant others and operate in the unconscious as archaic or deep motivation. LeVine comments: "most frustration comes from in-group members" (Levine & Campbell 1972:119). Frustrations that cause intrapsychic conflicts, however, do not happen out of the blue in adult life; they are always built up from experiences of previous frustrations involving a vertical deepening process. To escape an inner breakdown, personal symbols can help a person move beyond motivation and achieve new spiritual meaning.

Obeyesekere says,

> A progressive movement of unconscious thought involves the transformation of the archaic motivations of childhood into symbols that look forward to resolution of conflict and beyond that into the nature of the sacred or numinous (1990:17).

The original pursuit of the sacred in the attempt of the spirit mediumship episode was not abandoned; it only *shifted* to spiritual leadership! Chewe was effectively put in touch with the "sacred" in his leadership role in the church. He was moving from a regressive state of conflict to the resolution of conflict (cf. chapter six).

One aspect of manipulation of personal symbols is substitutability. Obeyesekere states that, "Symbols in principle, if not always in practice, show infinite substitutability" (1990:58). Chewe substituted *spirit mediumship* with *spiritual leadership*. Effective resolution of conflict achieves healing! Chewe experienced (psychic, inner) healing. The tensions of inner conflicts were removed. He coped with his *ntenda* condition within the context of his *intungulushi* role. There was new meaning in his life and his life experience. Bate, quoting Edgar Jackson, says healing is a "release from meaninglessness" (in Bate 1993:158). As the *umupashi/cikuni camfita* symbol had helped him counter-balance the *ntenda* status, moving out of his "social corner" at an earlier stage in his life, in the same way, his *spiritual leadership* reinforced this movement in 1991. His new role once again met the needs of the relevant social group. Obeyesekere states:

> The role resolution of psychic conflicts lands the individual ipso facto into a community. But landing in a community does not always mean acceptance by it: this depends on the consonance of the role with the needs of the community (1984:161).

There was consonance between Chewe's role and the needs of the community. He earned himself a reputation as a trusted marriage counsellor. Also, many times Chewe would be called to officiate at funerals and burials regardless of the denominational affiliation of the deceased and the family of the deceased. Though he never underwent formal training as a pastor, people called and recognized him as one! The church and the community in which he lived addressed him as *bakapyunga besu*, meaning "our preacher, pastor." He became a widely known man in his area. But still, one outstanding question hovers in the air. Did the healing extend to a full restoration of his physical condition? This question shall be addressed in the following section.

3.3 1994: Endurance Crisis – Confirmation of Role Resolution

From February 1994 until November of the same year, Chewe was continuously sick. One day in February, while weeding the maize field, he suddenly fell sick. He was unable to engage in real work and could only accomplish small tasks. When walking, he was short of breath and was tied to the vicinity of his house. Painkiller tablets showed no effect and people suspected him of suffering from HIV/AIDS. Some people assumed he was close to death. A most awkward pattern of sickness manifestations crystallized. He said:

> *Naleumfwa ukulwala sana ukufuma pali cimo ukufika pa cibelushi, lelo lyonse ilyo caleba pa Sunday ulucelo nshaleishiba ifyo Lesa alempeela amaka, icakuti naleenda nafika ku church no kuyabomba imilimo yonse bwino bwino.*

> I felt very sick from Monday to Saturday. But whenever Sunday came round, I don't know how, in the morning God gave me strength and I could walk to church and was able to accomplish all work in good manner.

3.3.1 The Crisis

Chewe would be sick from Monday to Saturday and was confined to the house, but on Sunday morning, he always acquired unexplainable strength, enough to walk to Church and lead the church service and walk home again.[9] After Sunday's work was done, the Monday-to-Saturday-routine commenced again. People attributed this situation to witchcraft that had befallen his household. He was advised to either shift his residence or to clear the house from *ubuloshi,* "witchcraft." He refuted both suggestions.

Fellow church members also proposed to him that he be sensible. By being sensible, they meant to try to acquire the services of a qualified *Shing'anga* (Healer). But Chewe refused to do this also, and said, "If I am to die, I will die, but you must promise me to continue with the work in the church."

---

[9] A distance of about 2 km going and coming!

In November 1994, his health improved miraculously! Because of his strong opposition against witchcraft and beer drinking, people thought some elderly persons of other persuasions of faiths had used witchcraft against him. It was a difficult time to go through. One of his relatives ran away to Ndola to escape from the rising tensions in the village, never to be seen again.

3.3.2 Interpretation of the Crisis

When I asked Chewe how he looked back at this difficult time, he commented that the "1994 experience" had helped him to come to a better understanding of God. He now (six years later) depended totally on God. "I don't use any medicine, I just pray. I do this even with my children. The sickness has helped me to establish a closer relationship with God."

Chewe had progressively moved toward inner healing. He was no longer under pressure to seek relief of his *ntenda* status by *ngulu* ritual, for *ngulu* ritual is a culturally provided defense mechanism and is dominated by motive. Instead, he submerged the *ntenda* symbol into the *intungulushi* symbol. Symbolization is culturally innovative and is governed by meaning. Meaning entails a self-defined goal. *Intungulushi* was the goal. There was a new dimension; a new meaning of himself, his sickness, and relationship with God was operative. This movement from motive to meaning, from symptom to symbol, is the work of culture; it is what Obeyesekere calls symbolic remove. The "Sunday-power-experience" gave him inner strength and confirmed him as leader; an even closer identification with the *intungulushi* symbol and *role resolution* occurred! His miraculous recovery and the way he handled this months-long ordeal of psychic conflict and physical sickness met the needs of the group, this time more particularly the needs of church.

The young church needed an example of God's sustaining power. They needed a "strong" leader. Church group members were met at a point of need where it mattered most: *fear that witchcraft could emerge as victor over one's faith in God.* The "1994 crisis" triggered a movement among young men in particular, who suddenly showed a much more sincere interest in the Christian faith than in the years before.

Almost six years later, Chewe was confronted with a crisis due to sickness that proved to be of an existential magnitude greater than he had ever before experienced. His faith and stance were put to the ultimate test. He could not pray for some time because of "great fear" that had beset him while he was in M-Clinic for treatment. What had happened?

3.4 2000: Existential Crisis – Inner Breakdown and Recovery

Chewe's third crisis in 2000 was far more acute existentially than were the two previous crises. He lay on his deathbed. His life was ebbing away. In this crisis, witchcraft was the main focus: the alleged cause of the whole sickness episode and all its effects and the upsetting of the whole treatment and therapy of his sickness that this entailed.

This third crisis was informed by witchcraft, a *negatively biased cultural symbol*. This time the link between cultural symbol and personal appropriation was much more complete. That is, the identification was so complete that it almost cost his life. His family had given up on him. He had given up on himself. The only comment, in fact the only meaningful word he spoke to me while I was in the village collecting him on the morning of a Wednesday in April 2000, was: "witchcraft." He was so earnest about it that he was sure that he would die from it, never to return again to his home.

Right from the very beginning, when he fell sick in March 2000, he had himself pursued identification with the cultural symbol of witchcraft. During most of his sickness, he did not sway from this course. He himself had demolished the inner blockade to resist the merge between cultural symbol and his personal experience, although this had been effectively fuelled by "significant others", most notably family members. Only after he had literally come back to life in May 2000, did he sway from the witchcraft symbol and allied himself once again to God.

- What caused his inner breakdown after he had so successfully and strongly withstood witchcraft proposals in 1994?
- What caused Chewe to identify himself so strongly with witchcraft in 2000?

To shed some light on these questions, I will present a short rundown of the events during the period of March to July 2000.

3.4.1 The Ethnographer: The View from the Outside

The diary records of this time contain much more material than can possibly be incorporated into this account. The "choices" I make in the selection of data might result in squeezing events too much. Moreover, it is not only data that matters, but also emotions and feelings (on his side as well as on mine) that count during this time of Chewe's sickness, which, if not presented, might distort this part of history. However, a selection of data is required and I will present what is most relevant here.

Wednesday, 5 April: I find Chewe feeling sick at his home. He complains of stomach pains. The following day, he comes to town and gets examined by a medical doctor, Dr. Frank, at one of the clinics. Medicine is prescribed and he returns home.

Saturday, 8 April: His condition has not improved. Chewe is admitted into L-clinic just across the river of his home. He has dysentery.

Monday, 10 April: My wife and I visit him. He is still suffering from dysentery. No improvement.

Wednesday, 12 April: Slight improvement. Dysentery has stopped. He looks weak but better than on Monday.

Thursday, 13 April: Message from the clinic. Chewe has had a relapse: Dysentery and severe stomach pains.

Friday, 14 April: We visit again but find the room at the clinic vacated. Proceed to the village and find him at his young brother's house. Situation is desperate. Chewe's condition has not improved. In fact, he is in great pain. I give him two aspirin tablets, but realize I have misjudged the situation when he vomits a short time thereafter. I am helpless and don't know what to do. I spent some time with him, pray and take leave. I request to be informed of his condition the following morning as somebody is coming to town.

At home, I contact Dr. Frank and ask him if he would be able to see Chewe on Saturday. The doctor agrees.

Saturday, 15 April: I go and collect Chewe from the village and take him to the doctor. Chewe is in a poor state. *Diagnosis*: Could be amoebic dysentery. Only a laboratory test could tell for sure. The situation is complicated by numerous incisions (*inembo*) spread all over his abdomen. At this stage, we do not know if he has also been given herbal concoctions to drink. Chewe is instructed to report to L-Clinic on the following Monday. A letter to explain his situation to the clinical officer is written.

Wednesday, 19 April: No news from Chewe for the last four days. "No news is good news," I think. Totally wrong! At arrival in the village, we find many people gathered at the house. Chewe is outside and is kneeling on the ground chewing some slices of oranges. He looks bad. He tries to get up, sit down, get up, and groans because of the severity of the pain. He says the pain is now all over his body. One of the very few words he speaks to me is: witchcraft!

We are struck by the gathering of the people. It looks like the funeral gathering has already commenced as sometime in the evening or during the night the funeral fire has been lit. By then it had been concluded that he would die soon. He is almost considered dead. People are waiting to see him die and breathe his last at any moment.

I am greatly agitated and confront his wife on the incisions to which she admits that it was her sister-in-law who made them and that it was also her who objected that somebody was sent to the clinic for the containers for testing the stool samples as instructed by the letter from the doctor.

My wife and I take leave and tell them we will come back later. In town, Dr. Frank is found. Chewe needs an immediate transfer to M-clinic. We return to A-village and find the people have dispersed. Chewe has been moved inside the house and we find him lying on the ground. I explain that we want to take him into town and see a doctor. He and his wife agree. Also, his sister consents after explanations are given. But his sister also wants to join us. We try to dissuade her, explaining that this might not be possible right now.

On the way into town, we learn that his sister has been giving him some kind of medicine (herbal concoctions) for a number of days, even this very morning. We collect Dr. Frank and proceed to the clinic. Chewe is examined and the doctor discovers a lump at the right side of Chewe's abdomen. Things don't look bright. The doctor assumes a perforation of the big bowel has occurred or is imminent. Fortunately, perforation has not yet happened but cannot be ruled out completely. It could still happen.

The vital life signs signal a positive message, although questions still hang in the air. The tentative diagnosis reads amoebic dysentery. When Dr. Frank mentions the lump on the abdomen, the "coin drops" and I begin to understand the situation. The lump was the key reason behind Chewe's talking about witchcraft, the behavior of his relatives, particularly his sister, the funeral gathering, the apathy of the people and their reluctance to undertake anything.

The lump on the abdomen is the symptom of *icuulu*, a sickness attributed to *ubuloshi* (cf. chapter three). Only a few weeks prior to Chewe falling sick, we had talked about this sickness. Now I understood why the funeral gathering had started during the night. There was no hope of his recovery at all. His death was final! His life had already ended though he was still alive physically.

I connect Chewe's own statement of witchcraft – which he had denounced so strongly during the past years – first, to the conclusion the assembly had arrived at during the early morning hours of the day. All I heard was magic and witchcraft. Second, he must have been thinking of his father and his two sisters, who had, according to his own reiteration some weeks earlier, also suffered from *icuulu* and died from it. I can hardly imagine the physical and psychological turmoil he must have undergone: No sleep for days, unrelenting pain, being close to a perforation of the large bowel, diagnosis of his state and pressure from family members, funeral procedures in process, the apathy of people sitting around him, and the memory of his father's and sister's illness and death.

When I take leave of him in the clinic in the afternoon, he looks better, though the chances of sustaining a perforation of the large bowel are still 50 to 50. An emergency operation cannot be ruled out. The operation would complicate the situation even more. His life is still in danger. I tell him to cling to life and not to let go, as there is still hope. We pray together. I hope the words can penetrate and console him.

When I talked of hope to him and his wife, I felt they could not really internalize my words. They were much too preoccupied with their own thoughts and feelings. I realized that in the context of illness such as icuulu, one is not only fighting the actual disease, but also the thoughts in people's minds.

Good Friday, 21 April: I am off to Mungwi for the Good Friday Church Service. Dr. Frank is with us. At arrival, he immediately visits the patient in the clinic. I can't because time does not allow.

But my thoughts are always wandering off thinking of the condition of Chewe. There are moments of fear that things have deteriorated. At one point, I am so anxious that I turn round to Mr. J. M. and ask him if he has any information on Chewe. My question: "Is he [Chewe] still alive?" His answer is positive. But he also says that he is weak. Some time later Dr. Frank enters the room. His facial expression doesn't betray any sign of positive developments – at least this is how I interpret it. Again, I am in fear. I feel that I am not able to stand in front of people and talk to them on the day of Good Friday. But I can't escape responsibility and decide to indicate to the congregation that I am emotionally touched by the situation in one of the rooms in the clinic.

After church service, I approach Dr. Frank. Contrary to my feelings and expectation, he says there is hope and there are signs of improvement. He substantiates his statement by saying that a lab test has been done and he himself has also looked at the slide, and he can now confirm that Chewe is suffering from amoebic dysentery. The treatment was correct and has to be continued.

I go and see him and find him seated on the bed. The church has also joined in and we sing some songs. Chewe is not a nice sight to see. He has lost quite a bit of weight. Apart from that, he has terrible hiccups shaking him to and fro. After each hiccup, he also groans and shakes his head. He is in the utmost pain. His wife is very much shaken, too. She is crying and doesn't say much. Her hope and confidence have also gone. When leaving, I go to Chewe and try to give him hope, explaining that we now know what the problem is and that medicine is available. He needs to gather strength physically and psychologically.

Easter Sunday, 23 April: In the afternoon, Dr. Frank and myself visit Chewe. His condition has markedly improved. What a different man he is! There is a smile on his face. He has been eating, drinking and has even managed to walk a few steps. Easter was indeed a victory over death for us and for him in the most literal sense. His other family members do not yet know where he is. I have deliberately withheld information from them, as we would like to avoid an "invasion."

We had anxious moments over Easter. Chewe would not have survived the day (19 April), had he not been "kidnapped" and put into responsible hands. On Good Friday he didn't look good, though he had improved slightly. Chances of survival were still slim. Good Friday proved to be the turning point! On Saturday, we had news that the hiccups had stopped as well as the vomiting and the bloody dysentery. He was able to eat small quantities of light but highly nutritious food.

Friday, 28 April: Chewe was discharged today and has moved in with friends who live near the clinic.

Sunday, 30 April: We visit Chewe and his wife. They are cheerful but he complains of light stomach pains. While returning home, we meet a friend and learn that people had brought food (*nshima,* stiff maize porridge, the staple food in Zambia) to Chewe and he had eaten. No wonder he developed stomach pains! I am irritated and angry that Chewe hadn't told me.

Tuesday, 2 May: Chewe is once again admitted. His condition is deteriorating. The doctor sees him. Treatment is changed. The following days become even more difficult. Each time he takes his tablets, he vomits them shortly thereafter. Discharge of bloody stool follows. The doctor is not in over the weekend. We fear for his life. We can only pray.

Wednesday, 10 May. Another doctoral visit to the clinic. Chewe is in bed and visibly discouraged. No words of hope or positive comments come from his lips. Dr. Frank speaks to him and poses questions which he answers. An examination is carried out. A relapse into amoebic dysentery is diagnosed. *We are back to square one!* There are no intravenous trips left, only tablets. If he cannot keep them down, we have run out of options. We crush the tablets into powder and mix it with tea and sugar. Chewe drinks the mixture. We stay on and wait for half an hour. No vomiting. There is hope. A couple of days without vomiting and the diarrhoea will stop and with it, the pain will subside.

I also had a long talk with him, trying to cheer him up. I emphasize his part in this process. This is the only and right medicine, and it is going to help him if he cooperates. He should look forward to the next period of time when he has to take the mixture instead of saying it won't work. The psychological boost did him good. As we leave, he sits outside in the sun bidding us farewell with a bright smile.

3.4.2 The Patient: The View from the Inside

It is understood that the "inside view" is derived from the data I gathered and, at the same time, is conditioned by the abstractions I undertake. However, I will mainly present the patient's own accounts at selected intervals during the period from April to July 2000.

Thursday, 18 May: I am visiting Chewe. He has been discharged from the clinic and is staying with friends nearby. No more vomiting; no more bloody diarrhoea. He is in the mood to recount some of the experiences he has gone through during the last weeks.

About two weeks (maybe even only one) before he first saw the doctor (6 April, 2000) in the clinic in town, he was working in the fields. Behind his house, next to an anthill, he had a field of sweet potatoes. As he was working, he stepped onto a certain place and instantly felt a sharp pain starting from his toes on the right foot, moving right up to the head. He was forced to take a break for a short while before he could continue with his work. After some time the same thing happened again; the same sharp pain rattled through his body. Chewe emphatically emphasized that he had stepped onto the *very same spot* again experiencing the same pain in the same fashion. He was forced to quit his work and to go back home. Returning home, he could not walk properly. He was limping on his right leg!

Some time after this incident, the day after he had seen the doctor in town (6 April, 2000), he again experienced the same kind of pain. It happened while he was going to the field and suddenly felt bowel movements. He passed blood and the very same day he was taken to L-Clinic. He described the pain as "lightning" (*akalumba*). Then, Chewe gave an explanation (his explanation) of the term *akalumba* and, indirectly with it, his view of the incident.

There are three contexts in which *akalumba* takes precedence.

1. *akalumba* is the name proper for "thunder/lightning." During the rainy season thunder and lightning often go together and strike objects such as trees.

2. *akalumba* is also used in the context of *ubuloshi*. When a wizard (*muloshi*) wants to strike a person, he or she does so by giving the targeted person a dream in which he or she sees a gun.

   I don't know why he specifically mentions a gun, but, from his life history, it is clear that the gun is an important and recurring object/symbol.

   When the person awakes and vomits blood then this indicates that the wizard has done his work. He "shot" his victim while asleep.

3. *akalumba* is used in the context of *ubuloshi* in a second way. A wizard with evil intentions can demarcate a particular place/spot and charge it with "power to strike." The expression used is *ukuteya kalumba* (*ukuteya* means "to set a trap" (e.g. a hunting trap for animals at a particular place where a person can be stricken with the "power of lightning", that is, *ubuloshi,* witchcraft).

The days from 16 to 19 April 2000 were dark hours. He himself had given up all hope. Even the Church had. That is why only few people came to his house during those days.

One will remember that one of the few words, spoken with much emphasis, that Chewe gave me on the morning when we collected him was "witchcraft." The connection to witchcraft is tied to the earlier experience of striking pain at the anthill. The *nature and manifestation of the pain* (sudden, unexpected, and unexplainable), the *particular spot* (near the anthill), and *the bloody diarrhoea* (the proof of a successful kill!) carried all the features of a "cultural ideology", a *Buloshi* attack.

When I asked him if the people who used witchcraft were strangers, he denied this strongly. "They are known people and can even be relatives. They are members of the community," he said. Then he related this witchcraft episode to earlier episodes in his life, the year 1989 in particular.

In 1989, when he had just started out in his Christian life, he and Paul M. (a relative from his mother's side) were active in church work and frequently spoke out against witchcraft and beer drinking, two prevalent evils in his village. One day, Paul M. was walking through the village when he overheard a band of elderly persons mentioning his and Chewe's name. They said this new church (the

Baptists) should not be allowed to continue with their work: They lure the people away from the Catholic Church. Furthermore, their outspokenness against witchcraft and beer drinking had to be stopped. The best way to do this would be to eliminate either of the two. When Paul heard all this, he hurried back to his mother and told her all he had overheard. She advised him to share this with Chewe and also to take them to court. The very same evening, Paul went to see Chewe and told him about the discussion and resolution of the "council gathering." Chewe replied that, if it was in his private interest, he as well could take legal action against them. But because of his involvement in God's work, they can do whatever they like. "God knows," he added. Paul, however, saw the matter from a different angle. He packed his bags and made his way to the Copperbelt city of Ndola, never to come back again!

Most of the persons who were part of the group have died except for one woman. When I asked him if it was this woman who he thought still had an interest in trying to eliminate him, he would not commit himself to a positive answer to my question.

3.4.3 The Ethnographer: The View from the Outside, Continued

Friday, 26 May. I am visiting Chewe in Mungwi. I was greatly aggravated and confused after my last visit with him. The reason was that on the same day I had seen him in the morning (18 May), Rita my wife, too, had passed by to see him in the afternoon. When she came home, she told me Chewe had confided in her that he had stopped taking his medicine for a short while. Also, his elder brother had come to see him and he brought him Bemba "medicine" for his healing. He complied with his brother's proposition and, as a result, developed pain in his stomach. However, he resumed following the clinic medication routine after he was spoken to. What bothered me was: Why had he not confided in me?

Today [Friday], I confronted him. Not with aggression, but just to let him know my position and the way I felt. He apologized for the interruptions his actions had caused during the bad time of his illness. I accepted his apologies as I felt they were genuine. I also posed some questions to him.

Robert: Did you have dreams during the time of your sickness?
Chewe: Yes, I had two dreams. I had them when I was in the clinic during my second internship. Each time I dreamed about a snake that wanted to kill me. In both instances, however, a person appeared and killed the snake. I shared these dreams with my wife.

In the first dream, his late mother appeared and killed the snake. In the second dream, it was a male person, a nearby neighbour in his village, who saved him from the deadly danger.[10]

Robert: What did the people in the village diagnose your sickness to be?
C: Some said "lightning" and others said *icuulu*. The latter was the *more prominent* (italics mine) option. That is why my sister made the incisions (*inembo*) on my abdomen. This was done in order to "trap *icuulu*" (*ukuteya icuulu*) by rubbing medicine into the cuts to stop *icuulu* from further movements in the body.

R: Did you ever connect your sickness to the sickness of your father who also suffered from icuulu sickness? (Cf. chapter four: icuulu sickness!)
C: Yes, I did! In fact, on the day before you picked me up (19 April), I was almost convinced it was like that. The nature of the sickness pointed very much into this direction. Moreover, my eldest sister (our firstborn) and my third eldest sister both died of the same sickness. Both had *icuulu*. So I thought I was following suit and was also going to die like them! (One will remember that Chewe had been very close to the third born sister.

Sunday, 28 May. Today it was arranged to take him, his wife and child to the village. It would be the *first time* since I had collected him on a Wednesday morning in April after more than five weeks of absence. The church was unaware of our coming! At our arrival, the church service had already commenced. The first person to meet him was his eldest daughter Chewe. Then, his son Chiti came to greet him. Chewe gave a great smile to his son, paused for a short while, and entered the room, which was full of singing and dancing. The women uttered instantaneous ululations and people stared at him with gaping mouths. Many songs were sung. Various people commented on Chewe's presence. One comment was that at one time the church had received rumours of his death. Also, they were disturbed by my refusal to tell anybody of Chewe's whereabouts for a long time and my staying away from the village and the church all this time. Be it as it may, they were now able to see that it had served a purpose and said I did well (*bacitile bwino*).

During the commencement of the service, I sensed Chewe's emotional excitement. I sat next to him. At one time, he was searching the hymnbook for a song and his hands were shaking. He tried to be

---

[10] Private conversation with Grace Mulenga, the wife of the late Chewe, Kasama, October 21, 2000.

composed as he was invited to come in front and address the congregation. He spoke of his departure on the said Wednesday morning when he believed he would not return alive. He spoke of the time away in the clinic, his sickness, and the need to return to the clinic this very day. I was under the strong impression he *is* an accepted and established leader. Several times people referred to him as *Bakapyunga besu,* our preacher, our leader.

In the early parts of June, he was on his way to recovery. The bloody diarrhoea had stopped and the laboratory test confirmed that he was cured of amoebic dysentery.

3.4.4 Interpretation of the *Ubuloshi* Episode

I take it that witchcraft implication in our case – and maybe in general ways too – sees the target person as a passive recipient, a victim of outside attacks. The nature of the sickness *icuulu,* according to the traditional concept, declared it to be a witchcraft case. In addition, the strong family context of *icuulu* left little to no room for alternative explanations. His father and two sisters – two of whom had been his closest significant others in his family – had supposedly died from *icuulu*. The anguish and inner turmoil Chewe must have suffered can only be imagined.

In contrast to *ngulu* spirit possession, the witchcraft context lacks the interaction or negotiation with the outside agency of the person himself. He is, so to speak, a mere receptor. Active participation in establishing possession status severely counterfeits Christian teaching and precepts. However, to become a victim of agencies whose allegiance one has not sought causes less discrepancy with one's Christian identity than the former. In addition, *ngulu* possession affects a few select members of the community (who have chosen to be involved!), (cf. chapter six: personal symbols and choice), whereas witchcraft could virtually affect the life of every individual of the community.

The juxtaposition of Christian beliefs and "witchcraft attacks" appears to have been generating a low-level inhibition in Chewe. It resulted in an emotional experience of utmost fear and inner tremor. In contrast, the juxtaposition of Christian beliefs and "possession experience" generated a high-level inhibition or anxiety in him. It prevented both from merging into a personal experience.

The *icuulu* and *ubuloshi* symbol sent taproots into his psyche. The *ngulu* episode was an affair between him, the *ngulu* community, and benevolent spirits. The Situation was now different. Witchcraft surfaces when relationships are affected. It always involved people who are known, who are close, with whom one interacts, but never strangers. This time it involved him, the family/social group, and destructive spirit forces.

As pointed out earlier, LeVine notes that, "most frustration comes from in-group members" (LeVine & Campbell 1972:119). Theoretically, his extended family could have had a share in forming the *ubuloshi* symbol into an emotional and rational reality (Chewe himself had hinted that). To my reckoning, his immediate young brother and a nephew who had once held responsibilities in the church but was later relieved of his duties due to misconduct were rarely seen at Chewe's side during his sickness. Their attitude could not have escaped his notice. Both of them pressed hard to have him taken to *Shing'anga* for treatment against witchcraft. Both somehow "trailed in his shadow." Childhood experiences with his brother – which had been marked by conflicts (betrayal and corporal punishment), emotions and frustrations – and with a disgruntled nephew are not insignificant factors in relationships. Who knows what elements (of archaic or adult origin) lay dormant in his and in their subconscious and could only be expressed indirectly through the *ubuloshi* symbol?

Initially, Chewe was unable to substitute witchcraft for another symbol powerful enough to move him out of the muddy mire of despair. When it was time for his discharge from the clinic, Chewe had, however, managed to surmount his personal anguish. The effects of the treatment were showing and he was feeling rather well.

It took considerable efforts of explaining, arguing and convincing to demonstrate that the root cause of the lump on his abdomen was due to an infection and to confirm that, given the right treatment, it could be flushed out of his body. Only after a serious relapse of amoebic dysentery in the early parts of May was there support from his side. Up to then, he had not really had faith in the medicine he received in the clinic.

With the help of others, he had conquered his fear and recovered physically and psychologically. Was he on the road to victory?

3.5 The Terminal Point: Chewe's Death

Thursday, 8 June: I go to the clinic and collect Chewe and his family. We have made arrangements for X-ray pictures in the Hospital in town. Other implications like stomach ulcers cannot be ruled out. I take the Chewes to Chiba to stay with his brother. On the following days we see each other regularly, have meals together and share ideas.

There was new life in him. Chewe reflected on the events of the past two months and commented that he had been in great fear during his hospitalization. He had not been able to pray. But the prayers of brothers and sisters, the counsel of friends, and the support of many other individuals had helped him to overcome the hours of darkness. Their concern for him gave him new aspirations and hope. He resumed his prayers. The Chewe I knew came back to life. It was during this time that he began to speak of future plans. For example, he talked about shifting residence and building himself a new and bigger house on a small hill at the back of his garden. He became quite inquisitive about my garden and spoke of doing this and that in his own. And of course, he harbored plans for the church (church building, evangelism, women groups etc.).

Thursday, 15 June: The x-rays have been made. I am keeping them in the house because the doctor is presently out of town.

Monday, 19 June: I meet his young brother in town. Bad news. Chewe vomited several times on Sunday. I advise him to take him to the nearest clinic.

I feel disturbed and wonder what has happened since I saw him last. Has he diverted from his diet again? Has he drunk unboiled water? I don't know what to say or what to do.

Tuesday, 20 June: Dr. Frank examines the x-rays. He indicates a problem in the stomach, possibly an ulcer causing an obstruction that would account for the vomiting. Moreover, the likelihood of a malignant ulcer cannot be ruled out.

The following days are not good for Chewe. He loses weight, vomits, and complains of stomach pains. We visit him regularly. I am under the impression that his fighting spirit has subsided and also that he is quite passive about his situation.

3.5.1 Death and Burial

Saturday, 1 July: Chewe is very ill. I go and find him lying on the ground outside the house. We take him to the nearest clinic. His elder brother accompanies me. On the way, his brother comments on Chewe's condition. He says it is just like it was with their father who was also "trapped by African magic" (*ukuteya ubuloshi;* attention is drawn to the "family context" of *icuulu,* cf. chapter four). The clinic renders first aid but cannot really help. Chewe gets a transfer to the Hospital.[11]

The weekend is rather difficult. Chewe's condition is deteriorating rapidly. Late afternoon on Sunday, I go and see him.

Sunday, 2 July: Chewe speaks very little. I pray with him and leave. This is the last time I meet him alive. He dies at one o'clock a.m. on July 3, 2000. He died of a bleeding stomach ulcer. Burial is arranged for

---

[11] I cannot give a full account of the clinic episode. Suffice it to say, it was not something I would like to experience every day.

Tuesday, July 4.[12] Together with my Zambian colleague, I have the privilege of burying him. His family declines addressing (usually done through a spokesperson) the assembly at the graveyard.

3.5.2 Afterthoughts

Chewe had been on the road to recovery when he moved in with his brother. He was showing confidence and looking forward to the future. But during the time Chewe stayed with his elder brother, especially after the vomiting had resumed, I felt he became quite passive about his situation. Also, from the time he had come to stay with his elder brother, his immediate young brother had come to visit him almost every day. Why now and not earlier in his sickness? Why was Chewe so positive and keen about moving to his elder brother in the first place? Did his two brothers share similar feelings about him, maybe the younger of the two because of their childhood days? Did both of them feel this way toward Chewe because he was the sole beneficiary of their father's estate? These are just two of the possible options that come to mind.

My interpretation: Chewe had experienced a return to life in highly dramatic circumstances. A new beginning had been offered to him. He wanted to distance himself from patterns which had brought confusion and emotional pain in his life (e.g. witchcraft and *icuulu,* strained and difficult relationships). Part of this process was to seek restoration of relationship with the two brothers. But he could not possibly confront them "openly" (putting feelings and thoughts into words) about these past events. For one reason, Bemba culture does not support confrontation. How could he make sure their relationship would not be further jeopardized, especially after what he had been through the past months?

Bührmann, in her study with Xhosa people in South Africa, writes, "preliterate people *act out* what western people *talk out* (italics in the original)" (in Bate 1993:82). I belief Chewe was acting out penance toward the two of them by "placing himself voluntarily into their hands." In the symbolic act, Chewe externalized psychological guilt. One constituent of psychological guilt is primary guilt, says Obeyesekere.

Primary guilt

> relates to those deep unconscious primary process emotions that trigger guilt-such as ambivalence and hatred for parents and siblings, oedipal conflicts, castration fears, sexual guilt over incestuous feelings, sibling rivalries, and similar emotions recorded in the psychoanalytic literature (1984:78).

---

[12] The author paid for most of the funeral expenses.

Chewe could not put his feelings in words because feelings of guilt (e.g. ambivalence and "hatred" for his brothers and sibling rivalries in our case) are beyond the reach of language;[13] "they are rooted in unconscious experience" (Obeyesekere 1984:80). By moving towards them, he, in a way, 'surrendered to them.' He hoped he could develop new rapport with his brothers. To leave his brother's place a healthy and restored man, what better new beginning of life could there be? But when his condition deteriorated within a short time, he had to mentally fight his sickness, as well as its implied context and his guilt!

Although guilt cannot be expressed in language idioms, an individual must nevertheless "be able to handle guilt, especially if it is acute, by externalization" (Obeyesekere 1984:80). One way of replacing the language idiom is by different kinds of signs: symptoms, dreams, and visions (Obeyesekere 1984:80). Obeyesekere defines symptoms as

> ... a culturally organized diagnostic system of bodily signs that formulate or encode unconscious motivations and inner states (1984:80).

From a cultural and from a Christian standpoint, he could not leave this world with unresolved guilt in his heart (especially now that his death was approaching). Neither could he afford that a row with his brothers go public. This would have added shame on them and increased his guilt. By his passiveness, Chewe regressed to the symptomatic pole of the *ntenda* symbol acting out penance.

Some days before his physical condition became acute, a church choir had come to visit him at his brother's home. Immediately after the choir had settled down, Chewe fetched a Bible and turned to Psalm 116:12-14, reading the verses out loud:

> How can I repay the LORD
>   for all his goodness to me?
> I will lift up the cup of salvation
>   and call on the name of the LORD.
> I will fulfil my vows to the LORD
>   in the presence of all his people.[14]

I asked him if he had also made a vow to the Lord, and if he intended to fulfil it. "There is one," he said; "To let others know of God's goodness."

---

[13] "Most languages have *not* [italics in the original] developed an idiom for describing guilt-ridden inner states" (Obeyesekere 1984:80).

[14] Actually, the whole Psalm is of interest. The Psalm covers much of Chewe's situation. See Appendix 1.

The unresolved conflicts with his brothers bothered him. Most probably there were feelings of guilt, a feeling of "owing them" restitution. Part of his "repayment" was to do penance for past events. The "repayment" was a vow, which he first tried to fulfil in the symbolic act of moving in with his elder brother, and later, as his body rapidly deteriorated, by bodily signs. A second element of fulfilling the vow was the "presence of people" (the choir, my wife and myself), who formed an audience as well as bearing witness to his penance. The (felt) relief of guilt, the release from its grip, is most appropriately indicated by a proclamation of "God's goodness."

4. A Concluding Reflection: Objectification – Yes but Subjectification – No

Major events of Chewe's life have been presented in this chapter. Three traumatic experiences after his father's death were described in detail. An interpretation of these events has been supplied. In a subsequent section, three life crises have come under review. The special characteristics of these crisis periods resulted from Chewe's conversion to Christ with an initial commitment to Him in 1988. His *ntenda* state triggered conflicting private emotions.

In Obeyesekere's theory on personal symbols, two sets of conflict resolution were listed. One set was objectification, and the other was subjectification. Both processes achieve the same result, but their mode of operation differs.

Objectification relays private emotions (often times of conflicting nature) to the public. This happens via cultural symbols, which are endowed with personal meaning. Initially Chewe used the *umupashi/cikuni camfita* cultural symbol, and, through personal appropriation, manipulated its meaning. Later he tried to employ an alternative cultural symbol (*ngulu spirit mediumship*), which failed because the institutional context of the symbol (the church) did not allow for its expression. I am quite positive that Chewe would have been able to achieve *Ngulu* status, had it not been for his Christian call. Instead, he *substituted* spirit mediumship with spiritual leadership. The substituted symbol helped him to express and resolve intrapsychic conflicts. There was no need for subjectification, or the establishment of his own religious order, church, or even institution, since he was able to integrate himself into an already existing social (Christian) body.

Burlington (2004), in his superb work on Emilio Mulolani of Bemba ethnicity who founded an African Initiated Church (AIC), shows how Emilio also canalized personal trauma in publicly available symbols. Emilio not only achieved objectification, the resolution of his personal trauma and maintaining integration with the relevant social group, but progressed beyond it, objectifying his inner conflicts by founding a new church "that accepted a unique set of meanings and developed its own institutionalized ways of conducting interpersonal relationships in terms of those meanings" (2004:260).

The resolution of conflict occurs in appropriating personal symbols, which work through the process of symbolic remove. One condition for the success of personal symbols is self-reflexion (cf. chapter six).

Chewe had great powers of self-reflexion, powers so necessary for healing of inner conflicts. He dove deeply into his cultural heritage to deal with the vices and mysteries of his life. Emotion and custom were linked in select cultural symbols endowed with personal meaning. Also, Chewe was literate. To some extent, the involvement and responsibility in the church were compensation for his "lost education," which he saw as an opportunity that had been denied him in life. He kept the church records meticulously; he wrote down the early history of the church, took care of most of the church's correspondence, and, apart from that, wrote autobiographical accounts.

The process of symbolic remove, the success of personal symbols, is interlinked with the resolution of role, the social role an individual has to perform. Chewe's role resolution in the *intungulushi* symbol enabled him to perform a meaningful social role.

His sickness in 2000, which lasted for four month and ended in his death in July, first caused an inner breakdown. The reason for his psychological and emotional breakdown must be attributed to the nature (*icuulu*) and the context (family and witchcraft) of the sickness. The recovery from amoebic dysentery as a result of the medical diagnosis of his lump (*icuulu*) on the abdomen was achieved through medication as well as, and equally important, through the dedication of individuals attending to his psychological and emotional needs.

The interrelatedness of psyche and body, health and society was shown insofar as the issue of guilt was a concern to Chewe after his discharge from the clinic. He acted out his guilt in the symbolic act of moving in with his elder brother. When his physical condition deteriorated, he became passive and withdrew. He regressed to symptom, acting out penance and thus fulfilled his vow to the Lord.

Chewe died from a bleeding stomach ulcer. Medical practice suggests that, for example in Zimbabwe (and Zambia should not be much different), stomach ulcers in people are often related to social stress. In contrast, people in many instances in Europe develop ulcers because of high-level performance stress.[15] Stereotype food and low levels of nutritious diets contributed to his stomach problem. But Chewe's ulcer(s) were also, probably to a major extent, a result of years of long-standing social stress.

The common notion that non-literate cultures or societies with a high level of group conformity must necessarily be viewed in terms of "group processes

---

[15] Private conversation with Dr. F. LeBacq, Kasama, May 5, 2000. Dr. LeBacq worked for many years as a medical doctor in Government Institutions in Zimbabwe as well as in Zambia.

rather than with individual motivation" (Obeyesekere 1984:1) is inadequate because, in review of this chapter, it becomes clear that man is not collective but individual!

Below, major themes of this chapter are illustrated in a graph with explanations provided where necessary.

Chapter 7: Identification and Interpretation of Personal Symbols

FIGURE 6: INTERACTION OF PERSONALITY, CULTURE AND SOCIETY

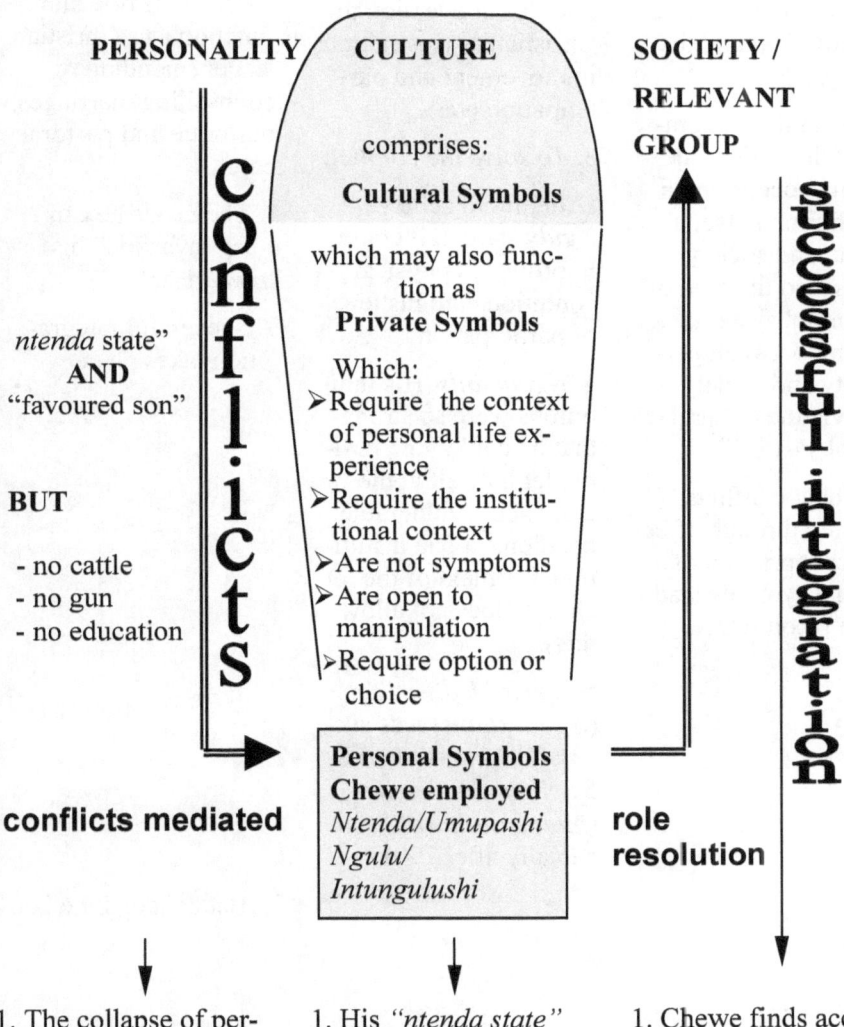

conflicts mediated	**Personal Symbols Chewe employed** *Ntenda/Umupashi Ngulu/ Intungulushi*	role resolution

1. The collapse of personality through psychic conflicts can be averted through personal symbols.

1. His *"ntenda state"* (the "exceptional other") was made bearable by his manipulation of the *umupashi/ cikuni camfita* symbol (extrapolating responsibility to the group).

1. Chewe finds acceptance in the community because there is consonance between his "role" and with the needs of the community. First in his role as a skilled handyman (repairing guns and bicycles, sewing

2. But personal symbols may not be sufficient to create a bridge between the individual and the group.

3. "Successful integration of the patient ideally must occur on all three fronts: personality, culture, and society. This is also the goal of the symbol systems ... The link between personality and society is often via the cultural symbol system."[16]

4. Psychic conflicts mediated through effective appropriation of personal symbols leads to role resolution.

2. His *ntenda* condition was still a conflict issue after his conversion to Christianity (restrictions in movement and participation etc.).

3. *To solve the conflict*:

(Attempt to achieve *Ngulu* status): it could improve his physical condition, and his level of participation.

4. *Ngulu fails*. His inhibitions were so strong that he could not possibly let himself come into such a vulnerable position.[17] (The institutional context of the church does not allow this).

5. *Spirit Mediumship* (*Ngulu status*) was successfully substituted by *Spiritual Leadership* (*intungulushi role*) especially after 1991.

clothes, doing bricklaying work, hunting). Later in his role and function as a Christian leader (mending & counselling marriages, pastorate and pastoral care).

2. The needs he can meet "override" his "*ntenda* status."

3. Successful integration takes place.

© R. Badenberg June 2001

---

[16] Obeyesekere 1984:160.
[17] Compare Obeyesekere 1984:162.

PART III:
THREE "C'S" – COMMUNICATION, CONVERSION, COUNSELLING – THE CASE STUDY APPLIED: A MISSIOLOGICAL PERSPECTIVE

Part Three of this thesis establishes the necessary link to missiology. When Nuckolls, in his introductory paragraph of *The Cultural Dialectics of Knowledge and Desire* (1996), set out to introduce his concept of culture, he suggested that this would manoeuver him into stormy weather in the terrain of anthropology. His attempt to define the term culture, which, it is emphasized, is the most difficult of all (1996:xxiii), would steer him there. In the same way, an attempt to step over from cognitive anthropology via social hermeneutics to missiology is not far from Nuckolls' predicament in anthropology. One could easily get into trouble. This is true for at least two reasons.

First, one could be charged with the fault of "selling off" theology via missiology to the humanities. Second, one could be in for an assault from the humanities camp with a charge of "abusing" their merits for non-genre purposes. I am not inclined to enter into a discussion to promote one at the expense of the other. It would be mere fallacy. There has been enough "damage" done by keeping theology/missiology, anthropology, and the social sciences apart from one another. Speaking of theology and anthropology in particular, Tippet describes their relationship as having "avoided each other like plagues" (1987:xii).[1] His words are loud and clear. There is, however, good evidence that noticeable progress has been achieved. Voices like Tippet's have provoked much thought and reorientation inside and outside academia.[2] I there-

---

[1] Speaking on the same issue, Rommen says, "Das Verhältnis zwischen christlicher Mission und Anthropologie ist immer problematisch gewesen." (The relationship between Christian mission and anthropology has always been a problematic one) (1994:37). Kraft writes: "For many Christians, the term *anthropology* [italics in the original] is either an unknown term or one that they associate with those who attack Christianity. It is often seen by them as a discipline that advocates evolution and ethical relativism and is often regarded as anti-Christian" (1996:2).

[2] Rommen observes that among missionaries a positive reorientation took place. Many missionaries saw the need to do courses in cultural anthropology. People like Eugene Nida, William Smalley in the 1950s, and Tippet and Kraft in the 1970s and later, as well as Lingenfelter and Hiebert were some of the evangelical scholars who introduced anthropology into the practical approaches of the Christian mission. In the words of Rommen: "Evangelikale haben also ihre zurückhaltende Einstellung den Sozialwissenschaften gegenüber weitgehend überwunden, doch ohne dabei ihre Überzeugung von der Notwendigkeit der Bekehrung preiszugeben" (Evangelicals have in general overcome their resentments toward the social sciences, but have firmly held on to their conviction of the necessity of conversion) (1994:38).

fore venture to provide such evidence. There is indeed no reason why that once profound indifference toward each other should be further encouraged, particularly when apparently all the sciences (theology in most certain terms), as Bock demonstrates, are seeking an answer to the question: "What does it mean to be human?" (Bock 1979:17).

This study is primarily concerned with this question as well. It is particularistic in answering it by empirical investigation of one person's life. Because human life and human existence is at the heart of this study's, Missiology, by virtue, is of necessity an integral part of this thesis. Why by virtue? If a definition of missiology were to be forged, Tippet's attempt would be the most appropriate one, I think. He says, "Missiology is the '*study of individuals* [italics mine] being brought to God in history'" (1987:xiii).[3] This definition is excellent on several counts.

First, to "study individuals" simply requires tools, theoretical frameworks to gain insights and results. There is no "one-multipurpose-universal-tool" to do the job, rather a toolbox of various and distinguished tools is needed to accomplish good work. That is why tools and insights of other disciplines have been incorporated into this thesis. Second, to "study individuals" requires a dimension beyond pure academic research, or the expansion of knowledge however valuable such enterprise might be. The dimension of God as creator and sustainer of this world, his love for and interest in individuals, is the basis of missiological concern because it ontologically addresses the question of what it means to be human. And third, the "study of individuals" occurs "in history." History refers to time and space, or, put differently, to context. Individuals live and experience their lives in time and space, individual time (life history) and individual space (society of a particular area with their cultural heritage). Just as context was fundamental when, for example, dealing with categorizing sicknesses in Bemba thought or studying personal symbols, the individual, societal and cultural context is fundamental to mission and missiology in order to bring individuals to God.

It should be clear now that Missiology belongs to an "interdisciplinary realm" which "draws from all the social and human sciences, and if the interaction is genuine something methodologically new will be born and missiology will

---

[3] Tippet's more academic definition of Missiology reads as follows: "Missiology is defined as the academic discipline or science which researches, records and applies data relating to the biblical origin, the history (including the use of documentary materials), the anthropological principles and techniques and the theological base of the Christian mission. The theory, methodology and data bank are particularly directed towards: 1. the process by which the Christian message is communicated, 2. the encounters brought about by its proclamation to non-Christians, 3. the planting of the Church and organization of congregations, the incorporation of converts into those congregations, and the growth and relevance of their structures and fellowship, internally to maturity, externally in outreach as the body of Christ in local situations and beyond, in a variety of cultural patterns" (1987:xiii).

expand" (Tippet 1987:xiii, xv). Consequently, Missiology is not an armchair science developed by armchair scholars and taught as a closed-circuit system in faculties and classrooms. Missiology "must be open-ended," as Tippet fervently appeals (1987:xvi). Again, he issues a challenge when he says that, "missiological theory has to come from the field, not from the West" (1987:xvii).

The following three chapters participate in missiological theory as it engages in three key areas of this discipline. Three missiological "Cs," Communication, Conversion and Counselling, are each reviewed in separate chapters.

Chapter eight addresses the question whether cybernetic communication models are adequately sufficient for communicating the Christian message. *Missio Dei, adoratio Dei,* and *imago Dei* make up the main corpus. Each topic will be discussed with a view toward possible missiological concerns that arise from the assumptions made.

In chapter nine, conversion is discussed with reference to the attention it is given by different disciplines. Missiological and psychological models are introduced and applied to the case study. Similarly, select features of changes Christian conversion entails are presented and demonstrated in Chewe's life.

Finally, issues pertaining to counselling will be spelt out in chapter ten. Next to a call for theological ethics as the base for Christian counselling, cross-cultural implications and complications are addressed. A theory on understanding people cross-culturally is discussed, leaning on Zeno Vendler, and inferences to the case study will be made. In a concluding section it will be shown that, in the case of Chewe, counselling had not reached its terminal point with his death. Instead, his "file" still concerns other people.

Chapter 8
A First Missiological "C": Communication

1. Introduction

Chewe's life was all about communication. The symbols he employed were a special way of communication because he endowed them with personal meaning. Personal symbols provided for conflict resolution, and at the same time, operated as means of communicating himself to others. However, had he not been able to rationalize his situation and to move out of communicating only to himself (failing to remove his inner travails by the employment of symbols), his inner conflicts might have driven him into fantasy or into committing suicide. This was not the case. The deployment of some cultural symbols, which attained personal meaning, not only brought him healing, but also provided an avenue for him to reach out to others. His personal symbols enacted a "symbolic remove" progressing away from intrapsychic conflict to resolution of conflict in the attainment of a new, meaningful social role. This move away from regression into the past and toward progression into the future brought him inner healing. Through personal symbols, Chewe was engaged in a horizontal communication process with others.

This chapter, however, moves beyond his self-communication and the horizontal communication process with the social group made up of his family, the village community, and the church. There was a third dimension, on a vertical axis, where communication took place: the personal encounter and communication Chewe had with God.

2. The Neglected Dimension in Communication Theories

Markus Piennisch draws attention to the fact that a multitude of communication theories – including theologically orientated models – only concern themselves with the cybernetic[1] use of communication (the theory of information) without including God's transcendental reality as the basis of communication (1995:19). He argues that cybernetic instrumentalized communication fails to deliver the ultimate reason of communication. This ultimate reason cannot adequately be addressed if one is only concerned with communication *between* (1995:21), that is, between inner-cultural as well as inter-cultural communication participants. Hendrik Kraemer, summarized by Piennisch, de-

---

[1] Cybernetics concerns itself with communication and control in machines, animals and man. A cybernetic communication model consists of the factors SENDER ==> MESSAGE (via canal) ==> RECEIVER (Piennisch 1995:16, 19).

scribed communication *between* as the basic fact of human existence.[2] Piennisch then points out that Kraemer emphasized that communication *between* is locked into the ultimate reason of communication, that is, communication *of.* By communication *of,* Kraemer means communication of God's revelation of himself to man (1995:21). The shared goal of communication *between* and communication *of* is the restoration of communication in all dimensions, both the divine-human axis as well as the immanent-human axis (1995:21).

How can the restoration of communication on both axes be realized? Lewis and Demarest point out that there is need to recognize that

> communication is inherent in the triune God eternally. Transcending the limits of space and time in the Godhead are personal relationships involving content-full communication (in Piennisch 1995:55).

That is to say that all communication has its roots in God's being. Second, the "content-full communication" within the Trinitarian being of God is evident in His creativity, manifested in the abundant diversity of creation (Piennisch 1995:88).

Third, inner-trinitarian communication is based on basic structures that determine God's gracious condescension to man (Piennisch 1995:88).[3] For Pöhlmann (1980), God's gracious condescension is the cardinal point in the history of creation and humankind. How else could we know anything about God, His character, or His intentions? Pöhlmann writes:

> Der christliche Gott ist nicht der Gott der *Transzendenz*, sondern der Gott der *Kondeszendenz* (italics in the original) (1980:124). (The Christian God is not the God of *Transcendence,* but the God of *Condescension*).

Therefore, communication is a "divinely created gift" based on the matrix of inner-trinitarian communication, "which is characterized by certain basic properties" (Piennisch 1995:212). These basic properties or structures are

---

[2] "Kommunikation "zwischen" bezieht sich auf die Grundtatsache menschlicher Existenz" (Piennisch 1995:21). Summary of Hendrik Kraemer 1958:6-7.

[3] "Die Kondeszendenz überwindet den Gegensatz zwischen Gottes transzendentem Wesen und immanenter geschöpflicher Wirklichkeit, so daß echte Kommunikation zwischen Gott und Mensch möglich ist" (God's gracious condescension overcomes the antithesis of His Transcendence and His Immanence that is manifest in the reality of creation, so that real communication between God and man is possible). Piennisch summarizing Herman von Bezzel in Joachim Ritter und Karlfried Gründer 1976 (IV): 942-946 (in 1995:10).

revealed in God's gracious condescension to man. What are the "basic structures" that unfold in God's gracious condescension?[4]

2.1 Five Constant Basic Structures of God's Communication

When Kraemer spoke of communication *of*, he did so in a general description of God revealing himself to man. Piennisch is not content with the general, but moves on to break communication *of* down into five specifics. Piennisch writes:

> *The eternal and immutable God stands in a mutual relationship of communication with man. Although this relationship demonstrates varying manifestations of God's gracious condescension, it is based upon constant basic structures of communication. These are love, spirit, word, deed and life* (1995:212).

The immanent Trinity of God is both the ultimate source as well as the enabling faculty of communication (Piennisch 1995:47). In a further abstraction of the inner-trinitarian communication, it can be said that the ultimate reason for communication is to govern the relationship between God and man as well as the relationship between man and his fellow-man expressed in the basic structures of love, spirit, word, deed and life. What is the context in which these five specifics determine the relationship between God and man and, in a second step, the relationship between man and man?

First, these five basic structures manifest in God's gracious condescension within the specific framework of a "salvation-historical longitudinal section" (Piennisch 1995:213). Without the context of space and time, history and geography/culture, the basic structures of the inner-trinitarian communication would not at all be tangible. And second, love, spirit, word, deed and life manifest in man's relationship with God in his worship and praise to God. In a particular way, they were first manifest in man's cultic-ritual service in the Old Testament. They are now manifested in the liturgical service of the Church in God's presence (Piennisch 1995:10, 213-214).

2.1.1 Love: Ubi Amor, Ibi Trinitas

Augustine states: *Ubi amor, ibi trinitas* ("Where love is there is trinity") (in Sauer 1951:19). God *is* Love (1 Jn 4:16). Love is *the* communication within the Trinity of God. Out of this love-communication among the Father, the Son and the Holy Spirit emanates the creativity of the Godhead. Love cannot rest and exist in enjoyment of itself. Augustine says, "If God is love, then there

---

[4] Condescension is derived from the Latin word *condescendo*. Meaning and usage of this term in Theology and Church History is broadly discussed in Piennisch 1995:10.

must be in him a Lover, a Beloved, and a Spirit of love" (in Sauer 1951:18). Love seeks exposure; it is therefore always focused on the "other." Outside inner-trinitarian communication, man is the "other," not the "awkward other," but the *imago Dei*.

Pöhlmann, summarizing P. Althaus, comments that the inner-trinitarian love of God is the pre-requisite for his love to us. Only because God *is* love, does he *act* in love (1980:119). Only because God is irrevocably *Abba*, does he deal with us as *Abba* in the Son and through the Spirit (Rom 8:15-17) (Pöhlmann 1980:120).

S*auer* writes, "Love is the deepest element of His life, the innermost fount out of which His nature eternally flows forth, the creative center that begets all His working and ruling" (1951:18). Love must beget. And life it must beget. The creation of life occurs in the unity of spirit, word and deed (Piennisch 1995:57).

2.1.2 Love-Communication in Creation and History

Because God *is* Love, He is necessarily the God in history.[5] H. Gese remarks that God's self-revelation to man is neither timeless nor is it confined to a certain point in time, but it walks a historical way inasmuch as man is a historical being.[6] Consequently, the inner-trinitarian communication structures are continued in creation as well as in history (Piennisch 1995:57).

Creation and history are the expression of the comprehensive creativity of the triune God. God the Spirit carries the Word of the Son who, in his creative speaking, brings about the realization of the word to manifest as deed. All is executed by the will of the Father who, out of his love, creates life (Piennisch 1995:62). Elsewhere, Piennisch puts it this way: All communication of God is rooted in his love. God's communication of his love is mediated by the Spirit and expressed in the word-deed whose final aim and content is life (1995:68).

2.2 Missiology and Communication: Three Dimensions

Having dealt with the neglected dimension in communication theories, it is now necessary to move on to explore in what way communication concerns missiology. From what was outlined in the previous section, we can say that missiology is in need of a communication concept encompassing three dimensions.

---

[5] Pöhlmann says: "Da Gottes Wesen Liebe ist, ist er *notwendig* ein *geschichtlicher* Gott, ein Gott, der mit dem Menschen *mitgeht*, ihm *nachgeht*, ihm *vorausgeht* ... (italics in the original)" (1980:37-38).

[6] Gese remarks: "Die Selbstoffenbarung Gottes an den Menschen ist weder zeitlos, noch auf einen Zeitpunkt beschränkt, sie geht einen geschichtlichen Weg, sowahr der Mensch ein geschichtliches Wesen ist" (in Pöhlmann 1980:38).

Missiology is to recognize that all communication has its beginning *in* God; secondly, that it is a creation-gift (*Schöpfungsgabe*) *of* God to man, and thirdly, due to its character and origin, seeks to ultimately connect creation (man in particular) *to* God. On the background of these assumptions, Piennisch poses three questions:

(1) How does God communicate with man? (2) How does man communicate with God? (3) And how does man communicate with man about God (1995:12)?

In pursuit of answers to these three leading questions, God's communication with man will be discussed in a "salvation-historical longitudinal section" with focus on the "fulfilment of God's communicative condescension in Jesus Christ" (Piennisch 1995:213). In other words: God's redemptive act in the *missio Dei*.

Man's communication with God in his liturgical service will be treated with focus on worship and prayer. In this area, Chewe will be featured.

Finally, the communicative relationship between man and fellow man needs to be exposed to a communication model that makes God an integral part of the communication process. For the inter-cultural communication section – which concerns the missionary – I will draw on Eugene A. Nida and his "three-language/culture model," though I will amend it by adding a fourth dimension.

3. Trans-cultural Communication: *Missio Dei* – The "Christ Incarnate Model"

God's communicative condescension to man culminated in Jesus Christ. Piennisch writes:

> In his incarnation, the communication structures of love, spirit, word, deed and life, which were given by God in times of the Old Covenant, become visible to their highest degree. Christ's person and ministry are God's final communication (1995:213-214).

Christ is the center of God's salvation communication to man on two counts. On the one hand, Christ is the *fulfilment* of the Old Testament revelation. And on the other hand, New Testament revelation has its roots and *beginning* in him (see (Piennisch 1995:138).

3.1 *Missio Dei*: Scriptural Grand Theme

The focus in the Old Testament is most notably on God's word-deed communication. God's utterance (Gn 1:3) at the beginning of his creative work includes creating as well as sustaining. Both elements, are inclusive in God's דבר (*dabar*) – God *spoke* and it *was*. *Dabar* must be understood in its dual meaning of *creative word* and *creative act* at the same time (Piennisch 1995:69).[7] The Old Testament climax of God's word-deed communication (*dabar*) was the cultic-ritual service, which first was introduced in the Tabernacle, and later continued in the Temple (see Piennisch 1995:138). God's word-deed communication is, however, in the constant accompaniment of his *ruach*. His *dabar* – in *creative word* and *creative act* – is carried by His *ruach* (Breath/Spirit).

The New Testament proclaims God's word-deed communication in the climax of Christ's incarnation as the *logos* (Jn 1:1). The *logos* communicates God's *dabar* to man in the unity of word and deed (Jn 1:3,14; Heb 1:2; 11:3). Just as the *dabar* of God in the Old Testament was carried by God's *ruach*, in the same way God's *logos* is carried by His *pneuma* in the New Testament (Piennisch 1995:139). The life-giving nature of *pneuma* is visible in its highest order in the resurrection of the incarnate word as well as in the life-dispensing gift of the Spirit to Believers (Jn 6:63) (Piernisch 1995:139). But already the incarnation of Christ as the word-deed required the presence of the Spirit of God. When the *logos* entered into the world, the Holy Spirit authoritatively exercised divine creative power to let the eternal word become deed in the Son of God (Lk 1:35; Jn 1:14) (Piennisch 1995:139).[8]

To sum up, both the Old Testament and the New Testament give primary attention to communication. Throughout Scripture, the tenet is that communication has its beginning in the Trinity of God. The trinitarian God *is* love. This love, in urge to expose itself to the "other," creates the world in word that is deed at the same time, because His spirit carries it in order to beget life. The *amor Dei* empties itself in a final act in the creation of man as the *imago Dei*, but culminates in the *missio Dei* – the incarnation of the Son, the *imago Dei* par excellence. Love, spirit, word, deed and life become therefore the grand theme of the Scriptures. The greatest act of God's communication was in the grand effort of sending the Son into the human habitat, a "broken world" (Smith & Barndt 1980:24). The *grand theme* of scripture, culminating in the *grand effort* of sending the Son to bring healing to a "broken world," is and remains the *grand model* for mission par excellence.

---

[7] Piennisch cites Ps 107:20 were God's *dabar* means deed. The context of v 19 and v 21 refers to God's intervention in a situation of desperation and distress. His rescue mission is described as *dabar*, that is, healing his people form a deadly disease. In response, the people are charged to give thanks to the Lord "for his unfailing love and his wonderful deeds for men (NIV)." God's *dabar* has healing power that manifests to man in a concrete deed (1995:71).

[8] Brown says: "The earth was void and without form when that Spirit appeared; just so Mary's womb was void until through the Spirit God filled it with a child who was His son" (in Piennisch 1995:139).

3.2 *Missio Dei*: Missiological Grand Model

In Christ, God entered into the human environment as a human. Although God's condescension to man took place in space and time, it is not confined to space and time. While Christ came to live in one specific culture, his incarnation affects each and every culture.

Any missiological model, if it seeks to be mission (sending) in the sense the term implies, must bear in mind from whence it comes, what its task is among people, and where it is going with people. It was G. Vicedom (1958) who uncompromisingly presented the concept of *missio Dei* in his work *missio Dei-Einführung in eine Theologie der Mission*. He says, summarized by Müller, "the nature of God is the starting point for the *missio Dei*" (Müller 1985:3). Mission comes from God's heart!

George W. Peters (1985), in his preface to his book *Missionarisches Handeln und Biblischer Auftrag: Eine Biblisch-Evangelische Missionstheolgie*, credits Vicedom with clarity on "biblical thinking" (1985:9). Quoting Vicedom, Peters writes that

> nach der Gesamtkonzeption der Schrift wird Gott nur eine Absicht zugeschrieben: die Menschen zu retten[9] (According to the overall conception of the Scriptures, God has but one prime intention: to save people) (in Peters 1985:9).

Mission in our "broken world" has its roots in God himself. It is anchored in his love and based on the *missio Dei* of his Son. It is charged with the task to restore to man the *imago Dei specialiter* through a personal relationship with Christ, the *imago Dei* par excellence.[10] Mission restores man to God!

And finally, mission looks ahead to the fulfilment of the end result of *missio Dei* which Peters describes as the glorification of the Father, the Son, and the Holy Spirit (Peters 1985:9). Mission brings glory to God! Is *missio Dei* still valid in our time and age?

---

[9] Vicedom, *Missio Dei*, 12 (in Peters 1985:9).

[10] Orthodoxy in particular showed concern with the anthropological *imago* term. Two *imago* forms of man are prominent. (1) *imago Dei improprie* or *generaliter* (image of God in a common sense) and (2) *imago Dei proprie* or *specialiter* (image of God in a special sense). Because of sin and the fall of man, the *imago Dei specialiter* was lost to man only to retain his *imago Dei generaliter* (Pöhlmann 1980:154, 167). The whole chapter (151-168) is recommendable!

3.3 *Missio Dei*: Outdated or Validated?

Missio Dei can neither be reduced to merely mean a historical event, nor can it be substituted by any other "mission model."[11] This is true whether based on theological grounds in which either God or the Holy Spirit is given primacy, or whether carried out on social grounds in attempts to deal with human calamities (e.g. injustice, misery, suffering etc.) with human force and wit. I want to advance just two arguments to show that *missio Dei* is far from being outdated and therefore dispensable.

3.3.1 *Missio Dei*: Love, Spirit, Word, Deed and Life at Work

Earlier it was shown that all basic structures of communication – love, spirit, word, deed and life – reached a climax in the Father's sending the Son, the Christ. But these structures were not frozen in Christ's person in order to be preserved for His return and reunion with the Father and the Spirit. Quite the contrary is true! The basic structures of communication of love, spirit, word, deed and life unfold in the ministry of Christ in correspondence to inner-trinitarian communication structures. John chapter 11 serves as an illustration of how all properties of these five basic structures shine forth in Jesus' ministry while on earth.

"Lazarus was sick," we read (v.1). Despite the urgent request to quickly come and extend His healing hand to the one He loved (v.3), Jesus delayed his departure in answering the sisters' call! While He delayed, Lazarus died, was buried and put to rest in a tomb. Jesus' view of the situation is incomprehensible to His disciples (v.7-15) who despair, charging Him with being unreasonable and endangering their lives (v.16). Also, His late arrival in Bethany earns Him a sharp reprimand and a straightforward proposition on what He should do now from Martha, one of the sisters (v.21).

The final word over Lazarus' life had been spoken. The final deed over his body had been done, so it seemed. An extraordinary situation develops. A promise is given (v.23). A confession is made (v.27). Emotions rise (v.32-35). Both sympathy and accusations fill the air at the same time (v.36-37). The context of the whole scenario, the precariousness of the situation, and the diversity of opinions and emotions of people could not have been compounded more. The bad odor from the cave, the bad mood of the crowd, all summed up to a bad combination of circumstantial factors. And Jesus only spoke words. The resemblance to Gn 1:1-2 can hardly be more striking. Darkness and confusion engulfed the earth in the beginning, and God's *dabar,* His word-deed – He *spoke* ... and it *was* – turned darkness into light and chaos into order (Gn 1:3ff). "Lazarus, come out!" (v.43): Christ's words penetrated

---

[11] For example, Thomas Thangaraj argues for a *missio humanitatis,* that is, mission that is anchored in humanity contrary to mission that is vested in *missio Dei* (in Ramachandra 2001:45).

darkness, death and the tomb as well as silenced the confusion among the audience. *The word-deed, rooted in love divine and carried by the spirit, returned Lazarus to life.*

How could the Christian mission ever do away with or replace love, spirit, word, deed and life? What better, more appropriate, more modern, more "down-to-earth" ministry can we give to a broken world, if not the very fount of the eternal God and the exemplary ministry of the exalted Christ!

3.3.2 *Missio Dei*: Community Focused Mission

W. Shenk, in his essay "Lesslie Newbigin's Contribution to Mission Theology," points out that for, Newbigin, Christ's community was the key to mission (Shenk 2000:59). Further, he summarizes Newbigin saying, "At the center of mission and unity stood Jesus Christ" (2000:59). Newbigin's theological vision was Jesus Christ and the community. Quoted by Shenk, Newbigin has this to say:

> It is surely a fact of inexhaustible significance that what our Lord left behind Him was not a book, nor a creed, nor a system of thought, nor a rule of life, but a visible community .... He committed the entire work of salvation to that community. It was not that the community gathered around an idea, so that the idea was primary and the community secondary. It was that a community called together by the deliberate choice of the Lord himself, and re-created in Him, gradually sought – and is seeking – to make explicit who He is and what He has done. The actual community is primary; the understanding of what it is comes second (in Shenk 200:59).

Missio Dei was and continues to be a community-focused mission. Jesus turned communities around in either way. There were those who followed Him and others who plotted against Him. But He certainly left behind a visible community of individual believers, and commissioned them to go forth as individuals to impact communities. How was this possible? Paul in his letters to the churches in Rome and Corinth puts it plainly enough. The driving force of mission is God's redemptive love in Christ (Rom 5:8). In turn, it is love that drives the Christian mission "because God has poured out his love into our hearts by the Holy Spirit, whom he has given us" (Rom 5:5). To do what? To steal people's hearts? To brainwash their minds? To superimpose a certain (mostly Western) Christian culture on the "heathen culture?"[12] Far from it!

---

[12] Kraft says: We are not called to win people to or to train people in whatever our own cultural approach to Christianity may be. The specific outworking of expression and behavior, the particular integration of emphases, values, and thematic configurations, must be discovered and

Love has but one law: "to *win* (emphasis mine) as many as possible" (1 Cor 9:19). These, regenerated by His *word-deed* in the creative act of the *Holy Spirit* (2 Cor 5:17), will receive *life* "and have it to the full" (Jn 10:10), and will become a visible Christ-centered community with a horizon extending to the ends of the earth "to make explicit who He is and what He has done."

3.3.3 Towards a Definition of Mission

The Christian Mission is anchored in the *Trinity* of God. The *missio Dei* is in search of the *imago Dei*. Mission is the effort to recognize the individual as *imago Dei generaliter* with the intention of restoring to him the *imago Dei specialiter* which he receives in Christ, the *imago Dei* par excellence. O'Donovan puts it this way:

> One of God's greatest purposes in mankind's salvation is to restore the holy image (the *imago Dei specialiter*, insertion mine) of God which was ruined by sin (Eph 4:24). This is one of the central themes in the Bible (1996:89).

Man is individual, but individuals form the church. Though inward-bound to promote faith, love and hope, the calling of the church is outward-bound for influencing and transforming communities. Mission is focused on *Community*. Shenk, summarizing Newbigin, remarks:

> The starting point must ever be God's initiative in Jesus Christ, the calling of the church to be the visible and witnessing community of the Gospel, the essential structure an unfolding narrative rather than an institutional system (2000:60).

Mission is *theology in action in the praxis of Missiology*. The tension and friction arising from the "tug-of-war" between Missiology and Theology, to decide which should gain the upper hand, is unnecessary to say the least. Paul's letter to the Romans should be heard and read anew. Unfortunately, doctrinal preoccupation of the church in its eras of Reformation, Orthodoxy, Enlightenment and so forth, have elevated this letter to a theological-doctrinal banner first and foremost.[13] A formal observation of the epistle to the Romans, however, will reveal that the starting point is not of doctrinal nature, but

---

worked out (perhaps with our assistance) by each and every society as it responds to the Gospel of Christ in its own unique fashion" (1996:446).

[13] "Der Römerbrief hat wie kein anderes neutestamentliches Buch in der westlichen Kirchengeschichte an Wegscheiden eine zentrale Rolle gespielt. Der Römerbrief stand jahrhundertelang im Zentrum dogmatischer Schlachten und wir haben uns angewöhnt, ihn ganz auf diesem Hintergrund zu lesen" (Schirrmacher 2000:109).

missiological concern. *The framework of Paul's theological mind is his missiological heart!*

Schirrmacher observes that before Paul digs into doctrinal issues (beginning from chapter one, verse 16), he first describes his task (v.1) and in v.5 in particular. This task is "to call people from among all the Gentiles to the *obedience* (italics mine) that comes from faith." What forms the focal point at the beginning of the letter (ch 1:5) also occupies the heart of Paul at the end of the letter (ch 15:18): "I will not venture to speak of anything except what Christ has accomplished through me in leading the Gentiles to *obey* (italics mine) God by what I have said and done."

Paul did not write this letter in the capacity of professor of theology – which is undoubtedly was – on a desk in the faculty of a university, but rather 'in the field' as an apostle and missionary!

4. *Adoratio Dei*: Man in Communication with God

In the introductory remarks of this chapter, the vertical axis of communication – Chewe in communication with God – was hinted at. At the same time, three leading questions for this chapter were formulated of which the second will be tackled here: How does man communicate with God? Chewe's communication with God is embedded in this inquiry.

4.1 Prayer: Conquest or Dialogue?

Prayer is a special form of communication insofar as it is communication proper with the supernatural. Prayer is neither a Christian invention nor specifically a Christian monopoly. People in all cultures, apart from communicating among themselves, are conversant with a reality beyond what can be seen with the eyes and perceived with the mind.

4.1.1 The Issue of Residue

In my years as a missionary working with Bemba speaking churches in the Northern Province of Zambia, interesting observations were made. Frequently during church services and other meetings, prayers are often spoken twice as fast as normal conversation would happen. Some people rattle along with incredible speed, unleashing a waterfall of words and phrases over the present assembly. One wonders how one could possibly think up such an impressive sequence of speech without stumbling or mumbling.[14] Putting aside the tech-

---

[14] As an example, I vividly remember participating in a Sunday morning Church Service held at Itinti (about 15km east of Kasama) on 24 September 2000, were the Service leader, Mr. Anton, closed the worship time in prayer and were I entirely failed to follow his words. He was not speaking in tongues, but with incredible speed so much that I lost track of what he was saying. It may well be that even some native speakers were challenged to follow him.

nical aspect of such a skill, I am more interested in finding out what the motive of such behavior could be. Is there a reason why people would behave this way? Underlying this question is the following: Is the performed Christian act of prayer related to or influenced by a traditional concept of prayer or interaction with the Transcendence? Is there cultural residue intermingled with the biblical data? In order to address these questions, we have to backtrack to some assumptions made in chapter two in the section of "conquering transcendental space."

In chapter two, it was noticed that there is ambivalence in traditional Bemba worldview concerning the Transcendence. Though the feeling of awe for the spirit world is felt, Bemba society manages to "conquer" this world by word and deed. Man is so profoundly in the center of Bemba worldview, that the concept of mutual understanding and intimate relation with the "other-world" is hard to perceive. The problem is: a "new Christian overcoat[15] hardly results in new thinking. The practice of prayer within the scope of the Christian churches in Bembaland is indicative of the fact that there are levels of possible cultural residue yet operative in prayer. Generally speaking, the concept of prayer, as dialogue with God from person to person is a subject still open for wider and deeper promotion.

4.1.2 A Personal Issue of Dialogue

Prayer in the Christian sense is not a transcending of space and a conquering of personal beings or impersonal forces, but a *dialogue* between creator and creature, between *Abba* and child. There is a marked difference between receiving through conquest and receiving through dialogue. The former seeks to intrude into the sphere of the supernatural realm by the sheer force of words and sounds laid down in the appropriate choice and order of words and their special intonations. Nida sees two prominent elements in this communication act, (1) words and special intonation serve as proof of the sincerity of the actor (Nida 1960:21), and (2) consequently, underscore "the worthiness of the worshiper" (Nida 1960:13). In contrast, the Christian form of communication with God is dialogue.

Dialogue with God has the promise of being heard (cf. Mt 21:22; Mk 11:24), of being granted answers to one's request because dialogue is locked into the experience and reality of a personal relationship with Him. Moreover, man is explicitly told to dialogue with God (cf. e.g. Mt 6:6; 9-13; Lk 18:1; 21:36). I

---

[15] "Christianity as offered by both Churches [United Free Church of Scotland, UFCS and Catholic] has hardly touched the traditional beliefs and related customs, so much so that, to the people themselves Christianity appears as a mere "overcoat"" (Oger 1991): summary at the back cover of the book. In the same book Oger says: "The Christian spiritual "import," with its aim at *"bringing men to their ultimate goal in heaven"* [italics in the original] may be a mere "overcoat" over traditional deep seated beliefs and customs leaving them undisturbed" (1991:231).

may receive answers to my request(s) by a degree of "convincing" or, if one may use the expression, "pestering" God, but I will never be able to take by force. God, in his gracious condescension, is ever present, but never subdued. He is the giver and provider, but can never be ordered about, nor can anyone take control over Him (cf. Gn 32:30; Ex 33:19) (see Piennisch 1995:121). "For the Christian, prayers are answered only on the basis of God's grace to the believer, for man has no righteousness (or worthiness) except that which God gives to him through Jesus Christ" (Nida 1960:21).

4.2 The Christian "Overcoat" Creates Cultural Ambivalence

The representatives of the biblical Transcendence (angels, cherubim, seraphim and the whole array of demonic spirit beings) create ambivalence in Bemba culture, because, except for one figure, Jesus Christ, they lack a tangible human history. But as sound is essential to conquering Bemba traditional transcendental space, emphatic and loud prayers appear to follow suit in the Christian context when shouting at the invisible spirits or deity also seeks to conquer. This is most prominent in tongue-speaking assemblies.

4.2.1 The Gap between Cultural Protocol and Liturgical-Service Practice

Such practice, however, constitutes a paradox because loud and emphatic words, raised voices, and shouting in addressing the human community is not allowed and is registered as impertinence in daily communication protocol. Particularly along the axes of age and respect as well as those of authority and status is proper protocol to be observed and appropriate voice level mandatory. A gap of ambivalent attitudes and behaviors is formed between improper communication protocol among the human community and observed church practice in worship and prayer of some Bemba church denominations. "Overcoat" and/or residue are not mere theoretical possibilities, but are realities that can be encountered. They continue to require renewed commitment to the liturgical service of the church community in worship and dialogue with the triune God.

4.2.2 Chewe: *Adoratio Dei*[16]

Chewe was a Bible reader. The Bible was one of the few books in his possession. Its companion was the Bemba Hymn Book. Many of the hymns it contains, he had mastered over the years, coming to know them by heart. A self-taught guitarist, he was always willing to lead the church in singing choruses and hymns.

Having been an introspective individual (cf. chapter seven), Chewe had his own idiosyncratic style of prayer. Most of the time, at least as far as I can say,

---

[16] *Adoratio Dei* is Latin meaning, "to worship, adore." I kindly acknowledge this information by Dr. Markus Piennisch. Private correspondence, December 14, 2000.

he was very contemplative and thoughtful in his prayers. One could sense his reflection upon whatever the content of the prayer was. Thankfulness and praise were important and dominant elements in his worship of God. He seemed to have grasped two essential truths about being human in the presence of God: to love and to praise.[17]

Adoratio Dei became a major theme in his life, especially after his miraculous recovery from many months of ill health in 1994 (cf. chapter seven). His worship was not characterized by the attempt to conquer God, but rather in dialogue to conquer with God. Chewe had great respect for people, treated them as *imago Dei* with great vigor in order to lead them into *adoratio Dei*.

5. Inter-cultural Communication: *Imago Dei* and the "Nida Model"

In the earlier parts of this chapter, a third leading question was introduced to frame an essential feature of communication: How does man communicate with man about God? Missiologists (e.g. Kraemer 1956, Hesselgrave 1978), linguists (e.g. Nida, 1960) and anthropologists (e.g. Kraft 1990) among others, have made communication a topic of academic study.

Piennisch has convincingly argued that the communicative aspect within the trinity of God is a neglected dimension in communication. This fact is obvious when communication theorists like Berlo observe, that "all communication occurs within a cultural context" (1960:164). The word "all" carries truth but is also short-sighted. It is true in the sense that, insofar as man is a cultural being, human communication must necessarily happen within a cultural context. In contrast, "all" is short-sighted insofar as it seems to suggest that the cultural context is the one and only reality with which we are confronted and with which we interact. That is not true. Kraft will provide further insight into what has been outlined above.

5.1 Kraft: REALITY vs. reality

Kraft counters Berlo by distinguishing between REALITY and reality. REALITY refers to "God as he is" (1996:19), or, in other words to "know *absolutely* (italics in the original)" (1996:19), as God does. R(r)eality is the *perception we have* of God, the world, and even of ourselves.[18] This perception, says Kraft, is conditioned by four factors: (1) The limitation of our senses shapes our experience (1996:21). (2) We work within the self-imposed

---

[17] Man is destined to love (Lv 19:17ff) and to praise (Ps 6:6). Is 38:18f reads: For the grave cannot praise you, death cannot sing your praise; those who go down to the pit cannot hope for your faithfulness. The living, the living-they praise you ... (see Wolff 1984:324-325, 328-330. Also, Pöhlmann 1980:168).

[18] Nida remarks: "... we do not perceive reality as it actually is" (1960:70).

limitation of being "highly selective in choosing the data we consider" (1996:21). (3) Next to personal selectivity, there is the "screening and filtering of REALITY" (1996:21) as the product of the society in which we grew up. And (4) our "human sinfulness" (1996:22) influences and distorts our perception of REALITY. Though we are barred from knowing REALITY (as God sees it), that is, in *absolute* terms, we can, however, know in *adequate* terms in order for us to plan for physical, social and spiritual survival (1996:19)

5.1.1 Paul and John: Partial Knowledge and Veiled Facts

The apostle Paul was well aware of our restricted perception of REALITY when he wrote to the Corinthian church:

> Now we see but a poor reflection as in a mirror; then we shall see face to face. Now I know in part; then I shall know fully, even as I am fully known (1 Corinthians 13:12).

In fact, other early Christian witnesses like John saw it much the same way as demonstrated when he says to his readers:

> Dear friends, now we are children of God, and what we will be has not yet been made known. But we know that when he appears, we shall be like him, for we shall see him as he is (1 John 3:2).

5.1.2 Weber: Reality – Beyond the Reach of Science

Max Weber, the renowned German sociologist, also acknowledges the fact that we have to live within the restrictions of imperfect knowledge, though science would prefer not to be restricted in any sense. In *The Sociology of Max Weber* (1968/1970), Julius Freund, summarizing Weber, writes:

> Weber's "basic assumption [is] that empirical reality is extensively and intensively infinite. This means, first of all, that reality surpasses our power of understanding, so that we can never come to the end of our exploration of events and of their variations in space and time or act on them all; next, that it is impossible to describe even the smallest segment of reality completely or to take into account all the data, all the elements and all the possible consequences at the moment of taking action...Neither any of the science nor all sciences taken together can give us perfect knowledge, because the mind is not capable of reproducing or copying reality, but only of reconstructing it with the aid of concepts. And there is an infinite distance between the

real and the conceptual. Thus we can never know more than fragments of the whole, for the whole is a singularity which defies the sum total of all conceivable singularities. It defies even the knowledge we have acquired, for that knowledge, no matter how solid in appearance, is laid open to question the minute a scientist discovers a new and hitherto unthought of point vantage (1970:7-8).

5.2 Nida: "Bible Culture," "Missionary Culture," "Host Culture"

Having given consideration to Berlo's "all-communication-within-cultural-context" and having pointed out that this perspective falls short by not taking into account REALITY, we can nevertheless learn much from his insights into communication theory *within* the cultural context. The following section attempts to elaborate on the process of communication within the cultural context. But first, let us set out the peripheries of the inquiry.

Communication is at the heart of the Bible. God communicates information. He wants us to know – actually we need to know – with the task to pass on to others. God communicated with man. The Scriptures are the result of this process. He communicated in time and space in specific localities, within specific cultures, in specific languages, in specific life contexts of people, and so on. But His communication also transcends time and space, transferring information to other places, other cultures, other peoples, other ages and so forth (compare Hesselgrave 1978:22). This makes communication the most profound fundamental facet of being human, but it also is the most complex task and challenge humans have to tackle.

5.2.1 Berlo: Man, Message and Meaning

All communication – here the word "all" is appropriate and comprehensive – can be ground down to six ingredients wedged between Purpose and Response (see Berlo 1960:30-31). Along the continuum of the communication process, the purpose (let's say it is on the far left) is interlocked with the communication source. The (1) *communication source* formulates a message on purpose or intent. The message must be packaged on its way, must be (2) *encoded* (through speech, writing, etc). The packaged, encoded (3) *message* is to be delivered, transmitted by certain means, or (4) *channels*. On delivery, the message must be appropriately handled, (5) *decoded* in order to impact the (6) *communication receiver* (Berlo 1960:23-39). When this happens, purpose found response.

With respect to the communication of Biblical times (or the "Bible Culture" – see Hesselgrave 1978:73), we have to identify these ingredients of the communication process. There is, first of all, the *communication source* – God and the Holy Spirit – who have "creative purposes and ultimate plans" (Nida

1960:221) or intentions to pass on information. The information has to be *encoded* – using speech and writing mechanisms (see Berlo 1960:32-34) of God and the Holy Spirit. Encoded information – the *message* – is transmitted via sound waves, the *channel*. The writers of the Old and New Testament, as firsthand *communication receivers, decoded* the message – using hearing and writing mechanisms – and responded by recording the message on some kind of storable material.

With respect to inter-cultural communication of the Christian Message, we again have to work with the same ingredients. Only the distance of space and time to the original "Bible Culture" adds to the burden and complexity of the communication process. "As a communicator, the missionary stands on middle ground," says Hesselgrave (1978:72). He is not the *communication source*, but looks to the Scriptures as the source of the original information which the *encoders* – the writers of the Old and New Testament – transmitted via the *channel* or medium of letters/books (albeit in languages that are no longer spoken today. In fact, the New Testament in the original Greek already is a translation of the Aramaic that Jesus most likely spoke while on earth[19]). Our hearing and reading mechanisms (ears and eyes) *decode* the message, which is then passed on to the central nervous system as the *receiver*. As we read, or hear what is read, we make responses to what has been read or heard.

The missionary in his "middle ground" position also looks at "the broken world" and its peoples. He sees people from his own culture, but his eyes are on the people of other cultures. His task: to communicate Christ across culture. He is not a member of the original "Bible Culture," but a member of his own culture ("Missionary's Culture") (Hesselgrave 1978:73-75), sent to engage in inter-cultural communication with the "Host Culture." This makes "communication the missionary problem *par excellence*" (Hesselgrave 1978:19).[20] The missionary's middle ground position poses several challenges to him.

First, the "Host Culture" will always remain his "*adopted culture*, never his *native culture* (italics in the original)" (Hesselgrave 1978:19).

---

[19] F. F. Bruce, the distinguished British New Testament scholar, writes: "For the Western world today the hardness of many of Jesus's sayings is all the greater because we live in a different culture from that in which they [the hard sayings of Jesus] were uttered, and speak a different language from his. He appears to have spoken Aramaic for the most part, but with few exceptions, his Aramaic words have not been preserved. His words have come down to us in a translation, and that translation – the Greek of the Gospels has to be retranslated into our own language. But when the linguistic problems have been resolved as far as possible and we are confronted by his words in what is called a "dynamically equivalent" version-that is, a version which aims at producing the same effect in us as the original words produced in their first hearers-the removal of one sort of difficulty may result in the raising of another" (1985:16).

[20] Kraft remarks: "Understanding and interpreting the Bible, couched as it is in the cultural patterns of other times and places. Since all that is reported there happened in societies other than our own, interpreting the Bible is a cross-cultural problem" (1996:9).

Second, he is not a primary, but a secondary source (Hesselgrave 1978:24). That leads to the third presumption: he must still learn if he is to teach, if he is to communicate Christ (Hesselgrave 1978:24). On the one hand, learning includes the usage of the techniques of exegesis and hermeneutics in order for him to properly decode the original message. And on the other hand, learning consists of (1) using the techniques of other disciplines, like anthropology and the social sciences, (2) to adequately exegete (acquire knowledge and try to understand cultural specifics), and (3) interpret (doing social hermeneutics) cultural patterns as well as to act upon the "Host Culture."[21]

5.2.2 Towards a Definition of Missionary

A missionary is a *student*. A student of the "Bible Culture" and simultaneously a student of the "Host Culture." In studying both, he learns much about his *own* culture and might hopefully be able "to avoid being crippled by the enemy within us – our own ethnocentrism" (Kraft 1996:xiii). A former colleague and missionary to Zambia said this:

> We are asked to take on too much responsibility and assume too much about people long before we really know anything about them. (What follows is:) It is kind of like "just do something even if it is wrong. God will make up for the rest and anyway, whatever *they* (italics mine) know and do is wrong while whatever we know and do is right."[22]

A missionary is a *person who is part of the message*. What is the message? The letters and words, the written texts of the Bible? Before we can answer that, Berlo asks: What are messages? Messages are "behavioral events that are related to the internal states of people," he says (1960:168-169). This might look strange to us at first glance. But one example will help: God sent his Son. Because God so loved the world (internal state), He sent his son (behavioral event). **This is the message**. Not on paper or clad in words, but in the act of the incarnation of the Son. The Scriptures describe this love related to the event in many different ways, pictures and words. Scripture's descriptions of God's internal state and His behavioral event, of love and act, is vouchsafed since it is θεόπνευστος-*theopneustos* (God-breathed) 2 Tim 3:16.

---

[21] This thesis attempts to present this second dimension of the learning process from a variety of angles in which missionaries ought to engage in if their *Communication of the Christian Faith* (to borrow Kraemer's title of his book) is to become meaningful to the people they have gone to "teach."

[22] Gary R. Burlington, Lincoln Christian College, ILL. Private correspondence, July 27, 2000.

What is the missionary's message? That God's internal state of love, as expressed in the behavioral event of the incarnation of His Son, has impacted the messenger's (missionary's) internal state, and has led to the behavioral event of allegiance to Christ. In turn, Christ, through his physical presence ("incarnation") in the Host Culture, expresses his intent (communicates) to impact the internal state of his hosts, so that they too may pledge allegiance to Christ. Is there not too much emphasis on the missionary as person? Not too much, but a great deal.[23]

A missionary is a *person who, despite being part of the message, is not himself the message.*[24] He comes with a message in the attempt to create *meaning* to his "other-culture" *imago Dei*. "The concept of meaning is central to communication," says Berlo (1960:169). He continues to say: "If (people) have no similarities in meaning between them, they cannot communicate" (1960:175). How then does the missionary's message convey meaning? Berlo again writes:

> *Communication does not consist of the transmission of meaning* [italics in the original]. Meanings are not transmittable, not transferable. Only messages are transmittable, and meanings are not in the message, they are in the message-users (1960:175).

The meaning the missionary puts in his message, does not necessarily create the same meaning (or may create no meaning at all!) in the respondent people. Because "meanings are not in messages ... meanings are in people" (Berlo 1960:175). Only if the message, injected with the source person's meaning, finds a receiver to whom the message makes sense (has meaning) can there be communication.[25]

Over and above, the missionary has reason to believe that the Holy Spirit helps him to be, or become, an inquisitive student with open eyes and ears, whose physical presence and conduct of life within his "Host Culture" is the message that creates meaning for his hosts,[26] with the purpose that they themselves engage in a personal communication process with God.[27]

---

[23] Martin Luther, the German Bible and Reformation; Bruce Olson among the *Motilone* of Columbia (see Olson 1978), the Elliot's among the *Aucas,* and Chewe among his own people, are just a very few individuals whose lives had meaning to others and the message of God's love and salvation was heard. See also Peters 1985:184-187. The New Testament has much to say about witnessing or personal advocacy.

[24] Olson expressed it like this: "How could I introduce them [the Motilone Indians] to Him [Jesus] for what He really was, independent of my own personality and culture?" (1978:136).

[25] For a discourse on "Language and Meaning" see Kraft 1996:240-241.

[26] Piennisch, summarizing Kraft, says, "... die verbale Mitteilung [muß] in Beziehung zur persönlichen Erfahrung der Empfänger gesetzt werden, damit die Botschaft ihr Ziel erreicht" (1995:25).

[27] "Bruce [Olson] "tied into" the Motilones, and as a result, the Motilones "tied into" God" (The Editors in Olson 1978:8).

5.2.3 Kraft: Timeless Communication Insights

Kraft remarks:

> Basic insights concerning issues such as ... communication (Nida 1954, 1990 [1960]) ... are, I believe, timeless and crucially important for cross-cultural Christian workers to consider, whether or not they are currently of interest to professional anthropologists (1996:xv).

Some basic timeless and crucially important insights of Nida concerning communication are depicted below (figure seven). His "three-culture-model" is described in his book *Message and Mission: The Communication of the Christian Faith* (1960:221-229).[28]

Hesselgrave (1978) and Kraft (1990) have both built on Nida's communication model. Summaries of both authors and their modifications of Nida's model are found in Piennisch, *Kommunikation and Gottesdienst* (1995:24-26).

The figure below shows an expansion of the above-mentioned authors' ideas in that it includes a fourth component, *"Those"* of the "Fourth Culture."

---

[28] Communication insights matter a great deal in Bible Translation because three sets of languages and cultures interact – "those of the original documents, those of the readers, and those of by which the Bible and the faith were mediated to the translator, "says Smalley (1995:61). He continues to say that up to the 1950s translators lacked "cross-linguistic and cross-cultural criteria by which to judge when a translation is both natural and faithful to the original" (1995:61). Smalley further states: "Ever since the Christian message was expressed in tongues other than its original ones in the first half of the first century, the Gospel has been clothed in multiple languages and has also been colored by those languages and by the cultures of which they are a part" (1995: 62).

FIGURE 7: "FOUR-CULTURE-COMMUNICATION MODEL"
(Based on Eugene A. Nida's Three-Culture-Model 1960)

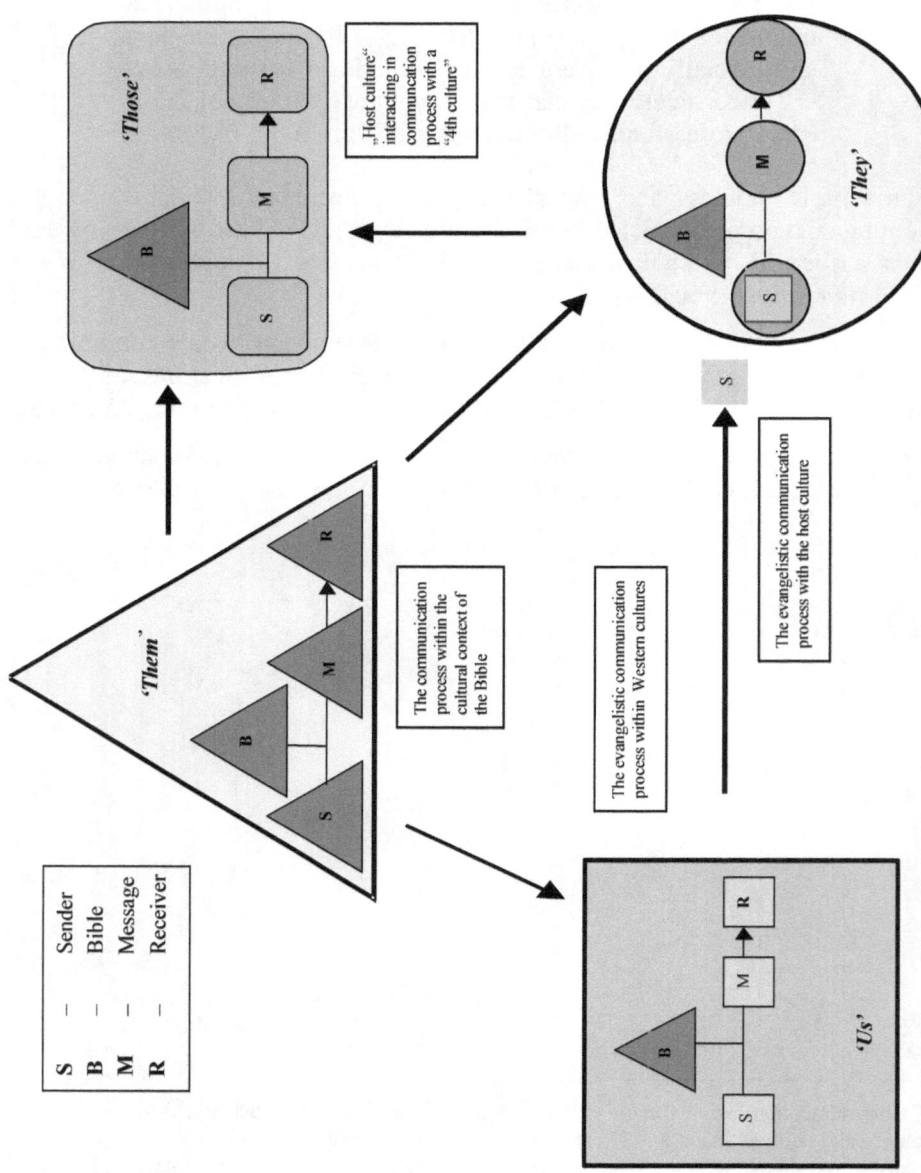

Based on Eugene A. Nida, *Message and Mission: The Communication of the Christian Faith* (New York: Harper & Row Publishers, 1960), 222; supplemented through inspiration by Robert J. Priest, Personal Notes Introduction to Hermeneutics," Fall Semester, Columbia International University, Deutscher Zweig, Korntal, 1998; further modified by the author, June 2001.

5.2.4 Beyond "Them," "Us" and" They" – "Those" and the Hermeneutical Circle

The hermeneutical circle in the communication process of the biblical message consisting of *"Them*," the "Bible-Culture" ⇒ *"Us*," the "Missionary's-Culture" and ⇒ *"They*," the "Host Culture" is successfully closed only when the "Host Culture" starts its own engagement with the Scriptures. This engagement includes exegesis, hermeneutics, as well as a formulation of faith, which should lead to meaningful engagement in mission within their own culture. This should eventually lead the members of the culture to become partakers in the global mission endeavour interacting in a communication process with *"Those"* of a "Fourth-Culture."

During the last two hundred-and-fifty years or so, Mission has been, to a great extent, a north-to-south, north-to-east and north-to-west movement. Whereas in theology, "home-grown" formulations and applications of the Bible have emerged in South America, Africa and South Asia, the three components of Nida's model are still predominant in missiological communication models. The "north-to-south/west/east mission movement" as well as the "home-grown" theologies of whatever labels in the south, west and east are all, however, in need of reformation. Neither the only "Us"-and-"They" axis in mission endeavour, nor the introverted concerns of "home-grown" theologies which focus chiefly on liberation and lack the "mission-horizon" live up to God's horizon of a time when *all* nations and *all* tongues "shall confess that He is LORD." The realization of *amor Dei* in search for man in *all* nations and of *all* tongues through the *missio Dei,* and the recognition of man as the *imago Dei generaliter* in need of the *imago Dei specialiter* in Christ, could help missiology and theology to become wholly committed to God's horizon. This horizon would be the greatest gift Christianity could offer to a "broken world."

6. A Concluding Reflection

The starting point of this chapter was Chewe. Apart from communicating with himself, his family, and the social group and church, he also was in communication with God.

Piennisch's concept of the inner-trinitarian communication among God the Father, God the Son and God the Holy Spirit has been found to be fundamental in correcting the shortcomings found in other communication theories.[29]

---

[29] Here I want to engage into a discourse with Nuckolls. He investigates the Western understanding of the relationship between explanatory logic (epistemology) and the origin of the world (ontology). Nuckolls starts his enquiry by relating explanatory logic to what he calls "biblical myth." The similarity between the Western drive for order, "distain for inconsistency and intolerance for ambiguity, and emphasis on "actor/agent as one distinct from the object he attempts to explain or create," finds a parallel in the biblical creation process. The sequence of

The reason is that this concept highlights the five basic structures of love, spirit, word, deed and life, which manifest in the creation and God's gracious condescension to man in a "longitudinal-historical section," first in the "cultic-ritual service" of the Old Testament, then culminating in the incarnation of Christ, and finally in the "liturgical-service" of the Church.

Communication in connection with missiology was then described as consisting of three dimensions: God to man, man to God, man to man about God. The *missio Dei* was presented as the *grand theme* of Scripture, and the *grand model* of Mission (Mission comes from God, Mission restores man to God, and Mission brings glory to God). An inquiry into whether the *missio Dei* for current mission practice is outdated was undertaken. A probing into Christ's ministry while on earth confirmed the five basic communication structures of love, spirit, word, deed and life. Further, it was noted that *missio Dei* is community focused. The result of the inquiry confirmed the validity of *missio Dei* as forming the grand model of mission practice for all times. Then, a definition or description of Mission was proposed: Mission is anchored in the Trinity of God; Mission is focused on Community; and Mission is theology in action in the practice of Missiology.

The man-to-God communication axis was examined with an attempt made to show that *adoratio Dei* is the basis of man's liturgical service and relationship with God. "Is prayer conquest or dialogue?" was the leading question. The practice among some Bemba speaking churches was questioned. The issue of cultural "residue" and Christian "overcoat" was addressed. Chewe's personal prayer practice showed a difference in that his introspectiveness and his intimate interaction with God made *adoratio Dei* a major theme in his liturgical service in the latter parts of his life.

Intercultural communication – man to man about God – in need to realize the distinction between REALITY and reality (Kraft) was reiterated and reinforced by biblical references (Paul and John). The restriction of imperfect

---

logical order in Genesis (Light-sun/moon, Firmament-birds/fish, Land-animals/man) finds a "soul-mate" in "formal scientific explanation." Of interest is his interpretation of the Genesis account. He says, "The early chapters of Genesis reveal the inner logic of creation. First, the universe has a unique beginning. Second, the creator is detached and emotionless – a disembodied spirit with no interior sensations" (Nuckolls 1996:98-100). I will skip his third injunction, as it won't concern us here. What is of interest is the second statement. What happens when the inner-trinitarian communication is pushed out of the enquiry is obvious here. The creator is "detached and emotionless." A sorry statement considering the fact that the creator showed keen interest in what he had created in each sequential stage. Especially, after he had finished all that he had made, God "saw ... and it was very good" (Gn 1:31). God cannot speak and create, cannot look at it and count it to be very good!, if he was "detached and emotionless," utterly deprived of "interior sensations!" If God were detached and emotionless in creating the world, there would have been no purpose in doing so. There must be motive and purpose to create something that is "very good." There must be love, the greatest of all emotions!

knowledge is a fact that not even all sciences taken together can solve (Weber). With regard to missiology, Berlo's insights into communication theory and Nida's three-culture/language model informed this section of the study.

Communication theorists such as Berlo argue that communication is not just about reaching out to another person. Communication has a purpose. By communicating to others, we want to become an "affecting agent" (1960:11). Not only that, we also purpose a response. Between purpose and response, Berlo identified six communication ingredients: communication source, encoding, message, channel, decoding, and communication receiver. Mission, however, does not just purpose any response per se. Mission also wants "to affect others" (1960:11): their thinking, their emotions, their behavior. *"In short, we communicate to influence – to affect with intent* [italics in the original]*"* (1960:12).

God, in love, spirit, word, deed and life, entered into a communication process with humankind. The climax was the *missio Dei* in sending Jesus Christ to come into "that which was his own" (Jn 1:11). God, exclusively and finally, "has spoken to us by his Son" (Heb 1:2). In Jesus Christ, God communicated to "influence – to affect us with intent" – to reconcile us to himself (Col 1:13-22), to move from a "cease-fire" toward a lasting and valid "peace treaty" (Rom 5:1) between himself and every individual on earth.[30]

To communicate Christ in this manner, the missionary's "middle ground" position (Hesselgrave) was highlighted and compared to Nida's model. The implications of message and meaning were outlined and a definition or description of missionary was proposed.

Finally, it has been pointet out that Nida's three-component model is not sufficient to close the hermeneutical circle in the communication process of the biblical message. Next to *Them* ("Bible-Culture"), *Us* ("Missionary's-Culture"), and *They* ("Host-Culture"), the horizon of *Those* ("Fourth-Culture") can help to move both missiology and theology out of a position of being in danger of paralysis.

---

[30] All definitions of God fall short of who He really is. There is only one definition that can express God: His self-definition in Jesus Christ. "Er ist *der, der am Kreuz für uns gesiegt hat, er ist der, der paradoxerweise als Opfer siegt, er ist der victor quia victima* [victor *because* victim]. Daß gerade der *Besiegte* der *Sieger* ist, daß der *Gekreuzigte* der Auferstandene ist, daß es einen Gott gibt, der diesen Umweg der Liebe geht, ist das Proprium des Christentums" (Pöhlmann 1980:117).

Chapter 9
A Second Missiological "C": Conversion

1. Introduction

In his essay "Conversion in Focus: Anthropological Views and Missiological Perspectives," Marc Spindler (1997:275-288) bemoans the fact that, while cultural anthropology is eagerly debating on Christian conversion, missiologists are discussing other issues.[1] And while conversion was the central theme of several recent conferences held by anthropologists,[2] missiological studies were neither quoted nor discussed (1997:279). This development should indeed receive attention. It is for this reason that Spindler proposes that "conversion deserves a place of honor in the contemporary missiological discussion" (1997:275).

Although Spindler may be right, I would like to remove the "sting" of his harsh, critical observations by making mention of The Consultation on Conversion, held in Hong Kong in January 4-8, 1988, which was left out of the considerations in his paper. The proceedings of the conference are compiled in *Papers of the Consultation on Conversion*[3] wherein we see a maximum of attention given to the issue of conversion, ranging from biblical, theological, historical, psychological and sociological, and cultural studies to missiological papers, presented by an equally wide range of authors including theologians and missiologists.[4]

However, facts are facts. Conversion is no longer only a theological/missiological issue but has moved into the spotlight of anthropology, the social sciences and psychology (Johnson & Malony 1982:9-11). Should missiologists crouch down and leave the field to other disciplines? But a "war"

---

[1] Spindler refers to the World Council of Churches' recent World Missionary Conference in Salvador, Brazil, 24 November-3 December 1996; topic: "The Gospel in Diverse Cultures." "The result (of the Conference) was that conversion disappeared from the missiological agenda" (1997:275).

[2] Conference on Conversion held at Boston University, Boston, Massachusetts, 14-18 April 1988. Discussions were edited by Robert W. Hefner, ed., *Conversion to Christianity: Historical and Anthropological Perspectives on a Great Transformation* (Berkeley: University of California Press, 1993); hereafter cited as Hefner, *Conversion to Christianity*. An international symposium of anthropologists in June 1994 was held by the University of Amsterdam together with the universities of Nijmegen and Leiden, the International Institute of Asian Studies in Leiden, and with the support of the Royal Academy of Sciences in the Netherlands. Proceedings of this conference were edited by Peter van der Veer (in Spindler 1997:279-280).

[3] *Papers of The Consultation on Conversion*, Hong Kong Conference, January 4-8, 1988 (Tübingen: Institut für Missionswissenschaft und Ökumenische Theologie, 1988).

[4] To name just a few: J. I. Packer, P. Beyerhaus, P. G. Hiebert, E. Rommen, K. Bockmuehl, and B. J. Nicholls all presented papers in Hong Kong.

between the disciplines will not be the solution, I believe. Just as missiology as a whole is interdisciplinary, (Tippet 1987, see Introduction to Part Three), so is conversion a subject with many frameworks. Jeeves (1988) believes that different frameworks of conversion have the potential to be "complementary accounts of the same events" (1988:183-206).

That leaves us with the question of how to proceed from here. Which frameworks should be considered and which should be left out? And in what ways are they complementary or contradictory? For reasons of space, a measure of selectivity is necessary.

2. Conversion: Review of Select Relevant Literature

Spindler summarizes the proceedings of two of the above-mentioned recent conferences of anthropologists (Boston, 1988 and Amsterdam, 1994), which were each edited by Hefner (1993) and van der Veer (1996) respectively.

2.1 General Theory on Conversion in Anthropology

Generally speaking, the Boston conference assessed "conversion to Christianity" as "largely positive," says Spindler (1997:279). In what way exactly was the conversion to Christianity perceived to be a step in a positive direction?

2.1.1 "The Boston Résumé"

Spindler presents Hefner's view of conversion to be a positive step toward "world-building."[5] Or in Spindler's own words, "Conversion means access to a new or larger macrocosm, to a new global awareness," [to what has been termed] "civilization" (1997:279). He continues:

> In other words, world religions, including Christianity, greatly contribute to the education of humankind, making humans members of a single moral commonwealth instead of members of local groups ignoring one another (1997:279).

Behind this theory, Spindler discovers the influence of Robin Horton (1971) who advocated the "elimination of the religious ingredients of conversion" (Spindler 1997:279-280). Horton claims that conversion as a shift of cosmological perspective could and can happen even without world religions (Christianity or Islam). Hefner, however, discards this "speculative hypothesis" on the grounds of "the historical role of world religions (which) ... cannot be understood outside their global scope" (in Spindler 1997:280).

---

[5] Hefner borrowed the term "world-building" from Berger 1967 (in Spindler 1997:279).

Theological Critique

In opposition to a conversion that contributes to an educated humankind which enjoys "a single moral commonwealth," Christian conversion, according to Spindler, is tied to the person of Jesus Christ. "The new Adam is personalized in Jesus and offered as a paradigm of personal existence to every human being" (Spindler 1997:284). And "personal conversion ... amounts to the birth of the new Adam in the human individual" (Spindler 1997:284).

2.1.2 "The Amsterdam Résumé"

Peter van der Veer (1996) accepts Hefner's conclusion, "namely the concept of the rationality of conversion" (in Spindler 1997:280). Van der Veer, summarized by Spindler, says: "Conversion is a progress towards the rationalization of an open, human world" (in Spindler 1997:284). In other words, Christian conversion is a

> technology of the self, ... which, under modern conditions, produces a new subjecthood that is deeply enmeshed in economic globalization and the emergence of a system of nations-states. Not only does conversion to Modern Christianity (both Protestant or Catholic) seek to transform the Self by changing its relations to Others, it enables a new organization of society (in Spindler 1997:280).

Theological Critique

First of all, what are the "modern conditions" that van der Veer wants to recognize? Our world is still a "broken world," and man is still a sinner. However "modern" conditions may be, we have not yet advanced beyond the need for this old Gospel message. Second, "conversion to Modern Christianity" has not and will never have inherent power to "transform the Self." The heart of man is not changed by the structure of modern Christian Institutions, but by God's grace and mercy alone (Acts 15: 11; Rom 3:24).

Despite the positive evaluation of conversion to Christianity by both Hefner and van der Veer, their frameworks have little potential of giving conversion a Spindler calls a "place of honor" in contemporary missiology.

2.2 A Sociocultural Theory on Conversion

Hiebert (1988) approaches conversion from a different angle. "Biblical conversion has to do with real people, consequently it is always in history" (1988:233). That is to say, conversion has a psychological (individual), sociocultural (corporate) and historical dimension. The sociocultural-historical dimension is discussed below; the psychological one later. Since there is this human dimension in conversion, Hiebert sets out to examine what the human side is. In a preliminary stage, he approaches the inquiry from three angles.

First, there is phenomenology. The word *conversion* can be found in many contexts: it has a religious tone, it appears in economic discussions (one currency is *converted* into another), and people speak of it in technical terms – "cars that can fold down their tops are convertibles" (1988:234).

Second, beyond phenomenology lies the question of ontology. What is the reality of conversion? How can we determine what is true and real? In reference to Christian conversion, it includes "reality testing – seeking to differentiate between genuine and spurious commitment, true and false statements, and authentic and inauthentic behavior" (1988:234).

Third, conversion is the concern of missiology. The concern is to help people to move from "where they are (phenomenology) to where God wants them (ontology)" (1988:234). At this stage, missiology is urged to look at the "principle of incarnation ... (because) we must begin where people are, not where they should be" (1988:234). Not only is it a question of *where* people are, but also one of dealing with them *as* they are (polygamists, thieves, singles, widowed, rich, poor, etc.).

Having dealt with the preliminaries, Hiebert moves on to point out that conversion as seen from a social science viewpoint involves two central concepts: culture and society (1988:234). Each culture (encompassing beliefs, feelings and values) has its own way of forming concepts and defining reality. Therefore, a central question is: "How do we define 'conversion,' and to what extent is our definition influenced by our cultural way of creating categories" (1988:235). Hiebert provides three sets of categories that influence the way conversion is defined and understood.

2.2.1 "Bounded Set" Categories

"Bounded sets" (things of the "same kind") are a dominant way of category formation in the West (1988:235). One outstanding characteristic of bounded sets is the clear demarcation of boundaries (e.g. private and public, work or leisure, friend or foe etc.). As a result: "Conversion has to do with the boundaries between categories" (1988:236): for example, to move from one category – Dollar – to the other category – Euro – or whatever other currency. "In religious terms it is changing from being non-Christian to being Christian" (1988:236).

But what do people mean by "being Christian"? One can either define the category "Christian" in terms of beliefs (deity of Christ, virgin birth etc.) or in terms of lifestyle (no drinking, no smoking, "well-behaved", distinct mannerisms, punctuality etc.) (1988:236). Conversion defined by bounded sets puts people either into one category (non-Christian) or into the other (Christian), each with its own underpinnings.[6] A middle ground position is out because of its ambiguous character.

Theological Critique

Bounded sets pose a problem to conversion because definition goes by intrinsic terms – what people are in and of themselves or what they are not in and of themselves. In this view, there is the danger of crediting people with their "achievement" in salvation (1988:239). Though there is the human side in conversion and salvation, God is the first and main actor in converting a person. Hiebert says: "Salvation and conversion refer to the same reality, but the former focuses more on the divine side of things, and the latter on the human dimension" (Mt 18:3; Lk 22:32; Acts 3:19) (1988:233).

2.2.2 "Fuzzy Set" Categories

"Fuzzy sets" allow for ambiguity. They have no sharp boundaries. For example, Hiebert says, "'day' and 'night' are fuzzy sets. One moves into the other without sharp break" (1988:237). One category may possess a varying degree of the characteristics of the other category. Thus, "fuzzy sets are often used to emphasize processes rather than states" (1988:237). Applied to conversion, a fuzzy set approach, however, "raises difficult theological problems," says Hiebert (1988:238). Can a person be both Hindu (or belong to any other "category" for that matter) and be Christian at the same time?

Theological Critique

Fuzzy sets also create theological difficulties. Conversion does not leave a person half in the "light" and half in the "dark." A person cannot be "half" *in* and "half" *out* of the Kingdom of God. Christian conversion is not based on truth as a mixture of Christian "ingredients" and some other kind of "ingredients." Despite the fact that fuzzy sets are process oriented, this process holds varying degrees of each of the categories within its set. It is a process *within* the boundary of "totally in" and "totally out." Christian conversion is not a process within a given set with varying degrees of characteristics from the other. In the end, Hiebert remarks, "fuzzy sets push us towards religious syncretism and relativism" (1988:238). But Christ is the one and only way to God.[7]

---

[6] For example, what are the *minimal* requirements to be counted "in" and how *high* is the bar placed for one to gain entry. Compare Hiebert 1988:236.

[7] John 14:6 says: Jesus answered, "I am the way and the truth and the life. No one comes to the Father except through me." The Greek *ego eimi* (I am) is emphatic and reinforces Jesus' claim insofar as it attributes exclusivity to Him.

2.2.3 "Centered or Relational Set" Categories

In this mode of thought, things are defined according to what they are in themselves (intrinsic definitions), but – and this is important, says Hiebert – in relationship to something else (extrinsic definitions) (1988:238). "In a centered set things related to the same 'center' or reference points are grouped together" (1988:238). For example, brothers and sisters are a particular group of people "not because of what they are intrinsically," but because of their extrinsic definition, that is, "because they are offspring of the same parents" (1988:238).

In centered or relational thinking, conversion means a change in direction and/or a change in relationships. "It is to leave one relationship for another. In religious terms it is to turn from one god to another. In Christian terms it is to turn from the god of self,[8] or any other god, and to make Jesus the Lord of one's life" (1988:238).

Category formation, based on cultural concepts, is an issue in missiology. The following section attempts to highlight the fact that missionaries need to be aware of the "grip" that categories (first and foremost their own) exercise on them.

2.3 Introductory Entry Point

About half way through Chewe's period of sickness from April to July 2000, the subject of conversion came up. Strangely, it was a one-sided affair. It was not that both of us entered into discussion on this subject. No, the subject crept in through the back door in *my* mind. How did this happen? Some of the developments taking place puzzled me in a way that a question formed in my mind: Is he (Chewe) really converted?

Comment: on several occasions, I could not quite understand his "behavior." For example, at times he was not fully compliant with medical advice – not sticking to instructions pertaining to food as he had been advised, taking alternative "Bemba medicine", "hiding" information from me, and, for a long time, insisting that *ubuloshi* (witchcraft) activities had been carried out against him and the deep seated fear this brought to him.

On the one hand, I thought of my reasoning as ridiculous because all the evidence of past years – and not least our long-standing friendship – quite clearly testified of his conversion and genuine commitment to Christ. I knew it was true. But on the other hand, there were questions! Why had his conversion become an issue with me? And why was it becoming one now? Why was it an issue as fundamental as conversion and not just one of "temporal darkness,"

---

[8] Some anthropologists view conversion as a "means to an end (continuity of purpose in life), and the end is self-determination and self-fulfillment governed by self-interest" (Spindler 1997:277).

or "a stint of confusion?" Obviously there was a cognitive dissonance that was influencing my thinking. A discrepancy between *what I saw* and *what I wanted or expected to see*. Perhaps, the bottom line was this: I was looking for "behavior," or "genuine" tangible points that would meet my own cognitive categories in terms of my understanding of conversion, manifesting in a particular "converted behavior." I truly had a problem on my hands. I realized I was gauging Chewe's *present* Christian converted behavior against my *own* perception of appropriate Christian converted behavior, of how he *should* behave in his situation. But, we were both converted. Why then cognitive dissonance?

3. Conversion: A Reading on Charles Kraft

Kraft in *Christianity in Culture* (1980) expresses concern over advocating "but a single method of entrance (conversion; addition mine) into the community of God" (1980:328). He argues that difference in theological convictions account for defending or propagating a "single method of entrance" such as "believers" baptisms or "infant" baptism, (1980:328) "sudden experience" or "radical conversion". The reason for a "single method of entrance" position is attributed by Kraft to the "lack of awareness of God's desire to adapt his approach to human beings to the cultural matrix in which they are immersed" (1980:328). Kraft terms single-method-of-entrance positions as "inadequate models" (1980:328). The question is: why are they inadequate? Precisely because of the cognitive-dissonance-effect such models promote. Does this mean that there are no biblical moorings for conversion? Does it mean that the relative elements (culture, psychology etc.) are the only precepts by which conversion can be measured?

3.1 Biblical Absolutes or Biblical Principles/Constants?

A "single method of entrance" may easily become a biblical absolute if predominant attention is given to "such dramatic examples of conversion as those of Paul (Acts 9), the Philippian jailer (Acts 16)" (Kraft 1980:333) and others.[9] Nevertheless, the few conversion records in the New Testament do not represent the whole conglomerate of people who converted to Christ. If the cited examples were to be termed "classical" or as the only "single-mode-conversion-experience," then Kraft says, the disciples, for example, could not positively be included in this group (1980:333). But undoubtedly the disciples *were* converted. Coming back to the question of whether there are no biblical moorings or precepts for conversion, Kraft arrives at two sets of precepts.

---

[9] Johnson and Malony look at the five grand examples (Paul, the Ethiopian Eunuch, Cornelius, Lydia, and the Jailer) of conversion as recorded in the book of Acts (1982:87-101.

3.1.1 A First Set: "Turning" or "Returning"

Consulting "primary biblical words (Heb. *shuv*; Gr. *epistrepho*)" (Kraft 1980:333),[10] Kraft concludes that, *"the central focus remains that of turning, changing direction, reversing the direction in which one is headed so that it is toward rather than away from God [italics in the original]"* (1980:333). Conversion is a turning *away* and turning *to* movement. The turning *away* "is coupled with the need for repentance (Gr. *metanoia*) from the error and wilfulness that led one astray" (Kraft 1980:333). Hiebert's "centered or relational set" supports Kraft's argument.

Biblical Approach to Categories

"Centered or relational sets were fundamental to Hebrew thought," says Hiebert (1988:240). *Shuv* "(used 1056 times in the Old Testament)" (Johnson & Malony 1982:77-78) ... conveys the idea of turning, turning away, turning back (Hiebert 1988:240). Christopher Barth writes:

> The Hebrew word shuv refers to the occurrence of "turning" in the opposite direction. The direction in which a man went or looked and which determined his plans and actions is changed into a new, the opposite direction. It means the "re-orientation" towards a goal from which one has moved away previously. Equally in relation both to concrete and abstract things, shuv indicates a "return"; geographically it means returning to a former position; circumstantially, it means "restoring a former state" (in Hiebert 1988:240).

Metanoein and *epistrephein* are used in the New Testament to convey the same meaning of "to turn around," "to proceed in a new direction" (Hiebert 1988:240; also Johnson & Malony 1982:78-79). The emphasis is on dynamic rather than on Greek static categories (Hiebert 1988:240).[11]

Is this focal point of "turning," "turning around" or "returning" apparent in the disciples of biblical times? How did "turning" and *metanoia* manifest in their lives?

As a key figure among the initial twelve disciples whom Jesus called into discipleship and ministry, Simon Peter will be singled out for a case study.

---

[10] *Shuv* is more than 1000 times mentioned in the Old Testament. Some 120 times it occurs in the context of "turning," "turn round" or "returning" with reference to God. See Fiedler 1982, s.v. "Buße/Bekehrung." On *epistrepho* see Packer 1988, s.v. "Conversion."

[11] For example, Luke uses *epistrephein* to denote physical movement (nearly 20 times). Also Paul uses *apostrephein* and *anastrephein* (Eph 4:22, 1 Tim 1:12), both of which carry the idea of turning and then walking (Hiebert 1988:240).

"Turning" and Metanoia: Simon Peter

In the introductory part of *Simon Peter: From Galilee to Rome*, Charsten P. Thiede (1986) makes the point that the prominence of Paul "in the history of Christendom" might not really be justifiable (1986:10). Featuring in all four Gospels and receiving ample space in the Book of Acts, it is Peter, not Paul, "who stands out most clearly as a character in his own right, with all his strengths and shortcomings" (1986:10). Furthermore, Thiede reminds Bible readers "that conveniently tucked away near the end of the New Testament are two invaluable documents purporting to come from Peter himself (1986:10)."

Peter's life story, as we know it from the episodes recorded in the New Testament, was a process of "turning" and "returning." In an initial encounter with Jesus at Bethany across the Jordan, Peter's attention is first "turned to" Jesus as the Messiah (Jn 1:28, 41). This encounter at the Jordan River, and the subsequent journey to Galilee of Jesus, John, Andrew, Simon Peter, Philip, and Nathaniel, was but the beginning of a lifelong journeying together. In Capernaum, where Peter had made his home and run his fishing business, he helps Jesus to preach to the crowd from his boat. Chronologically, Luke 5:1-10 contain Peter's "first words in the gospels" (Thiede 1986:23). The miraculous catch of fish was a second, significant "turning point" in the life of Peter based on a manifestation of Jesus' Messiahship. While still in the boat, Simon Peter realizes the radical difference between himself and Jesus. He falls on his knees, calls Jesus "Lord", and acknowledges his "extraordinary powers" (Thiede 1986:23). Right there, he receives his missionary title and missionary call: he is to become "a fisher of men." From that time forward, Peter's house became a base for Jesus' ministry (Thiede 1986:23-24).

A decisive event of "turning even closer" to Jesus was Peter's proclamation of Jesus being the Christ (Mk 9:29), though he did not yet fully realize the full content of His Messiahship. Peter, mistaking the Messiahship as the fulfillment of a political role, rebukes Jesus who reacts sharply to Peter's words. (Mk 9: 32-33).[12]

After having moved together with Jesus for a considerable length of time and having witnessed Jesus' ministry from close range, Peter denies him three times in the courtyard of the palace after Jesus' arrest. When he realized what he had done, Peter, having earlier so confidently proclaimed that he would lay down his life (Jn 13:37),[13] was "shattered to pieces" (Thiede 1986:86), left the

---

[12] The NIV rendering "Get behind me, Satan!" could mean something like "go and think about what you have said and *do* follow me as a believing disciple (italics in the original) (Thiede 1986:33-34).

[13] Mk 14:31 says: But Peter insisted emphatically, "Even if I have to die with you, I will never disown you." "Emphatically (ἐκπερισσω"ς-*ekperissos*) occurs only here in the whole Greek Bible and indicates how shocked and hurt he (Peter) must have felt" (Thiede 1986:70).

scene and wept bitterly (Mk 14:72; Mt 26:75; Lk 22:62). Was Peter converted when he denied the Lord three times just within a few hours? In this instance, we have Jesus' own view of Peter's situation. Jesus talks of Peter "turning back" (ἐπιστρέψας-*epistrepsas*)[14] or "returning" to Him even long before the incident in the courtyard actually happens. The emphasis is not on conversion as other translations seem to suggest[15] but on Peter's "human frailty (as a follower of Jesus turning back), against which the forgiveness of Christ would shine even brighter" (Thiede 1986:86).

3.1.2 A Second Set: "Relational Interaction"

A second set that emerges from Scriptures in regard to conversion is the "biblical focus (that) is upon a relational interaction that may be entered into a number of culturally and psychologically appropriate ways" (Kraft 1980:333-334). Is there evidence that "relational interaction" had taken into account culture and personality, say, for example, in the life and ministry of the disciple Peter?

Cultural Background of Simon Peter

Peter was not a dumb, backward, uneducated, and simple Galilean fisherman as it is sometimes commonly assumed. Galilee had been permeated with Greek culture and language for several centuries. The Romans and their dominating presence, too, had imprinted their language and culture on Jewish life (Thiede 1986:17-20). Thiede counters the argument that a man like Peter "could not possibly have written the elaborate Greek of the first epistle that bears his name" (1986:20), by pointing out that both Peter and his brother Andrew, as well as their associate Philip, had Greek names indicating the strong influence of Greco-Roman culture upon their families.[16] The socio-economic situation (major trade routes touching the Sea of Galilee, and the fishing industry and trade) made it obligatory that Peter spoke fluent Greek.[17] And, of course, Aramaic and his mother tongue Hebrew were also at his disposal (Thiede 1986:20-21). Peter, like any other Jew, would have enjoyed a similar educational upbringing: attending elementary school, "usually until the age of fourteen"; and mastering "reading, writing and effective memorization techniques, (which) were common features" (Thiede 1986:22). His multi-language skills along with his multi-cultural exposure were part and parcel of

---

[14] "But I have prayed for you, Simon, that your faith may not fail. And when you have turned back, strengthen your brothers." Lk 22:32 (NIV).

[15] "Ich aber habe für dich gebeten, daß dein Glaube nicht aufhöre. Und wenn du dereinst dich bekehrst, so stärke deine Brüder." Lk 22:32 (Lutherbibel Standardausgabe, revidierte Fassung von 1984).

[16] "Apparently, their parents had absorbed enough hellenistic influence to find it quite natural to give their sons non-Aramaic names" (Thiede 1986:21).

[17] "The area was marked by cultural cross-fertilisation and multi-lingualism" (Thiede 1986:20).

Peter when he first turned to Jesus and also later in his apostolic ministry. His conversion to Christ neither blotted out his multi-cultural heritage nor required him to get rid of his cultural package as "worldly" excessive baggage. Quite the contrary! The person, apostle and missionary Peter put his multi-cultural-heritage, all his skills, as well as his multi-cultural knowledge systems[18] into service for Christ!

The Person Simon Peter

The gospel of Mark reports that Peter and Andrew were the first disciples. Mark's account (1:19) of the calling the two brothers is quite extraordinary, to say the least. Why would they just leave behind everything, and follow Jesus' call that had reached them "out of the blue"? The answer is that this was not Peter's first encounter with Jesus. They had first met in Bethany where John the Baptist had made his camp to baptize people in the river Jordan (Jn 1: 28). Peter's spontaneous reaction after the miraculous catch of fish (Lk 5:1-11) was not an instant conversion, but rather a significant boost toward trusting and committing himself to Christ.[19]

Looking at the sketch of Peter from the scriptural accounts, one character trait stands out: *spontaneity*. Whether it was spontaneous protest (Lk 5:5),[20] or spontaneous action (Jn 13:8-9),[21] Peter was quick to speak and act. He must, however, have enjoyed the trust of his fellow disciples as their *spokesperson* and as occupying a leading role among them.[22] Other characteristics with which Peter can be credited, are his *voluntary submission* under the authority of Jesus (Thiede 1986:23) (Lk 5:5) and his *fighting spirit* (Mt 26:51; Mk 14:47; Lk 22:50; Jn 18:10). In Gethsemane he did not shy away from using physical power; in fact, "Peter was the only one to show actual physical courage" (Thiede 1986:78). Also, he was *willing and open* enough to cross cultural thresholds as when he was introduced to the Gentile mission in a vision (Acts 10:9-23).

---

[18] As an example, see Acts 10:9-23.

[19] One must not forget that some time prior to going fishing, Jesus had healed Simon Peter's mother-in-law from a high fever. It could not have escaped his notice. Peter had already had a "share" of Jesus' power when he was confronted with the miraculous catch (see Lk 5:38-39). Psychologically, his degree of awareness for Jesus was considerably greater than at their first meeting at the Jordan River.

[20] Simon answered, "Master, we've worked hard all night and haven't caught anything." (NIV).

[21] "No," said Peter, "you shall never wash my feet." Jesus answered, "Unless I wash you, you have no part with me." "Then, Lord," Simon Peter replied, "not just my feet but my hands and my head as well!" (NIV).

[22] Mark 3:13-19, Matthew 10:1-4 and Luke 6:12-16 all mention Peter first.

In closing, Peter's initial encounter with Christ developed into a lifelong commitment to Christ, which recognizably *transformed* the fisherman Peter, but did not *superimpose* a specific, stereotype Christian personality[23] on him.

4. Conversion: A Psychological Model

Johnson and Malony (1982) have dealt with conversion from a biblical and psychological perspective. Christian conversion is a "change from one faith to another" (1982:21) or a ""change of lords"" (Hiebert 1988:233). Such a change is comprised of God's side and the human side. God's side, his part and work in conversion is, however, out of reach for us. Nevertheless, the immediate question that surface is of a historical nature. When did/does this event of "change" become history in the life of a person? Did/does conversion happen in a moment (like changing a shirt), or did/does it involve a process over time? The answer is not an easy one. Johnson and Malony have shown this in their introduction to conversion, saying that interest in the subject "(even) gave birth to a new discipline, the psychology of religion" (Johnson & Malony 1982:21).

4.1 Moment or Process?

Just as a person does not live in a vacuum; neither do changes – Christian conversion among them – occur in a vacuum. Man, being a being of culture who exists in a web of social relationships is certainly imprinted by culture and society (category formation as discussed above shows this influence clearly). Therefore, conversion is no exception.

Engel and Norton (1975) and Tippet (1976/1977) have each attempted to produce a model that would account for these influences across cultures.[24] The emphasis "across cultures" is vital inasmuch as a concept or category of one single culture may, and actually does, result in distorting the way conversion takes place with different people in different cultures. "A single-act experience (and) ... the tendency in Western Evangelical Christianity to see conversion as a private, static, once-for-all event divorced from a cultural context is called into question" (Johnson & Malony 1982:22).[25]

---

[23] Johnson and Malony affirm that, despite Ferm's (1959) suggestion that "Christian conversion brings about a radical change in personality," there has not been much evidence "to support Ferm's (1959) contention that conversion results in a radical change in personality in the individual" (1982:65). Court has this to say: "Hence, at this point, it is not clear whether reference to someone becoming a new person in Christ, or being born again, which are clearly radical in their *spiritual* content, mean the same thing as saying that they undergo a personality change – a psychological phenomena" (1988:222).

[24] Johnson & Malony and Kraft have both adapted Tippet's model (Johnson & Malony 1982:23; see also Kraft 1980:336).

[25] Hiebert makes a similar assertion (1988:249, 263).

The previous section dealt with two essential elements in conversion: *turning round* to face and *relating* to the center, Jesus Christ. Tippet's conversion model complements these two elements by widening the scope, looking at the change of "faith" or "lords" as a dynamic sequence of events.

FIGURE 8: THE DYNAMIC SEQUENCE OF EVENTS IN CONVERSION
(Based on Johnson & Malony 1982; Adapted from Tippet 1976)

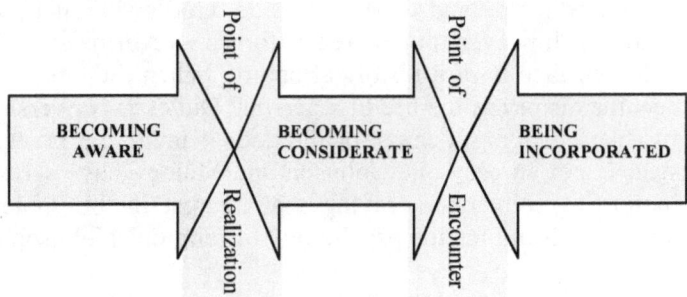

4.1.1 Becoming Aware

All changes have to do with context or, rather, contexts. One cannot experience change of any kind if there is no awareness of one's present state (present context) and, at the same time, of some other, different way of life, a new context. Awareness of, or becoming conscious of, a new context may come as a natural development, as an internal crisis, or as a result of direct advocacy (see Tippet 1977:203-221; also Johnson & Malony 1982:23-30).

Chewe developed growing awareness for the Christian faith in 1988, when he was put in touch with a group of Christians. His *ntenda* status and the three traumatic experiences (no cattle, no gun, and no education) had left a deep "scar" and conflict inside him. His marriage in the same year and his drinking habits had added further weight to the burdens he had to cope with in his life. When the new context first intruded on him, he was not immediately struck by its new properties.

But strong and direct advocacy by Paul (a Zambian), his Christian mentor, and others helped him to see the new "faith," the new "lord" as a context with potential to change. Over a period of several months, Chewe was "fed" with information of the new context. Chewe came to the *point of realizing* that the new context was not merely an idea but a real possibility.[26]

---

[26] Tippet says: "There comes a moment when it suddenly becomes apparent that the passage from the old context to the new is not merely an idea. It is possibility" (in Johnson & Malony 1982:30-31).

4.1.2 Becoming Considerate

"It is significant to note that anthropological (Tippet) and psychological (Austin) research demonstrates that people are influenced by significant others in the conversion experience" (Johnson & Malony 1982:32). This was undoubtedly true in the life of Chewe (cf. chapter seven). Significant others helped him to begin considering the new faith. Often, decisions are made during this period of consideration (Johnson & Malony 1982;30).

Chewe's first "turning point" was the Wednesday afternoon Bible study at his house. The new context had become reality to him. After a troublesome night,[27] he "turned round" to face and *relate* to Christ. The *point of encounter* with Christ was embedded in a resolution to stop drinking. He made an initial commitment to Jesus, a "*conscious allegiance (faith commitment) to God* (italics in the original)" (Kraft 1980:334) that grew with the years, but was put to the test in a number of instances. The 1991 crisis with the *ngulu* episode proved to be a decisive period in "turning back" to Christ. Similarly, the 1994 crisis turned out to be a "turning toward" the center Jesus Christ. Lastly, the year 2000 tested his faith and relationship with God more than ever before. The events (cf. chapter seven) during the months of sickness were also characterized by "turning" to Christ "anew."

4.1.3 Being Incorporated

Missiological (Tippet 1976) and anthropological (Arnold van Gennep 1961, "rites of passage") literature describes incorporation into the new context (church) as taking place in an act (Johnson & Malony 1982:36).[28] Incorporation affirms a person's stance and formal status in the group followed by a process of consolidation. "The process of incorporation is an ongoing process in which the person grows in a biblical faith" (Johnson & Malony 1982:37).

In Chewe's case, there was no formed, organized church body, which would have enacted a certain rite to be followed. By then, the group was a band of individuals, led by a layperson, who got transferred in September 1988. Chewe's incorporation was in form of taking up leadership of the group as "immediate successor" to Paul, his mentor. The leadership was transferred to him by God (as he saw it), and was acknowledged by the group even up to his death.[29]

---

[27] See chapter 7 and Footnote 3!

[28] Tippet says: "The Act of Incorporation should be a confirmation and consummation of the change of religious faith,"... (in Johnson & Malony 1982:36). Kraft mentions baptism as a means to enact incorporation (1980:328-344).

[29] See chapter seven and the section "1991: Role Resolution Crisis-A Change of Symbols." Baptism followed later and was performed by the author.

Does a psychological model of conversion make God's part redundant and lead us to favor a model that emphasizes man's active searching and responding? Johnson and Malony, summarized by Hiebert, postulate an interactive situation in which "God is seen as the author of conversion but we cooperate in the experience" (1988:229).[30]

4.2 Individual or Corporate?

Tippet, Hiebert and probably others place high value on the socio-cultural situation in which conversion occurs. Next to cultural givens (e.g. category formation), there are the social dynamics (family and kinship structure, clans, etc.) that play into the discussion of change. "The importance of group dynamics in conversion" (Hiebert 1988:250) is, for example, seen in "Oceanic peoples who have become Christians [mostly] so by group movements" (Tippet 1977:204).

Can a decision as important as conversion be solely an individual's decision in societies with a high grid of group conformity? Hiebert and Tippet are in support of the importance of the group. Spindler stresses the individual. He says:

> I see in present mainline missiology a great reluctance to deal with personal conversion in real theological depth. We are so persuaded of the wrong of individualism and pietistic reduction, and so well instructed that non-Western cultures are not individualistic but community-oriented, by nature apt to solidarity and mutual love, that we can no longer believe that human beings are indeed individuals and should be approached as individuals (1997:282).

Both positions have implications for missions. The polarization of the individual may tear him out of his existing social networks, whereas group movements may include individuals who do not share the decision, and elements of syncretism creep into the church (see Hiebert 1988:251, 253).

It has been one of the main scopes of this study to be particularistic concerning emphasizing the individual (e.g. see chapter six and the culture concept of Nuckolls and chapter seven, Chewe's life). Private and public are interlocked with a firm grip on each other yet both make an imprint on one another. No individual will totally submerge into group-conformity. He would not be a human being, if he did not exercise agency upon his context, trying to give meaning to his very own life. In the same vein, there is little value in promoting the individual and with it individualism above almost anything and everything in life. If we are liberated from "anything" and "everything," we have become strangers to ourselves.

---

[30] Kraft's second constant in the conversion process: "*a dynamic interaction between God and human beings*" hints at the same (1980:335).

Our world is a changing world. "World-exposure" endorses rapid changes to even the most remote societies on our planet. Societies with beliefs in and values for "group conformity" are challenged by the hour. But cultures are generally quite conservative about massive changes.[31] What can be proposed is that it is no longer – and probably never was – a case of personal *or* corporate, but one of personal *and* corporate partaking in the event and process of change – and conversion.

Chewe exercised a great deal of individual influence on his context and on the social group around him. His conversion did not, however, tear him out of the existing social networks. But he certainly did take up a new stance and occupied a new social role. He did not wait for the approval of the group (the extended family, and the village community) to take this deliberate step of changing from one faith which was a mixture of traditional and catholic beliefs to another, protestant understanding of faith). But he certainly gauged other people's feelings and tried to influence as many persons from his extended family as possible to become part of and join the new church. Some did; others remained aloof. Obeyesekere is probably right when he stresses the fact that a decisive element of individual vs. group is the potential and capacity of meeting the needs of the group (the wider social group) that an individual agency generates in change, decision or Christian conversion (cf. chapter seven). Group conversions are not "out-of-the-sky" dynamics but develop their dynamic force through the personality of individuals of the group.[32]

5. Conversion: New Context – New Values and New Perspectives

Change to a new context also means change to new context values and beliefs. The New Testament is rather strong and particular about new values in a person's life in relationship to Christ. Jesus discusses some of them in Matthew chapters 5-7 declaring them as Kingdom Ethics in "present time" (Ridderbos 1986). Paul was equally explicit about a relationship with Christ that was in accord with a new life in Christ (Rom 6:4; 7:6; 12:1-2; Eph 4:24; Col 3:12 or 1 Thess 5: 12-28; 2 Thess 3: 6-14). High emphasis is placed in New Testament teaching on relationships with others, for example, keeping peace and keeping unity.

---

[31] "Kulturen stellen festgefügte Systeme dar, ausgestattet mit einer natürlichen Trägheit, die allzu schnellen Veränderungen Widerstand leistet und Zusammenbrüchen entgegenwirkt" (Käser 1997:282). "The inventory of a culture is, of course, very large. Even though many things may be changed from generation to generation, many things remain pretty much the same" (Kraft 1996:360-361).

[32] The "1994 crisis" triggered a movement among young men to open up to the Christian faith. At least five of them moved beyond initial interest in Christ. They are all strong Christians today with various responsibilities in their local church (cf. Chapter seven, "Interpretation of the Crisis"). There was a "group movement," albeit the size of the group did not encompass whole social units.

5.1 Chewe and New Values

New Values took root in Chewe's life through interaction with the Scriptures. As mentioned earlier, he was a Bible reader. In March 2000 (just months before his death), he shared with me about values that had become important in his Christian life. He made particular reference to one book in the Old Testament and one Hymn.

5.1.2 David: No Revenge!

Chewe: The book of 1 Samuel is important to me. I find a lot of encouragement through the life of David. He didn't give up despite pressure, persecution and family pressure. I read it regularly!

- When Saul was chasing after David, Saul was in the hands of David who had reason to kill him for all he had done to him. But David did not regard the encounter in the cave as an opportunity of vengeance. [No *revenge!*]

- David and his son Absalom. Even after being found guilty of conspiracy, David wanted to spare Absalom's life. [No *revenge!*] In my life, I have experienced people who were against me like my "elder brother" Patrick M. (cousin). [Though he did not particularly mention the name of his immediate young and elder brother, his life story implied them both, too]. So, one time this elder brother insulted me badly while he was drunk. The next morning I went to see and greet him. He felt very shy and ashamed. I greeted him regularly in order to extend friendliness to him. After some time he came to my house and we discussed the issue. Since then, we enjoy a good relationship. What David experienced and what he went through, I can relate to it personally in my life. This is when I am helped to handle difficult situations in life.

The "no-revenge attitude" shines especially bright against the events that took place during the last weeks of his life. It will be remembered that he had decided to move in with his elder brother (cf. chapter seven). I then understood that Chewe wanted to restore relationships with them and to do penance for past wrongs. Keeping peace; no revenge! Chewe kept his focus on this one "new-Kingdom-value."

5.1.3 "The Shepherd Hymn"

Robert: What is your most favorite Hymn?
Chewe: The Song found in *Inyimbo sha Kulumbanya Lesa,* No. 97: *Lesa e Kacema wandi* (The Lord is my Shepherd).[33]

R: Why is this song so special to you?

---

[33] Complete Hymn in Appendix 2.

C: The whole of my life reflects the words of the Hymn. Each time I go through the verses, the words are always new; they speak to me afresh. When I am sick or when I am in need of something, then this is the song that comforts me most.

[*Comment*: a week before this interview was taken (mid-March 2000), Chewe had been quite sick for four days]

> V2: In times of problems and feeling of giving up, God restores my heart (*umutima*/psyche).

> V3: This verse speaks of death. In the past, I feared death very much. The Hymn helps me to conquer the fear of death. The words also correspond with Jn 5:24:

>> I tell you the truth, whoever hears my word and believes him who sent me has eternal life and will not be condemned; he has crossed over from death to life. (NIV)

> V4: At times I ask myself why God has chosen me; why he has brought me close to his *cintamba* (altar). [*Comment*: could be connected to his parents who wanted him to become a Priest, but could not pursue this career because of his poor health].

> V5: This verse speaks of encouragement. Someone should be on good terms with people here on earth. This will help me to understand that I am a child of God.

The Hymn stresses Chewe's focus on a new value system brought about by his conversion to Christ.

5.2 Chewe and New Perspectives

Christian conversion not only includes new values and beliefs, but also a new future perspective. The apostle Paul, in clear and uncompromising words, presents the story of the Thessalonian church emphasizing:

> how you turned to God from idols to serve the living and true God, and to wait for his Son from heaven, whom he raised from the dead-Jesus, who rescues us from the coming wrath (1Thessalonians 1: 9-10). (NIV)

The "turning-to-God-from-idols" axis is immediately linked to a future dimension, the "coming of the Son from heaven." The future dimension is qualified by waiting – not idly sitting around, but rather actively participating in the affairs of Christ with his Church on earth. And secondly, to be assured of Christ's intervention "from the coming wrath."

Bemba culture too places great emphasis on relationships and looking forward to the "future." As documented in chapter two, "the East signifies the future, hope and expectation, light and happiness" (Hinfelaar 1994:3). Chewe's future, hope and expectation were however concrete. Christ guaranteed him a future. Christ would give him life eternal, not life that was dependent on the memories of the human community.

5.2.1 John: Eternal Life

Chewe: In the Gospel of John, Jesus talks very much of the Kingdom of God. Especially chapters 14 and 16 contain words of encouragement. For example, Jn 16:20 provides total encouragement to me.

> I tell you the truth, you will weep and mourn while the world rejoices. You will grieve, but your grief will turn to joy. (NIV)

There are times when there is pressure from the family and other people. Then I consider these words that grief [sorrows] will be turned into joy at the end. Sometimes we think too much of our present life here on earth. This is when many people give up hope and faith. I have seen many people losing their faith in Jesus Christ because they were just looking at their present life.[34]

5.2.2 A Bemba Chorus

Chewe: There is a vernacular chorus I like very much. The words are:

| *Yesu nshila ya mweo,* | Jesus is the way of life, |
| *Mwana Lesa* | The Son of God |

These words correspond very much with Jn 14:6 where Jesus says he is the way, the truth and life; life here on earth, and eternal life with Him in the time to come. Chewe had a perspective that reached far beyond his life on earth. Little did he know that he was going to be confronted by the words of the song and scripture just so soon after he had stated them to me in March 2000.[35]

5.3 A Word to Missionary Workers

One must be aware of one's own cultural package and own theological inheritance when engaged in intercultural ministry. Otherwise, misjudging people might not only be a "theoretical possibility," but could turn out to be a reality with harmful implications and consequences.

---

[34] Interview on March 22, 2000 on the veranda of his house in A-village.

[35] Interview on March 22, 2000 on the veranda of his house in A-village.

In "introductory entry point" of this chapter, I said that Chewe's "converted behavior" at one time raised questions of his conversion in *my* mind. There were "blanks" in my conversion picture of him. In other words, knowing he was converted and the difficulty I had with some of the observed behavior, caused a situation of ambiguity to arise. Duane Elmer remarks,

> when someone does something that we do not understand, and an explanation is not quickly forthcoming, we actually provide our own explanation (1993:19).

We fill in the "blanks" with our own culturally and personally conditioned data. Sadly, "the interpretation we provide virtually always attributes a *negative* (italics in the original) characteristic and motivation to the other person," says Elmer (1993:19-20). This negative attribution[36] toward another person's behavior poses a serious problem. Negative attribution works in all areas of our lives. It usually is the first reaction toward "strangeness" and unfamiliarity, especially when different cultures meet.

In particular, the Western mind seeks to close ambiguities fast, says Elmer, and in doing so, people are quick "to attach some deficiency to the other person" (1993:20). This happened to me. What was the "damage?" The damage, I would say, was minor in this particular case. It was something that affected only *me* and only for a short period of time. It could have caused serious damage to our relationship, had I not consciously tried to maintain our friendship and relationship. I knew enough facts about his life (although I am in no way saying I had the "whole picture") to provide me with clues toward understanding his situation and with a push to move on with him. This is a theme I will take up in the following chapter when dealing with counselling.

6. A Concluding Reflection

Conversion is a highly debated matter across a range of different disciplines. Controversial individual opinions may always accompany the study of change – and conversion – but there is really no need to make conversion a matter of sharp controversy between disciplines. Missiology can benefit from other viewpoints, especially if conversion remains or again becomes a prominent missiological feature in its own right. If Spindler is right, then missiology needs to do its homework for this to take place.

This chapter has highlighted some opinions on conversion of several disciplines. A general anthropological view of conversion as proposed in Boston and Amsterdam was found to be inadequate. Theological critiques for each view were given.

---

[36] Elmer points out that social scientists call this *"the negative attribution theory."* Part of an address Elmer delivered to a Missionary Assembly in Dobel, Germany, April 1999.

Conversion concerns a person in reference to his worldview and his social networks. Hiebert's socio-cultural proposals were reviewed. Cultural factors, such as category formation, were seen to influence people in regard to their definition and understanding of conversion. The "bounded set" and the "fuzzy set" categories were each looked at and evaluated as dissatisfactory for categorizing Christian conversion. The author's own example was given as a demonstration of the fact that concepts and categories do indeed influence a person in judging the meaning of Christian conversion for an individual from a different culture.

Biblical moorings for conversion were considered on reading Charles Kraft and his proposal of two sets operative in Christian conversion. Hiebert's "relational" or "centered" set category was presented as a complement to Kraft's model. "Turning" and "returning" forms the first set and "relational interaction" the second set of Christian conversion. In a case study of Simon Peter, both sets were validated.

Concerning one's socio-cultural environment, conversion also concerns a person as an individual – his own psychological "wiring." The Tippet/Johnson & Malony psychological model – growing awareness, consideration of the new faith, and incorporation into the church as a process of dynamic sequences – allows for a cross-cultural application and understanding of Christian conversion. Part of this process could be a crisis that creates in the person a problem-solving perspective (adolescence and the search for identity) or a crisis experience (sickness, divorce and so forth). Advocacy plays a large part in the decision-making process.

Chewe's conversion was a dynamic process within culturally defined parameters. This process had its beginning in an initial commitment to God, a turning point – one day in 1988 – towards Christ. The intrapsychic conflicts of his previous life and the meaninglessness of living at that time provided the entry point to an awareness of Christ and an acknowledgement of him as his Lord, who, by Chewe's following him, would give him a new outlook on life. Subsequent events (1991, 1994 and 2000) challenged his conversion and allegiance to Christ, but each time Chewe regained his focus on Him, even amidst culturally conditioned contexts and reaffirmed his relationship with Him until his death.

The question of whether Christian conversion is an individual or a corporate decision in societies where the group is a social dominant was answered by saying it is a mixture of both. Individual agency and values held by the group (e.g. conformity) interact in dialectical manner. Another issue that was – admittedly briefly – addressed was that of the new values and perspectives entailed by Christian conversion were addressed. This was done by presenting reference points of Chewe's Christian life. Although the human side in conversion was considered, it must be noted and stressed that Jesus Christ is the "author and perfecter of our faith" (Heb 12:2).

Chapter 10
A Third Missiological "C": Counselling

1. Introduction

Communication and conversion could easily be treated as separate entities in their own academic – or missiological – right. But this study portrays a real person in real life contexts, and a missionary confronted with both. Advocacy is defined as a person-to-person proclamation of God's Good News to help people to convert to God (or to help those who are already converted to go on with God). This moves subject and missionary to yet another plane of interaction. Relationships and personal friendships spring up in the course of time. But how does one relate to another when life is getting tough and when light turns into darkness? Life is not always smooth and even. Neither are relationships always easy-going and simple. Counselling is as much a missiological concern as the two previously mentioned areas of communication and conversion.

This chapter is interested in establishing a basis of counselling in a call for theological ethics. A bond of true and genuine human solidarity is the beginning of counselling ethics since the formation of this bond prevents us from treating people as "cases." Nevertheless, true solidarity must have God at the center while the basic communication structures of love, spirit, word, deed and life are at work.

Counselling across culture means trying to understand people in their context of culture and life experience. Z. Vendler's theory on understanding people will inform this section. It will be shown that knowledge, understanding, and empathy form an intertwining relationship. The case study and the author's own experience are at the heart of this section.

There are reasons why we fail to understand people. Three possible causes are offered and solutions proposed. An "Afterthought" and a section titled "Aftermath" conclude this chapter. In "Afterthought," a special, additional viewpoint on Chewe's life context receives attention. "Aftermath" provides hints indicating that closing the file on one individual person does not necessarily mean the file is closed in relation to other people.

Because of the circumstances under which the counselling theme came into focus, this chapter purposely lacks extensive engagement with theoretical frameworks pertaining to the field of counselling, although they are not entirely absent.

1.1 Setting the Stage

When faced with the critical situation of Chewe's four months of sickness (April to July 2000), I also underwent emotional stress. On two occasions when he faced imminent death, I was thrown into inner turmoil. In addition, the relationship we had and the helplessness I felt when visiting during these hours of darkness, caused questions to form in my mind. Some questions were just loose strains of thoughts, others evolved into words. I present some of these questions below:

1. Am I maintaining contact with this person and persons in general in order to keep up appearances, so that others might say that I am "a sympathetic fellow," or "a nice person"?

2. Am I maintaining contact in order to maintain a given "role"? (The community knows that I am a missionary, consequently they expect me to act like one).

3. Am I content with just fulfilling my duties? (Since "visiting the sick" is part of the work I have been charged with, and because I am being paid for this work, I will just do it).

These questions provide ample ground for internal battles. No doubt, very often when "duty," "life," or "friendship" confront us with the problems, maladies, and struggles others have, we also struggle. Sometimes, when caught up in such a situation, there is no escape. We simply have to look the situation squarely in the eye. "Keeping up appearances," "maintaining a role," or "fulfilling one's duties" are indeed powerful, compelling forces. But are these the only choices or strategies that are left to us? I believe that what is needed is a compelling force that is tied to a common history with the person we are dealing with – however long and intense this common history may be or may have been. The awareness that our common history as human beings can make something happen between two persons is the beginning. I am referring to a perceived and profound sharing of a common humanness. In other words, do I relate to someone as a person, or as a "case"? Am I relating to a being with emotions, fears and conflicting desires, or to an object that no longer receives (or has never received) my respectful attention "as a unique, esteemed human being designed by God?" (Elmer 1993:19).

However, to conclude that the goal of all counselling is to achieve solidarity between human beings as an end in itself would be to depart from missiological concerns and to misread the content of scripture. *In meeting man as man, man's maker cannot be declared redundant.*

1.2 Demarcating the Field

These few introductory notes have already demarcated the complex field involvement in counselling practice. Counselling is not something which one does or offers to another person as a mere service. Counselling is not a sterile exercise in which technicalities are settled, roles fulfilled, or duties performed. Counselling is a person-to-person interaction that involves ethics.

2. A Call for Theological Ethics

The compelling force referred to above is ethics. Some may call it "morality", others "sympathy", and again others "solidarity."[1] However, these labels neither express satisfactorily the kind of ethics that are applicable to the counselling of a single person, nor the kind of ethics that is needed to further the cause of missiology. What is needed, I believe, is ethics that is rooted in *theos*, in God himself, and that derives its compelling force from His *logos*, His love-word to us.

Piennisch (cf. chapter eight) asks what the communicative basic structures of love, spirit, word, deed and life mean for counselling (1995:193).

2.1 "Shepherd-Attitude": A Basic Structure of Counselling

The structure of love comes to light in counselling being a service – but not merely a service! – because it is rendered to an individual in the "Shepherd-attitude" as demonstrated in the ministry of Jesus to his disciples (Mt 9:36-38; Mk 6:34) (see Piennisch 1995:195). Jesus as the self-declared Good Shepherd (Jn 10:11) does not shy away from efforts to go and seek the one "sheep" that has gone astray (Mt 18:12-13). Jesus demonstrates this "Shepherd-attitude" to the extent that he gives his life for his "sheep" (Jn 10:11-15). The ethics of counselling, and its communicative component, is grounded in love that originates in God (Piennisch 1995:195).

2.1.1 "Shepherd-Attitude": A "Fruit of the Spirit"

Love as the binding element between counsellor and counsellee is the result or "fruit" of the Spirit's pouring out God's love into our hearts (Rom 5:5). This fruit, however, is in need of "intentional cultivation" (2 Cor 2:8) and has its origin and example in God's sacrificial love in Christ His Son (Rom 5:8) (Piennisch 1995:195).

2.2 "Shepherd-Service": Mandate of the Church

When Jesus prepared for his return to the Father, he specifically requested the Spirit, the "Counsellor" (Jn 14:16), to continue the ministry of guiding and counselling (Jn 14:26) the disciples after His departure from them (Jn 14:12). Along with teaching and preaching, the disciples are to continue Jesus' ministry of counselling the weak, the sick and the broken-hearted. The Church as a

---

[1] Piennisch points out that counselling cannot be reduced to mere interpersonal solidarity (1995:194).

whole has received the mandate to continue Jesus' "Shepherd-Service" in the Spirit. In what ways does the Church's "Shepherd-Service" of counselling manifest?

2.2.1 "Shepherd-Service": Spirit-Word Ministry

The New Testament speaks of the "Shepherd Service" of the Church as a Spirit-word ministry given to one another. For example, in the epistle to the Philippians, Paul exhorts the church to give encouragement in Christ, comfort of His love, fellowship with the Spirit, tenderness and compassion (Phil 2:1). It is especially comfort in love that represents the communicative dimension of counselling one another and is a sign of fellowship made possible in the power of the Holy Spirit (Piennisch 1995:196).

2.2.2 "Shepherd-Service": Word-Deed Ministry

Next to the Spirit-word ministry, the Church is equally mandated to exercise the "Shepherd Service" as a word-deed ministry. Paul, for example, says if someone is caught in a sin, others should "restore him gently" (Gal 6:1). This may require corrective words as well as corrective action. Likewise, Paul reminds the Galatian church to "carry one another's burdens" (Gal 6:2) in fulfillment of Christ's law of love (Piennisch 1995:197). The burdens people carry are many-faceted. But whatever the burden may be, the counsellor's aim is always to help a person to become whole again in all aspects of live, and to be united or reunited with God.

2.2.3 "Shepherd-Service": Ministry unto Life

All "Shepherd Service" has the goal of reconciling man to God, says Piennisch (1995:199). He continues that reconciliation becomes effective when a person realizes the love of God and enters into a peace relationship with Him, with himself and with others (1995:199). Counselling is therefore a ministry unto life. It is a "Shepherd Service" carried by love. It is "Shepherd Service" that touches a person through the spirit-word ministry of encouragement, comfort, tenderness, and compassion. And finally, it is "Shepherd Service" that comes to a person in the word-deed ministry of forgiving him of his sin and carrying his burdens. Such "Shepherd Service" is rooted in love, carried by the Spirit in word and deed, and returns life and wholeness to the sinner, the weak, the sick and the broken-hearted.

3. Walking Frontiers: Counselling Across Cultures

The previous section outlined a theological basis of counselling. The five-fold elements of the communication structure are a tremendous challenge to coming to terms with one's own culture. Even more profound are the demands in a cross-cultural situation. But just as with communication where the missionary takes on a "middle-ground" position, so it is with counselling. A missionary (assuming his background is culturally distinct from that of his host culture) also takes a middle-ground position in the ministry of counselling. On the one hand, he looks for guidance from the Bible – a culturally conditioned perspective. On the other hand, he sees the individual of the host culture in need of help – a data conditioned perspective.

3.1 The Quest: What are the Points of References?

Dealing with other people, especially when they are faced with difficult life situations, is always a quest for "what is appropriate"? What are the things one can do, and what words can one say to help? What reservoir can one draw from? What is good counsel? These issues become even more complex when counselling takes place in an intercultural situation.

Not on few occasions did I ask myself what the proper "thing" to do or not to do was, when Chewe was agonizing in pain. This was even more the case during the periods when death was hovering over his life. What counsel would penetrate his inner state and sooth, or positively remove, his fear of witchcraft implications? How could I possibly help him to conquer his fear? The answer to these issues is more complex than is apparent at first glance. Of course, I know fear from my own personal experience. But still, is a personal knowledge of fear sufficient ground to reach out to another person?

Chewe had great fear. I was able to relate to in a certain way to the emotion of fear and the disturbance this brought in his thinking and his behavior. But only in a *certain* way! What I could not relate to was the context of his fear. I had never had a personal encounter with fear triggered by the *icuulu*/father and *icuulu*/*ubuloshi* (witchcraft) context. So, how could I relate to it? It is useless to simply denounce such fear as unsubstantiated, ridiculous, or "unworthy of Christian standing." The depth of understanding someone can demonstrate toward a person is dependent on the extent to which he has access to that person's context. Renewed relational interaction is a result of this depth of understanding.

3.2 Common Human Properties – Expressed in Unique Ways

Nuckolls, in investigating Bateson's famous account of the Iatmul ritual *Naven,* makes reference to Bateson's attempt to define emotions. According to Nuckolls, "for Bateson, emotions are self-implicating motivational phenomena with direction and force, organized in relationships of opposition, and constitutive of a dialectic" (1996:64).

Elaborating on emotion, Nuckolls states that as human beings we are all born "with the same repertoire of basic emotions" (1996:64). Falling back on Bateson and his discussion on Iatmul "pride," Nuckolls concludes that "Iatmul "pride"... is still pride as we know it, but to understand it is to take into account the *unique ways* (italics mine) in which it has been elaborated by Iatmul culture" (1996:64).

This viewpoint is a workable theory. There is a direct line to the problem of fear as demonstrated above with Chewe. His fear was fear as I know it, but to understand and to deal with it, I had "to take into account the unique ways" the context in which his fear manifested and encroached on his personal life, as well as the greater context of Bemba culture. If I had not known him and his life in his personal-psychological context as well as in his socio-economic context to the extent to which I did, I would have been barred from further influencing and consoling him. A dreadful thought indeed.

Counselling across the culture barrier is like walking a frontier and crossing from the "known" into the "unknown." To cross over into the "unknown" presupposes love for the "unknown." Yet, the bigger difficulty comes once the frontier is crossed, when one is to come to terms with understanding what the "unknown" is made of and why things are the way they are.

Without love and the will to learn the "world across," the "other world" will remain unintelligible and strange even after one has taken the initial strides across. In a cross-cultural counselling set up, the basic structure of love shines forth in trying to understand people in their world and "intentionally cultivate" (see 2 Cor 2:8) relationships especially when cognitive dissonances become a hindrance to relating to one another. Counselling people requires an attitude of openness for people and the right information to understanding people in their "other world" context.

Jesus was the Counsellor par excellence; he "knew all men" (Jn 2:24), that is, he had the whole picture of their lives. He understood people in the entirety of their personal, social and cultural context. He had no need to acquire any information about man "for he knew what was in a man" (Jn 2:25). However, we are not like Jesus. We are His disciples, learning from Him to try and understand people with Him at our side. But are we prepared to learn? How can we learn?

4. A Theory on Understanding People

In "Understanding People," Zeno Vendler develops essential insights for understanding people. In starting out on this subject, Vendler asks why "no scientific model can fully represent, and no covering law adequately explain, man in his inner life and free activity?" although human beings are part of the physical world, and therefore are "observable entities." (1984:200).[2] The answer is that persons are "not merely objects but also subjects of experience – of sensation, feeling, thought and action" (1984:200).

---

[2] Elsewhere Vendler continues to say: "... thus science has no foothold on subjective states" (1984:201).

Being object and subject at the same time means a double representation that cannot fit into any scientific model because a person can objectively register the sensations, feelings, thoughts (when uttered) and actions of another person. But, beyond that, a person can also imagine what the experience of that sensation, that feeling, that thought and action of the subject is *like* (1984:201). As a rational being, a person can represent another person "in imagination, as a subject of experience" (1984:201). Because this representation in imagination is a "subject of experience," it lacks a methodological framework and hence exists outside of science.

Vendler says:

> Thus the connection between subjective states and overt manifestation is to be found in one's experience alone: And this is not a scientific datum. Yet, it enables one to represent, in imagination, the state of another mind. Without the power of the imagination we all would be solipsists [we would have knowledge only of the self; addition mine] (1984:201).

The ability to imagine what it must be like in such and such a situation or emotional state is, however, not conclusive in itself. For the full representation of the experience of another person's agony, guilt, or fear and so forth, the input of contextual information is needed. It is due to the absence or the presence of information that we either understand or do not understand a person. No wonder such statements as "I don't just understand what made him or her do this" are so often part of our daily life experience.

4.1 To Know and To Understand: Related and Yet of a Different Kind

Vendler draws attention to the fact that a significant difference exists between *to know* and *to understand*. He brings out the difference by saying that to "*know* takes both simple and complex objects, ...(because) to know takes all kinds of wh- clauses as complements. (To) *understand* is restricted to more involved objects; ... *understand* can take only *why* and *how* but not *who, what (whom), when,* and *where*" (1984:203-204).

What, when and *where* and to *whom* something happened are observable and can therefore stand on their own. As for *why* and *how*, they require reasons or explanations, which are hidden in the person. In order to extract *why* and *how* details, one either has to elicit them from the subject or one has to imagine what the *why* and *how* details are. "The dimension of understanding opens up after the facts are known" (Vendler 1984:205). Berlo comes close to Vendler's position when he says that, when we say we know someone, "we imply that we understand people" (1960:119). But this can only happen when we can predict how one behaves.

When I went to see Chewe on that Wednesday morning in April 2000, he was in great pain and terrified that witchcraft was responsible for his condition. We rushed him to the clinic where the Doctor diagnosed a lump on his abdomen. There and then, I understood why the family had started with funeral preparations, and why Chewe was petrified with fear. The family diagnosed the lump as *icuulu* and its accompanying cultural context and explanation. Only after I had the fact of *icuulu* and its implications, did the pieces fall into place. I began to understand and was prepared to move closer to him. Had I known about the swelling a few days earlier, I could have predicted what was going to happen. But I did not know those facts to be in that position.

Understanding presupposes a whole lot of *who* and *why* information that can put one in a position to act, beginning by taking interest in the other person. "Understanding requires a constructive effort of the mind to supplement features that are not observable to the senses" (Vendler 1984:205). Vendler advances a rather descriptive example. He remarks:

> The etymology of the word *understanding*, no less than of its Latin equivalent *intelligere* is usually revealing. The metaphor behind the English word suggests the idea of support or foundation, whereas the Latin verb, a combination of *inter* and *legere*, literally means "reading between the lines." Just to play with words: To understand is to "read" what does not appear in the lines yet gives sense to what does (1984:206).

Counselling does not only take into account the information that is disclosed in words. To get to know what words do not give away, a good measure of "reading-between" will be of the greatest service in keeping the lines off communication open between counsellor and counsellee. "Reading between the lines" requires a fair amount of information, both of a person's cultural context and of a person's life context. However, knowledge of the information might not be enough to understand the situation.

4.2 A Call to Move from *Know*-ing towards *Understand*-ing

Knowing the facts should enable one to be considerate and able to place the person in the proper perspective instead of putting him into a different "drawer" or "cabinet." By taking the facts of a person's life into consideration, one is in a much better position to understand his behavior and actions. "Indeed, when talking about understanding people, we *never* mean human bodies at rest performing biological functions. People act; organs only do things. Therefore, it is people who need to be understood" (Vendler 1984:207).

4.2.1 Personal Projection

How does this understanding come about and what does it consist of? Vendler proposes that understanding is to "generate" or "regenerate" in my mind "the mind of a free agent, that is, his thoughts, feelings, desires, and intentions in the unity of one consciousness" (1984:208). Explaining further, he says that it is not enough to accumulate knowledge of observable facts or the sum of a person's behavior.

We must proceed and try to explain his actions

> in terms of reasons, motives, intentions, and the likes, that is to say, in terms of factors belonging to the subjective consciousness rather than to the objective and observable features of his body, behavior, or physical surroundings (1984:208).

Obeyesekere asks: "May not my personal projections help me understand what goes on in the minds of others?" (1984:9). Yes, this is more easily achieved with a person of one's own cultural background. But personal projection taking place in another culture requires knowledge of culture and, more importantly, intimate knowledge of a person in order to achieve understanding of what goes on in his mind.

Personal projection asks: *What* would *I* do in a life-threatening situation where medical explanations of the abdominal swelling (imminent perforation of the intestine caused by amoebic bacteria), and culturally supplied explanations (*icuulu* caused by witchcraft) mixed with family history (death of his father and two of his sisters) of the same sickness are competing with one another? To achieve anything in getting closer to the person with a view toward helping him, "we have to try to understand the subject" (Vendler 1984:208). But understanding involves a further dimension.

4.2.2 Total Transference

It is one thing to try to understand a person by asking what *I* would do if *I was confronted* with the *icuulu* complex. Yet, it is quite another thing to ask what I would do if *I were he* in *his* circumstances. To imagine what I would do in that situation merely means to look for solutions from my own repertoire of rationale, beliefs and emotions. But this is not enough because the subject can only access his own repertoire of rationale, beliefs and emotions in his attempts to chisel out a solution.

> We always can project, or at least try to project, ourselves into the situation in which the agent finds himself by imagining what it must be like for him to be in that situation.

What would *I* feel, how would *I* [italics in the original] react, if I were he? (Vendler 1984:208-209).

Vendler calls this projection "total transference" (1984:209). This means that, apart from imagining what I would do, I have to "try to assume in addition our subject's beliefs, values, prejudices, hang-ups, and the rest" (1984:209). In conclusion, it can be said:

> The understanding of an agent requires empathy, that is, the reproduction, by means of imaginary transference, of the agent's consciousness in one's own mind so that this conduct may appear as a result of free, but rational, choice (1984:209).

The required empathy, the power of sharing another person's feeling, Vendler stresses, is an intentional act of the mind. In the Christian sense, it is a deliberate act of love. An act that requires "intentional cultivation" as hinted earlier on. To be able to move anywhere close to understanding a person, we are well advised to furnish ourselves with the right kind of information. The facts will put us in a position to imagine that person's circumstances (fear, guilt, discouragement, etc.). To project oneself in such a way as to "put on the shoes" of the other person – total transference – requires a deliberate decision, either to retreat *from* the person or to advance *with* the person.

4.3 Theories on Empathy

Berlo asserts that a human being has the ability to understand how another person "operates as a psychological entity – as a person with thoughts, feelings, emotions, etc." (1960:119). In other words, we have "skill in ... *empathy – the ability to project ourselves into other people's personalities* (italics in the original)" (1960:119). How do we develop the ability to project ourselves into other people's personalities? Strictly speaking, says Berlo, there are three main views on empathy. The first view holds that "there is no such thing" (1960:120) and learning is simply a stimulus-response communication. Berlo dismisses this view because human communication behavior is much more complex (1960:120). We are all entangled in a triangular relationship of (a) in what ways our behaviors (b) impacts the behaviors of other people and (c) how their behaviors influence in our behaviors return (1960:121). Every human being has empathetic ability but there are individual differences.

Berlo then proceeds to describe the two remaining theories on empathy, one psychologically-[3] and the other sociologically-oriented.[4]

---

[3] This theory is informed by the work of Solomon Asch (1952), *Social Psychology* (in Berlo 1960:122).

(1) Empathy is an inference theory. "We empathize by using the self concept to make inferences about the internal states of other people ... the self-concept determines how we empathize" (1960:127).

The inference theory implies that the observation of my own behavior related to my internal psychological states – my feelings, thoughts, emotions and so on – cause me to interpret my own physical behavior. As a result, man "develops a concept of *self* (italics in the original) by himself, based on his observations and interpretations of his own behavior" (1960:122). From this interpretation of self-experienced psychological states, man makes inferences about the inner world of others.

The trouble with the inference theory lies in its assumptions, namely, (a) self-experienced internal states are first-hand evidence while other people's internal states are second-hand experience, (b) other people express a certain internal state by the same behavior as oneself, and (c) one can only understand those internal states of which he has experienced himself (1960:123). We all know that our reading and interpretation of other people's behaviors is erroneous, even to the extent that it may result in a communication breakdown. This is a serious issue, I believe, in counselling a person.

(2) Empathy is a role-taking theory. "The concept of self does not determine empathy. Rather, communication produces the concept of self and role-taking allows for empathy" (1960:127).

Which theory are we to believe? Berlo opts for a combination of the two latter theories. Both are valuable because "*man utilizes both these approaches to empathy* (italics in the original)" (1960:127). Berlo suggests that a human being is first engaged in role-taking developing "a concept of the generalized other" (1960:127). Our own concept of self is determined by how we perceive others. While growing up and becoming mature, a person develops a concept of self. We then operate on the basis of the concept of self, that is, "we now begin to make inferences about other people, based on our own concept of self" (1960:127-128).

4.4 "What Happens to *Verstehen* when *Einfühlen* Disappears?"

So far, it has been established that knowing another person significantly moves a person toward understanding that other person. Knowing the struggles and anxiety of someone opens the door to his heart. Yet, over and above knowing the facts and understanding what those facts do to a person in distress, there is another dimension, which Geertz so aptly alludes to in asking "What Happens to *Verstehen* when *Einfühlen* Disappears?" (Geertz 1984:124). Knowing the circumstances that weigh someone down, and under-

---

[4] The major source of this theory is the work of George H. Mead (1934), *Mind, Self and Society* (in Berlo 1960:124).

standing *why* and *how* they cause him to behave the way he does, can be a rather technical affair. It is very possible to merely take note of a person's present situation without getting any closer to him, or even to retreat.

Counselling is an act of love. To put it in another way: *Einfühlen* is the intentional effort to project what goes on in another person's mind, or what it must be like to be in such and such a situation, and sending a positive signal of openness towards the other. Applying this to the case study, one could say that it is not enough to take note of a person's fear which has been caused by witchcraft implications. One must try and pinpoint *why* witchcraft implications are operative and *how* they affect a person.

For example, when Chewe was critically ill and already a candidate for death, we took him to the clinic (cf. chapter four and chapter seven). The examination by the doctor revealed an abdominal swelling which meant different things to different people. To the doctor, it indicated a serious, immediate *medical problem* which he was charged with handling: the impending perforation of the large intestine. The family of Chewe diagnosed the lump as *icuulu* being the result of witchcraft activity of a person within the community. To them it was a *family, relational and cultural problem*. To Chewe it meant following his sister's and father's illness and fate. It was an *existential – no hope – problem*. To other missionary colleagues and outsiders, it posed a *strange, defuse and complex problem*. How to give counsel amidst so many varied viewpoints? Should one make a strong case for the doctor by favoring the medical details, denouncing and ridiculing witchcraft associations, over the family? Should one agree to everything and anything the subject says and feels in order to not upset him any further?

4.4.1 Decision Time

When in early May 2000, Chewe's conditioned again deteriorated after he had come out of a life threatening situation over Easter, I was informed that Chewe had complained that the doctor and I had apparently forgotten about him. Why else had we not come to visit him for over a week?! I was not pleased and felt he was doing me (and the doctor) an injustice after all we had invested in him. To compound matters even further, I came to know that, during this time, family members had visited Chewe. Somehow, they had managed to create the impression that he was not properly looked after. Furthermore, since western-type medicine had not yet healed him, he should rather take some "real (Bemba) medicine," which he then did. He did not get any better. On the contrary! He suffered a full-blown relapse of amoebic dysentery. Only this time the clinic had completely run out of intravenous medication. Tablets were the only medicinal option left, but Chewe frequently vomited everything that entered the stomach.

When confronted with the complexity of Chewe's situation, I was not only confused, I was truly angry. Not only was I angry, but I was also confronted with the question of whether I wanted to commit myself any further. Was I willing to demonstrate the act of love of staying at his side? Or should I leave him to the medical personnel to deal with his medical problem?

4.4.2 More than a Matter of Etiquette

Falling back on Geertz's question: What happens to *Verstehen* (understanding) when *Einfühlen* (what must it be like to be that person in those conditions) disappears? We could answer by saying that one might opt for "role-fulfillment" or *Pflichterfüllung* (doing one's duty). Following the path of "role" and "duty" can be a workable solution that might result in some good. But counselling is not about being disciplined in "role" and "duty" (although this does not mean there is no code of conduct!) and doing some good. The issue really is: How about the "Shepherd Service" and the "Shepherd attitude?" Because of the close relationship we had developed over the years, the months of Chewe's sickness were tough times for me psychologically and emotionally. Yet, the ethical question remained: etiquette or heart? Furthermore, counselling does at times have a double effect: it (hopefully) restores the other person to life. At the same time it might well help the counsellor to come to grips with some of his own problems. Etiquette and heart concerned me, not the counsellee!

4.5 Two Reasons for Failing to Understand a Person

Despite the ability of personal projection and total transference, one might still fail to understand a person. The failure can be due to two reasons: "ignorance of some relevant circumstances and failure to capture some features of the subject's mind (passions, beliefs, perceptions, etc.)" (Vendler 1984:210).

When it comes to the "ignorance of some relevant circumstances," not even the great amount of knowledge or facts that one could gather can explain why and what someone did. With regard to the failure to capture some features of another person's inner state, Vendler advances three factors that can be responsible: "insensitivity, lack of experience, and difference in background" (1984:210).

(1) Insensitivity: The degree to which people are able to *einfühlen*, to empathize, with their fellow men varies from person to person.

(2) Lack of experience: This regards lifestyles or behaviors. Exposure to, and interaction with, persons with different lifestyles usually narrows the gap in favor of better understanding. However, there are also those experiences which are outside the mainstream experience of the "common man," such as the experiences of mystics, addicts or the like (1984:211).

(3) Difference in background: "…this presents the crucial difficulty in understanding people belonging to another culture, from either the past or the present" (1984:211).

Is there a way to eliminate these factors? Vendler says sensitivity can be improved, though insensitivity "can hardly be removed" (1984:211). What about lack of experience? Here the factor of learning comes into play. Experience gathered over time improves one's ability to understand, hence the "lack of experience is usually remedied in time" (1984:211). The "difference-in-background" factor is the hardest to overcome. Vendler knows of but one solution to eliminate the cultural differences: "study and effort" (1984:211).

4.6 Afterthought

Why were the months of Chewe's sickness so complex and at times so bewildering to me despite the longstanding friendship between us? I try to answer by saying: the deeper we enter into the culture and the person's life, the more complex that which we know becomes. Moreover, what we know is challenged, revised, and, at times, produces new questions to which an answer is out of reach. (The sciences in general provide the best examples for this conclusion). I will add one more viewpoint which I believe plays into the discussion of the above-raised question.

Chewe was rather "traditional" and "conservative." I use these labels with much care and do not mean to stress their negative aspects! Although, through the church and working with foreigners like me, he was in touch with a big, progressive and open world, he essentially lived in a "closed world" in his village. One has to recall that, for twenty years, he had not been to the Capital City of Lusaka which, I presume, had changed dramatically. And he had traveled to the Copperbelt Province only once in his lifetime five months before he fell sick! One's level of progressive and "liberalized" thinking is closely linked to the extent of one's exposure to foreign worlds and concepts. Even a city in one's own country can be utterly strange and foreign. This is when worldviews are being touched. I am not saying his worldview had remained the same after his conversion to Christ. Most certainly not! But just as our worldviews as Christians, missionaries and other traveling folks are enriched or changed while we are traveling the world and interacting with people from other life-worlds, so it is with the people we work with in our host-culture. And just as someone from a western country can be tied up in the "four corners" of his own village and yet be a Christian (I'm referring to the peasant farmer village community in my native Bavarian rural area in Germany), so was Chewe a Christian in his "closed world." His world was the village with all its values, burdens and conflicting elements. His horizon was the setting sun. These were the points of reference that were at his disposal when he was critically ill. These were the points of reference I had to come to terms with. But in this "closed-village-world," God was no stranger. God spoke to him. God also helped me and others to speak to him and more precisely, to render "Shepherd Service" unto him with the goal of reconcile him with God and life. Chewe clung to God. Being reconciled with God, he wanted to reconcile with his brothers (cf. chapter seven). Just the day before his departure from this world, he stated to the author his readiness to go this last – though difficult – part of his life's journey.

4.7 Aftermath

Although my counselling of Chewe reached its terminal point with his death, counselling was not over concerning the widow and the church at large that had been stricken by the "Chewe story." After the burial of Chewe, rumors were spread in the villages. One rumor said that, since the church's leader had died, the church itself would die (*Chafwa yalafwa* is what was heard and is a play of words. *Chafwa* is the name of the village but also represents the church that congregates there, which was going to die, or *-fwa*, in the near future).

This is neither the place to describe in detail what then happened, nor is it essential to the concern of this chapter. Suffice it to say that the intimate relationship I had with Chewe and the contextual information of his life and culture was a tremendous asset on my side as I strove to support the church and do my share to keep them going as a church amidst loss and hostility. What crystallizes, however, is the fact that counselling an individual is not necessarily an end in itself. What we gain and what we miss from that one experience might also have beneficial or disastrous repercussions for others. Hence, there are missiological implications and also, possibly, complications. Vendler's call for study and effort is one that deserves undivided attention.

5. A Concluding Reflection

The way we look at people often determines the way we relate to people. In the field of counselling, the question of ethics cannot be ignored. "Shepherd service" and "Shepherd attitude" view people as persons loved by God, separated from God and in need of being reconciled to God. People are not "cases."

Next to the theological perspective, we need additional contexts in order to "see" the other person. That is, to "see" him as person is to "see" him in his cultural and personal contexts. To do so in a cross-cultural situation is like crossing boundaries with the intention of crossing from the "known" into the "unknown." To gather information and facts about the subject's "external circumstances" (Vendler 1984:211), one has to cross the "culture and mind frontier" of the person with whom one is interacting. Doing so enormously enhances one's chances of understanding a person. The external circumstances are, however, more easily grasped than the inner dimension or, so to speak, the internal circumstances under which a person acts.

To know a person means to understand why the external circumstances made him behave the way he does or did. But an understanding of why a certain behavior is triggered by certain external circumstances requires what Obeyesekere calls personal projection: to imagine what it must be like to live in such and such a context. Vendler expanded on that dimension by adding, "what it must be like to be *that* person in *those* conditions" (Vendler 1984:211). He calls this total transference. At this point a crossroad is reached. If I am anywhere near to seeing or understanding (!) what it is like to be *that* person in *that* situation, the question of empathy is most relevant. On the topic of empathy, two relevant theories – inference and role-taking – were described. Berlo proposed a synthesis of both as the most acceptable. We first develop categories of perceiving others (role-taking). Then, later in life, we develop a concept of self based on which we make inferences about other people.

The result of seeing, or at least approximately seeing myself in the counsellee's shoes, can be confusing, terrifying or even repulsive. At this point, Christian counselling must include an intentional act of love on the part of the counsellor who is to stay with the counsellee in accordance with "Shepherd service" and the "Shepherd attitude."

The degree to which one has the ability to empathize varies from person to person. In the Christian context there is also the issue of the gifts that God gives to his people. However, there is always room to improve on sensitivity. Exposure and interaction over time can usually remedy a lack of experience. Vendler's plea for "study and effort" will hopefully become a passionate appeal to those who, like me, are involved in "walking the frontiers" of culture, and who – once those frontiers have been crossed – try to make the most of what is beyond.

Chapter 11
Conclusion and Outlook

1. Conclusion

This study began with a brief description of historical events and cultural elements concerning the Bemba people with special reference to space and time (cf. chapter two). It was shown that man is at the center of Bemba worldview. This anthropocentric view is expressed in the beliefs and values that cover the lifetime as well as the afterlife of Bemba people. In addition, such a man-centered view of the world presupposes a concept of person in his physical existence. Elements such as *umupashi*, (*spirit double*), outlines of the concept of body (cf. chapter three) and categories of illnesses as well as ideas on treating them in order to achieve healing, were presented (cf. chapter four).

What needs to be emphasized, however, is the fact that any discourse on sickness and healing must include a focus on the person who experiences sickness. To omit this focus would be to show concern only with describing the culturally conditioned cognitive dimension of sickness and healing. Such an approach would, in my view, suffer from serious shortcomings. As much as we may want to give an account of the traditional lore of sickness, we must also make an effort to understand how the individual is affected physically, psychologically, and socially, and what he is doing about it medically, psychologically and culturally. This active participation of the patient is essential because it provides insights into *how culture works,* and also addresses the question of *why a person exercises individual agency in this particular manner* from among a whole array of other possibilities at his disposal since this influences our rapport with one another. It was a main aim of this study to investigate the knowledge system of an African culture and describe this aspect of participation and active involvement in sickness and healing by presenting an in-depth study of Chewe's life.

Chewe's agency in dealing with his life and *ntenda* condition unearths two salient features about human life in general and about him in particular: context and conflict. Chewe was *ntenda* in his particular cultural *context*. His striving to exchange a condition of sickness for a condition of well being – to achieve healing – was not a smooth process, but rather one characterized by *conflict*.

In the conclusion of his book studying the life of the Prophet Simon Kimbangu and the history of the Church of Jesus Christ on the Earth (EJCSK) in the former Zaire, Wyatt MacGaffey emphasizes the fact that, to understand Simon Kimbangu as person, prophet, and leader of a church movement, one cannot succeed by compartmentalizing him, the social structures and the historical events. MacGaffey writes:

> To understand Kimbanguism we must consider its adherents concretely in terms of their *specific situations and prospects within the context* (italics mine) (1983:247).

I have followed up on MacGaffey's assumption on the "specific situations and prospects within the context." Chewe's "specific situation" as *ntenda,* as a person stricken with illness, his "prospects" of being healed as viewed within the context of social structures, and the cultural knowledge system within which he acted, all triggered conflict on the personal-psychological and the socio-cultural levels. What MacGaffey asserts for Kimbanguism – the need for compromise, the reality of paradox, ambivalence, and the need for continued adjustment (1983:247) – is equally applicable to Chewe's situation. The engagement of cultural symbols that were infused with personal meaning *was* "continued adjustment" in his attempt to manage internal conflicts, in his quest for healing, and in his efforts to make sense of his life. The personal symbols he employed helped him to move away from the symbols' archaic motivation, and move on to communication and integration with the social group. The cultural context and his action in resolving conflicts led him to experience inner healing.

According to MacGaffey, the tensions or conflicts arising from the above-mentioned mixture of Kimbanguist properties call for situating them "in a holistic, historical study integrating event, individual action and motive with culture and structure" (1983:247). We must undertake to account for Chewe's situation of sickness and his quest for healing in the very same fashion.

The presentation of his life history does not – and should not – try to explain away these tensions. Rather, it seeks to present an account of those tensions, "holistic" and "historical" in nature, and Chewe's striving to obtain healing in "individual action and motive with culture and structure," as demonstrated by his employment of personal religious symbols.

1.1 Man in Context

A major feature and message of this study was, therefore, the emphasis on context. I want to further outline this emphasis on context in a brief review of the material presented.

Obeyesekere asks: Are the meanings of symbols contained in the symbols themselves or in the persons in the culture who employ the symbols? His answer: Personal symbols have to be studied within the *larger institutional context* and *personal life experience.*

Berlo states that "all communication occurs within a cultural context" (1960:164). Question: Is the meaning of words (which are symbols) in the words themselves or in the person who uses the words (symbols)? He answers by saying that meaning is not in the *word-context*, that is, in the words themselves, but in the *person-context*, in the person who uses the words.

Kraft points out that Christian conversion takes place within the *cultural and psychological context* of a person.

And Vendler remarks: "One knows words but understand sentences" (1984:204) – because of words, grammar, and syntax. You know a person, but you understand him in context. Counselling requires more than knowing the facts. One has to *understand the facts in context*.

Whatever subject is put under scrutiny or chosen for scientific investigation, the two basic properties of context and conflict will always emerge. Cognitive anthropology, the social sciences, and theories of communication, to name just some of the disciplines that informed this study, all require context. Missiology is no different. It works in context. We come to people – in the act of carrying out the Christian mission – in context. And we understand God in context, at least to such degree as to be sure about his intentions with this world, with every individual, and with mankind as a whole. We gain understanding of Him in the context of creation, of His interaction with people seen in the longitudinal-salvation history, of His self-revelation in Jesus Christ, of His historical interaction with the Church from the time of Christ's resurrection to the present time, and in the context of the experiences we undergo in our personal life. And last but not least, we proclaim, teach and preach God and Christ in the context of our own personal faith experience and cultural heritage, as well as the entire structures of the host culture.

1.2 Man in Conflict

It is true that missiology cannot operate outside the parameter of context. It is just as true that it can neither escape from conflict nor brush it aside.

A missionary is a messenger or ambassador. But the missionary as an ambassador of Christ engages in a protocol of give-and-take. Conflict is part of his task of winning adversaries, of gathering the scattered, and rescuing the lost. At the core of this undertaking must be what Weber called *verstehen* or "understanding."

Understanding begins when one is fully coming to grips with the human condition. Nuckolls, summarizing Obeyesekere, says: "For Obeyesekere, dialectical conflict is the truth of our human condition" (1996:xxxiii-xxxiv). While we give credit to Obeyesekere's superb description of "dialectical conflict" as the "truth of our human condition," we cannot end there. It will simply not do to place a full stop after stating the conditions all human beings commonly share. Rather, we must proceed and ask why we are in "dialectical conflict."

In the same way we ask for the origin of personal symbols in the life of individuals experiencing psychic conflict, so must we ask for the origin of "dialectical conflict" of "our human condition" as a plurality of human beings. The question of origin is one of necessity.[1]

Yes, we are in conflict with ourselves. Yes, we are in conflict with our fellow man. And yes, most significantly, we are in conflict with our Creator. What is the root cause of our "dialectical conflict" as the "truth of our human condition"? Edward Yarnold describes it this way:

> [It is] the disharmony in man's aspirations, the "war" in man's personality, which arises from his drive both toward God and away from God towards himself ..." (1964:282) (see Romans 7: 13-25)

Acknowledging this fount of the dynamics and dialectics of our human condition – context and conflict – and seeing and understanding their features across cultural boundaries, paves the way for engaging in three important missiological concerns: communication, conversion, and counselling. Only then is one involved in doing mission. This is, in my view, missiology defined.

1.3 What's in for Missiology?

What new insights concerning missiology did this study unearth? Perhaps none. But it is firmly hoped that, first of all, it can fulfill Tippet's plea for a genuine interaction between missiology and the social sciences. He emphasizes that, if the interaction "is genuine, something methodologically new will be born and missiology will expand" (1987:xv). The methodology applied in this thesis might make a contribution towards this kind of expansion of missiology. The Christian mission is not a neutral endeavor because it is conditioned by the messenger and based upon a specific theological understanding of the Christian mission. Neither is the Gospel "preached into a vacuum"

---

[1] Obeyesekere himself makes a passionate appeal for origins in his own discipline of social anthropology and the social sciences. A neglect of origins makes one "more primitive than those we study, for, right through human history, imaginative men in almost every culture have sought the origins of their society and institutions and, often enough, the origins of life on earth" (1984:15). The reason for this neglect might be that origins land scientists "in the despised area of pseudohistory" (1984:15). Following Obeyesekere's own plea for origins, we must extend our research and studies to the origin of man himself. If social anthropology is not be afraid of landing itself in pseudohistory when probing and searching for origins, then, similarly, there is no reason whatsoever that, in studying the origins of man, one should be afraid of criticism that missiological research might be landing itself in pseudoreligion. The Holy Scriptures are not suggesting any form of pseudoreligion. They are a valid source of genuine religious experience. More than that, they reveal that part of God's heart, which we cannot know by our human mind. For more, see Obeyesekere1984:15-18.

(Ramachandra 1994:409). We will always have to deal with already existing concepts on the side of the host culture.

Secondly, this study has attempted to achieve a synthesis of psychology, sociology, anthropology and theology in the sense suggested by missiologist Hans Kasdorf when he says that a missiologist seeks to combine the interests of all these disciplines (1989:110). A missiologist seeks to acquire an interest for the individual. For this purpose, he draws on psychology. He also sees the need to understand the social structures and their dynamics. That is when he engages in sociology. Then he makes an effort to understand how social dynamics influence the individual in his relationship to culture. At this point, the missiologist works with anthropological concerns. And, finally, he includes the theological interest of man in relationship with God.

Third, I hope this thesis has made a contribution toward efforts that give missiology and the social sciences an equal share in theology departments, in the faculties of universities or, indeed, in any other Christian institutions of learning. What we need is not so much theology carved out in reputable institutions, but a Theology of Missions whose thrust comes from God, the Holy Scriptures *and* from where mission actually happens: in the field.

Fourth, perhaps this study has placed a finger on a sore spot of the Christian mission in general. Mission practice – and my own experience as a missionary – seem to suggest that we assume far too much about the people we go to teach, and, similarly, that we take up responsibility long before we really know anything about them. There must be an even greater effort on the side of the agents of Christian mission to make use of information that can – and will – help in the pursuit of more intelligent engagement in intercultural ministry. Our efforts to communicate the Gospel, the greatest gift to humankind, should be carried out with the most meaningful and strongly-charged thrust they can possibly be given in order to impact communities around the globe.

2. Outlook

This study has attempted to show a valid interdependency of three scientific disciplines: anthropology (cognitive anthropology in particular), sociology (social hermeneutics in particular), and missiology. Missiology does profit from, and can greatly exploit, the rich insights of cultural anthropology and the social sciences. Hendrik Kraemer, a missiologist, acknowledged this more than six decades ago although cognitive anthropology and social hermeneutics had not yet taken off the scientific ground. Nevertheless, here is what he said:

> A real grasp of the structure of "primitive" and an intelligent application of this knowledge in the work of building the Church, is as indispensable as good linguistic attainments. Here comes in the great value of the results of an-

thropological research for the Christian Mission. In this respect a large part of the missionary body has still to learn open-mindedness, not for the sake of anthropology, *but for the sake of doing the missionary task well and making the Christian approach an intelligent, constructive one* [italics in the original] (1947:341).

Kraemer's call still reaches us as fresh, clear, and valid as ever. It is exactly "for the sake of doing the missionary task well and making the Christian approach an intelligent, constructive one," that missiology continues where anthropology and social science have reached their ends. Charles Kraft, a missionary anthropologist, reiterated Kraemer's plea six decades later:

> Anthropologists have taught us a great deal about the need to take everyone's culture seriously. As committed Christians we need to combine this insight with something we could not learn from them: the fact that God desires us to use human cultures to interact with His creatures, to change their allegiances, their perspectives and their behavior in the direction of His ideals. Our commitment to Christ requires that we see culture as context and instrument rather than as an end in itself (1996:xiii).

As long as people inhabit this planet, the Christian mission has a mandate from God to follow and missiology has a task to do. The basis of this task is the desire to bring individuals to God. The task carried out by studying how best these individuals can be brought to God in the context of their life-history, as well as in the context of their cultural and social structures. This is underlined in Tippet's definition of missiology when he says "missiology is the *study of individuals* (italics mine) being brought to God in history" (1987:xiii). When one keeps this perspective clearly and uncompromisingly in mind, anthropology and the social sciences become, when handled well, complementary tools in achieving this goal.

2.1 *Imago Dei* – Metatheory for Missiology, Anthropology and the Social Sciences

The complementary features of these tools do not so much shine forth in their technical aspects (methodology of investigation) or their specific interests (objects, institutions, material culture etc.), but rather in their attempt to study the same subject: the human being in its entirety of existence. Despite the divergence of technicality and interest, there is broad consensus among the various disciplines when it comes to defining the human being.

We are of the same human matrix, or, as social scientist Obeysekere puts it, "constituted of the same essence" (1984:8), and share a common human "wiring", or, as psychoanalytic anthropologist Spiro writes, "human feelings are determined...by the transcultural characteristics of a generic human mind" (1984:334). Therefore, all credit should be given to the biblical premise of the *imago Dei* which includes all human beings regardless of race or culture.

Caudill adds his support, saying that "all human beings are somehow the same and yet somehow different" (Caudill 1976:25-26). Differences, says Caudill, come about as a result of the interplay or inter-relatedness of the social-structural, cultural, psychological, and biological dimensions.

Obeyesekere's "same essence," Spiro's "generic human mind," and Caudill's common humanness all lobby for the biblical *imago Dei*. The *imago Dei generaliter* in need of the *imago Dei specialiter* that is attained through Christ and through Him alone! – this forms the missiological metatheory, accompanied by complementary tools enabling connection to other life-forms.

2.2 Personal Final Comment

There is no reason why Missiology should be gripped by a fear of losing out to other disciplines. Equally, there is no need to shy away from learning from one another, since learning does not necessarily mean losing.

One only loses if he is not certain about what he has and falls into a protective stance over what he *thinks* he has, thus missing out on what he *could* have. Giving up fear and protectionism might indeed prove to be a valuable means of moving forward. And advance we must! Because neither time, nor cultures, nor academic disciplines, nor the Church – nothing, apart from God's desires to bring individuals of all cultures to Himself, remains stagnant.

Edward Yarnold says it this way:

> The Church being in transit, must not identify herself with any particular culture. We should not, for example, look back wistfully to the middle ages as the realization *par excellence* [italics in the original] of the christian ideal. The cultural milieu in which the Church must fulfill her mission in any particular age is never part of the Church's own essence, even though this culture may have derived its inspiration from Christianity. Therefore we should not imagine that we are serving the Church by trying to re-create, or retain in fossilized form, the political, philosophical or aesthetic fashions of another age. (The same is true of arts: each age has its own style, and the artist of integrity cannot and will not try to work in the style of earlier times) (1964:287).

We can be certain about God and his ideals for every individual in every culture, *though we are in transit*. We can also be sure about His commitment towards his messengers to help individuals from every culture to achieve these ideals *while we are in transit*.

The expansion of Missiology will depend on messengers who are willing to invest more in moving forward, than "trying to re-create, or retain in fossilized form, the political, philosophical or aesthetic fashions – or indeed missiological patterns – of another age." May God help us not to become crippled by stagnant mindsets by giving us fresh awareness of our transitory situation in carrying out the Christian mission. And, to borrow Kraemer's words, may He help us in *"doing the missionary task well and making the Christian approach an intelligent, constructive one"* (1947:341) until Christ comes (1 Thess 3:13).

Appendix 1

PSALM 116

[1] I love the LORD, for he heard my voice;
he heard my cry for mercy.

[2] Because he turned his ear to me,
I will call on him as long as I live.

[3] The cords of death entangled me,
the anguish of the grave came upon me;
I was overcome by trouble and sorrow.

[4] Then I called on the name of the LORD:
"O LORD, save me!"

[5] The LORD is gracious and righteous;
our God is full of compassion.

[6] The LORD protects the simplehearted;
when I was in great need, he saved me.

[7] Be at rest once more, O my soul, for the LORD has been good to you.

[8] For you, O LORD, have delivered my soul from death,
my eyes from tears, my feet from stumbling,

[9] That I may walk before the LORD in the land of the living.

[10] I believed; therefore I said,
"I am greatly afflicted."

[11] And in my dismay I said,
"All men are liars."

[12] How can I repay the LORD
for all his goodness to me?

[13] I will lift up the cup of salvation
and call on the name of the LORD.

[14] I will fulfill my vows to the LORD
in the presence of all his people.

[15] Precious in the sight of the LORD
is the death of his saints.

[16] O LORD, truly I am your servant;
I am your servant, the son of your maidservant;
you have freed me from my chains.

[17] I will sacrifice a thank offering to you
and call on the name of the LORD.

[18] I will fulfill my vows to the LORD
in the presence of all his people,

[19] in the courts of the house of the LORD –
in your midst, O Jerusalem.
Praise the LORD. (NIV)

Appendix 2

Hymn

(*Lesa e Kacema wandi*[1] / The Lord is my Shepherd)

Lesa e Kacema wandi,	The Lord *is* my Shepherd,
Nshakakabile pe;	I shall never be in want;
Ku mulemfwe alentwala,	To green pastures, He leads me,
Ku menshi ya bumi.	To the waters of life.
Umutima ambwesesha,	My innermost, He restores to me,
Mu lwendo angafwa,	On the journey through life, He guides me,
Mu nshila sha bololoke,	In paths which are straight,
Pe shina lyakwe fye.	For his name's sake alone.
Lintu nkenda mu mfwa ine,	Though I will walk in the face of death,
Nshakatine kantu,	I shall not fear anything,
Pantu imwe mulensunga,	For You are the one who keeps me safe,
No kunsansamusha.	And joy, You cause me to have.
Cintamba mwanungikila,	A table you have prepared for me,
Mu cinso ca babi,	In the presence of evil,
Umutwe wandi mwansuba,	My head, You do anoint,
Nkombo shaisula.	Filled are the cups to capacity.
Busuma bweka no luse,	Only goodness and mercy,
Fyakulankonka pe,	Shall surely follow me all my life,
Na mu ng'anda yakwa Lesa,	And in the house of the Lord,
Nkekalililamo.	(In there) I shall dwell for evermore.

Translation by Author, April 2001

---

[1] From the Hymnbook *Inyimbo sha Kulumbanya Lesa: Mu CiBemba,* Song No. 97 (Luanshya: Zambia: African Christian Books, n.d.; reprint 2000), 45.

Appendix 3

Glossary

Ababenye	the Sacred or Royal Relics of Bemba chiefs
Abantu	persons (in particular Africans)
Akapopo	fetus (sing.)
Bakalamba	a grown up, mature person; an Elder
Balunshi	flying insects
Bashimatongwa	original inhabitants of the Northern Plateau. People who settled in present day Northern Zambia prior to the conquest of the BaBemba
Bena Ng'andu	the "Crocodile clan," the Royal Clan of the BaBemba
Buloshi	witchcraft
Butuntulu	state of wholeness, completeness, perfection; harmony
Chitemene	slash and burn system of agriculture
Chitimukulu	Paramount Chief of the BaBemba people
Cifimba	term to describe malnutrition in children; the technical term is *kwashiorkor*
Cisungu	the initiation rite of Bemba girls
Icibanda	evil or malevolent Spirit; the malevolent *spirit double* of a person
Icuulu	mysterious sickness caused by witchcraft
Ifikulaika	all creeping insects
Ifipapa	medicine made from the barks of trees
Ifipaso	jumping insects
Ifishimba	medicine made from living creatures (prepared only by the traditional healer)
Ifishishi	tree and plant insects
Imfumu	a Bemba chief
Imibele	the specific character traits of a person (sg. *Umubele*)
Imyumfwikile ya mubili	"the feelings of the body." The body sensations
Imyumfwikile ya mutima	"the feelings of the Heart." The emotions
Inembo	incisions in which medicine is rubbed
Intifu	persistent hiccup
Intungulushi	(1) a guide, leader; (2) leadership
Isabi	collective term for fish

Kabilo	Royal Councilor
Katuutuu	(sing.) a newborn baby before it has received its name (not yet a human being)
Kukushe ngulu	*"strengthening the person who has established contact with ngulu spirits."* Second preliminary stage of establishing *ngulu* spirit mediumship
Kunwa amenshi	first stage of *ubupyani* (succession)
Kupyana	to succeed a dead person (family member)
Kupyanika	second stage of *ubupyani* (succession)
Kutundule ngulu	*"unplugging" of the ngulu spirit/s.* First preliminary stage of establishing *ngulu* spirit mediumship
Kwinika ishina	"naming;" name giving ceremony
Mbusa	the sacred emblems used in the initiation rite of Bemba girls
Mealie Meal	Maize flour (used to cook the stable food *nshima* or *ubwali*)
Mipashi	Collectively: the ancestral spirits of a family or clan
Mitanda	temporary residency in huts build near the gardens
Mu nda	the immaterial spot inside the abdomen. In certain circumstances a synonym for *umutima* and may be rendered as "inner-being," "innermost"
Mucapi	witch-cleanser
Muloshi	(sing. wizard, sorcerer)
Mumbi Makasa Liulu	lit. "*Mumbi* who steps down from heaven." Founder Queen of the Bemba *Bena Ng'andu* Dynasty
Mupashi Mukankala	"A rich and generous spirit/forbear." An important ancestral spirit being of the family, who will again be assigned to a family member to become his spirit double
Mupashi Wamushilo	the Holy Spirit
Mwine calo	the "owners of he land"
Mwine wa mushi	The headman of a village
Ngulu	(1) a spirit or spirits possessing humans. (2) a person who has attained *Ngulu* status
Ntanda bwanga	A lingering or incurable and much feared disease. Often times confirmed Tuberculosis
Ntenda/uwalwalilila	Person suffering from chronic ill health

Appendix 3   265

Ntuse	(1) a person suffering from chronic malnutrition; (2) a dwarf, stunted person
Shimwalule	the highest non-Bemba office holder who oversees the burial of Bema chiefs and also guards the royal burial ground
Shing'anga	traditional healer
Ubufyashi	(1) parenthood; (2) sexuality
Ubulwele bwa Ngulu	mysterious spirit sickness
Ubupyani	"succession"
Ubushilu	madness
Ubuumba	impotency
Ukondoloka	term to describe malnutrition in children; the technical term is *merasmus*
Ukukowesha	"contamination" caused by the breach of a taboo
Ukuteya kalumba	"to set a trap of lightning," meaning to bewitch a person with the intention to kill
Ukuwilwa	to be possessed by a spirit
Ulunse	term to describe malnutrition in children due to the early resumption of sexual relations of the mother
Umubili	general term for the body of humans and animals
Umukowa	Clan (pl. *imikowa*)
Umusamfu	fits or epilepsy
Umuti	(1) the word for tree; (2) also the collective term for medicine
Umutima	(1) anatomically: the heart (pl. *imitima*). (2) the seat of emotions, seat of intellectual processes and sole reference to the personality of a person; in short: the psyche
Umweo	"life-force" of a person
Uwawilwa	a spirit possessed person

Abbreviations

Africa	Journal of the International African Institute
AJET	Africa Journal of Evangelical Theology
em	evangelikale missiology
EMQ	Evangelical Missions Quarterly
GRZ	Government of the Republic of Zambia
GRZMH	Government of the Republic of Zambia Ministry of Health
IBMR	International Bulletin of Missionary Research
JAH	Journal of African History
JRA	Journal of Religion in Africa
JRAI	Journal of the Royal Anthropological Institute
Missiology	Missiology: An International Review
RAI	Royal Anthropological Institute
RRR	Review of Religious Research
Soc. Sci. Med.	Social Science and Medicine
Soc. Anthrop. Med.	Social Anthropology and Medicine
TaJH	Transafrican Journal of History
ZfMR	Zeitschrift für Missionswissenschaft und Religionswissenschaft

Bibliography

Altaus, Paul. 1965. *Die Christliche Wahrheit.* 7. Aufl. Gütersloh: Mohn.

Archdiocese of Kasama. 1970. "Commission for the Study of Customs: *Ngulu.*" TMs (photocopy). Kasama.

Asch, Solomon. 1952. Social Psychology. In *The Process of Communication: An Introduction to Theory and Practice.* David K. Berlo. 1960. New York, NY: Holt, Rinehart and Winston, Inc.

Aschwanden, Herbert. 1987. *Symbols of Death: An Analysis of the Consciousness of the Karanga.* Gweru: Mambo Press.

Austin, R. 1977. "Empirical Adequacy of Lofland's Conversion Model." *RRR* vol. 18, no. 3: 282-287. In *Christian Conversion: Biblical and Psychological Perspectives.* Cedric B. Johnson and H. Newton Malony. 1982. Zondervan Publishing House.

Badenberg, Robert. 2007. *Das Menschenbild in fremden Kulturen: Ein Leitfaden für eigene Erkundungen.* edition afem, mission specials vol. 8. Nürnberg: VTR. Bonn: VKW.

Badenberg, Robert. 1999. *The Body, Soul and Spirit Concept of the Bemba in Zambia: Fundamental Characteristics of Being Human of an African Ethnic Group.* Edition afem, mission academics, Bd. 9. Bonn: Culture and Science Publ., Dr. Thomas Schirrmacher.

Barnes, H. 1922. "Survival after Death among the Ba-Bemba of North-Eastern Rhodesia." *MAN* 22: 41-42.

Barth, Christoph. 1967. "Notes on "Return" in the Old Testament." *The Ecumenical Review* vol. 19: 310-312. In "Conversion: A Sociocultural Analysis." In *Papers of The Consultation on Conversion.* Paul G. Hiebert. 1988. Hong Kong Conference, January 4-8, 1988, 233-267. Tübingen: Institut für Missionswissenschaft und Ökumenische Theologie.

Bate, Stuart Clifton. 1993. "Inculturation and Healing: A Missiological Investigation into the Coping-Healing Ministry in South African Christianity." D.Th. thesis, University of South Africa.

Bateson, Gregory. 1958. 2nd edition. *Naven.* Stanford: Stanford University Press.

Berger, Peter L. 1967. The Sacred Canopy: Elements of a Sociological Theory of Religion. In "Conversion in Focus: Anthropological Views and Missiological Perspectives." Marc Spindler. *ZfMR* vol. 81, no. 4 (1997): 275-288.

Berlo, David K. 1960. *The Process of Communication: An Introduction to Theory and Practice.* New York, NY: Holt, Rinehart and Winston, Inc.

Boahen, Adu A., ed. 1990. *General History of Africa*. Vol. VII. "Africa under Colonial Domination 1880-1935." Abridged edition. London: James Currey; Berkerley, CA: The University of California Press; Paris: UNESCO.

Boas, Franz. 1940. *Race, Language and Culture*. New York: Macmillan.

Bock, Philip K. 1979 (3d ed.). *Modern Cultural Anthropology: An Introduction*. New York, NY: Alfred A. Knopf, Inc.

BookNotes for Africa. 1997. "Notes on Recent Africa-related Publications of Potential Interest for Theological Educators and Libraries in Africa." No. 4 (October): 1-21.

Brelsford, Vernon. 1942. " *"Shimwalule"*: A Study of a Bemba Chief and Priest." *African Studies* vol. 1, no. 3 (September): 207-223.

Brelsford, Vernon. 1944. *The Succession of Bemba Chiefs: A Guide for District Officers*. Lusaka: Government Printer.

Brown, Raymond E. 1977. *The Birth of the Messiah: A Commentary on the Infancy Narratives in Matthew and Luke*. In *Kommunikation und Gottesdienst: Grundlinien göttlicher Zuwendung in Bibel und Verkündigung*. Markus Piennisch. 1995. Studium Integrale Theologie, edition pascal. Neuhausen-Stuttgart: Hänssler-Verlag.

Bruce, F. F. 1985. *The Hard Sayings of Jesus*. The Jesus Library, ed. Michael Green. London: Hodder and Stoughton.

Bruner, Edward M. 1976. "Tradition and Modernization in Batak Society." In *Response to Change: Society, Culture, and Personality*, ed. George A. DeVos, 234-252. New York: D. Van Nostrand Company.

Bührmann, M. V. 1989. "Religion and Healing: the African Experience." In *Afro-Christian Religion and Healing in Southern Africa*, eds. G. C. Oosthuizen, S. D. Edwards, W. H. Wessels, et al, 25-34. In "Inculturation and Healing: A Missiological Investigation into the Coping-Healing Ministry in South African Christianity. Stuart Clifton Bate." D.Th. thesis, University of South Africa, 1993.

Burlington, Robert Gary. 2004. "I love Mary": Relating Private Motives to Public Meanings at the Genesis of Emilio's Mutima Church. D. Miss. diss., Faculty of the School of Intercultural Studies, Biola University. Ann Arbor, MI: ProQuest Information and Learning Company.

Carey, Francis. 1986. "Conscientization and In-Service Education of Zambian Primary School Teachers." Ph.D. thesis, Department of International and Comparative Education, Institute of Education, University of London.

Carmody, Brendan. 1988. "Conversion and School at *Chikuni*, 1905-39." *Africa* vol. 58, no. 2: 193-209.

Caudill, William A. 1976. "Social Change and Cultural Continuity in Modern Japan." In *Responses to Change: Society, Culture, and Personality*, ed. George A. DeVos, 18-44. New York: D. Van Nostrand Company.

Chanda, Alex G. 1982. "Shamanism and People's Belief among the BaBemba of Northern Zambia." (Research Paper) Saint Paul University, Ottawa.

Chomsky, Noam. 1957. *Syntactic Structures.* The Hague: Mouton.

Corbeil, J. J. 1975. "Bemba Medicines." TMs (photocopy). Mbala, Zambia: Moto-Moto Museum.

Corbeil, J. J. 1982. *Mbusa: Sacred Emblems of the Bemba.* Mbala, Zambia: Moto-Moto Museum; London: Ethnographica Publishers.

Court, John H. 1988. "Psychological Factors Affecting Conversion." In *Papers of The Consultation on Conversion.* Hong Kong Conference, January 4-8, 1988, 207-232. Tübingen: Institut für Missionswissenschaft und Ökumenische Theologie.

Coxhead, J. C. C. 1914. "Native Tribes of N.E. Rhodesia." *RAI,* Occasional Papers, No. 5. In "Bemba and Related Peoples of Northern Rhodesia." In *Ethnographic Survey of Africa.* Wilfred Whitely. 1950. Ed. Daryll Forde, 1-54. London: International African Institute.

Crawley, A. E. 1909. *The Idea of the Soul.* London: n. p.

Crawley, A. E. 1911. *Encyclopedia of Religion and Ethics,* s.v. "Doubles."

Cunnison, Ian G. 1969. *History of the Luapula.* Rhodes-Livingstone Paper No. 21, first published by the Rhodes-Livingstone Institute, Northern Rhodesia, 1951. London: Oxford University Press.

Cunnison, Ian G. 1959. *The Luapula Peoples of Northern Rhodesia.* Manchester: University Press.

D'Andrade, Roy G. 1984. "Cultural Meaning Systems." In *Culture Theory: Essays on Mind, Self, and Emotion,* eds., Richard A. Shweder and Robert A. LeVine, 88-119. Cambridge: Cambridge University Press.

D'Andrade, Roy G. 1984. "Problematic 2: Meanings, Conceptions, and Symbols: What are Ideas and Where do you Find Them." In *Culture Theory: Essays on Mind, Self, and Emotion,* eds., Richard A. Shweder and Robert A. LeVine, 1-24. Cambridge: Cambridge University Press.

D'Andrade, G. Roy. 1995. *The Development of Cognitive Anthropology.* Cambridge: Cambridge University Press.

Devereux, George. 1980. "Normal and Abnormal." In *Basic Problems in Ethnopsychiatry,* trans. B. M. Gulati and George Devereux. In *The Work of Culture: Symbolic Transformation in Psychoanalysis and Anthropology.* Gananath Obeyesekere. 1990. The Lewis Henry Morgan Lectures 1982. Chicago and London: The University of Chicago Press.

Dillon-Malone, Clive. 1988. "*Mutumwa Nchimi* Healers and Wizardry Beliefs in Zambia." *Soc. Sci. Med.* vol. 26, no. 11: 1159-1172.

Dixon-Fyle, Mac. 1976. "Politics and Agrarian Change among the Plateau Tonga of Northern Rhodesia, 1924-63." Ph.D. diss., University of London.

Doucette, Joseph Melvin. [1997]. *The Clans of the Bemba and of some Neighbouring Tribes*. Kasama, Zambia: Malole Parish, Archdiocese of Kasama.

Elmer, Duane. 1993. *Cross-Cultural Conflict: Building Relationships for Effective Ministry*. Downers Grove, Illinois: InterVarsity Press.

Engel, James F. and Wilbert Norton. 1975. *What's Gone Wrong with the Harvest? A Communication Strategy for the Church and World Evangelism*. Grand Rapids, MI: Zondervan.

Etienne, Fr. Louis. 1948. "A Study of the Babemba and Neighbouring Tribes." TMs (photocopy). Ilondola: Language Center.

Etienne, Fr. Louis. 1949. "Dieu, les *Ngulu*, les *Mipashi*," TMs, Ilondola Language Center. In "Spirit Possession among the Bemba: A Linguistic Approach." Louis Oger. Paper presented to the Conference on the History of Central African Religions. Lusaka, 30 August-8 September 1972.

Fallers, Lloyd. 1957. "The Predicament of the Modern African Chief: an Instance from Uganda." *American Anthropologist* 290-305. In *Response to Change: Society, Culture, and Personality*. Edward M. Bruner. 1976. "Tradition and Modernization in Batak Society," ed. George A. DeVos, 234-252. New York: D. Van Nostrand Company.

Ferm, R. 1959. *The Psychology of Christian Conversion*. In *Christian Conversion: Biblical and Psychological Perspectives*. Cedric B. Johnson and H. Newton Malony. 1982. Zondervan Publishing House.

Fiedler, Klaus. 1982. *Brockhaus Biblisches Wörterbuch*. Hrgs. Fritz Grünzweig, Jürgen Blunck, Martin Holland, Ulrich Laepple, Rolf Scheffbuch, s.v. "Buße/Bekehrung." Wuppertal: R. Brockhaus Verlag.

Frankenberg, R., and J. Leeson. 1976. "Disease, Illness and Sickness: Social Aspects of the Choice of Healer in a Lusaka Suburb." In *Social Anthropology and Medicine,* ed. J. Loudon. New York: Academic Press.

Freund, Julien. 1970 (reprint). *The Sociology of Max Weber*. Trans. Mary Ilford. London: Allen Lane The Penguin Press.

Frey, Reinhard. 2000. "Conversion among the Bemba in the Context of the Zambia Baptist Association in Central Part of the Northern Province of Zambia: An Empirical Study." University of Malawi, Department of Theology and Religious Studies, Ph.D. module III, 2001. Kasama, November.

Frost, Mary, Sr. 1977. "*Inshimbi* and *Imilumbi*: Structural Expectations in Bemba Oral Imaginative Performances." Ph.D. diss., University of Wisconsin.

Gann, L. H. 1964. *A History of Northern Rhodesia: Early Days to 1953*. London: Chatto & Windus.

Ganoczy, Alexandre. 1973. "New Tasks in Christian Anthropology." In *Humanism and Christianity*, trans. David Smith, ed. Claude Geffré. The

New Concilium Religion in the Seventies, no. 86, 73-85. New York: Herder and Herder.

Garrec, N. 1917. "Croyances et Coutumes Religieuses des Babemba." Rome: White Fathers.

Geertz, Clifford. 1984. "'From the Native's Point of View:" On the Nature of Anthropological Understanding." In *Culture Theory: Essays on Mind, Self, and Emotion,* eds., Richard A. Shweder and Robert A. LeVine, 123-136. Cambridge: Cambridge University Press.

Gese, Hartmut. 1977. Zur Biblischen Theologie. In *Abriss der Dogmatik.* Horst Georg Pöhlmann. 1980 (dritte, verbesserte und erweiterte Auflage). Gütersloh: Gütersloher Verlagshaus Gerd Mohn.

Goodenough, Ward Hunt. 1956. "Componential Analysis and the Study of Meaning." *Language* 32: 195-216.

Goodenough, Ward Hunt. 1957. "Cultural Anthropology and Linguistics." In *Report of the Seventh Annual Round Table Meeting on Linguistics and Language Study,* ed. Paul Garvin. Georgetown University Monograph Series, *Language and Linguistics* 9. Washington, D.C.: Georgetown University.

Gouldsbury, Cullen and Herbert Sheane. 1911. *The Great Plateau of Northern Rhodesia.* London: Edward Arnold.

Gray, Richard. 1990. "Christianity." In *The Colonial Moment in Africa: Essays on the Movement of Minds and Materials, 1900-1940,* ed. Andrew Roberts, 140-190. Cambridge: Cambridge University Press.

Guthrie, Malcom. 1962. "Some Aspects of the Pre-History of the Bantu Languages." *JAH* vol. 3, no. 2: 273-282.

Habermas, Jürgen. 1971. Knowledge and Human Interests. Transl. Jeremy J. Shapiro. In *The Work of Culture: Symbolic Transformation in Psychoanalysis and Anthropology.* Gananath Obeyesekere. 1990. The Lewis Henry Morgan Lectures 1982. Chicago and London: The University of Chicago Press.

Hefner, Robert W., ed. 1993. Conversion to Christianity: Historical and Anthropological Perspectives on a Great Transformation. In "Conversion in Focus: Anthropological Views and Missiological Perspectives." Marc Spindler. *ZfMR* vol. 81, no. 4 (1997): 275-288.

Hesselgrave, David J. 1978. *Communicating Christ Cross-Culturally: An Introduction to Missionary Communication.* Grand Rapids, MI: Zondervan.

Hiebert, Paul G. 1988. "Conversion: A Sociocultural Analysis." In *Papers of The Consultation on Conversion.* Hong Kong Conference, January 4-8, 1988, 233-267. Tübingen: Institut für Missionswissenschaft und Ökumenische Theologie.

Hinfelaar, Hugo F. 1994. *Bemba Speaking Women of Zambia in a Century of Religious Change (1892-1992).* Studies of Religion in Africa, eds., Adrian Hastings and Marc R. Spencer. Leiden: E. J. Brill.

Hoch, E. 1992. *Bemba Pocket Dictionary.* Ndola, Zambia: The Society of the Missionary for Africa (White Fathers).

Hochegger, Herman. 1965. "Die Vorstellungen von "Seele" und Totengeist bei Afrikanischen Völkern." *Anthropos* 60: 273-339.

Horton, Robin. 1971. "African Conversion." *Africa* vol. 41: 85-108. In "Conversion in Focus: Anthropological Views and Missiological Perspectives." Marc Spindler. *ZfMR* vol. 81, no. 4 (1997): 275-288.

Ipenburg, At. 1992. *"All Good Men:" The Development of Lubwa Mission, Chinsali, Zambia, 1905-1967.* Studies in the Intercultural History of Christianity, founded by Hans Jochen Margull, eds., Richard Friedli, Walter J. Hollenweger, Jan A. B. Jongeneel und Theo Sundermeier, Vol. 83. Frankfurt am Main: Peter Lang.

Jackson, Edgar N. 1981. The Role of Faith in the Process of Healing. In "Inculturation and Healing: A Missiological Investigation into the Coping-Healing Ministry in South African Christianity." Stuart Clifton Bate. 1993. D.Th. thesis, University of South Africa.

Jeeves, M. A. 1988. "The Psychology of Conversion." In *Papers of The Consultation on Conversion.* Hong Kong Conference, January 4-8, 1988, 183-206. Tübingen: Institut für Missionswissenschaft und Ökumenische Theologie.

Johnson, Cedric B. and H. Newton Malony. 1982. *Christian Conversion: Biblical and Psychological Perspectives.* Zondervan Publishing House.

Kambole, R. M. 1980. *Ukufunda Umwana Ukufikapo.* Lusaka: Zambia Educational Publishing House.

Kasdorf, Hans 1989. *Die Umkehr: Bekehrung in ihren Theologischen und Kulturellen Zusammenhängen.* Hg. Arbeitsgemeinschaft der Mennonitischen Brüdergemeinden in Deutschland (AMBD). N.p.: logos.

Käser, Lothar. 2004. *Animismus: Einführung in seine begrifflichen Grundlagen.* Bad Liebenzell: Verlag der Liebenzeller Mission. Erlangen: Erlanger Verlag für Mission und Ökumene.

Käser, Lothar. 1977. "Der Begriff Seele bei den Insulanern von Truk." Ph.D. diss., Geowissenschaftliche Fakultät, Albert-Ludwigs-Universität Freiburg i. Br.

Käser, Lothar. 1989. *Die Besiedlung Mikronesiens: Eine Ethnologisch-Linguistische Untersuchung.* Berlin: Dietrich Reimer Verlag.

Käser, Lothar. 1997. *Fremde Kulturen: Eine Einführung in die Ethnologie für Entwicklungshelfer und kirchliche Mitarbeiter in Übersee.* Erlangen: Verlag der Ev.-Luth. Mission; Lahr: Verlag der Liebenzeller Mission.

Käser, Lothar. 2004. *Animismus: Einführung in seine begrifflichen Grundlagen.* Erlangen: Verlag für Mission und Ökumene; Lahr: Verlag der Liebenzeller Mission.

Keller, Edmond J. 1986 (second edition). "Decolonization, Independence, and Beyond. In *Africa,* eds., Phyllis M. Martin and Patrick O'Meara, Bloomington: Indiana University Press.

Kemp, Roger Francis. 1987. "South African Baptist Missionary Society in Zambia: A Missiological Evaluation." D.Th. thesis, University of South Africa.

Klass, Morton. 1995. *Ordered Universes: Approaches to the anthropology of religion.* Boulder, CO: Westview Press.

Ki-Zerbo, J., ed. 1990. *General History of Africa.* Vol. I. "Methodology of African History." Abridged version. London: James Currey; Berkerley, CA: The University of California Press; Paris: UNESCO.

Kraemer, Hendrik. 1947. *The Christian Message in a Non-Christian World.* London: Edinburgh House Press.

Kraemer, Hendrik. 1956. *The Communication of the Christian Faith.* Philadelphia: Westminster. Germ. 1958. *Die Kommunikation des christlichen Glaubens.* Zürich.

Kraft, Charles H. 1980 (second printing). *Christianity in Culture: A Study in Dynamic Biblical Theologizing in Cross-Cultural Perspective.* Maryknoll, NY: Orbis Books.

Kraft, Charles H. 1996. *Anthropology for Christian Witness.* Maryknoll, NY: Orbis Books.

Kroeber, Alfred L. and Clyde Kluckhohn. 1952. *Culture: A Critical View of Concepts and Definitions.* Papers of the Peabody Museum of American Archaeology and Ethnology, vol. 47. Harvard.

Labrecque, E. 1931. "Beliefs and Religious Practices of the Bemba and Neighbouring Tribes." TMs (photocopy). Ilondola: Language Center.

Leach, Edmund R. 1958. "Magical Hair." *JRAI* 88: 147-164.

LeBacq, Frank (with E. Chisakuta, D. Mutale, M. Mubanga and W. Mulubwa). [1998]. "Community Based Health Promotion: An Opportunity within the Zambian Health Reforms for a New Cultural Approach to a Generic Community Based Health System in Kasama District, North-Central Health Region, Zambia." Kasama: n.p.

Lee, Dorothy. 1959. *Freedom and Culture.* Harvard University: Prentice-Hall, Inc.

LeVine, Robert A. and Donald T. Campbell. 1972. *Ethnocentrism: Theories of Conflict, Ethnic Attitudes, and Group Behavior.* New York: John & Sons, Inc.

LeVine, Robert A. 1984. "Properties of Culture: An Ethnographic Interview." In *Culture Theory: Essays on Mind, Self, and Emotion*, eds., Richard A. Shweder and Robert A. LeVine, 67-87. Cambridge: Cambridge University Press.

Lewis, Gordon R. and Bruce A. Demarest. 1987. Integrative Theology, I: Knowing Ultimate Reality / The Living God. In *Kommunikation und Gottesdienst: Grundlinien göttlicher Zuwendung in Bibel und Verkündigung*. Markus Piennisch. 1995. Studium Integrale Theologie, edition pascal. Neuhausen-Stuttgart: Hänssler-Verlag.

Lewis, I. M. 1971. Ecstatic Religion: An Anthropological Study of Spirit Possession and Shamanism. In *Modern Kongo Prophets: Religion in a Plural Society*. Wyatt MacGaffey. 1983. Bloomington: Indiana University Press.

Lienhardt, Godfrey. 1966 (second edition). *Social Anthropology*. Oxford: Oxford University Press.

Linton, Ralph. 1936. *The Study of Man*. New York: Appleton, Century, Croft.

Livingstone, David. 1970 edition. *The Last Journals, Vol. 1 and Vol. 2*. Ed. H. Waller. Connecticut: Westport Greenwood Press.

MacGaffey, Wyatt. 1983. *Modern Kongo Prophets: Religion in a Plural Society*. Bloomington: Indiana University Press.

Makopa Joel L. 1998. "Providing Complete Traditional Education to a Young Person." Transl. of R. M. Kambole, *Ukufunda Umwana Ukufikapo*. Lusaka: Zambia Educational Publishing House, 1980. Handwritten notes, Chinsali.

Marcuse, Herbert. 1955. *Eros and Civilization*. Boston: Beacon Press.

Maxwell, Kevin B. 1983. *Bemba Myth and Ritual: The Impact of Literacy on an Oral Culture*. American University Studies, Series XI Anthropology / Sociology, vol. 2. New York: Peter Lang.

Mbiti, John S. 1969. *African Religions and Philosophy*. London: SPCK.

Mead, George H. 1934. Mind, Self and Society. In *The Process of Communication: An Introduction to Theory and Practice*. David K. Berlo. 1960. New York, NY: Holt, Rinehart and Winston.

Meebelo, Henry S. 1971. *Reaction to Colonialism: A Prelude to the Politics of Independence in Northern Zambia 1893-1939*. Manchester: Manchester University Press.

Metuh-Ikenga, Emifie. 1991a. "The Concept of Man in African Traditional Religion: With Particular Reference to the Igbo of Nigeria." In *Readings in African Traditional Religion: Structure, Meaning, Relevance, Future*, ed. E. M. Uka. Bern: Peter Lang.

Metuh-Ikenga, Emifie. 1991b. *African Religions in Western Conceptual Schemes: The Problem of Interpretation*. Studies in Igbo Religion. 2nd edition. Jos: IMICO Publishers.

Middleton, John. 1973. "The Concept of the Person among the Lugbara of Uganda." In *La Notion de Personne en Afrique Noire*. Organisé dans le cardre des Colloques Internationaux du Center National de la Rechercher Scientifique, à Paris, du 11 an 17 Octobre 1971, par Madame G. Dieterlen, Directeur de Recherche au C.N.R.S. Paris: Editions L'Harmattan.

Mulenga, Kapamba. 1998. *Blood on their Hands*. Lusaka: Zambia Educational Publishing House.

Müller, Klaus W. 1985. "The *Missio Dei*: An Introduction to a Theology of Mission by Georg V. Vicedom." Paper presented to the University of Aberdeen, February 7.

Musambachime, Mwelwa C. 1992. "Colonialism and the Environment in Zambia, 1890-1964." In *Guardians in Their Time: Experiences of Zambians under Colonial Rule 1890-1964*, ed. Samuel N. Chipungu, 8-29. London and Basingstoke: MacMillan.

Musonda, Damian Kanuma. 1996. *The Meaning and Value of Life Among the Bisa and Christian Morality*. Roma: Pontificia Universitas Lateranensis, Academia Alfonsiana, Institutum Superius Theologiae Moralis.

Nangawe, Eli, et al. 1997. "Applied Health Research, Malnutrition in Under Fives in Kasama District: Intervention Phase Analysis Report," GRZ M[inistry] o[f] H[ealth].

Nangawe, Eli, et. al. 1998a. *Determinants of Action Against Malnutrition in Under Five Children Kasama District-Northern Province*. Applied Health Research, Series 2. Lusaka: ZPC Publications.

Nangawe, Eli, et. al. 1998b. *People-Centered Analysis and Intervention*. Lusaka: ZPC Publications.

Needham, D. E., E. K. Mashingaidze and N. Bhebe. 1991. *From Iron Age to Independence: A History of Central Africa*. New edition, ninth impression. Harlow: Longman.

Newbigin, Lesslie. 1954. The Household of God. In "Lesslie Newbigin's Contribution to Mission Theology." Wilbert R. Shenk. *IBMR* vol. 24, no. 2 (April 2000): 59-64.

Ngubane, Harriet. 1977. *Body and Mind in Zulu Medicine*. London: Academic Press,

Nida, Eugene A. 1960. *Message and Mission: The Communication of the Christian Faith*. New York, Evanston, and London: Harper & Row Publishers.

Nuckolls, Charles W. 1996. *The Cultural Dialectics of Knowledge and Desire*. Madison, WI: The University of Wisconsin Press.

O'Donovan, Wilbur. 1996. *Biblical Christianity in African Perspective*. Carlisle: The Paternoster Press.

O'Shea, Michael. 1986. *Missionaries and Miners*. Ndola, Zambia: The Missionaries of Africa, Mission Press.

Obeyesekere, Gananath. 1984 (paperback). *Medusa's Hair: An Essay on Personal Symbols and Religious Experience*. Chicago and London: The University of Chicago Press.

Obeyesekere, Gananath. 1990. *The Work of Culture: Symbolic Transformation in Psychoanalysis and Anthropology*. The Lewis Henry Morgan Lectures 1982. Chicago and London: The University of Chicago Press.

Oger, Louis. 1972a. "Spirit Possession among the Bemba: A Linguistic Approach." Paper presented to the Conference on the History of Central African Religions. Lusaka, 30 August-8 September.

Oger, Louis. 1972b. "The Bemba of Zambia: Outlines of their Lifecycle and Beliefs." TMs (photocopy). Ilondola: Ilondola Language Center.

Oger, Louis. [1987 or later]. "Historical Approach to *Ngulu*." TMs (photocopy). N.p., n.d.

Oger, Louis. 1991. *"Where a Scattered Flock Gathered," Ilondola 1934-1984: A Catholic Mission in a Protestant Area (Free Church of Scotland) Chinsali District, (Zambia)*. Ndola: The Missionaries of Africa on the Occasion of the Centenary of the Catholic Church in Zambia.

Ogunboye, Peter, with Lois Fuller. 2000. "The Human Soul in Yoruba/Igbo Tradition and the Bible." *AJET* vol. 19, no. 1: 75-86.

Olson, Bruce E. 1978. *Bruchko*. Second printing. Carol Stream, ILL: Creation House.

Ong, Walter J. 1982. *Orality and Literacy*. New York: Methuen Press.

Ortigues, M. C. and E. 1966. Oedipe Africain. In *Modern Kongo Prophets: Religion in a Plural Society*. Wyatt MacGaffey. 1983. Bloomington: Indiana University Press.

Packer, J. I. 1988 (reprint). *The Illustrated Bible Dictionary, Part One: Aaron-Golan*, s.v. "Conversion." Leicester: Inter-Varsity Press.

Parker, Melissa. 1995. *Africa* vol. 65, no.4: 506-523.

Parrinder, Geoffrey. 1976 (3d edition). *African Traditional Religion*. London: Harper and Row Publishers.

Parsons, Talcott. 1964. *Social Structure and Personality*. New York: Free Press.

Pell, Rodney George. 1993. "Relevant Patterns for Urban Baptist Churches in Zambia: A Missiological Exploration." M.Th. diss., University of South Africa.

Peters, George, W. 1985 (2nd revised edition). *Missionarisches Handeln und Biblischer Auftrag: Eine Biblisch-Evangelische Missionstheolgie.* Bad Liebenzell: Verlag der Liebenzeller Mission.

Piennisch, Markus. 1995. *Kommunikation und Gottesdienst: Grundlinien göttlicher Zuwendung in Bibel und Verkündigung,* Studium Integrale Theologie, edition pascal. Neuhausen-Stuttgart: Hänssler-Verlag.

Pöhlmann, Horst Georg. 1980. *Abriss der Dogmatik.* Dritte, verbesserte und erweiterte Auflage. Gütersloh: Gütersloher Verlagshaus Gerd Mohn.

Pueth, Eugen. 1910/11. "Äussere Mission." In *Afrika Bote: Nachrichten aus den Missionen der Weissen Väter.* Trier: Verlag des Missionshauses der Weissen Väter.

Ramachandra, Vinoth. 1994. "The Honor of Listening: Indispensable for Mission." *EMQ* vol. 30, no. 4 (October): 404-409.

Ray, Benjamin. 1976. African Religions. In "The Concept of Man in African Traditional Religion: With Particular Reference to the Igbo of Nigeria." In *Readings in African Traditional Religion: Structure, Meaning, Relevance, Future.* 1991. Ed. E. M. Uka. Bern: Peter Lang.

Richards, Audrey I. 1939. *Land, Labour and Diet in Northern Rhodesia: An Economic Study of the Bemba Tribe.* London: Oxford University Press.

Richards, Audrey I. 1940. *Bemba Marriage.* Lusaka: Rhodes-Livingstone Institute.

Richards, Audrey I. 1970 (reprint). *Mother-Right Among the Central Bantu.* Westport, CT: Negro Universities Press.

Richards, Audrey I. 1982 (reprint). *Chisungu: A Girl's Initiation Ceremony among the Bemba of Zambia.* Paperback. London and New York: Tavistock Publications Ltd.

Ridderbos, H. N. 1986 (reprint). *The Illustrated Bible Dictionary, Part One: Aaron-Golan,* s.v. "Kingdom of God, Kingdom of Heaven." Leicester: Inter-Varsity Press.

Ritchie, J. F. 1968. *The African as Suckling and as Adult: A Psychological Study.* The Rhodes-Livingstone Papers No. 9, first published by the Rhodes-Livingstone Institute, Northern Rhodesia, 1943, second impression for the Institute for Social Research University of Zambia. Manchester: Manchester University Press.

Ritter, Joachim und Karlfried Gründer. (Hg.) 1976. Historisches Wörterbuch der Philosophie, s.v. "Kondeszendenz." Darmstadt: WB, IV: 942-946.

Roberts, Andrew D. 1970. "Chronology of the Bemba (N. E. Zambia)." *JAH* vol. XI, no. 2: 221-240.

Roberts, Andrew D. 1973. *A History of the Bemba: Political Growth and Change in North Eastern Zambia before 1900.* Madison: University of Wisconsin Press.

Roberts, Andrew D., ed. 1990. "Preface." In *The Colonial Moment in Africa: Essays on the Movement of Minds and Materials, 1900-1940*, 1-2. Cambridge: Cambridge University Press.

Rommen, Edward. 1994 (2., erweiterte Auflage). *Die Notwendigkeit der Umkehr: Missionsstrategie und Gemeindeaufbau in der Sicht evangelikaler Missionswissenschaftler Nordamerikas*. Giessen: Brunnen Verlag.

Sauer, Erich. 1951. *The Dawn of World Redemption: A Survey of Historical Revelation in the Old Testament*. Trans. G. H. Lang. London: The Paternoster Press.

Schirrmacher, Thomas. 2000. "Gemeinde und Mission im Römerbrief." *em* vol. 16, no. 3:109-110.

Schoffeleers, J. Matthew, ed. 1999 (reprint). "Introduction." In *Guardians of the Land: Essays on Central African Territorial Cults*, 1-46. Gweru: Mwambo Press.

Shenk, Wilbert R. 2000. "Lesslie Newbigin's Contribution to Mission Theology." *IBMR* vol. 24, no. 2 (April): 59-64.

Shweder, Richard A. and Edmund J. Bourne. 1984. "Does the Concept of the Person Vary Cross-Culturally?" In *Culture Theory: Essays on Mind, Self, and Emotion*, eds., Richard A. Shweder and Robert A. LeVine, 158-199. Cambridge: Cambridge University Press.

Slikkerveer, L. Jan, and K. L. Slikkerveer. 1995. "Taman Obat Keluarga (TOGA): Indigenous Indonesian Medicine for Self-Reliance." In *The Cultural Dimension of Development: Indigenous Knowledge Systems*, eds., D. Michael Warren, L. Jan Slikkerveer, and David Brokensha, 13-34. London: Intermediate Technology Publications.

Smalley, William A. 1995. "Language and Culture in the Development of Bible Society Translation Theory and Practice." *IBMR* vol. 19, no. 2 (April): 61-71.

Smith, Louis A., and Joseph R. Barndt. 1980. *Beyond Brokenness: Biblical Understandings of Mission*. New York: Friendship Press.

Snelson, Peter. 1990 (second edition). *Educational Development in Northern Rhodesia 1883-1945*. Lusaka: Kenneth Kaunda Foundation.

Spindler, Marc. 1997. "Conversion in Focus: Anthropological Views and Missiological Perspectives." *ZfMR* vol. 81, no. 4: 275-288.

Spiro, Melford E. 1965. "Religious Systems as Culturally Constituted Defense Mechanisms." In *Context and Meaning in Cultural Anthropology*, ed. Melford E. Spiro, 100-113. New York: Free Press.

Spiro, Milford E., and Audrey G. Spiro. 1975 (revised edition). *Children of the Kibbutz: A Study in Child Training and Personality*. Cambridge, MA and London, England: Harvard University Press.

Spiro, Melford E. 1982. *Oedipus in the Trobriands: The Making of a Scientific Myth.* Chicago: University of Chicago Press.

Spiro, Melford E. 1984. "Some Reflections on Cultural Determinism and Relativism with Special Reference to Emotion and Reason." In *Culture Theory: Essays on Mind, Self, and Emotion*, eds., Richard A. Shweder and Robert A. LeVine, 323-346. Cambridge: Cambridge University Press.

Spradley, James P. 1979. *The Ethnographic Interview.* New York: Holt, Rinehart and Winston.

Tanguy, F. 1996 (reprint). *Imilandu ya Babemba.* Lusaka: Zambia Educational Publishing House.

Tanguy, F. 1954. "The Bemba of Zambia: Beliefs, Manners, Customs." Ilondola: Language Center, Edited by The Language Center. (TMs photocopy). The Society of Missionaries of Africa. Ilondola, 1983.

Taylor, Steven J., and Robert Bogdan. 1984 (second edition). *Introduction to Qualitative Research Methods: The Search for Meanings.* New York: John Wiley & Sons.

Thangaraj, M. Thomas. 1999. *The Common Task: A Theology of Christian Mission.* Nashville: Abingdon Press; reviewed by Vinoth Ramachandra. *IBMR* vol. 25, no. 1 (January 2001): 45-46.

Thiede, Carsten Peter. 1986. *Simon Peter: From Galilee to Rome.* Exeter: The Paternoster Press.

Tippet, Alan R. 1976. The Phenomenology of Cross-Cultural Conversion in Oceania. In *Christian Conversion: Biblical and Psychological Perspectives.* Cedric B. Johnson and H. Newton Malony. 1982. Zondervan Publishing House.

Tippet, Alan R. 1977. "Conversion as a Dynamic Process in Christian Mission." *Missiology* vol. V, no. 2 (April): 203-221.

Tippet, Alan R. 1987. *Introduction to Missiology.* Pasadena, CA: William Carey Library.

Turner, T. O. 1970. "The Agricultural History of Zambia." Paper presented in the Workshop on the Teaching of Central and East African History. Lusaka, August.

Tyler, Stephen A., ed. 1969. *Cognitive Anthropology: Readings.* New York: Holt, Rinehart and Winston.

Van Binsbergen, Wim M. J. 1999 (reprint). "Explorations in the History and Sociology of Territorial Cults in Zambia." In *Guardians of the Land: Essays on Central African Territorial Cults,* ed. J. M. Schoffeleers, 47-88. Gweru: Mwambo Press.

Van der Veer, Peter., ed. 1996. Conversion to Modernities: The Globalization of Christianity. In "Conversion in Focus: Anthropological Views and

Missiological Perspectives." Marc Spindler. *ZfMR* vol. 81, no. 4 (1997): 275-288.

Van Gennep, Arnold. 1961. The Rites of Passage. In *Christian Conversion: Biblical and Psychological Perspectives*. Cedric B. Johnson and H. Newton Malony. 1982. Zondervan Publishing House.

Vendler, Zeno. 1984. "Understanding People." In *Culture Theory: Essays on Mind, Self, and Emotion,* eds., Richard A. Shweder and Robert A. LeVine, 200-213. Cambridge: Cambridge University Press.

Vicedom, Georg F. 1958. *Missio Dei-Einführung in eine Theologie der Mission.* Munich: Christian Kaiser Verlag.

Weber, Max. 1969. "Objectivity in Social Science." In *The Methodology of the Social Sciences,* edited and translated by Edward A. Shils and Henry A. Finch, New York: Free Press.

Wendland, Ernst R. 2000. *Preaching that Grabs the Heart: A Rhetorical-Stylistic Study of the Chichewa Revival Sermons of Shadrack Wame.* Kachere Monograph no. 11. Blantyre: CLAIM (Christian Literature Association in Malawi).

Werner, Douglas. 1971. "Some Developments in Bemba Religious History." *JRA* vol. IV, no. 1: 1-24.

Werner, Douglas. 1999 (reprint). "*Miao* Spirit Shrines in The Religious History of The Southern Lake Tanganyika Region: The Case of *Kapembwa*. In *Guardians of the Land: Essays on Central African Territorial Cults,* ed. J. M. Schoffeleers, 89-130. Gweru: Mwambo Press.

Willis, Roy. 1999. *Some spirits heal, others only dance*. Oxford, New York: Berg.

White Fathers. 1991 (revised edition). *The White Fathers Bemba-English Dictionary.* Ndola, Zambia: The Society of the Missionaries for Africa (White Fathers).

Whitely, Wilfred. 1950. "Bemba and Related Peoples of Northern Rhodesia." In *Ethnographic Survey of Africa,* ed. Daryll Forde, 1-54. London: International African Institute.

Wolff, Hans Walter. 1984 (4., durchges. Auflage). *Anthropologie des Alten Testaments.* Munich: Christian Kaiser Verlag.

World Bank. 1994. "Zambia Poverty Assessment." Vol. 1. Report No. 12985-ZA, Cap 7, 162-170.

Yarnold, Edward. 1964. "The Mission of the Church." *The Way* vol. 4, no. 4: 278-288.

Subject Index

Adoratio Dei 26, 191, 202, 204, 214
Acculturation 94
Akanwa (pl. *utunwa*) 53-54
Amala 58, 60, 68
Amalgamation 106
Amalwele ya kulowekwa: diseases caused by witchcraft (*ubuloshi*) 81ff
Amalwele ya Makowesha: diseases caused by violation of traditional laws 74ff
Amalwele ya Mipashi: diseases caused by spirits 89ff
Ameno (sg. *ilino*) 53-54
Amor Dei 197, 213
Anthropocentric: Bemba religion 40, 253

Bashimatongwa 36, 110, 113,
Bemba: "House-religion" 104, 129; language 11, 41, 44, 50, 59; medicine 221, 248; migration 28-30; Royal Charter Myth 130; tradition 32; traditional culture 27, 124, 165; tribe 15, 27, 83, 110; women 28, 77, 104, 105-06, 115; worldview 29, 32, 40, 203, 253
Bena Ng'andu 36-37, 104, 108, 110-115, 129-130, 263-264
Bible 183, 201, 204, 207; culture 8, 207ff, 215; reader 204, 224, 232; Translation 32,
Body: human 41, 44, 46, 70f, 133; social 24, 44, 70-71, 107. *See also umubili*
British 106; rule 129; South Africa Company 102; government 106

Categories 15, 25; knowledge and 43f; concept of body and 46f, 62; illnesses and 72ff; formation of 219; "bounded set" 219f; "fuzzy set" 220; "centered or relational set" 221; biblical approach to 222ff
Catholic 29, 109, 129; Church 105, 108, 177, 218; faith 120, 127; scholar 29
Character traits, *see Imibele*
Chewe 16-26; 84, 100, 117, 119-130, 153-, 185, 187, 191-192, 196, 202, 204-205, 213f, 221-236, 241-252; and fear 160, 169, 233, 241f; his life before 1978, 154; his death 16, 84; 179-186; the Christian 16, 154, 250; Shimfwamba 126, 127, 159-180
Chitapankwa, Bemba Paramount Chief 111, 112, 114, 130
Chitimukulu 28, 37, 102, 104, 108f, 111, 114
Chitemene 102-103, 107, 115, 129

Christ 15, 184, 196-199, 200-206, 208-211, 215, 221-236, 253, 259f
Christian: beliefs 164, 179; call 184; Church 120, 127; churches 108, 159, 203; community 200; conversion 191, 216ff, 220-229, 231, 233; 236, 250, 255; counselling 191, 252; culture 200; faith 16, 105, 169, 211, 228; identity 166, 179; mentor 162, 229; message 107, 191, 208; mission 26, 200f, 255ff; "overcoat" 203f, 214; prayers 204; teaching 104, 129, 179; values 165
Christianity 105, 108, 115, 129f, 154, 213f, 217ff, 222, 259; conversion to 188; evangelical 227; Bemba women and 103-108
Cifimba 75-78
Cisungu 29, 32, 63-64, 68, 78, 80f
Cognitive anthropology 18, 42, 189, 255, 257
Colonial: powers 28; administration 101, 106f, 129; imperialism 104; office 105; personnel 28; rule 102, 129; Zambia 101
Communication: cybernetics 189; inner-trinitarian 26, 193ff, 213; of deep motivation 149
Componential Analysis 18, 42f. *See also* Cognitive anthropology
Conversion: in Christianity 17, 184, 188ff, 216ff; in anthropolgy 26, 217ff; in psychology 26, 216; missiological models of 26, 216ff; sociocultural theory on 218ff; "turning" or "returning" in 223ff; "relational interaction" in 225ff; psychological model of 227ff
Copperbelt 15, 105, 120, 177, 250
Counselling 18, 25f, 188f, 235, 237ff, 241ff, 255; cross-cultural 240ff, 251; ethics of 191, 237, 239, 251
Culture and personality 20, 130, 152, 225; "Bible" 207ff, 213ff; host 15, 207ff, 213ff, 241, 250, 255ff; "Missionary" 207ff; paradigms 131f, 152; "behavior paradigm" 131; "idea paradigm" 131; "Idea-knowledge-meaning" paradigm 132
Cultural standard/goal 96-98, 187-188

Deed 26, 38, 194-203, 214ff, 237, 239f; in the sacrifice 39

Deep motivation 19, 100, 135f., 140f., 144f., 147ff., 151ff., 159, 167; symbolic representation of 136ff.
Defense mechanism/s 145, 147, 153, 169
Dialectic 17, 25, 130, 241; between culture and the individual 20, 25, 101, 130, 133-134; concept of 152; dialectical conflict 94, 96, 255-256; dialectical opposition 95; dialectical relationship 74, 97, 100, 134; of desire and demand 139
Divine 114; access to the 66f., 99, 104; authority 104, 114; creative power 197; descent 112; "gift of parenthood" 67; intervention 114; side of things 220
Dreams 30, 33, 48, 117, 126, 165, 177, 183
Drums 91, 117f.
Dynamics 25, 35, 100, 256; group 230; of meaning ascription 18; personal psychological 16, 100; social 230, 257; social cultural 16, 100

Empathy 237, 246ff., 252
Ethics 26, 233, 239, 251; Kingdom 231; theological 191, 237, 239ff.
Ethnocentrism 15, 209
Ethnographer 21, 23, 142, 170, 177; as person 24; and science 21; and informant 22; and language 22; and time 22
Emotions 62, 82, 132, 142f., 146, 150, 170, 180, 182, 199, 215, 238, 241, 246f.; Chewe and 16; conflicting private 184; God and 213f.; of the Ethnographer 23-24, 170f.; of the spirit double of a person 33-34, 39; seat of 44, 59, 61; definition of 241f.; painful 164
Emotional experience 142f., 153, 160, 164, 179
Enculturation 94, 149
Estrangement 19, 146, 153

Fantasy 146ff., 192
Federation of Zimbabwe, Zambia and Malawi 106
Female initiation rite, see Cisungu
Fire 55, 67f., 75, 77, 80, 93, 118, 124; "cease- 215; fireplace 66, 77ff., 81; firewood 127, 161; funeral 171; "polluted" 79; root metaphor 67; sex/sexuality and 67, stick 126

Guilt 145, 182ff., 232, 243, 246

HIV/AIDS 17, 67, 79, 81, 98, 168
Heart 24, 38f., 43f., 51, 55, 58ff., 83, 92, 183, 202, 218, 233, 247, 249; God's 198. *See also umutima, psyche, SEIC.*

Hermeneutics 21, 205, 211; hermeneutical circle 209, 211; social hermeneutics 17, 21, 25, 186, 205, 253
Hiatus 19, 136
History 28, 29, 36, 42, 119, 170, 190, 255; God in 195; life history of Chewe 16f., 100, 125f., 129, 141, 176, 245, 254; literature on the Bemba 27; longitudinal-salvation 255; science of 28; of the Bemba people 27f., 101, 112; "of the Church of Jesus Christ on the Earth" 253; oral 40
Hut-tax-System 100f., 129

Icifu 58, 60
Icuulu: sickness of 25, 74, 82-86, 172f., 179, 244; explanatory models of 83-84; treatment of 86-88; symptom of 172; "trapping" of 178; witchcraft and 182, 245, 248
Idiom 48f., 51, 146, 166; language or symbol 82, 148f., 183; public 146, 150, 165f.; symbolic 147, 153
Imfumu 68, 130; Mukulumpe Mubemba 112; etiquette 113, 130, 165 ; institution 113
Inhibition 126, 166, 177, 179, 188
Internalization 138, 141; of cultural symbols 153; of object-relations 140
Ilinso (pl. *amenso*) 51ff.
Imago Dei 26, 191, 195, 197f., 201, 205, 210, 258ff.; *generaliter* 201, 213; 259; *specialiter* 198, 201, 213, 259
Imibele 33f., 38f., 61f.
Intrapsychic conflicts 19, 24, 137, 151, 159, 167, 184, 236
Intungulushi 19, 160, 163, 166f., 169, 185, 187f.

Kasama 27, 74, 80f., 93, 114, 119f., 126, 155; Archdiocese of 93, 114; Police Station 156
Katuutu 30, 33
Kukushe ngulu 118f.
Kutundule ngulu 117f., 125
Kwashiorkor 75ff. *See also Cifimba*
Kwinika ishina 30

Leisure [principle] 147ff., 153
Love 26, 63, 138, 140, 161, 194, 196; counselling act of 246, 248; Chewe from his parents 121, 158; Chewe for his father 154; God is 194ff., 197; God's love in our hearts 200, 239; Chewe from his mother 158; of God 190, 192, 195, 240

Subject Index

Malnutrition 67, 74, 77, 80ff.; acute 75f., 77; in adults 78f.; chronic 79f. *see Stunting;* and dialectical conflict 96; and "Compartmentalization" 96f.
Manipulation: of personal symbols 144, 149, 153, 167, 187; of psychogenetic symbols 142
Mbusa 63f.
Mediumship: *ngulu* spirit 19, 25, 124ff., 129f., 162, 164, 166f., 184, 188
Missio Dei 26, 191, 196-201, 213-215
Missiology 25f, 189-191, 195f., 201, 213ff., 217-221, 230, 235, 239, 255-260
Missionary 15, 17f., 23, 27, 196, 202, 208, 210, 215, 237f. 240, 255, 257f. culture 207f., 213; definition of 209-210; era 28; St. Paul the 202; Simon Peter the 224, 226; task 260; worker 234f.
Mitanda 56, 68, 102f., 107, 115, 129; huts 102
Mporokoso, Bemba Chief 102; town 27
Mu mutima 24, 38f., 58ff., 62ff
Mumbi Makasa Liulu 112-114; founder mother of the *Bena Ng'andu* dynasty 130
Mu nda 59-63, 68
Mupashi Mukankala 19, 32, 34
Mutuntulu 71f., 160
Mwine Mushi 37f., 69
Mwine wa Mushi 37f.

Ndusha 58
New Testament 26, 196f., 208, 222ff., 231, 240
Ngulu possession 25, 93, 107f., 110-115, 117-119, 125, 129f., 164-166, 179 phenomenon a 101; ritual *see kutundule ngulu* and *kukushe ngulu;* sickness 74; status 25, 115, 117-119, 122, 125f., 130, 147, 162-166, 184, 188; upsurge of 103-104, 106
ngúnúnngaw 32
ngúnúyéech 32f.
ngúún 32
Ntenda 16, 18f., 123, 126f., 159-169, 183-188, 227, 253-254. *See also uwalwalilila*

Objectivity 21, 23f.
Objectification 100, 134, 150-153, 184
Oedipus complex 153; with regard to personality development 100; family structure and 137; Malinowski and 137; Spiro and 137; Obeyesekere and 138; personality and society 140; gender and 140; generation and 140

Paradox 94-99, 204, 254; cultural 74

Participant observation 22, 42
Penance 182ff., 232
Performance principle 148
Personal symbols 18, 20, 22, 25, 100, 190, 256; Chewe and 154-188; 254; significance of 142; Obeyesekere's theory on 14, 100, 135-153; "Objectification and Subjectification" and 150ff.
Ponde, Bemba Chief 102
Prayer 166, 180, 196, 202ff., 214
Prostestant 105, 108, 129, 218; missionaries 32; Missions 105 ; understanding of faith 231
Psyche 24, 33f., 39, 44, 58f., 179, 185, 233 definition of 59-63. *See also Heart and SEIC.*
Psychogenetic symbols 141f., 159

Reality principle 148
Reconciliation 240
Reflexivity: self- 149-150
"Reincarnation" 34
Role resolution 161, 167ff., 185, 187f.

Sense organs 43, 50ff.; *ukumona* 50, 52; *ukununsha* 50, 57; *ukumfwa* 50, 56f.
SEIC 24, 33f., 38f., 44, 58f. 62f. *See also Psyche.*
Sexuality 63f., 66, 97, 138
"Shepherd-Service" 239-240
Shing'anga 83-88, 91, 118f., 124, 129, 160, 168, 180; *Ngulu* 119, 124, 162; Shimpala 125f., 165f.
Shimwalule 36f, 108
Spirit double 19, 27, 30, 32ff., 38, 40, 89f., 116, 128, 130. 160f., 165, 153
Stunting, *see* chronic malnutrition
Subjectification 100, 134, 150-153, 184
Symbols 19f.; cultural (public) 18f., 131ff.; embedded in the context of culture 18; dialectic between culture and personality 20, 25; meanings of 83; of death 73; personal 14, 22, 100, 135ff., 141ff.
Symbolic remove 100, 135, 147ff., 153, 169, 185f., 192
Symptoms 83, 91f., 96, 107, 162; personal symbols and 143; definition of, 183, 187; of sickness 116f.

Transcendence 27, 32, 38, 99, 108, 114, 193, 203; biblical 204; transcendental space 36, 38-40, 203f.; via dreams 30
Transference 146; total 245f., 249, 252
Trauma 157, 159; personal 141, 151, 153, 184; traumatice experience 142, 145, 163f., 184, 228

Ubuloshi 81, 84, 88, 90, 128, 160, 168, 172, 176, 179-181, 221, 241
Ubulwele bwa Ngulu: *"Spirit Sickness"* 91-92; symptoms of 91-93
Ubufyashi, see Sexuality
Ukondoloka (Merasmus) 76ff.
ukuwa 68, 116ff., 130
Ululimi (pl. *indimi*) 53, 55ff., 127
Ulunse 75ff.
Umubili 31, 43-47, 84
Umulopa 58
Umulu 113
Umupashi 19; definition of 30-33; name 128; personal symbol 19, 25, 161, 187; "reincarnation" and 34; spirit double 19, 27, 34f., 38ff., 89, 160, 165, 253;

Umusamfu 88, 116; treatment of 89; interpretation of 90-91
Umutima 24, 34, 43f., 58-63, 233. *See also* Heart, Psyche and *SEIC*.
Umutwe (pl. *imitwe*) 43, 46, 48ff., 88
Umweo 28, 31
Uwalwalilila 16, 123, 159, 161. *See also* Ntenda

Witchcraft 73, 81ff., 86, 88, 90, 127f., 160f., 168ff., 176f., 179ff., 185, 221, 241, 244f., 248. *See also Ubuloshi*
Work of culture 20; 100; 135; 144ff.; 153; 169

Zambia 15, 21, 27-42, 74f., 79, 81, 89, 94, 101ff., 120, 129, 166, 174, 185, 202

Name Index

Abel, Robert 73
Althaus, Paul 195
Asch, Solomon 246
Aschwanden, Herbert 73
Austin, R. 229

Badenberg, Robert 18; 30; 33f; 43; 58; 104; 188
Barndt, Joseph R. 197
Barnes, H. 31
Barth, Christoph 223
Bate, Stuart Clifton 73; 167; 182
Bateson, Gergory 95f.; 241
Beaufort, Justice 102
Berger, Peter L. 217
Berlo, David K. 132; 205ff; 243ff; 255
Beyerhaus, Peter 216
Bezzel, Herman 193
Boahen, Adu A. 101
Boas, Franz 42; 113
Bock, Philip K. 190
Bogdan, Robert 42f.
Brelsford, Vernon 27
Brown, Raymond E. 197
Bruce, F. F. 208
Bruner, Edward M. 18f; 95; 132
Bührmann, M. V. 182
Burlington, Gary R. 184, 209

Campbell, Donald T. 167; 180
Carey, Francis 17; 27f.; 32; 94; 101; 109; 129
Carmody, Brendan 102
Caudill, William A. 259
Chanda, Alex G. 117
Chomsky, Noam 132
Corbeil, J.J. 64f.
Court, John H. 227
Coxhead, J. C. C. 28
Crawley, A.E. 30
Cunnison, Ian G. 37; 109f

D'Andrade, Roy G. 43; 46; 132f.
Demarest, Bruce A. 193
Dervereux, George 149
Dillon-Malone, Clive 63; 88
Dixon-Fyle, Mac 102
Doucette, Joseph Melvin 104
Durkheim, Emile 35; 131; 135; 139

Elmer, Duane 235f.; 238
Engel, James F. 227

Etienne, Fr. Louis 27; 109f.; 129f.

Ferm, R. 227
Fiedler, Klaus 223
Frankenberg, R. 63
Freud, Sigmund 136ff.; 145
Freund, Julius 131; 206
Frey, Reinhard 163
Frost, Mary 121
Fuller, Lois 34

Gamitto, 28
Gann, L. H. 102
Ganoczy, Alexandre 133
Garrec, N. 27
Geertz, Clifford 247f
Gese, Hartmut 195
Goodenough, Ward Hunt 42; 132f.
Gouldsbury, Cullen 27
Gray, Richard 105
Gründer, Karlfried 193
Cunnison, Ian G. 37, 109, 111
Guthrie, Malcolm 27

Habermas, Jürgen 149
Hefner, Robert W. 216ff.
Hesselgrave, David J. 205; 207ff.; 211; 214
Hiebert, Paul G. 218ff.; 230; 236
Hinfelaar, Hugo F. 28f.; 32; 37; 66; 68; 104; 107ff.; 111f.; 121; 129f.; 165; 234
Hoch, E. 90
Hochegger, Herman 31
Horton, Robin 217
Huggins, Godfrey 106

Ikenga-Metuh, Emifie 34
Ipenburg, At 27; 32; 36; 105

Jackson, Edgar N. 167
Jeeves, M.A. 23; 217
Johnson, Cedric B. 26; 216; 223; 227ff.; 236

Kambole, R.M. 64-66
Kapombole, Fr. Bonaventura 93
Käser, Lothar 32ff.; 42f.; 131; 231
Kasdorf, Hans 257
Kaunda, Kenneth 107
Keller, Edmond J. 107
Kemp, Roger Francis 107
Ki-Zerbo, J. 28f
Klass, Morton 34
Kluckhohn, Clyde 131

Kraft, Charles H. 26; 132f.; 186; 197; 202; 205f.; 209ff.; 214; 222; 223ff.; 229; 236; 255; 258
Kraemer, Hendrik 192ff.; 205; 257ff.
Kroeber, Alfred L. 131

Labrecque, E. 27
Lacerda, 28
Leach, Edmund R. 95; 136; 143
LeBacq, Frank 73; 75; 77; 79f.; 185
Lee, Dorothy 70
Leeson, J. 63
Lenshina, Alice 106
LeVine, Robert A. 167; 180
Lévi-Strauss, Claude 133
Lévy-Bruhl, 23
Lewis, Gordon R. 193
Lewis, I. M. 138; 193
Lienhardt, Godfrey 23; 135
Linton, Ralph 133
Livingstone, David 28; 113
Lupunga, Dawson 96
Luther, Martin 210

MacGaffey, Wyatt 40; 100; 112ff; 135f.; 139ff.; 253f.
Makopa, Joel L. 65f.
Malinowski, Bronislaw 42; 137f.
Malony, H. Newton 26; 216; 222; 223ff.; 236
Marcuse, Herbert 148
Maxwell, Kevin B. 29, 31f., 36; 39f.; 67; 107ff.; 112
Mbiti, John S. 40
Mead, George H. 139; 247
Meebelo, Henry S. 102f.
Middleton, John 30; 34; 41
Miller 132
Mulenga, Kapamba 105f.
Müller, Klaus W. 198
Musambachime, Mwelwa 102f.
Musonda, Damian Kanuma 33; 67; 96

Nangawe, Eli 74-81; 96
Needham, D. E. 106
Newbigin, Lesslie 200f.
Ngubane, Harriet 73
Nicholls, B. J. 216
Nida, Eugene A. 26; 196; 203ff; 207-211; 213; 215
Norton, Wilbert 227
Nuckolls, Charles W. 25; 94ff.; 100; 113; 131; 133f.; 145ff.; 152ff.; 189; 213f.; 230; 241; 255

Obeyesekere, Gananath 19-25; 35; 82; 95; 100; 113; 115; 132-154; 159f; 164; 167; 169; 182ff.; 231; 245; 252.; 254ff.; 258.
O'Donovan, Wilbur 201
Oger, Louis 27; 31; 91; 93; 104f.; 107; 110ff.; 114ff.; 130; 203
Ogunboye, Peter 34
Olson, Bruce 210f.
Ong, Walter J. 29
O'Shea, Michael 35
Ortigues, M.C. and E. 139

Packer, J. I 216; 223
Parker, Melissa 23f
Parrinder, Geoffrey 81
Parsons, Talcott 100; 115; 139
Pell, Rodney George 35; 95
Peters, George W. 198
Pinto, Fr. 28
Pitiloshi, Gabriel 41
Piennisch, Markus 26; 192-197; 204ff.; 211; 213; 239ff.
Pöhlmann, Horst Georg 193; 195; 205;
Pueth, Eugen 103

Ramachandra, Vinoth 199; 257
Ray, Benjamin 34
Richards, Audrey I. 27f.; 31; 64; 67; 122
Ridderbos, H. N. 231
Ritchie, J. F. 75
Ritter, Joachim 193
Roberts, Andrew D. 27f.; 101; 110
Rommen, Edward 189

Sauer, Erich 194f.
Schirrmacher, Thomas 202
Schoffeleers, J. Matthew 31
Sheane, Herbert 27
Shenk, Wilbert 200
Shweder, Richard A. 132f.
Simwanza, H. 86
Slikkerveer, K. L. 74
Slikkerveer, L. Jan 74
Smalley, William A. 189; 211
Smith, Louis A. 197
Snelson, Peter 27f.; 105
Spindler, Marc 216ff.; 230; 235
Spiro, Audrey G. 163
Spiro, Melford E. 137; 163
Spradley, James P. 42; 132

Tanguy, F. 27f.; 31; 113
Taylor, Steven J. 42f.
Thangaraj, M. Thomas 199
Thiede, Carsten Peter 224-226

Tippet, Alan R. 26; 189ff.; 217; 227ff.; 236; 256; 258
Turner, T.O. 103
Tyler, Stephen A. 132

Van Binsbergen, Wim M. J. 37; 106f.
Van Gennep, Arnold 229
Van der Veer, Peter 216ff.
Vendler, Zeno 21; 26; 191; 237; 242-246; 249ff.; 255

Vicedom, Georg F. 198

Weber, Max 20; 43; 113f.; 135f.; 152; 206f.; 215; 255
Wendland, Ernst R. 29; 40
Werner, Douglas 27f.; 31; 109f.; 129f.
Willis, Roy 118
Whitely, Wilfred 27f.
Wolff, Hans Walter 205

Yarnold, Edward 256; 259

www.ingramcontent.com/pod-product-compliance
Lightning Source LLC
Chambersburg PA
CBHW032002220426
43664CB00005B/116